COMPARATIVE LAW BEFORE
THE COURTS

COMPARATIVE LAW
BEFORE THE COURTS

Edited by

Guy Canivet, Mads Andenas
and
Duncan Fairgrieve

BIICL
BRITISH INSTITUTE OF
INTERNATIONAL AND
COMPARATIVE LAW
www.biicl.org

Published and Distributed by
The British Institute of International and Comparative Law
Charles Clore House, 17 Russell Square, London WC1B 5JP

© The British Institute of International and Comparative Law 2004

British Library Cataloguing in Publication Data
A Catalogue record of this book is available from the British Library

ISBN 0–903067–62–5 (H/Bk)
ISBN 0–903067–89–7 (P/Bk)

Reprinted 2005

Typeset by Cambrian Typesetters
Frimley, Surrey
Printed in Great Britain by Biddles Ltd,
Guildford and King's Lynn

Foreword

The Rt Hon Lord Goff of Chieveley, DCL, FBA

I am honoured to be invited to contribute a Foreword to this book on Comparative Law before the Courts. It shows you some of the work of the British Institute of International and Comparative Law. The Institute continues to pursue a mission established in 1895 to understand and influence the development of law on a global rather than merely national basis. Today, a knowledge of comparative law is not just a scholarly virtue. It is an essential feature of modern legal life. Bringing together judges and practitioners, academic lawyers, and civil servants, the British Institute is uniquely situated to play a role in the promotion of knowledge about comparative law.

It is a particular pleasure for me as President of the British Institute of International and Comparative Law to note that this book is illustrative of our developing institutional links. We are pleased at the Institute to continue and develop our association with the French judiciary through collaboration with the Premier Président of the Cour de cassation, Monsieur Guy Canivet. Not only has Monsieur Canivet been a regular and distinguished speaker at a number of our recent conferences and research events, but also it is through his initiative that we have started a new collaboration with the Société de Législation Comparée, which is in many ways the sister organization of the British Institute. Founded in 1869, the Société was one model for the Society of Comparative Legislation, the precursor of the British Institute. It is thus gratifying that there is a renaissance in the relationship between the two Institutes. Monsieur Canivet was a keynote speaker at the conference in February 2003 which gave rise to this book, and we are honoured that he is co-editor of this collection.

The February Conference was organized jointly with the Institute of European and Comparative Law at Oxford University, of which Professor Mark Freedland was then the Director. This is one of a number of joint ventures between the two Institutes, and so it is especially appropriate that Professor Freedland should provide an introduction to the collection of essays.

The subject matter addressed in this book is at the centre of the interests of the Institutions associated with this venture. Comparative law is increasingly recognized as an essential reference point for judicial decision-making.

The English courts have long been open to considering how legal problems are solved in other jurisdictions. The recent case of *Fairchild v Glenhaven Funeral Services Ltd* has reinforced this further. Lord Bingham conducted a comparative law survey on a point of causation and declared that:

Development of the law in this country cannot of course depend on a head-count of decisions and codes adopted in other countries around the world, often against a background of different rules and traditions. The law must be developed coherently, in accordance with principle, so as to serve, even-handedly, the ends of justice. If, however, a decision is given in this country which offends one's basic sense of justice, and if consideration of international sources suggests that a different and more acceptable decision would be given in most other jurisdictions, whatever their legal tradition, this must prompt anxious review of the decision in question. In a shrinking world ... there must be some virtue in uniformity of outcome whatever the diversity of approach in reaching that outcome.[1]

There have been parallel developments across the Channel. At our Grotius lecture in November 2002, Monsieur le Premier Président Guy Canivet spoke about the role of comparative law before Supreme Courts. He said that:

Citizens and judges of States which share more or less similar cultures and enjoy an identical level of economic development are less and less prone to accept that situations which raise the same issues of fact will yield different results because of the difference in the rules of law to be applied. This is true in the field of bioethics, in that of economic law and liability. In all these cases, there is a trend, one might even say a strong demand, that compatible solutions are reached, regardless of the differences in the underlying applicable rules of law.'

It is heartening to see that comparative law is gaining in utility and relevance in the decision of the courts. This book is thus a timely offering, bringing together a collection of essays by distinguished jurists from the judiciary and academia. It should prove to make an important contribution to analysis of this topic. I gladly commend this publication.

---

[1] [2002] UKHL 22, para 32. Lord Rodgers also observed that '[t]he Commonwealth cases were supplemented, at your Lordships' suggestion, by a certain amount of material describing the position in European legal systems... The material provides a check, from outside the common law world, that the problem identified in these appeals is genuine and is one that requires to be remedied' (para 165).

Preface

The aim of this book is to examine the use of comparative law by national and international courts. Authoritative contributions cover both common law and civil law jurisdictions from the viewpoint of both practitioners and theorists.

Comparative law is increasingly recognized as an essential reference point for judicial decision-making. The challenge to judges and counsel is considerable. Legal scholarship has an important role in making comparative material available in a systematic manner. At the present stage there is also a need to discuss the role of comparative law in the judicial process. One extension of this discussion of legal method is how legal scholarship can assist. The discussion ranges from jurisprudential questions of the relevance and weight of comparative law arguments, to the practical aspects of how to present those arguments to a court or where and how to access the source material. Parallel developments in different jurisdictions justify a comparative approach to the use of comparative law. There may be lessons to learn from other jurisdictions.

The origin of this book was a BIICL conference organized jointly with the Institute of European and Comparative Law, University of Oxford, and the Société de Législation Comparée, France, which took place in February 2003.

Many of the chapters published here were originally presented as papers at that event to an audience of academics and practitioners. We would like to thank the participants at that conference, who, through their contributions, have helped to influence the shape of the chapters in this book. Some of the contributions to this collection have previously appeared in other publications. Chapter 9, Paul Mahoney's 'The Comparative Method in Judgments of the European Court of Human Rights: Reference Back to National Law', is an updated version of an article first published in *The Role of Comparative Law in the Emergence of European Law* (Swiss Institute of Comparative Law 2000).

Many thanks also to the staff of the British Institute of International and Comparative Law who have overseen the production process, in particular to Olivia Skinner, the Institute's remarkable publisher.

GUY CANIVET
MADS ANDENAS
DUNCAN FAIRGRIEVE

Contents

List of Contributors

Professor Guido Alpa, Full Professor of Civil Law at the University of Rome 'La Sapienza'.

Dr Mads Andenas, Director, British Institute of International and Comparative Law.

Michael Brooke QC, Four New Square.

Mr Justice Burton, High Court Judge; President of the Employment Appeal Tribunal; Chairman of the Central Arbitation Committee.

Judge Joaquín Martín Canivell, Tribunal Supremo de Justicia, Spain.

Monsieur le Premier Président Guy Canivet, Premier Président de la Cour de cassation, France.

Judge Jean-Paul Costa, Vice-President of the European Court of Human Rights.

Monsieur le Conseiller Olivier Dutheillet de Lamothe, Member of the French Conseil Constitutionnel.

Roger Errera, Conseiller d'État Honoraire.

Dr Duncan Fairgrieve, Fellow in Comparative Law, British Institute of International and Comparative Law; Maître de Conférences, Sciences Po, Paris.

Professor Bénédicte Fauvarque-Cosson, Professor of Law, Université Paris II (Panthéon-Assas).

RG Fentiman, Reader in Private International Law, University of Cambridge.

Ian Forrester QC at the Scots Bar, White and Case LLP.

Professor Mark Freedland, Director of the Institute of European and Comparative Law, University of Oxford; Fellow of St John's College, Oxford.

Professor H Patrick Glenn, Peter M Laing Professor of Law, McGill University; Visiting Fellow, All Souls College, Oxford University.

The Rt Hon Lord Goff of Chieveley, House of Lords.

Professor AS Hartkamp, Procureur-Général at the Supreme Court of the Netherlands, Professor of Private Law, University of Amsterdam.

Sir Sydney Kentridge QC, Brick Court Chambers.

Judge Koen Lenaerts, Judge of the European Court of Justice and Professor of European Law at the University of Leuven.

Paul Mahoney, Registrar of the European Court of Human Rights.

Professor Horatia Muir Watt, Professor at the University of Paris I (Panthéon-Sorbonne).

Professor Dr Paul Oberhammer, Professor of Civil Law, Civil Procedure, and Commercial Law, Martin Luther University Halle-Wittenberg, Germany.

Bernard Rabatel, French *Magistrat de liaison* in the United Kingdom.

Professor Geoffrey Samuel, Professor of Law, Kent Law School; Professeur *associé*, Université de Panthéon-Sorbonne (Paris I).

Professor Aldo Sandulli, Professor of Administrative Law, Faculty of Political Sciences, University of Urbino 'Carlo Bo'.

Dr Hannes Unberath, Institute of International Law—Comparative Law—Ludwig-Maximilians-University Munich; Visiting Fellow, University College London.

Nicholas Underhill QC, Fountain Court Chambers.

Introduction: Comparative and International Law in the Courts

*Mark Freedland**

As Lord Goff begins his Preface, so I begin this Introduction by saying that it is an honour to have been invited to contribute some opening words to this symposium of papers on comparative law in the courts, the product of a colloquium which took place in February 2003 at the British Institute of International and Comparative Law. Dr Mads Andenas was kind enough to invite the Oxford Institute of European and Comparative Law to be associated with the colloquium and with this consequent symposium publication. That provides me with a welcome opportunity to celebrate the state of comparative law studies in the United Kingdom at large but especially in London and in Oxford, and among those who are associated with comparative law endeavours in both places. The ensuing papers give much cause for that celebration.

To engage in that celebration has become unexpectedly controversial. For Professor Markesinis, in his recently published work on *Comparative Law in the Courtroom and the Classroom*,[1] has characterized the great English comparatists of the twentieth century as having eventually led their students and successors into an isolated and enclosed intellectual ghetto, from which he sees little prospect of their escaping.[2] I am sorry to find myself greatly at variance in this respect with a comparatist of such distinction, and moreover the founding Director of the Oxford Institute of European and Comparative Law. Writing as an occasional comparative lawyer, not a professionally dedicated one, I nevertheless identify several of those great comparatists as having been among the major intellectual influences upon me, almost as much so as Professor Kahn-Freund as the *doyen* of British labour law, and I venture to advance a set of reasons for being quietly proud of the comparative heritage with which they endowed our law schools, and for being confident that it is well maintained as a source of enlightenment to students and scholars alike.

---

* Professor of Employment Law and Director of the Institute of European and Comparative Law, University of Oxford.
[1] (Oxford Hart Publishing 2003).
[2] See 4–26, especially 25–6.

One of the main attributes of that heritage is the idea or perception that comparative law is not in any way a separate or ring-fenced area of legal studies; it has open borders, so that legal scholars can enter or leave the state of comparative law without elaborate identity papers. Thus Otto Kahn-Freund himself, who enjoyed a good paradox as well as a bit of gentle self-deprecation, said that 'the Professor of Comparative Law suffers from the problem that the subject he professes has by common consent the somewhat unusual characteristic that it does not exist'.[3] He went on to explain that the point is that comparative law is 'not a topic but a method', or rather 'the common name for a variety of methods of looking at law, and especially of looking at one's own law'.

I find this idea of a variety of methods very helpful, and I think of comparative law as a broad *genre* of legal scholarship, unified obviously by the choice or commitment to make comparisons between different legal systems or components of different legal systems, but diversified firstly as to the *techniques* of comparison, and secondly as to the *purposes* of comparison. I think I can discern five main techniques, and, by happy coincidence, five main purposes, though I am far from suggesting that there is a direct or even a neat relationship between particular techniques and particular purposes. Moreover, it seems to me that exponents of comparative law may devise complex combinations of those techniques and those purposes, and indeed that the great comparatist scholars have done precisely that in various subtle ways.

Anyway, the five main *techniques* which I think can be identified are those of, first, general taxonomy and synthesis of legal systems; secondly, comparative legal sociology; thirdly, comparative legal history; fourthly, general civil law and common law comparison, and fifthly, specific topical comparison. The five main *purposes* seem to me to be those of, firstly, articulating systems of *ius commune*; secondly—and rather in contrast—identifying areas of national or ethnic legal particularism; thirdly, legislating in a rational and informed way; fourthly, enhancing the quality of judicial decision-making; and fifthly, increasing the analytical depth of legal education. I think that British comparative law scholars have on the whole tended away from the first two alternatives and towards the latter three alternatives on each of those lists; but they have generally refrained from defining comparative law in a way which excludes the other preferences.

I have tried to devise a metaphor in which to identify these alternatives and these preferences. That said, I acknowledge that comparative lawyers can disagree profoundly about the way in which to deploy a particular

---

[3] In 'Comparative Law as an Academic Subject', originally his inaugural lecture as Professor of Comparative Law at Oxford delivered on 12 May 1965; (1966) 82 LQR 40 at 40.

metaphor. I am much struck by the diversity of argumentative uses to which the metaphor of the 'legal transplant' has been put. It is fascinating to me how, at a particular turning point in the history of the development of surgical techniques of transplantation, Otto Kahn-Freund could invoke the idea of the transplant to warn of the negative risks of organic rejection of imported legal solutions,[4] while Alan Watson could deploy the same notion to draw attention to the positive potential for legal portability.[5] So I can see that we have to be careful of drawing on similes from the field of bio-technology.

Nevertheless, I shall take that risk. So let me invoke the analogy of the genome projects and the way that scientists are making progress on the basis of those projects. A genome project, as I understand it, is a project for establishing a fully detailed map of the genetic make-up of a particular organism; you can choose simple organisms or higher more complex ones. It first required scientists of enormous imagination and insight to understand the basic structure of the component genes. It then requires colossal computing power to draw up these genetic maps. Once they have been drawn up, new ways of studying the functioning of the organism become possible. In legal studies, the computer is in a sense rapidly providing a kind of genome, a body of legal data gathered and made immediately accessible to an extent that no legal scholar or law librarian has remotely been able to achieve in the past.

But, in legal science as in biological science, the informativeness of these vast bodies of information can easily be exaggerated. They are essentially bodies of raw data, and their sheer magnitude means that the skills of the analyst are called upon more than ever. Here one is reminded of the admittedly rather sweeping assertion that all forms of higher knowledge consist of comparison. This is where the comparatist comes into his own or her own. It is he or she who makes the legal database reveal new things by perceiving that there are interesting relations or interactions between particular parts of the structure. These perceptions may take the form of grand taxonomical sweeps, or of very specific but no less momentous discoveries or analyses. Both kinds of perception contribute to the science of comparative law. It might appear that when academic theorists interact with judges, or even with legislators, their exchanges tend usually to be of the latter, very specific, kind. The practical law-maker or adjudicator might seem to look to the legal scholar for very highly focused learning. Nevertheless, I think that something more significant than the presentation of encapsulated recipes can and does take place on such occasions; and I

[4] In 'On Uses and Misues of Comparative Law' (1974) MLR 1.
[5] In, most notably, *Legal Transplants: An Approach to Comparative Law* (Scottish Academic Press 1974; American edn University Press of Virginia 1974).

suggest that the present colloquium, which consists essentially of a set of exchanges between judges, advocates and jurists, has just such a deeper significance.

The present work is also fruitful and promising in another very significant respect. It occurs at that increasingly important point of intersection between comparative law and international law, especially private international law. Moreover, and I think this is a crucial point, behind the cameos which are painted by the twenty-odd papers in this symposium, we can discern quite clearly the emerging shape of a body of European/comparative law—a new legal genome of its own, if I dare pursue that metaphor further. This begins to be a coherent conception at a quite a profound level. It is something both more and less than the mere combination of European Law with comparative law. It is less than the combination of European with comparative law, because it is concentrated upon the comparative law of the European region, rather than being concerned with comparative law in its more general *sans frontières* sense.

However, the conception of European/comparative law which I am exploring here is also both greater and different, in important ways, from the simple combination of the two elements. I make that suggestion on the basis of the following theorem, some proof of which is I think afforded by many of the papers in this symposium. The whole of *European/comparative law* is greater than (and different from) the sum of its parts for the following reasons. Let us for this purpose identify European law as having several layers, especially a supra-national layer consisting of European Union law and the law of the European Convention on Human Rights, and a national layer consisting of the domestic legal systems of European States (there being also regional and sub-national layers). European law as thus understood is formed and developed in a way which is both *comparative* and *interactive* as between those different elements or constituent parts.

By this I mean that the different elements of European law, although they begin life autonomously from each other, are seen increasingly to develop by means of comparison and interaction between them. In particular, European supra-national law, which can easily be understood as an exogenous creation superimposed upon national legal systems is often, on the contrary, better analysed as a process of formation by comparison between and distillation from national and even sometimes sub-national legal norms and structures. Stimulated by those interactions, moreover, the development of European national legal systems tends itself to become more comparative and mutually reflexive. That is not for a moment to suggest that this is a universal or all-pervasive model of development—far from it; but it is an increasingly influential one the importance of which has not yet been fully appreciated. It applies with some force in the fields of public law, competition law, consumer law and employment law. I suspect that the great current struggles about the development of European contract law represent the conflict between this new model and an older one in which the assertion of national legal autonomy has been especially strong in this particular field.

We always have to be careful about imagining entire classical temples from small fragments of stone and tile, but nevertheless I have found that the ensuing papers are very encouraging of the view that the kind of structure of European/comparative law which I have sketched out above is indeed taking shape in the course of the dialogue between academics and practitioners which they represent. This dialogue is more than a polite exchange of information; it provides evidence of mutual inspiration too. The papers have been elegantly ordered by the learned editors, and divided into four parts, in such a way that I have found that the theme which I have sought to articulate in this Introduction emerges as a natural progression from each paper, and each part, to the next one. What follows is a brief indication of the sense in which that is the case, rather than a summary of the argument of each individual author.

In the first part of the symposium, entitled 'Conflicts and Comparisons', the scene is set by some general indications of the problems and possibilities of comparative law in the courts, that is to say in the process of judicial adjudication and enunciation of the law at a national level. These indications are furnished in the context of discussion which ranges from the problems of proof of foreign law in national courts to legal borrowings and institutional mechanisms for international judicial cooperation in national courts. There is a strong sense of comparative law being on the increase and on the move as an aspect of judicial methodology.

In the first two papers, Bénédicte Fauvarque-Cosson and Richard Fentiman are concerned with the proof of foreign law in national courts. Professor Fauvarque-Cosson's argument is that whereas the respective approaches to the proof of foreign law of the English and the French courts seem to present a sharp and crude contrast between foreign law regarded as fact (and therefore external to the knowledge of the judge) and foreign law regarded as law (and therefore internal to the knowledge of the judge), the reality is a much more convergent one in which, from each theoretical starting point, the court eventually tends to engage in an essentially comparative exercise in order to arrive at an understanding of the foreign law which is in question, so that '[n]either in England, nor in France, nor in any other legal system can foreign law be considered as mere fact or as pure law. Its real nature is hybrid.'[6] Mr Fentiman makes a similar point. He draws attention to the extent to which the English courts have remained relatively impervious to less insular approaches in other jurisdictions to the methodology and conceptualization of the proof of foreign

[6] Ch 1, at 11.

laws. Hannes Unberath, on the other hand, feels that, eventually '[c]ompara-tive law is able to ensure that convergence between the different legal systems will emerge gradually and organically'.[7]

An even stronger sense of comparative law as being on the march from the law libraries into the courts themselves is exhibited by the other two papers in the first part of the work, those of Horatia Muir-Watt and Bernard Rabatel. Professor Muir-Watt looks at the recent breakthrough whereby the French courts used a form of extra-territorial injunctive relief in insolvency proceedings which was inspired by British practice and circumvented deeply entrenched French resistance to this kind of extra-territoriality; she remarks how 'comparative law was put to constructive use in a sphere usually thought to be the seat of insoluble conceptual differ-ences between civil and common law worlds relating to the very process of adjudication'.[8] Bernard Rabatel draws attention to the growing practice in several countries, including France about which he principally speaks, of appointing 'liaison magistrates', visiting from their native jurisdiction to import expertise in the law of that jurisdiction. He concludes that '[a]t the point at which linguistic and technical barriers disappear, the barrier which exists too often in the minds of those participating in the legal systems must also be removed in order to give way to confidence: in their own way liai-son magistrates are dedicated to achieving this aim.'[9]

In the first part of the work there were hints that this intensification of comparative law methodology in the courts might be attributable to the growth and impact of European supra-national law; Rabatel, for example, remarked that '[t]he development of Community law and the jurisprudence of the European Court of Human Rights . . . have profoundly changed the way in which judges have, up until now, viewed the operation of their legal systems.'[10] In Part II on European Law, that suggestion becomes explicit, and is explored in a number of dimensions. Thus Michael Brooke and Ian Forrester draw upon their experience as advocates in the recent leading British case concerning the problem of contaminated blood transfusions to engage in important consciously comparative reflections about the way in which that issue is handled, both substantively and procedurally, by the courts of the United Kingdom, France, and Germany; the interesting point is that the focus and starting point for this exercise in comparative law is the EU Product Liability Directive 85/374/EEC. This is really a study in the implementation of and general impact of that Community legislation in those respective Member States.

The next three chapters thoroughly hammer home this crucial observa-tion. Thus Jean-Paul Costa, writing as the Vice-President of the European Court of Human Rights, explores the way in which the European

---

[7] Ch 21, at 316. [8] Ch 3, at 35. [9] Ch 4, at 54. [10] Ch 4, at 49.

Convention on Human Rights and its interpretation through the case-law of the Strasbourg court become a factor in the harmonization, though not in his view the unification, of the laws of European countries. For him, there is a sound rationale for this, consisting in the aim of 'progressively raising the level of protection in the field of human rights in Europe'; for which purpose he is 'convinced that the Court's jurisprudential policy should be to place itself in an intermediary position between judicial activism and judicial self-restraint'.[11]

The point here is that the many variants, as between European States, in the implementation or integration of supra-national European law, themselves become a study in comparative methodology, with regard not merely to specific areas of substantive law, but also with regard to the underlying constitutional relationship between the legal system of the national state and the supra-national norms and institutions. This idea is elegantly explored by Olivier Dutheillet de Lamothe; behind his charming account of an arranged marriage, divorce, and subsequent amicable co-existence between European law and the French Conseil Constitutionnel is the very important observation that the Conseil's review of the '*conventionnalité*' of national legislative proposals is a very special kind of scrutiny, a new and special kind of constitutional review in which the issue is 'compatibility with international rule'.[12]

If the national systems respond to European supra-national law in complex, so too does that supra-national layer itself produce a complex response to the legal methodologies and approaches of different Member States (as well as, inevitably, to political considerations in the broadest sense). This emerges strongly from the papers of Koen Lenaerts, a Judge in the European Court of Justice, and Paul Mahoney, Registrar of the European Court of Human Rights. The former paper evokes the notion, quite central to the argument advanced in this Introduction of the *interlocking* between the different elements of European/Comparative law; he observes that 'the comparative law method, when applied by the Community judge, is driven by a single leitmotif, and that is to find through the examination of other legal orders the solution which best suits the objectives of the Community'.[13] The latter writer makes a very similar observation with regard to the methodology of the Strasbourg court, valuably adding the notion that:

The ECHR establishes a two-way bridge between international law and national law: in one direction flows the international obligation for the Contracting States to make their national orders compatible with specified common standards; in the other direction, the inspiration and continuing source of those standards on the whole derive from principles already recognized under the domestic law of all democratic countries.[14]

---

[11] Ch 6, at 89.   [12] Ch 7, at 94.   [13] Ch 8, at 105.   [14] Ch 9, at 135.

Part III of the work takes the argument into the field of administrative law. This has been an area which has traditionally been relatively impervious to comparative cross-fertilization between European States; for example, the doctrinal foundations of English constitutional law were constructed by Professor Albert Venn Dicey partly on the basis of an elaborate exercise in negative comparative law, consisting in the root and branch rejection of what he somewhat mistakenly understood to be the central tenets of French *droit adminstratif*. It is therefore encouraging to see the main argument of this Introduction more than vindicated in this particular sphere. The two papers in this part of the work testify to the growth of comparative method in, respectively, the French Conseil d'Etat and the Italian public law courts. Moreover they bear out the idea that this growth is in part attributable to the interaction between these national legal systems and the supra-national layer of European law. Roger Errera comments that 'the European perspective is paramount' and that

[i]nside the EU today the words 'cross-fertilization', 'harmonization of legislation', and *'ius commune'* are widely used by lawyers wherever they meet and discuss issues of comparative law. [. . .] a new approach, a new frame of mind, is perceptible. [15]

Aldo Sandulli comments of the Italian experience that

[t]here are numerous cases where comparative law has made an impact through the filter of Community law. Some of the most important ones are to be noted for the way they have introduced the notion of bodies governed by public law into the Italian order when applying Community legislation.[16]

The papers in Part IV of this work concern a widely diverse set of topics in the field of general and mainly private law. Although I expected that it would become more difficult to pursue into this more diffuse area the main argument of this Introduction, about the growth and intensification of European/comparative law, I was surprised at the extent to which it continued to resonate from almost each and every one of these chapters. There is no doubt of this, for example, in the paper of Guy Canivet. As the Premier President of the French Cour de cassation, he conveys much the same sense of an increasing Europeanization of the thinking of that court as Roger Errera did for the Conseil d'Etat. Thus he asserts that

the Cour de cassation has by now become familiarized with the comparative law methodology via its normative commitment to the European legal order. We must not be oblivious to the fact that European legal integration, together with the first signs of an emergent European legal culture, not only results from authoritarian black-letter unification, but also involves gradual internalization of common values by each of the national legal systems.[17]

---

[15] Ch 10, at 162. [16] Ch 11, at 172. [17] Ch 12, at 189.

In the next paper in Part IV, Guido Alpa comes to similar conclusions from his broad historical survey of the role of 'Foreign Law' in Italian legal culture. He notes how the current period of development of that legal culture reflects 'the rise of the law of the European Union and therefore the necessary circulation of the models of the Member States of the Union, which are merged in the regulations, directives, and the very language used by the European legislator and by the Court of Justice of the European Community'.[18] To like effect, though less specifically oriented towards European supra-national laws, are the papers of Joaquín Martín-Canivell and AS Hartkamp. Speaking from their positions in the Supreme Courts of, respectively, Spain and the Netherlands, they both remark upon a gradually increasing engagement in comparative law looking to other European jurisdictions.

Thus Judge Martín-Canivell opines that '[a]n increase in the resort by the Spanish courts to foreign legal doctrines and norms may be expected in the near future';[19] while Professor Hartkamp equally predicts that '[i]n the light of developments in present-day Europe with its 'gradual convergence' of private law systems, comparative law before the [Dutch Supreme] Court and in the judgments of the Court will become increasingly important'.[20] In much the same way, Paul Oberhammer in his paper records that, while there has in general been, in the Austrian courts, a pragmatic and intuitive application of comparative law focused on German law, 'there are also decisions in which the desire for European legal unification is stated as a reason for using comparative law for the purposes of argumentation. This notion has become particularly important in Austria in the area of procedural law'.[21]

It would be quite tendentious and misleading to suggest that all the papers in this work are Euro-centric in the way that this Introduction is. Two very important contributions, those of Patrick Glenn and Sidney Kentridge, are as much focused upon North America and, in the latter case, South Africa, as upon European jurisdictions. Whether despite that or because of that, they too provide powerful tangential support for the thesis about European/comparative law which is advanced in this Introduction. Professor Glenn has a most significant argument about the emergence of 'new forms of transnational law and 'transgovernmentalism'' and thinks that 'comparative legal reasoning is an essential element in these processes'.[22] He notes that in European legal theory

[t]here is renewed interest in comparative legal reasoning before the courts, since comparative law, in its static, taxonomic dimension is not that which is now being urged. It is rather a more dynamic process of comparative legal reasoning which has become relevant, in which local law and foreign models are assessed against one another, for purposes of application in a given case.[23]

---

[18] Ch 13, at 199.   [19] Ch 14, at 216.   [20] Ch 16, at 233.
[21] Ch 18, at 246–247.   [22] Ch 15, at 219.   [23] Ibid

Sir Sidney Kentridge for his part presents human rights jurisprudence as an area in which in which the use of comparative law is particularly prominent and appropriate. He advances as one of the reasons for that 'the close family relationship between modern domestic bills or charters of rights'.[24] The European Convention on Human Rights and its counterparts in the legal systems of European states of course constitute an important part of the family within which that close relationship exists.

The concluding papers in Part IV revert more straightforwardly to European fora. There is an interesting tension within these papers, slight flashes of which have appeared in earlier chapters of this work but which is more generally evident in these concluding contributions. On the one hand, their authors, Geoffrey Samuel and Hannes Unberath, are as convinced as the generality of the contributors to this symposium of the onward and upward progress of what I have presumed to identify as European/comparative law. In the first of his two papers, Professor Samuel evokes the notion of a 'long-term relationship between English case-law and the civil law tradition' which 'gives rise to what might be called a hidden comparative law, the expression embracing the idea of an unconscious as well as a conscious aspect'.[25] In the second of his papers, he considers the notion of a legal 'interest' on a comparative basis as between English law and the laws of various continental European countries, especially France. He notes that the incorporation of the ECHR into English law is the 'only aspect of the European dimension to law that will have possibly a profound influence on the traditional interrelationship of the various established interests', European Union law being another such aspect.[26] Finally, Dr Unberath, whose focus is upon comparative law in the German courts, notes how its significance

is rapidly growing with the infiltration into German law of European law, especially in the field of private and private international law, and the increased importance of international conventions. In short: private law in Europe is in the process of reacquiring a transnational character.[27]

On the other hand, those final papers in the sequence voice some doubts and difficulties about the deployment, even about the status, of comparative law; those doubts and difficulties form the starting point for some brief concluding remarks to this Introduction. Professor Samuel in his first paper emphasizes how problematical it is to establish a definition of and approach to comparative law methodology which are sufficiently context-sensitive and structurally sophisticated to be intellectually coherent. He stresses that

great care must be taken when one talks of comparative law in the courts. Often one is not actually talking of comparative law. What is meant is that foreign material is

---

[24] Ch 17, at 235.   [25] Ch 19, at 255.   [26] Ch 20, at 279.   [27] Ch 21, at 307.

being considered by the court which may, or may not, draw conclusions obtained through methods that can properly be described as comparative.[28]

Mr Fentiman concludes that the problem of applying foreign law in national courts

raises in acute form the epistemological puzzle at the heart of comparative law, what may we truly know of foreign laws? . . . Doubtless scholars of comparative law can master the laws of other countries. But how can counsel and the courts acquire the familiarity with foreign law necessary to apply it efficiently and fairly in the course of real proceedings?[29]

As I have said, this set of doubts—which are actually Professor Kahn-Freund's worries about legal transplants writ large—is voiced elsewhere in this symposium. For instance, Mr Fentiman points out that 'the proof of foreign law may ultimately raise the most fundamental of all comparative law questions: how far can we truly comprehend foreign law?'[30] Moreover, it is a set of doubts which we have especially to keep in mind when thinking about the sort of European/comparative law construct which I have been putting forward in this Introduction, and which I have suggested emerges strongly from the papers presented in this symposium. That is because an integrative and comparative approach to European law has a special attractiveness to those who believe in the possibility and importance of legal solidarity and community within the European region. This may mean that, for such enthusiasts, among whom I count myself, there is always the risk of assuming rather than proving that projects coming from such an approach have a natural intellectual and practical coherence.

All that said, a most encouraging feature of this symposium is that it does not by any manner of means consist of a series of lectures to legal practitioners or judges by legal theorists or academics as to how to and when not to make use of comparative methodology. I come back to the point that it is, on the contrary, a general conversation in which the ascent of a learning curve is a mutual and shared enterprise. Nicholas Underhill's postscript to the paper of Brooke and Forrester is only one of a number of contributions in which the practitioners add to our understanding both of the difficulties and possible superficialities of comparative law in the specifically forensic context, and of how to avoid those difficulties and superficialities. In this symposium the theorist and the court practitioner are working hand in hand; indeed, the two characters are often combined in individual authors. It is not as if the academic as performer is presenting foreign law or comparative methodology to the practitioner or the judge as the audience; the script is being written by all of them jointly.

I conclude with a different but no less important point. This Introduction

---

[28] Ch 19, at 254.   [29] Ch 2, at 31.   [30] Ch 2, at 14.

may have appeared to represent a summary, even a *rapport de synthèse*, of the symposium as a whole. That would be a misleading representation in two significant senses. First, as I have indicated, I have sought to extract from the succeeding papers an argument, even a continuous thread of argument, about the emergence of European/comparative law. Of course I hope that this argument will appear as a convincing one, and that the successive chapters of this work will seem to support it. But it would be quite tendentious to suggest, and I do not suggest, that the learned contributors to this volume were directing themselves to such an argument, or even that they would necessarily agree with it. Secondly, it is even more strongly to be borne in mind that to view my extracts and quotations from the ensuing papers as amounting to exact summaries of them would be entirely to miss the variety of perception and experience within the broad field of comparative law and private international law which they represent. I hope and confide that the exposure to that variety of perception and experience will be as much of a pleasure for the readers of this volume as it has been for me in preparing this Introduction to it.

Introduction: Finding a Common Language for Open Legal Systems

Mads Andenas[1] and Duncan Fairgrieve[2]

I. COMPARATIVE LAW IN THE COURTS

Courts make use of comparative law, and make open reference to it, to an unprecedented extent. This book provides many different complimentary perspectives, and a wealth of material from many areas. There are a number of reasons for the new and important role of comparative law, and this introduction will look at some of them.

The conclusions concern the consequences this development has for the system of sources of law and for legal argument. They also point to the role that courts are playing in a legal system no longer adhering to twentieth-century positivist and national paradigms, and no longer restricted by outdated national doctrines of statutory interpretation or precedent. In the new more open legal systems it is left to courts to weigh and balance more complex sources of law than ever before. The courts will also have competing claims to legitimacy. The sources of law may still be supported on a unitary, nationally based, rule of recognition. But the way in which courts deal with the more complex issues of validity of norms and their hierarchy has one outcome. That is an opening up of the legal system, mainly through the recognition of sources of law from outside the traditionally closed national system.

Comparative law has become a source of law. Comparative law also offers assistance with many of the new issues of method that courts have to resolve in the more open legal systems. How does one deal with comparative law? When is it relevant, what weight should it have, how does one sort out the many practical problems that arise? Comparative law can assist courts in dealing with other issues: international law, European law, or for that matter, the relationship of courts with the legislatures as

---

[1] Director of the Institute of International and Comparative Law, London; General Editor of the *International and Comparative Law Quarterly* (OUP); Secretary of the UK Committee of Comparative Law and of the UK Association of European Law; Secretary General of Federation International de Droit Europeen.

[2] Fellow of Comparative Law at the Institute of International and Comparative Law, London; Maître de Conférences, Sciences Po, Paris.

parliamentary supremacy (in the sense of one national legislature's supremacy) is eroded.

Comparative law is one of several new types of challenges that courts have to deal with. A situation with sources of law with competing claims to legitimacy leaves a whole set of issues to be determined by the courts.[3] The traditional form of a unitary rule of recognition (if it ever applied fully anywhere)[4] did simplify the picture. The possible recourse to a clear hierarchy, resolving conflicts between norms, seemed to leave the major issues for determination by the legislature. The present, more complex constitutional systems of validity of norms and their hierarchy leave courts with many new issues. There are certain constitutional issues that traditionally have been left to practice. On the macro level, this applies to the relationship between legal orders. On the micro level, it applies to remedies protecting private parties against the State. These are issues that have come to the fore in most jurisdictions, with courts rapidly developing the law.

Courts are to an increasing degree involved in dialogues with one another across the traditional jurisdictional divides. A horizontal exchange between national courts is becoming very active, both on an informal level with meetings and systems for the provision of information. At another horizontal level, the International Court of Justice, the European Human Rights Court and the European Court of Justice are involved in dialogues with one another. At a vertical level, the dialogues between the international and national courts are developing and are also formally recognized in a way they would not have been a few years ago. One may talk about an international market place for judgments,[5] where the form of judgments may be influenced by the increased use of comparative law.[6]

All of this has developed the constitutional role of the courts. The increased constitutional role of courts seems to be a rather universal feature. The dynamic way in which comparative law is used is only one of several developments.

---

[3] What Hart termed the 'secondary rules', representing the constitutional arrangements of any particular society, are undergoing fundamental change. The 'primary rules' are also changing in a way that reflects the change of the secondary rules, developing rights of individuals, harmonizing the laws of European countries over a very wide field etc. See HLA Hart *Concept of Law* (Oxford OUP 1961) 151 about 'secondary rules'.

[4] See the brief setting out of the case against a universal rule of recognition, or Austin's illimitable and indivisible sovereign, or traditional statehood concepts in M Andenas and J Gardner 'Introduction: Can Europe Have a Constitution' in (2000) 11 KCLJ 1.

[5] Lord Rodger 'The Form and Language of Judicial Opinion' (2002) 118 LQR 226, 247. See Lord Goff of Chieveley 'The Future of the Common Law (1997) 46 ICLQ 745, 756–7 on the accessible form of common law judgments.

[6] The court websites that provide translations of important judgments may be another. The British Institute maintains one such website, on judgments on product liability, see <http://www.biicl.org>.

II. COMPARATIVE LAW SCHOLARSHIP

Comparative law is no longer an impractical academic discipline. Comparative law is more actively used, and its use more openly acknowledged, not only by courts, but also in teaching, scholarship, and in statute law reform. This new awakening puts the academic discipline under some pressure. One response is the growing scholarship on the purposes and methods of comparative law.

A generation ago, there were disagreements about the purpose and method in academic comparative law. Looking back, the prevailing impression is of an established academic discipline with a high degree of cohesion. There were parallel discourses across jurisdictions, mostly dominated by private lawyers, but with important contributions made by public and criminal lawyers.[7]

Comparative law has now lost its common language. This is one consequence of the expansion of the discipline: it does not have the coherence of the academic discipline of a generation ago. It is a current and rather pressing challenge to engage comparative law scholars in a discourse on what can be agreed upon as the core issues. The growing scholarship on the purposes and methods of comparative law is a good beginning, although the present phase demonstrates the wide range of views, some rather fundamentally opposed to one another.[8] There is much left before the academic discipline can emerge from this phase with some agreement on fundamental issues. Then much of the very active comparative law discourse may rediscover a common language. It requires this common language to have full impact.

---

[7] Sir Thomas Bingham '"There is A World Elsewhere": The Changing Perspectives of English Law' (1992) 41 ICLQ 513, 527, reprinted in T Bingham *The Business of Judging* (Oxford OUP 2000) 87, sets out how the academic comparative law discipline and the courts have interacted in the English tradition, in particular after the Second World War.

[8] See the following authors representing some of the divergence in the current comparative private law scholarship: P Legrand 'European Systems are not Converging' (1996) 45 ICLQ 52; M Bussani and U Mattei, 'The Common Core Approach to European Private Law' (1997/98) 3 Columbia Journal of Comparative Law 339; W van Gerven, J Lever, and P Larouche *Tort Law* (Oxford OUP 2000); B Markesinis *Foreign Law and Comparative Methodology: A Subject and a Thesis* (Oxford Hart Publishing 1997); B Markesinis *Always on the Same Path: Essays on Foreign Law and Comparative Methodology* (Oxford Hart Publishing 2001); B Markesinis *Comparative Law in the Courtroom and Classroom* (Oxford Hart Publishing 2003); A Peters and H Schwenke 'Comparative Law beyond Post-Modernism' (2000) 49 ICLQ 800; H Muir Watt 'La Fonction Subversive du Droit Comparé' RIDC 2000.503; R Sacco 'Legal Formants, A Dynamic Approach to Comparative Law (I)' (1991) 39 American Journal of Comparative Law 1; (II) (1991) 39 American Journal of Comparative Law 343; A Watson *Legal Transplants; an Approach to Comparative Law* (London 1993); R Zimmerman 'Savigny's Legacy: Legal History, Comparative Law, and the Emergence of a European Legal Science' (1996) 112 LQR 576; K Zweigert and H Kotz *An Introduction to Comparative Law* (3rd edn Oxford OUP 1998).

III. THE USE OF JUDGMENTS FROM OTHER JURISDICTIONS

A. *Foreign Judgments in Supreme Courts*

English courts have long been open to consider how legal problems are solved in other jurisdictions. Lord Cooke of Thorndon recently stated that

the common law of England is becoming gradually less English. International influences—from Europe, the Commonwealth and even the United States, sometimes themselves pulling in different directions—are gradually acquiring more and more strength.[9]

Since the 1960s English courts have paid more and more respect to decisions by courts from other common law jurisdictions. For some 30 years many important cases have included detailed discussions of the case law of a number of the most influential common law jurisdictions, in particular those of Australia and New Zealand.[10]

During the 1990s Lord Goff of Chieveley, the Senior Law Lord, made extensive use of European materials, in particular German case law.[11] In extra judicial writings, Lord Goff, and many other leading English judges, committed themselves to the use of comparative law in their judicial work.[12] Lord Woolf, while he was Master of the Rolls, said that

there was a time when English lawyers, if they were prepared to seek help from another jurisdiction, would only look to other common law jurisdictions. This is now changing.[13] The House of Lords and the judiciary in general now recognize that civil jurisdictions have much to offer . . . there is, I believe, a real process of harmonisation between the civil and common law legal systems.[14]

Lord Bingham, while he was Lord Chief Justice (the most senior English judge), said that judges in English courts were developing the practice to

---

[9] Lord Cooke of Thorndon 'The Road Ahead for the Common Law' (2004) 53 ICLQ 273, 274.

[10] Some parallel may be found in the German speaking courts' use of one another's decisions.

[11] In the case of *White v Jones* [1995] 2 AC 207, Lord Goff, recognizing the challenges posed by comparative law, opined that 'in the present case, thanks to material published in our language by distinguished comparatists, German as well as English, we have direct access to publications which should sufficiently dispel our ignorance of German law and so by comparison illuminate our understanding of our own' (263).

[12] Lord Goff of Chieveley 'The Future of the Common Law' (1997) 46 ICLQ 745. Lord Goff has also been a pioneer in the establishing regular meetings between senior judiciaries in different jurisdictions to discuss developments in the law of mutual interest.

[13] Sir Thomas Bingham '"There is A World Elsewhere": The Changing Perspectives of English Law' (1992) 41 ICLQ 513, 527 says that 'in showing a new receptiveness to the experience and learning of others, the English courts are not, I think, establishing a new tradition but reverting to an old and preferable one'. Reprinted in T Bingham *The Business of Judging* (Oxford OUP 2000) 87.

[14] Foreword to Steiner and Ditner *French for Lawyers* (London 1997).

'use case law from other European countries in much the same way as we use Commonwealth authorities'.[15] This is supported by numerous other writings by judges of the highest UK courts.[16]

In the case law, an important breakthrough came in *Fairchild v Glenhaven Funeral Services Ltd.*[17] Lord Bingham, by now the Senior Law Lord (president of the highest United Kingdom court), conducted a comparative law survey on a point of causation. He stated that:

Development of the law in this country cannot of course depend on a head-count of decisions and codes adopted in other countries around the world, often against a background of different rules and traditions. The law must be developed coherently, in accordance with principle, so as to serve, even-handedly, the ends of justice. If, however, a decision is given in this country which offends one's basic sense of justice, and if consideration of international sources suggests that a different and more acceptable decision would be given in most other jurisdictions, whatever their legal tradition, this must prompt anxious review of the decision in question. In a shrinking world ... there must be some virtue in uniformity of outcome whatever the diversity of approach in reaching that outcome.[18]

There have been parallel developments in most other jurisdictions.

The Premier Président of the French Cour de cassation (the French court of last instance), Guy Canivet, has stated:

Citizens and judges of States which share more or less similar cultures and enjoy an identical level of economic development are less and less prone to accept that situations which raise the same issues of fact will yield different results because of the difference in the rules of law to be applied. This is true in the field of bioethics, in that of economic law and liability. In all these cases, there is a trend, one might even say a strong demand, that compatible solutions are reached, regardless of the differences in the underlying applicable rules of law.[19]

---

[15] Introductory speech at the launch of W v Gerven *Tort Law: Scope of Protection* (Oxford Hart Publishing 1998) in Gray's Inn, May 1998.

[16] Sir Thomas Bingham '"There is A World Elsewhere"': The Changing Perspectives of English Law' (1992) 41 ICLQ 513, 527, reprinted in T Bingham *The Business of Judging* (Oxford OUP 2000) 87. These two articles were based on Grotius lectures at the British Institute of International and Comparative Law. The 2002 Grotius lecture (not published) was delivered by Lord Rodger on 'Comparative Law in the Courts'. Other contributions include Sir Jonathan Mance 'Comparative Law', University of Texas Journal of International Law, forewords in Basil Markesinis's books by Sir Stephen Sedley, Lord Phillips, book review in ICLQ by Sir Konrad Schiemann.

[17] *Fairchild v Glenhaven Funeral Services Ltd* [2002] UKHL 22, [2003] 1 AC 32; *McFarlane v Tayside Health Board* [2000] 2 AC 59, 73 and 80-1; *Henderson v Merrett Syndicates* [1995] 2 AC 145, 184.

[18] [2002] UKHL 22, [2003] 1 A.C. 32, para 32. Lord Rodgers also observed that '[t]he Commonwealth cases were supplemented, at your Lordships' suggestion, by a certain amount of material describing the position in European legal systems. . . . The material provides a check, from outside the common law world, that the problem identified in these appeals is genuine and is one that requires to be remedied' (para 165).

[19] In an address at the British Institute in November 2001 under the chairmanship of Lord Bingham.

In French administrative law, foreign law sources are becoming an increasing reference point for judicial decision-making. In doctrinal terms it remains a somewhat overlooked factor.[20] In the case of *Kechichian*,[21] which concerned administrative liability for failure to supervise banks and was heard by the Plenary Chamber of the Conseil d'Etat, Commissaire du Gouvernement Alain Seban started his detailed and impressive *conclusions*,[22] with a survey of comparative law, covering Germany, America, and England,[23] concluding with the remark that 'despite the different legal and administrative traditions, the same features may be found [in the three systems].' Noting the English courts' tendency to broaden the tort of misfeasance in public office,[24] the Commissaire du Gouvernement concluded that the comparative law survey highlighted the 'liberalism of French administrative law'.

Similarly, in two recent decisions concerning wrongful life actions brought independently before the Conseil d'Etat and Cour de Cassation, both courts were referred to comparative law solutions respectively in the *conclusions* of Commissaire du Gouvernement Pécresse,[25] and Avocat Général Sainte-Rose.[26]

A recent Conseil d'Etat decision provides the first occasion for this court to expressly cited a foreign judgment of a national court in its own decision. In the case of *Techna SA*,[27] the Conseil d'Etat made reference to a decision by the English High Court concerning labelling requirement under EU law, and held that the relevant European directive should be suspended in France. It explicitly cited the English case as support in giving the reasons underpinning the need to suspend the directive.

Of course these examples by no means entail that the English and French courts are systematically having recourse to comparative law in decision-making. They do however highlight the fact that in certain circumstances foreign legal systems are accepted by the courts as an important reference point in tackling domestic problems.

---

[20] One could expect doctrine to provide this kind of comparative material that courts find useful in their decision making. In fact, it is the courts that lead the way. It is for doctrine to follow in the countries that we have studied.

[21] See further discussion of this case in D Fairgrieve *State Liability in Tort* (Oxford OUP 2003) ch 4, s 3.2.1.2. See also M Andenas and D Fairgrieve 'Misfeasance in Public Office, Governmental Liability and European Influences' (2002) 51 ICLQ 757.

[22] The court subsequently adopted the solution which CG Seban proposed in his *conclusions*.

[23] Including an analysis of the most recent House of Lords decision in *Three Rivers DC v Bank of England* [2001] UKHL 16.

[24] See further ch 4, s 2.2.1.

[25] CE 14 Feb 1997, *Epoux Quarez*, RFDA 1997.375, 379–80.

[26] Cass Ass Plen 17 Nov 2000, *Perruche, Gazette du Palais*, 24–25 Jan 2001; D 2001 Jurisprudence 316.

[27] N° 260768 Techna SA 29 Oct 2003.

A strong tradition of transnational jurisprudence is emerging also in the United States. Justice Breyer's address to the 2003 annual meeting of the American Society of International Law marks this important development.[28] He said that 'comparative analysis emphatically is relevant to the task of interpreting constitutions and human rights'. He continued that nothing could be 'more exciting for an academic, practitioner or judge than the global legal enterprise that is now upon us'.

Justice Breyer has indeed made use of comparative law and commented upon it in several judgments. In *Knight v Florida* he stated that the 'Court has long considered as relevant and informative the way in which foreign courts have applied standards roughly comparable to our own constitutional standards in roughly comparable circumstances'.[29] In *Printz v United States* he went into some further detail:

Of course, we are interpreting our own Constitution, not those of other nations, and there may be relevant political and structural differences between their systems and our own . . . But their experience may nevertheless cast an empirical light on the consequences of different solutions to a common legal problem—in this case the problems of reconciling central authority with the need to preserve the liberty-enhancing autonomy of a smaller constituent governmental entity.[30]

In *Lawrence et al v Texas*[31] the use of foreign law makes a notable breakthrough. In this case the majority overruled an earlier Supreme Court decision in *Bowers v Hardwick*,[32] which had upheld Georgia's sodomy law as constitutional. For the first time the court (as individual justices such as Kennedy himself had previously done) relied on international human rights law and practice. Justice Kennedy observed:

When homosexual conduct is made criminal by the law of the State, that declaration in and of itself is an invitation to subject homosexual persons to discrimination both in the public and private spheres. The central holding of *Bowers* has been brought into question by this case, and it should be addressed. Its continuance as precedent demeans the lives of homosexual persons.

In *Lawrence* also Justice Scalia found occasion to express his views on foreign law. Justice Scalia, with whom Chief Justice Rehnquist and Justice Thomas agreed, said that the majority had signed up to what he called the homosexual agenda. He observed:

The court's discussion of these foreign views (ignoring, of course, the many countries that have retained criminal prohibitions on sodomy) is . . . meaningless dicta. Dangerous dicta, however, since this court . . . should not impose foreign moods, fads, or fashions on Americans.

[28] S Breyer 'Keynote Address' (2003) 97 *ASIL Proceedings* 265.
[29] 528 US 990, 997 (1999). [30] 521 US 898, 921 (1997).
[31] Judgment of 26 June 2003. [32] 478 US 186 (1986).

However, 'Justice Scalia himself has been far from consistent in insisting upon the irrelevance of foreign and international law'.[33] He too has looked to other jurisdictions when they offered support, in Scalia's case for limiting constitutional rights.[34]

The Supreme Court of the United States is much cited internationally. It has had a notable impact on the constitutional law of most jurisdictions.[35] As we see, not all the justices of the US Supreme Court are reciprocating.

Contemporary written constitutions now offer one example where comparative law is received as a formal source of law. In the South African Constitution of 1996, Article 39 (c) states that when interpreting the Bill of Rights, a court, tribunal or forum may consider foreign law. Several of the new constitutions in the former communist countries also provide other and interesting examples in this respect.

B. European and International Courts

Comparative law has also been given formal recognition in the case law of the European Court of Justice and the European Court of Human Rights. The approach is generally that 'autonomous' concepts are developed but they are building on national law. Article 288 EC Treaty on tort liability of Community institutions supports this approach. It states that

in the case of non-contractual liability, the Community shall, in accordance with the general principles common to the laws of the Member States, make good any damage caused by its institutions or by its servants in the performance of their duties.

In many instances the Court of Justice will refer to the 'legal traditions', the 'constitutional traditions',[36] the 'legal orders', the 'legal notions' or the 'legal principles' common to 'all' Member States or, at least, to 'several' Member States. The Court will usually be supported by comparative surveys and analysis in the opinions for the Advocate General and in submissions by the Commission or other parties.[37] There will very rarely be any material about the national courts' application of Community law. The interest is limited to their practice on national law. The Court rarely cites

---

[33] HH Koh 'International Law as Part of Our Law' [2004] AJIL 43, 47.

[34] See *McIntyre v Ohio Election Commission* 514 US 334, 381 (1995).

[35] In particular its due process and freedom of press jurisprudence.

[36] Which is used in the EU Charter of Human Rights and in the draft EU Constitution.

[37] K Lenaerts 'Interlocking Legal Orders in the European Union and Comparative Law' ch VIII below. See also W v Gerven 'The Emergence of A Common European Law in the Area of Tort Law: The EU Contribution', in D Fairgrieve, M Andenas, and J Bell *Tort Liability of Public Authorities in Comparative Perspective* (London British Institute of International and Comparative Law 2002) 125.

doctrine, and new internal court guidelines attempt to restrict this also in the opinions of advocates general.[38]

The European Court of Human Rights goes further, and it cites national case law on the European Human Rights Convention. There are interesting examples of dialogues with national courts in the Human Rights Court's recent practice.

Public international law recognizes State practice as a primary source of law. This entails close study of court decisions as an expression of State practice. The International Court of Justice cites national court decisions, in particular in their application of public international law.

One may talk about the emergence of an international market place for judgments. This introduction and book is, among other matters, about the demands that are put on comparative law to assist courts. Lord Rodger has recently pointed out some consequences for the form of judgments from the House of Lords and the Privy Council,

which once could command assent merely by their position. In [the] new world, where courts may pick and choose among a variety of authorities . . . the form in which the judges have expressed their view may well play a significant role in determining which of those view ultimately win acceptance.[39]

So the form of judgments may also be influenced by the increased use of comparative law.[40]

C. Foreign Law

To complete the picture of courts dealing with foreign law, reference should be made to private international law. To a large extent, national law recognizes party autonomy in commercial law, so that parties can choose the national law that shall govern the contract. A court may then be bound to apply the law of another jurisdiction when it makes its decision. Before the nineteenth-century nation state, courts would in most countries regularly apply another law than the local law. In the British Empire, the Privy Council, as a centralized court of last instance, applied the laws of a large number of jurisdictions. The present Privy Council, still based in London, is the court of last instance for a number of former British colonies.

Private international law has a new importance in a globalized economy where the trans-national contract is no longer an extraordinary occurrence. The courts will as a consequence be ever more strongly exposed to foreign

---

[38] This is for resource reasons: it affects the length of the texts that are to be translated into ever more languages.

[39] Lord Rodger 'The Form and Language of Judicial Opinion' (2002) 118 LQR 226, 247.

[40] The court websites that provide translations of important judgments may be another.

law. The use of judgments from other jurisdictions is also for this reason becoming more usual.

There are several new indirect entry points for judgments of other jurisdictions. Some of these are new or have increased in importance in recent years. The emergence of international human rights standards, the European Convention of Human Rights, and the European Union are important such entry points. Already Lord Denning cites judgments of German and Dutch courts on the application of Article 234 EC on references from national courts to the European Court of Justice.[41] This, as noted above, is not something the European Court of Justice would have done.

In our own work on tort liability of public authorities we have analysed how the application of the law of the European Convention of Human Rights and the European Union provide indirect entry points for judgments from other jurisdictions.[42] We have noted the influence of European Community law, which has both focused attention upon the illegality–fault relationship in English law,[43] and provided an example of alternative ingredients for determining State liability, most notably with the 'sufficient seriousness' test.[44] It is interesting to note that not only have the courts adopted the Community law test for State liability with equanimity, avoiding the protectionist language that has often marked the domestic law, but the application of Community law has also led certain judges to go through remarkable metamorphoses. This is illustrated by Lord Hoffmann's views on State liability. In the well-known case of *Stovin v Wise*,[45] Lord Hoffmann was in a restrictive frame of mind regarding the conditions of public authority liability. This case concerned an allegedly negligent failure of a local authority to exercise a statutory power to direct a private landowner to remove an obstruction from his land in order to improve visibility at a dangerous road junction. In rejecting the claim, Lord Hoffmann held that

---

[41] *Bulmer v Bullinger* [1974] ch 401. See also Lord Goff of Chieveley 'The Future of the Common Law (1997) 46 ICLQ 745, 757 on the use of a French judgment to determine whether a question was *acte claire* under the Art 234 EC procedure.

[42] M Andenas and D Fairgrieve 'Misfeasance in Public Office, Governmental Liability and European Influences' (2002) 51 ICLQ 757.

[43] See D Fairgrieve *State Liability in Tort* (Oxford OUP 2003) ch 3, s 3.3.1.

[44] P Craig 'The Domestic Liability of Public Authorities in Damages: Lessons from the European Community?', in J Beatson and T Tridimas *New Directions in European Public Law* (Oxford 1998). See ch 4, s 2.2.3. See generally W Van Gerven, J Lever, and P Larouche *Tort Law* (Oxford 2000) ch 9.   [45] [1996] AC 923.

the trend of authorities has been to discourage the assumption that anyone who suffers loss is prima facie entitled to compensation from a person (preferably insured or a public authority) whose act or omission can be said to have caused it. The default position is that he is not.[46]

He later described *Stovin v Wise* as one of an established line of cases denying financial compensation for claimants who had failed to receive a benefit from public services.[47]

In a different case, looking again at the topic of State liability but this time through the lenses of Community law, Lord Hoffmann was in more liberal mode. When the *Factortame* litigation returned to the House of Lords on the issue of liability for damages, he upheld the lower court's decision that the enactment of the Merchant Shipping Act 1988 constituted a sufficiently serious breach of Community law.[48] In a crucial part of his judgment, Lord Hoffmann declared that

I do not think that the United Kingdom . . . can say that the losses caused by the legislation should lie where they fell. Justice requires that the wrong should be made good.'[49]

In the United Kingdom, another avenue for the introduction of comparative law influences, and perhaps even the changing of mindsets, is the Human Rights Act 1998 (HRA). The jurisprudence of the European Court of Human Rights has clearly been influenced by civil law systems. This can be seen in various fields, including the articulation of the rules concerning just satisfaction. In terms of loss the Court has, in contrast with English law, made monetary awards for a wide variety of non-pecuniary loss, as well as taking a broad approach to the recovery of pure economic loss, and lost chances.[50] In its apparently open attitude to the heads of loss for which compensation can be awarded, the Court is probably closer to the French law tradition[51] than the common law. In formulating the rules governing damages under the HRA, the English courts must take account of this more liberal attitude.[52] In turn, this might well prompt a more general re-evaluation of the present stance of the courts in respect of pure economic loss and moral damage in light of practice under the HRA, through the first-hand application of concepts shaped by foreign law influences. In a broader

---

[46] Ibid, 949.
[47] 'Human Rights and the House of Lords' (1999) 62 MLR 159, 163.
[48] *R v Secretary of State for Transport ex p Factortame Ltd (No 5)* [2000] 1 AC 524.
[49] At 548.
[50] See, eg, *Allenet de Ribemont v France* (1995) 20 EHRR 557 (compensation inter alia for loss of business opportunities); *Pine Valley Developments Ltd v Ireland* (1993) 16 EHRR 379 (loss of value in land).
[51] Bell, Boyron, and Whittaker *Principles of French Law* (Oxford 1998) 393.
[52] Section 8(4) HRA.

sense, it has been argued that the HRA is challenging orthodox common law philosophy of State liability, with the introduction of a rights-based approach, rather than the traditional focus on defining tortuous wrongs by reference to duties,[53] and not rights.[54]

V. CONSEQUENCES FOR SCHOLARSHIP AND COMPARATIVE LAW
AT THE BRITISH INSTITUTE

The relationship between the traditional disciplines of law is more than ever in need of exploration. International law, European law and national legal orders are now perhaps best understood as open systems coexisting without any clear hierarchy. Beyond that their relationship remains unresolved at the most fundamental levels. The relationship between disciplines within the different legal orders or systems is of increasing importance, and distinctions, such as those between private and public law, become difficult to maintain. There is a clear need to see this in context, and to provide an institutional framework and support for academic research and legal practice dealing with the many issues that arise.

There is another problem common to all countries. The well-established legal approaches, limited by narrow definition of disciplines and by national traditions, do not meet the present needs. In comparative law the encyclopaedic collection and organization of materials is still useful but not sufficient. The traditional teaching and scholarship in public international law, and indeed in the still relatively young discipline of European law, are equally inadequate.

An additional problem here is the focus on one's own national approaches (for instance to public international law and to EU law), which, while practically important, need to be done with a broader perspective. Fundamental assumptions about the nation state based on nineteenth century thinking still rule. The way that international, European and domestic legal systems open up and recognize one another, gives rise to fundamental questions and provides a fertile ground for research and policy discussion.

The core function of the British Institute is to promote international and comparative law. Two important themes of the Institute's work have been dictated by recent events. They both lead to fundamental questions about the foundations for international and national legal orders and their relationship. One theme is the impact on the international legal order of the

---

[53] See eg N McBride and R. Bagshaw *Tort Law* (London 2001) ch 1.
[54] See T Hickman 'Tort Law, Public Authorities and the Human Rights Act 1998', in D Fairgrieve, M Andenas, and J Bell *Tort Liability of Public Authorities in Comparative Perspective* (BIICL London 2002).

events leading up to and following the military intervention in Iraq. The other important current theme of the Institute's work follows from the Convention on the Future of Europe. What would be the best constitution for Europe? Research in this field requires involvement not only of international and European lawyers but also constitutional lawyers. There is need for broader exchange and discourse to create a public sphere for resolution of the constitutional issues that arise. Comparative research has an important role in explaining constitutional features of the different national traditions and assisting in the creation of meaningful concepts at the European level.

This discussion gives rise to a more general question. How can one respond to the increasing need for an international and European institutional basis for research and policy discussion? One response is in cooperation and networks involving existing institutions. The British Institute has a role to play here, and it is in the process of increasing its involvement in this form of cooperation where it has long and important traditions. It is also possible to make a greater and even more distinct contribution if additional funding is obtained to strengthen the research staff and institutional support at the Institute. The international, trans-Atlantic, Commonwealth, and European dialogues in the different areas of law require a forum for policy discussion support by research. The Institute's research projects are aimed at fulfilling the mission of the Institute to move freely over, and break down, the boundaries between the fields of law in which the Institute has its work. They are in the broad field of transnational law. The projects or programmes are usually initiated because there is a practical need to resolve a problem. They will often lead to theoretical inquiries of a fundamental nature. A problem may require the organization of larger projects that only an institution dedicated to research can undertake. They make a contribution to the understanding of our international and national legal orders and their relationship.

The Society of Comparative Legislation, when it was founded in 1894 (marking the beginning of the British Institute), was part of a European movement of comparative law. The aims and reception of comparative law has changed much up though the years. John Austin wrote in 1834 about 'general or comparative jurisprudence' as the process of ascertaining the 'principles common to maturer systems,' in order to establish a system of universal principles of positive law.[55] Sir Frederick Pollock, in 1905, attacked the 'high priests of a moribund utilitarian orthodoxy' for their rejection of comparative law. For 'comparative research within the last twenty or thirty years . . . have revolutionised our legal history and largely transformed our current text-books'. He continued that 'the work of the

---

[55] *Austin on Jurisprudence* (London 1869) ii, 1107.

present generation in the field of comparative jurisprudence is mostly work of detail. . . . But there is no rest for knowledge, . . . and there will again be a time of large adventure'.[56]

Comparative law scholarship has again reached such a time of large adventure. The European constitution is one of several developments that require a new form of comparative research. In the work of the courts and the legislator, comparative law is moving ever more into the foreground, both in the application of international and European law, and also in the areas left that are not directly affected by anything but domestic concerns. It is for scholarship to provide the method or range of methods. To be able to do so, it must regain some kind of common language. Scholarship can then provide the material and analysis that the courts and the legislators need in their work. Right now, as the chapters in this book show, the courts are pioneers in the use of comparative law. It is for scholarship to follow the lead and take up this challenge.

[56] F Pollock 'The History of Comparative Jurisprudence' [1903] Journal of the Society of Comparative Legislation 74.

PART I

Conflicts and Comparisons

1

Foreign Law Before the French Courts: The Conflicts of Law Perspective

Bénédicte Fauvarque-Cosson

The question of how foreign law is pleaded and proved before national courts is a crucial one, and at first sight it seems to be one of the questions where the difference between common law and civil law countries is most drastic.[1] Some authors even advocate European regulation of conflict of laws since 'an enormous diversity reigns in Europe, in theory as well as in practice'.[2] While in English law this question tends to be treated as a mere procedural matter, in most civil law countries it lies at the conceptual core of private international law. In English law the rule is that the law must be pleaded and proved as a matter of fact to the satisfaction of the judge by expert evidence (or sometimes by other means), while in most civil law countries the rule is that foreign law should be treated as law. This usually implies that judges should apply it *ex officio*, in other words even if the parties have not pleaded and proved it. Yet, if this is true in most countries that have recently codified their conflict of law rules, it is not true in France, where there has been no such codification and where major private international law questions such as pleading and proof of foreign law are settled by the French Cour de cassation, the Supreme Civil Court.[3]

---

[1] For a comparative survey, see TC Hartley 'Pleading and Proof of Foreign Law: The Major European Systems Compared' (1997) ICLQ 271; ThM de Boer 'Facultative Choice of Law: The Procedural Status of Choice-of-Law Rules and Foreign Law' (1996) 257 Recueil des cours 223–447; M Reimann *Conflict of Laws in Western Europe: A Guide Through the Jungle* (New York Transnational Publishers Inc Irvington 1995) 159 ff; for an English perspective, R Fentiman *Foreign Law in English Courts* (Oxford OUP 1998); and for a French perspective, B Fauvarque-Cosson 'Le Juge français et le droit étranger', Recueil Dalloz [2000]125; P Mayer 'Les procédés de preuve de la loi étrangère' in *Etudes offertes à Jacques Ghestin* (Paris LGDJ 2001) 617 ff.

[2] O Remien 'European Private International Law, the European Community and its Emerging Area of Freedom, Security and Justice' CML Rev [2001] 78.

[3] As a sign of its importance, it should be noted that this question was dealt with three times in the Annual Reports of the French Cour de cassation: A Ponsard 'L'Office du juge et l'application du droit étranger' *Rapport de la Cour de cassation* (Paris La Documentation française 1989) 11; J Lemontey and J-P Rémery 'La Loi étrangère dans la jurisprudence actuelle de la Cour de cassation', Rapport (1993) 81; J-P Ancel 'Le Juge français et la mise en oeuvre du droit étranger' Rapport (1997) 33.

In fact, the English and the French approaches to foreign law are not as different as they may at first seem. In English law foreign law is a question of fact of a particular kind. Conversely, in French law it is a question of law (as decided by the Cour de cassation in 1993),[4] but a question of law of a particular kind. It benefits from specific treatment, which is not easy to define. Since the mid-1980s, a series of cases of the French Cour de cassation have completely reshaped French law's approach to foreign law. The case-law has had its twists and turns, and there have been numerous decisions of the Première chambre civile of the Cour de cassation. The position now seems to be settled, but for how long?

Three questions can be distinguished, although they are so interrelated that they are not always dealt with separately by the courts. The questions are as follows:

- Should the French choice of law rule be applied *ex officio*?
- When the choice of law rule designates a foreign law, is it for the parties or for the judges to determine the exact content of the applicable law?
- To what extent can the parties agree to the application of the *lex fori* and, in so doing, prevent the judge from applying *ex officio* the choice of law rule which designates a foreign law?

In order to simplify matters, most French authors refer to the application *ex officio* of foreign law. In reality, this is not strictly accurate. In fact, there are two different questions that should always be clearly dissociated: first, is the judge bound to apply *ex officio* the choice of law rule? Secondly, if this rule designates a foreign law, who is to determine the content of this law? By referring to pleading and proof of foreign law, it seems to me that English law better dissociates these two stages than French lawyers usually do.

I. SHOULD THE FRENCH CHOICE OF LAW RULE BE APPLIED *EX OFFICIO*?

For a long time the following principle prevailed in French law: the choice of law rule was not applicable *ex officio* by the courts. The principle was established in 1959 by the famous *arrêt Bisbal*[5] and, although much criticized, lasted until 1988.

In October 1988 the rule was reversed and the opposing principle was

---

[4] Civ 1ère 13 jan 1993 *Coucke* [1994] Rev crit 78, note B Ancel.
[5] Civ 1ère 12 mai 1959, *Bisbal* Rev crit 62 note Batiffol; [1960] Journal du dr int priv 810 note [1960] Sialelli D 610 note Malaurie; (1960) JCP 11733 note Motulsky; B Ancel and Y Lequette *Grands Arrêts de la jurisprudence française de droit international privé* (4th edn Paris Dalloz) no 32.

put forward: a judge must always apply the choice of law rule, even *ex officio*.[6] This strict approach for French judges was based upon Article 12 of our Civil Procedure Code ('le juge tranche le litige conformément aux règles de droit qui lui sont applicables').

The great majority of French commentators applauded this important overruling. However, it was itself overruled two years later, on 4 December 1990, in a case called *Coveco*.[7] This case reaffirmed the *Bisbal* principle: French judges are not bound to apply choice of law rules *ex officio*. Yet it introduced two exceptions that, in practice, deprived the principle of nearly all its substance.

The first of these exceptions was founded upon the origin of the choice of law rule: if it originates in an international convention (for instance, the Rome Convention), French judges should apply it *ex officio*. This exception was based upon the idea that once the French government has ratified an international convention, it is bound to apply it and its responsibility may be engaged if it does not do so. True as this may be, this assertion does not explain why, from a mere procedural point of view, international choice of law rules should benefit from a greater authority than mere internal rules. Either judges must apply *ex officio* their own choice of law rules, and in this case all of them should be so applied; or alternatively they are not bound to do so, and there is no reason why choice of law rules that originate from an international treaty should receive different treatment (unless the treaty itself so decides, although the Hague conventions are silent on this point). This exception was abandoned in 1999.[8]

The second exception still survives. The Cour de cassation decided that judges must apply choice of law rules *ex officio* when the parties do not have 'the libre disposition de leurs droits'. This expression is difficult to translate as it is hard to know exactly what it means in French! Basically, it refers to matters, such as family law matters, where parties cannot freely dispose of their rights. On the other hand, the rights of the parties to a contract are 'disponibles'. Mr Richard Fentiman translates it by using the

---

[6] Civ 1ère 11 oct 1988 *Rebouh* [1989] Rev crit 368; [1989] Journal du dr int priv 349, note D Alexandre and chr D Bureau 317, JCP 1989 II 21327 note Courbe [1989] Rép Defrenois 310 obs Massip; Ancel and Lequette (n 5) no 71; Civ 1ère 18 oct 1988 *Schule* [1989] Rev crit 368; [1989] Journal du dr int priv 349 note D Alexandre and chr D Bureau; JCP 1989 II 21259 note J Prévault; Ancel and Lequette (n 5), nos 74–8.

[7] Civ 1ère 4 déc 1990, *Société Coveco*, [1991] Journal du dr int priv 373, note D Bureau; Rev crit 558 note M-L Niboyet-Hoegy; Ancel and Lequette (n 5) nos 74–8.

[8] Civ 1 26 mai 1999 *Mutuelles du Mans* Bull Civ I, no 172, 113; (1999) 4 JCP 2325; Rev crit 707 note H Muir Watt; Fauvarque-Cosson (n 1). However, a distinction based upon the European origin of the choice of law rule could be necessary if national judges were obliged to apply *ex officio* European Community Law. On this debate, see G Canivet and J-G Huglo 'L'Obligation pour le juge judiciaire national d'appliquer d'office le droit communautaire au regard des arrêts Jeroen van Schijndel et Peterbroeck' (avr 1996) 1 Europe 3.

expression the parties' 'indefeasible rights'.[9] This translation offers the advantage of being just as mysterious as the French concept itself. More recently Mr Fentiman has also referred to the concept of 'inalienable rights'. He has also provided a new key to understanding this French distinction: 'the distinction mirrors that between fact and law. Where inalienable rights are in question, questions of foreign law are treated in a "legal" fashion. But where the rights are alienable the treatment of foreign law resembles (to common law eyes) the treatment of facts.'[10]

This concept of 'indefeasible rights' has become the main key to understanding the French system, which does not treat all questions of foreign law equally. It explains its originality and complexity, especially as it applies to the second question: who is in charge of determining the content of the foreign law?

II. WHO IS IN CHARGE OF DETERMINING THE CONTENT OF THE FOREIGN LAW?

From a conceptual point of view the question of the application *ex officio* of French choice of law rules needs to be distinguished from the problem of who bears the burden of proving the foreign law. However, from a practical point of view it seems logical to apply similar principles to solve this problem. It is for this reason that the French Cour de cassation has adopted the following solutions:[11]

- Where the parties' rights are indefeasible, the judge is not only bound to apply *ex officio* the French choice of law rule, he must also determine its content. In this respect he must examine all relevant sources of law: case-law, statute law, custom etc. If he does not do so, his decision can be quashed by the Cour de cassation on the basis of article 3 of the Code civil.
- Where the parties' rights are not indefeasible, the burden of proof rests upon the party who is pleading that the applicable foreign law is different from the *lex fori*. This eases the identification of 'false conflicts'.

It would appear that the line is clear-cut. In reality, however, it is often blurred.

- On the one hand, when the judge must determine for himself the content of the foreign law, the judge's duty amounts to a mere 'obligation de moyens'[12] (best efforts). In other words, if the judge encounters too many obstacles (such as the impossibility of ascertaining the

---

[9] Fentiman (n 1) 285.
[10] See Fentiman Ch 2 in this volume.
[11] Com 16 nov 1993 *Amerford* [1994] Rev crit 332 note P Lagarde [1994] Journal du dr int priv 98 note J-B Donnie; Ancel and Lequette (n 5) no 82.
[12] Ancel and Lequette (n 5) no 82.

exact content of the foreign law), he can revert to the *lex fori* as long as he justifies his decision. Moreover, in order to ascertain the content of the foreign law, he can ask for the parties' help. In fact, he may even reject the parties' claim if the latter does not help him (Article 11, Civil Procedure Code).

- On the other hand, when the burden of proof rests upon the parties, the judge is not completely freed from all investigation. Proof of the foreign law is usually made by means of 'certificats de coutume', and the judge must check that these documents properly reflect the state of the foreign law. The Cour de cassation exercises very strict control as over the way in which the judge writes his decision when applying the foreign law. Strangely, it does reduce this control when the parties' rights are defeasible.

- In addition, if the judge decides to apply *ex officio* the French choice of law rule (for even though he is not bound to do so he is always free to do so, unless the parties have reached an agreement to prevent him from applying the foreign law), he is then bound to determine the content of the relevant foreign law.

In my opinion the distinction between defeasible and indefeasible rights is inappropriate. In practice the party who has an interest in proving the content of the foreign law will most often do so. More fundamentally, this distinction is irrelevant and should be rejected when defining the judges' duties, not only as far as proving foreign law is concerned, but also as regard the *ex officio* application of the choice of law rule. Indeed, the French choice of law rule is a rule of law, like any other rule of law, and as such it should receive the same procedural treatment, based upon Article 12 of the Civil Procedure Code. It would seem better, therefore, to abandon this distinction and to turn back to a single regime according to which French judges would be under a double duty: first to apply *ex officio* the choice of law rules, and secondly, to determine the content of the foreign law. Some recent cases of the Cour de cassation could be interpreted as following this direction, at least as regards the question of who is in charge of establishing the content of foreign laws.[13]

It is important to be aware that the Cour de cassation's reluctance to proceed in such a way is based upon the need not to encourage litigants to use dilatory tactics. Indeed, it is inadvisable that, after the case has been heard twice (at first instance and on appeal), a litigant should be allowed to go before the Cour de cassation and ask for the lower court's decision to be reversed because it had not applied *ex officio* the choice of law rule which designated a foreign law. In the vast majority of cases, if this litigant failed

---

[13] Civ 1ère 18 juin 2002 18 sept 2002 22 oct 2002 [2003] Rev crit 86 note H Muir Watt.

to plead and prove foreign law, this was not out of sheer ignorance but because he knew or at least assumed that the result would be identical.

A drastic solution to this problem would be to resort to the English doctrine of estoppel: at this late stage of the proceedings one should be estopped from invoking the application of a foreign law.[14] Another, less radical, device has recently been adopted by the Cour de cassation. It is known as the 'théorie d'équivalence'. When the two laws in conflict are identical, the Cour de cassation allows first instance or appellate judges not to specify in their judgments which law they apply, in spite of their duty to apply *ex officio* the choice of law rule.[15] The application of the theory of equivalence is more demanding than the doctrine of estoppel for it implies some investigation of the content of the foreign law. In fact, it is doubtful whether the Cour de cassation may use it at all: in principle it is not supposed to engage upon such investigations. As useful a device as it may be—especially if, one day, the *ex officio* application of the choice of law rule was generalized to those cases where the parties' rights are 'disponibles'— the theory of equivalence should be very narrowly construed. Otherwise it may seriously undermine the mandatory application of choice of law rules.

The theory of equivalence in many ways resembles the doctrine of the *Antikiesregel*, which was first adopted and then rejected by the Bundesgerichthof.[16] According to this doctrine, when all laws lead to a similar result, the judge is not obliged to choose between them. In condemning this doctrine, the Bundesgerichthof referred to the parties' interest in knowing which law is applicable, especially as regards the question of the control of the interpretation of the law by the Supreme Court (for there is no control of the interpretation of foreign laws). Moreover, in countries where the doctrine of precedent is particularly important, it is essential to know whether judges have based their decision upon their own law or upon a foreign law. The theory of equivalence also reminds us of some American doctrines, based upon the notion of false conflicts, or 'non-conflicts'.[17] These doctrines consider that, if the contents of laws are identical, there is no real conflict.

The theory of equivalence could be rooted in the famous presumption of similarity between the foreign law and the *lex fori*, which is traditionally the case in most common law countries, in order to justify the application of the *lex fori*. In all common law countries, however, this presumption has

---

[14] For a comparative perspective on the doctrine of estoppel, see B Fauvarque-Cosson 'L'estoppel du droit anglais', in *L'Interdiction de se contredire au détriment d'autrui* Études juridiques (Paris Economica 2001) 3.

[15] Civ 1ère 13 avr 1999 [1999] Rev crit dr int priv 698 note H Muir Watt; [2000] Journal dr int priv 315 note B Fauvarque-Cosson; 3 avr 2001 [2001] Rev crit 513 note H Muir Watt.

[16] 3 May 1988 [1988] IPRax 231.

[17] Ehrenzweig *Private International Law* (General Part) (Sijthoff Leiden and Oceana New York 1967) sect 36, 86.

been criticized as being a mere fiction.[18] Moreover, it has never been treated as a universal rule: thus, English judges have sometimes refused to apply it when the foreign law does not belong to a common law country. Some authors have said that this mode of reasoning is yet more inappropriate when the *lex fori* has been modified by statute. All these criticisms could lead to question the idea, which was once put forward in comparative law, that there is a general *praesumptio similitudinis* between the conflicting laws, that is to say, a presumption that the practical results are similar.[19]

Recently, the French Cour de cassation has also discovered another technique, based upon the parties' agreement not to apply the foreign law. At first sight it could be compared to the doctrine of estoppel or to the theory of equivalence since it leads to the same result: it is used in order not to quash lower courts' decisions which have not applied the applicable foreign law. Yet, it is very different and does possess another justification, founded upon the parties' greater freedom of action when their rights are 'disponibles'.

III. THE PARTIES' RIGHT TO AGREE UPON THE APPLICATION OF THE *LEX FORI*

The parties' right to agree upon the application of the *lex fori* and, in so doing, to prevent the judge from applying the choice of law rule which designated a foreign law has emerged as a major topic over the last fifteen years. It is very closely linked to the judge's duty to apply *ex officio* the choice of law rule. Indeed, if the judge is not under a duty to do so, he most probably will not do so, and therefore it is less necessary to make an agreement aimed at preventing him from applying *ex officio* the choice of law rule. This may be the reason why the parties' right to agree upon the application of the *lex fori* was not asserted by the French Cour de cassation until 1988, when it overruled the long-standing *Bisbal* case and decided instead that judges were bound to apply *ex officio* the French choice of law rule.[20]

---

[18] Fentiman (n 1) 147 and 148, questioning the 'plausibility of equating English and forein law'.

[19] K Zweigert 'Méthodologie du droit comparé', in *Mélanges Maury* (Paris 1960) vol 2, 579; K Zweigert and H Kötz *Introduction to Comparative Law* (3rd edn Oxford Clarendon Press 1998) 40. Compare Fentiman, questioning the 'plausibility of equating English and foreign law' (n 1) 148.

[20] Civ 1ère 19 avr 1988 *Roho c Caron* [1989] Rev crit 68, note H Batiffol; [1988] D. Somm 345 obs B Audit; 6 mai 1997 *Hannover International* [19927] Journal du dr int priv 804 note D Bureau; [1997] Rev crit 514 and note; Ancel and Lequette (n 5) no 84; Civ 1ère 1 juillet 1997 *Sté Karl Ibold GMBH* [1998] Rev crit 60 esp 2ème note P Mayer. On this evolution, see B. Fauvarque-Cosson *Libre Ddisponibilité des droits et conflits de lois* (Paris LGDJ 1996), préf Y Lequette.

The parties' agreement has been called 'accord procédural'.[21] Such an agreement is aimed not at choosing the applicable law, but at putting aside the foreign law that is normally applicable. As indicated by its name, it is made during the procedure and must therefore be distinguished from a choice of law based upon parties' autonomy in contract matters (by contrast, this agreement is named 'accord de fond'). Its effects are limited to the matters that are being discussed; if, for instance, it intervenes between two parties to a contract, it concerns not the whole contract but only the specific issues that are being litigated.

Originally, an accord procédural was subject to three conditions:

- it had to occur once the litigation had begun before the courts;
- it could only be valid if the parties' right were 'disponibles';
- it had to be expressed.

While the first two conditions have been reaffirmed by the Cour de cassation, the third one is disappearing. Some recent cases have decided that failure to plead the application of foreign law amounted to a procedural agreement in favour of the *lex fori*. The Cour de cassation has done so in contract matters, at a time when judges were obliged to apply the choice of law rule *ex officio* because it originated in the Rome Convention. In fact, it has done so in order to save some judgments that had not applied the choice of law rule *ex officio*.

This new approach is subject to criticism. Indeed, there is some inconsistency in stating, first, that judges are bound to apply *ex officio* the choice of law rule and admitting, afterwards, that they can be relieved from this obligation on the mere basis that, in remaining silent, the parties have agreed to the application of the *lex fori*. In such situations silence may result from ignorance or deliberate manoeuvre of one party; it is not necessarily the expression of an agreement between parties whose interests are in conflict. Unless there is a case of false conflict, one of these parties is interested in the application of the foreign law. In the French inquisitorial system the judge should always have the duty to inform this party that, by virtue of the French choice of law rules, a foreign law is applicable.

The question might appear to be less important now because, when parties' rights are 'disponibles', the judges have no duty to apply *ex officio* the choice of law rule. However, it acquired a new dimension when recent cases applied the same device in order to elude the Vienna Convention on International Sales Contracts. Having decided that this Convention constitutes French law and must, as such, be applied *ex officio*, the Cour de cassation has ruled that the parties' silence as to this Convention amounts

---

[21] The first person to use this terminology was Professor Paul Lagarde, in his comment of Civ 1ère 4 oct 1989 *de Baat* [1990] Rev crit 316.

to an agreement to avoid it and to choose internal French rules of contract law.[22]

If, as now appears to be the law, such an agreement can be inferred from the mere silence of the parties, the French system is not very far from the English principle according to which, in the absence of pleading and proof of foreign law, the court will apply the *lex fori*. In fact, it comes very close to this solution. The only difference is that under French law the parties' rights must be 'disponibles' for such an agreement to be implied, while in English law such a requirement is irrelevant. In his book[23] Richard Fentiman has very clearly demonstrated that English law's treatment of foreign law is not always within the parties' 'untrammelled control'. Conversely, in countries such as France, where foreign law is in principle treated as a matter of law and where the judge should consequently be under a duty to apply it *ex officio*, this is not always so. Various means do exist in order to alleviate this duty. Two of them are particularly important: the equivalence theory, aimed at tracking false conflicts, and the parties' implied agreement to revert to the *lex fori*. The extent of the judges' duties depends on the use, moderate or otherwise, which the supreme courts will make of such devices.

IV. CONCLUSION

Neither in England, nor in France, nor in any other legal system can foreign law be considered as mere fact or as pure law. Its real nature is hybrid. More precisely, its procedural treatment depends on three very different factors. The first—and only one related to the foreign law itself—is the type of foreign law at stake: could a French lawyer consider Belgium law (strongly influenced by the French Civil Code) to be as 'foreign' as English law? Further, in those fields that have been harmonized via the implementation of EC directives, could this same French lawyer consider English law to be as 'foreign' as, for instance, Japanese law?

The two other factors are 'exterior' in so far as they have nothing to do with the foreign law itself. As previously mentioned, one is linked to the distinction between *disponibles* and *indisponibles* rights. Yet, this factor is not overriding; it even becomes irrelevant when it comes to determining the extent of the Cour de cassation's control over lower courts' decisions. The other factor is linked to the judges' initiatives: if the judge decides to apply *ex officio* the French choice of law rule, even though he is not bound to do

---

[22] Civ 1ère 26 juin 2001 [2002] Rev crit 93 note H Muir Watt; [2001] Journal du dr int priv 1121 note A Huet; [2001] D 3607 note Cl Witz.

[23] See n 1.

so, he must then determine the content of the relevant foreign law which should otherwise have been proved by the parties whose rights were 'disponibles'. Therefore, not only does the complexity of the French solutions regarding the treatment of foreign law in national courts rest upon the fact that 'not all foreign laws are the same';[24] it also rests upon the fact that during the litigation the judges' duties vary according to factors which relate not to the foreign law as such but to the parties' and judges' enterprises.

In this book, dedicated to the use of comparative law before national and international courts, it seems necessary to end this contribution with a more general view of the complicated relationship between comparative law and conflicts of laws.[25] The discipline of conflict of laws depends to a large extent on comparative law. At the same time it provides the latter with one practical legitimacy. This is particularly true in countries such as Germany, Italy, Switzerland, Austria, and, to a lesser extent, France, where judges are required to apply foreign law *ex officio*. Although this is not comparative law in the strict sense, as rightly noted by Mr Fentiman, it also 'truly raises a question of comparative law' for it is a 'matter not of know-ledge but of understanding'.[26] In fact, even if judges eventually turn back to the *lex fori*, the part played by comparative law in the process of applying a choice of law rule is considerable. For indeed, even before reaching the final step, which raises the questions of pleading and proof of foreign law, various comparative insights may be needed. Devices such as characterization, adaptation, and public policy require review of some foreign internal rules; the doctrine of renvoi implies reference to the choice of law rules of another jurisdiction. Last but not least, the recent development of true content-oriented choice of law rules[27] have made comparative investigations occasionally necessary at a preliminary stage, that is to say, in order to apply the forum's conflicts rules.[28]

---

[24] See Fentiman ch 2 in this volume.

[25] Fauvarque-Cosson 'Comparative Law and Conflict of Laws: Allies or Enemies? New Perspectives on an Old Couple' (2001) 49 AJCL 407.

[26] See Fentiman ch 2 in this volume. On this informational role of comparative law, see also M. Reimann, 'Parochialism in American Conflicts Law' (2001) 49 AJCL 369, 371.

[27] As to the development of such choice of law rules in codified private international law systems, see S Symeonides *Private International Law at the End of the Twentieth Century: Progress or Regress?* (Kluwer 1999), 48.

[28] See AT Von Mehren 'The Contribution of Comparative Law to The Theory and Practice of Private International Law' in International Law in Comparative Perspective WE Butler (ed) (Sijthoff & Noordhoff 1980) 153, 159 (topic of 10th Congress of Comparative Law Budapest 1978).

2

Foreign Law in National Courts

RG Fentiman

The remarks made in this chapter are concerned with an important way—perhaps the most important way—in which problems of comparative law arise in national courts. Their concern is with the proof of foreign law, with those cases where one country's courts are required to apply another country's laws.

The need to apply foreign law arises whenever the rules for choice of law provide that the law governing an issue is foreign. Alpha may sue Beta in England for a tort committed in France. Or Gamma may sue Delta in Germany under a contract expressly governed by English law. In the first case the law of the place of the tort will doubtless govern; in the second, the law chosen by the parties will likely be applied. But the application of foreign law begs questions of some difficulty and practical importance. These belong to private international law, or perhaps to the law of international civil procedure. But they also speak to the most fundamental of all questions of comparative law: what may we truly know of the laws of another country?

I. PRELIMINARY

The purpose of these remarks is to identify the nature of the foreign law problem, and sketch its implications for the conflicts lawyer and the comparatist. But three broader issues must first be addressed.

First, given the theme of these proceedings, it is necessary to ask whether the proof of foreign law truly raises a question of comparative law. Some may say that informing oneself as to foreign law is a matter of information not comparison; that *knowing of* foreign law is not to *compare with* foreign law. But the proof of foreign law is seldom a matter of acquiring information; it requires one country's courts to adjudicate questions involving another country's laws. Certainly, to understand foreign law, as the proof of foreign law requires, inevitably involves some degree of mental accommodation (or compromise) between the familiar concepts of one's own law and the unfamiliar concepts of foreign law. In all but the simplest cases, in which foreign law can be derived from a textbook, counsel and the courts must inevitably make judgments about foreign law, delve into its conceptual substructure, and adopt the thought processes of the foreign lawyer. If legal argument and adjudication under foreign law is not comparative law, it is hard to know what is. Indeed, the proof of foreign law may ultimately raise the most fundamental of all comparative law questions: how far can we truly comprehend foreign law? And it does so in a uniquely important and arresting way. Comparatists may debate the accessibility of foreign law. But whether we can grasp the true nature of a foreign system only has real significance, and is only truly tested, when the rights and duties of litigants depend upon it—when one country's courts are required to apply another country's laws.

Secondly, we should register the debt owed by the conflict of laws to comparative law. But we should also note how little the proof of foreign law in England has been influenced by trends abroad. At least in common law systems the conflict of laws is largely a product of comparative law— or, more exactly, of legal transplantation.[1] Unlike most departments of English law, for example, the subject did not evolve gradually. It originated instead in a flourish of judicial creativity in the nineteenth century. This was assisted by direct appeal both to foreign writers (such as Story,[2] Savigny,[3] and Huber) and to English writers (such as Westlake[4] and Dicey),[5] who themselves drew heavily on foreign commentators.[6] Recent history also provides some striking examples of legal transplantation. In the leading case of *Boys v Chaplin*[7] the House of Lords refashioned the rules for choice of law in tort by drawing directly from the approach of the American Restatement. And in *The Spiliada*,[8] the source of the modern doctrine of *forum non conveniens*, the House of Lords borrowed freely from the approach of the Scottish courts—with dramatic consequences for the English law of jurisdiction.

Interestingly, however, English law has been influenced not at all by developments in other jurisdictions regarding the proof of foreign law. The resilience of the principle that foreign laws are facts (with all that traditionally implies) contrasts with the rejection of the fact doctrine in the United States.[9] And there is little trace in English law of the debates about

[1] See further, Sack 'Conflicts of Law in the History of English Law' in *Law: A Century of Progress 1835–1935* (1935), 342.

[2] *Commentaries on the Conflict of Laws* (1834). All but three of the authors whose influence Story acknowledged in his preface were continental jurists.

[3] Significantly, Savigny's *System of Modern Roman Law* appeared in English translation in 1869.

[4] *A Treatise on Private International Law* (1858).

[5] *Conflict of Laws* (1896).

[6] An example is the treatment of domicile in *Whicker v Hume* (1858) 7 HL Cas 124.

[7] [1971] AC 356 (HL).   [8] [1986] AC 460 (HL).

[9] Miller 'Federal Rule 44.1 and the "Fact" Approach to Determining Foreign Law: Death Knell for a Die-Hard Doctrine' (1967) 65 Mich L Rev 613.

the foreign law problem visible in America, Germany, and France. Why this is so is itself an interesting question. As we shall see, the insularity of the English approach is no doubt explained by the way the foreign law problem is perceived in most common law systems (America excepted), and the circumstances in which it arises.

Thirdly, what follows must be put in context. The comparative law problems associated with the proof of foreign law are universal, matters of emphasis and idiom aside.[10] And the following remarks are not intended merely as an account of English law.[11] But they reflect the perspective of an English lawyer, and so need qualification. It is especially important to recall that the common law starts from the assumption that foreign laws are facts to be proved, not laws to be applied. This assumption is not shared by all common law jurisdictions (it has been rejected in American federal practice).[12] And it has been qualified in important ways elsewhere (as in English law, where foreign laws are facts 'of a peculiar kind').[13] But it colours the approach of the common lawyer. Not least perhaps it makes common lawyers relatively sanguine about cases where foreign law is 'incorrectly' applied, provided the evidence has been properly introduced and assessed.

Then there is the common lawyer's adversarial view of adjudication. Common lawyers tend more readily to regard adjudication, whether under foreign law or under their own, as a process of argument, not of discovery.[14] The right answer to a question of law (local or foreign) is perceived as emerging from an inquiry which is dialectical, not investigative. For this reason perhaps they tend to regard the use of single experts as an unsatisfactory means to establish foreign law, by comparison with one in which a court is required to decide between the competing testimonies of the parties' experts. And for this reason no doubt they are less concerned with whether foreign law is 'correctly' applied, in some objective sense, than with whether the process of proof is full and fair.

It must also be emphasized that in the English experience private international law is, or has become, a branch of commercial law—in stark contrast with many civil law systems in which disputes concerning marriage

---

[10] See, further, Hartley 'Pleading and Proof of Foreign Law: The Major European Systems Compared' (1996) 45 ICLQ 271.

[11] For accounts of English law, see, Dicey and Morris *The Conflict of Laws* (13th edn 2001) ch 9; R Fentiman *Foreign Law in English Courts* (Oxford OUP 1998); O'Malley and Layton *European Civil Practice* (1989) ch 9.

[12] Federal Rules of Civil Procedure, Rule 44.1; Wright and Miller *Federal Practice and Procedure: Civil 2d* (1995) vol 9 sect 2441.

[13] *Parkasho v Singh* [1968] 233; *Dalmia Diary Ltd v National Bank of Pakistan* [1978] 2 Lloyds's Rep 233 (CA); *MCC Proceeds Inc v Bishopsgate Investment Trust plc* [1999] CLC 417 (CA).

[14] An approach described by some as 'rhetorical': see Perelman and Olbrechts-Tyteca *The New Rhetoric* (1969).

or children are the norm.[15] This may explain why English lawyers are ready to endorse a system for establishing foreign law that is relatively costly, over which the court has relatively little control, and which in most cases allows litigants to choose whether to plead foreign law at all.[16] In such an environment the considerable cost of applying foreign law is perceived as a burden that can be absorbed by well-funded litigants. And the decision whether to introduce foreign law is regarded as a proper strategic choice for sophisticated parties who are likely to be well advised. Moreover, the only policy considerations in such an environment are likely to be respect for party autonomy, and the desirability of allowing litigants to minimize the cost of litigation—which argue for giving parties the choice whether to plead foreign law.

Finally, there is the important consideration that disputes involving substantive questions of foreign law arise relatively seldom in English law. This is not to deny that commercial disputes with foreign elements are common—indeed they are more common than in most jurisdictions. And it is true that such disputes are hard fought in preliminary proceedings concerning jurisdiction and interim relief. But it is less common for questions of foreign legal liability to go to trial. Why this is so is itself a complex, interesting question: one reason is that once the question of jurisdiction is resolved the parties are in a position to settle; another may be the expense of taking a case to full trial (especially under foreign law). But it means that the role of foreign law in establishing jurisdiction is a matter of particular importance to English lawyers.[17] And it means that the problem of applying foreign law has received rather less attention (which may explain the English lawyer's somewhat conservative approach to the problem).

But the relative infrequency of cases involving foreign law does not diminish the importance of the problem for the English lawyer. Infrequent as they are, such cases of course occur (as the following section illustrates). The foreign law problem also arises indirectly in an important way. As we have seen, the difficulty, and the possibility, of establishing foreign law can be decisive in identifying the *forum conveniens*. Again, even if cases under foreign law seldom go to full trial, the parties and their advisers are bound to act as if they will. The preparation of such cases, and the strategic decisions made by the parties, will take account of the likely outcome under foreign law and the difficulty and expense of proving it. Moreover, the relative infrequency of such cases may be a thing of the past. Legislation in the

---

[15] Broadly, this is attributable to the large number of cases before the English Commercial Court having a foreign element, combined with the fact that most matters affecting marriage and children are governed exclusively by English law, no conflicts issue therefore arising.

[16] R Fentiman 'Foreign Law in English Courts' (1992) 108 LQR 142.

[17] Id 'Foreign Law and the Forum Conveniens' in Symeonides and Nafziger (eds) *Law and Justice in a Multistate World: Essays in Honor of Arthur T von Mehren* (2002) 275.

area of choice of law in tort has brought new clarity to the law,[18] and has already generated a growing case-law in an area where cases were once few. More importantly, the increase in cross-border travel, communication, and commerce (partly facilitated by the Internet) is likely to increase the incidence of conflicts cases in future. And because many such cases may involve consumers, they may raise novel questions about the efficiency and fairness of the proof of foreign law. Such questions cannot be answered by assuming that issues of foreign law arise only between parties who are well funded and well advised, and that party autonomy is the only policy imperative.

II. THE FOREIGN LAW PROBLEM

The rights and duties of the parties may sometimes depend upon a law other than that of the forum; in such cases foreign law must be established, and (as difficult an issue) applied. This process is the very object, the terminus of the choice of law process, yet it is fraught with difficulty, and in the eyes of some may be impossible. The difficulty may be illustrated by contrasting two English cases: *The Spirit of Independence*[19] and *City of Gotha and the Federal Republic of Germany v Sotheby's and Cobert Finance SA.*[20]

1. The Spirit of Independence

The Spirit of Independence, a cross-Channel ferry, was arrested in Boulogne on the instructions of a shipyard that had not been paid by the charterer for repairs to the vessel. The charterer was insolvent. The question was whether the owners were entitled to the release of their vessel from arrest without assuming liability for the charterer's debts. There was agreement that the question was one of French maritime law. But the answer under French law was profoundly unclear. The relevant legislation supplied no clear guidance. And both courts and commentators were divided. So the parties deployed expert evidence in support of their rival positions. Both sides employed experts of acknowledged eminence, both of whom supplied lengthy reports and were examined and cross-examined at length.

Because the point was a novel one, as yet unresolved in French law, Rix J clearly felt himself in some difficulty. He remarked on 'how invidious a position this Court finds itself in, having to resolve what appears to be a

---

[18] Private International Law (Miscellaneous Provisions) Act 1995.
[19] [1999] 1 Lloyd's Rep 43.
[20] 9 Sept 1998 (unreported).

crux of the French law of arrest'.[21] Nonetheless, Rix J surveyed the *jurisprudence*, the *doctrine*, and the expert testimony with consummate care and skill, essaying the evidence in a tautly reasoned judgment of some twenty pages. But this impressive forensic exercise led in the end to a profoundly awkward conclusion. The evidence was tied. Although diametrically opposed, the rival positions adopted by each of the parties were equally plausible and compelling. Neither was obviously wrong, neither obviously right. Nor was one more persuasive than the other. How then was the court to resolve the impasse? Rix J's solution is both striking and revealing. He concluded, uncontroversially, that French law dictated no result either way. More creatively, he judged (without evidence) that a French court in such a case would favour whichever result was more just—which here meant releasing the vessel from arrest without penalizing the shipowner.

None could doubt that *The Spirit of Independence* provides a lesson in the proof of foreign law. Distinguished experts offered comprehensive, impartial evidence to a judge sensitive to the foreign law problem, who ultimately achieved a just result. But a nagging doubt remains: was French law really applied? In reality the evidence of French law was inconclusive, and Rix J reached his final decision not by applying French law (other than notionally), but by doing what justice required.

More precisely, the case is troubling—and revealing—for four reasons.

First, it highlights the cost and complexity of establishing foreign law.[22] In one sense the point is an obvious one. The protracted examination and cross-examination of experts is a costly, time-consuming process. And in one sense it need cause no particular concern: litigation is expensive, and complex litigation is more expensive still. But the point acquires added meaning if we accept that in *The Spirit of Independence* French law was never applied at all, save in a notional sense. For it is rightly a matter of concern if so intensive, and so expensive, a process ultimately yields no result. And the cost of establishing foreign law creates a further problem. It is not so much that is exposes the parties—or the losing party—to substantial costs. It is that the potential expense may deter litigants from pursuing or defending claims, and thus discourage or deny access to justice.

Secondly, *The Spirit of Independence* suggests that in some cases the difficulty in applying foreign law is a matter not of knowledge but of understanding. It shows that a court, however well informed about foreign law, may be unable to adopt the legal methods and habits of thought of a foreign lawyer. None could doubt the quality and comprehensiveness of the expert

---

[21] 65.
[22] Concerns about the cost and inefficiency involved often surface in common law jurisdictions in cases involving the doctrine of *forum non conveniens*; see, further, Fentiman (n 17) 275.

evidence in *The Spirit of Independence*. Rix J thought himself 'fortunate to have had the assistance of such experts, and grateful for the wealth of analysis and citation which they provided'.[23] But he also recognized the unreality of the task in which he was engaged, in so far as he was required to approach French law using the methods of the English lawyer. There is no reason why foreign canons of interpretation, and foreign legal methods, cannot themselves be proved (or agreed) in an English court. But in *The Spirit of Independence* both parties had presented the relevant French case-law as they might have relied upon English cases in a purely English dispute. They did so although the craft of reconciling and distinguishing cases, and the doctrine of precedent, are unknown (in the English sense) in France. As Rix J was aware, this inevitably distorted his inquiry into French law. As he said: 'to derive my decision from the material presented to me is to do something which a French Court would be unlikely to do'.[24]

Similar problems of method were also encountered by Hirst J in *The Nile Rhapsody*,[25] a case concerning the staying of actions that turned partly on the difficulty of applying Egyptian law in England. The difficulty lay not in the content of Egyptian law so much as in the techniques necessary to establish it. An amalgam of French civil law, 'custom, the principles of Islamic law, and the principles of natural law and equity',[26] Hirst J clearly considered Egyptian law to be especially inaccessible to those not familiar with its principles and the hierarchy existing between its various sources. The problem was compounded by the difficulty to an English judge of giving appropriate weight to juristic writing, case-law (in a system without precedent), and the decision of the Court of Cassation (not being a true court of appeal).[27] Such difficulties of approach meant that the issues in dispute 'were pre-eminently more suitable for decision in Egypt than here'.[28]

Thirdly, *The Spirit of Independence* highlights the uncomfortable truth that in some cases foreign law is beyond proof. More precisely, it suggests that some hard cases[29] cannot be resolved except by a court with a deep, perhaps instinctive, grasp of something more than the letter of the law. Some questions can only be answered by reference to underlying principles, which may remain unstated (and so beyond proof), or by recourse to techniques of analysis that can only be learned by long experience (and not merely by hearing evidence). The problem is only hinted at in Rix J's unease about applying English legal methods to a question of French law. It is perhaps best revealed in his (forgivable) inability to resolve the impasse in the evidence before him—other than by juridical sleight of hand. For it is at such a juncture in any legal system that the process of adjudication depends

---

[23] 47. [24] 66. [25] [1992] 2 Lloyd's Rep 399.
[26] 411. [27] 413. [28] 412.
[29] In Professor Dworkin's sense: see, further, R Dworkin *Taking Rights Seriously* (London Duckworth 1977) ch 4.

upon experience and the exercise of informed judgment—matters not read-ily amenable to the process of proof.

In this respect *The Spirit of Independence* recalls *Du Pont de Nemours v Agnew*,[30] which contains a classic statement of the foreign law problem. Famously, the case concerned the effect of public policy on a contract of insurance governed by English law. Asked whether a court in England or in Illinois was the most appropriate forum in which to resolve the dispute, Lord Bingham CJ alluded to the problems that a foreign court would encounter in handling the English doctrine of public policy. As he concluded:

This Court is necessarily better placed than any other to rule on that question . . . There is no decided authority in English law which denies them an indemnity. If English public policy is to be held to deny the right to indemnity in these circum-stances, then this Court and no other must so hold. I do not regard this as a ques-tion capable of fair resolution in any foreign court, however distinguished and well instructed . . . that is a question which I do not think any foreign Judge could consci-entiously resolve with any confidence that he was reaching a correct answer.[31]

Fourthly, *The Spirit of Independence* illustrates how difficult it is to handle those cases (however rare) in which foreign law cannot meaningfully be applied. What was Rix J to do, given the impasse presented by the tied evidence of the rival experts? In most cases English law admits of only two alternatives.[32] A court may in principle apply English law by default, a result sometimes justified by reference to the perplexing fiction that English and foreign law are deemed to be the same unless the contrary is proved. More commonly, a court can disregard the expert testimony and look for a solution in any legislation, commentaries, or decided cases relied upon by the experts.[33]

In *The Spirit of Independence*, however, the documentary evidence clearly offered no solution; it too was divided. Nor was it a case in which it would have been possible for the court to apply English law by default. For under English law arrest founds jurisdiction on the merits, and success-ful claims on the merits can always be executed against the arrested vessel. Whether or not a shipowner may secure release by giving security for a charterer's liabilities is therefore never an issue. As Rix J said, 'the ultimate question which exercises the parties in the present case under French law . . . simply does not arise under English law'.[34] As this suggests, it was always going to be necessary to find a novel solution to the problem of a

---

[30] [1987] 2 Lloyd's Rep 585, 596 (CA).

[31] 595.

[32] Where the issue goes to full trial; where questions of foreign law arise in interlocutory proceedings several provisional solutions are possible: *The Polessk* [1996] 2 Lloyd's Rep 40.

[33] *Bumper Developments Corpn v Commissioner of Police* [1991] 1 WLR 1362 (CA).

[34] 52–3.

failure in proof. But, however subtle that novel solution, it is hard to escape the conclusion that resort to such devices is always a signal of failure. It is not a means to apply foreign law, but an admission that the application of foreign law is impossible.

2. City of Gotha v Sotheby's

This is not to say that foreign law can never be applied satisfactorily. Indeed, the nature of the foreign law problem comes into sharper focus if we examine a case in which the proof of foreign law was apparently successful. Consider *City of Gotha v Sotheby's*,[35] which repays study in so far as it represents at first sight a counterweight to *The Spirit of Independence*.

City of Gotha turned on a difficult question of German law, on the effect of §221 of the *Bürgerliches Gesetzbuch*. The dispute concerned title to a painting, originally owned by the ducal family of Saxe-Coburg-Gotha, which disappeared in the closing days of the Second World War. The city of Gotha and the German government claimed title to the work when it was put up for auction at Sotheby's. The success of the claim depended upon whether the thirty-year limitation period in German law had expired. This in turn depended on §221, which governs the limitation of proprietary actions in the event that a third party acquires possession. The effect of §221 had never been considered by a German court. But it was a matter of much debate among German commentators. Following a comprehensive and supple treatment of the academic sources, and the evidence of the parties' experts, Moses J found that the city's action was not time-barred.

The case appears to be a model of how foreign law should be applied. And so it is. But the reason is worth exploring. It was a case where all that was involved was the interpretation of foreign legislation assisted by expert opinion and academic commentary. Matters of idiom and conceptual differences aside, the proof of German law depended simply on assessing on their face the strength of the competing views. But this did not involve issues about the relationship between unfamiliar legal sources. Nor were any arcane principles or any peculiarities of German legal method involved. No more was needed than the judge's own skill at weighing the rationality and persuasiveness of the arguments—matters within his inherent knowledge and expertise. Moses J had a clear view of the correct methodology to be adopted under German law, a methodology which was far from being foreign. As he said, in a revealing passage:

There is no dispute as to the approach the German court would take to issues in respect of which there is no judicial precedent. It would have regard to commen-

[35] 9 Sept 1998 (unreported).

taries on the German Civil Code ('BGB'). It would not feel bound by the mere fact that the majority of commentators took a particular view or by the most recent statement of opinion. It would take into account the quality of the arguments, the consistency of the statements and the reputation of the authors.[36]

Admittedly, in one respect German legal method differed from that of English law. As Moses J noted, 'German Courts adopt a teleological approach.' But such an approach is far from being unfamiliar to an English court, and is easily comprehensible. It is a universally understood form of reasoning, not an impenetrable aspect of foreign legal method.

As *City of Gotha* confirms, even the hardest questions of foreign law (or the most novel) are sometimes capable of resolution. Like *The Spirit of Independence* the case involved a novel question of foreign law which admitted of competing solutions. But *City of Gotha* is different in two telling ways. It was clear, as it was not in *The Spirit of Independence*, how a foreign court would approach the problem. And, decisively, that approach depended upon universal methods of adjudication, not any distinctive methodology. Although formally a matter of foreign law, it was within the knowledge and expertise of the English judge.

III. PRACTICAL RESPONSES

Because of the difficulties exemplified in cases such as *The Spirit of Independence* all legal systems have developed strategies for responding to the foreign law problem. A comprehensive survey of these strategies is beyond the scope of these remarks. But it is possible at least to outline what measures are available to solve (or to ease) the difficulty of establishing and applying foreign law. Each, however, as we shall see, has its limitations.

1. Four Responses

There are four practical responses to the foreign law problem.

(a) Perfecting the Process of Proof

An obvious response is to develop appropriate mechanisms for adjudicating foreign law questions—such that the difficulties encountered in *The Spirit of Independence* never (or seldom) arise.[37] Broadly, legal systems differ between those that adopt an adversarial approach to foreign law and those that favour an investigative approach. In the former it is for the

---

[36] Para I.2.
[37] See, further, Mayer 'Les Procédés de preuve de la loi étrangère' in *Études offertes á Jacques Ghestin* (2001).

parties to provide evidence supporting their position on foreign law, although it remains of course for the court to adjudicate upon that evidence. In the latter, foreign law is generally established (or a solution proposed) either by a single court-appointed expert or by the court itself following its own researches.

To ask which approach is best—or which variation of which approach—is an idle question, since each must be viewed against the background of the conceptual assumptions and procedural machinery available in each system. Certainly, the two approaches may reflect rival perceptions of the adjudicatory process in general. The adversarial approach has obvious appeal for those who see legal 'truth' as emerging from a process of argument; who see legal reasoning as dialectical, even rhetorical. By contrast the investigative approach reflects the assumption that adjudication is a process of discovery, a view which in an extreme (if fanciful) form perhaps assumes that it is possible scientifically to discern the correct answer to a question of law.

But it is perhaps appropriate to say that any successful regime for handling such questions (whether in the civil law or common law tradition) is likely to recognize that not all disputes about foreign law are the same. Certainly, it would be unwise to assume that, say, a case involving merely the interpretation of a foreign statute is on the same footing as one involving conflicting case-law or academic opinions. Nor is it sensible to assume that the law of a cognate legal system can be treated the same as that of a system that reflects an entirely distinct legal tradition.

This has two consequences. First, any successful regime is likely to be eclectic, offering a variety of mechanisms for establishing foreign law, each appropriate to the circumstances. Perhaps the American approach offers the best example. Certainly, Rule 44.1 of the Federal Rules of Civil Procedure permits resort to any available means to establish foreign law. In response, US courts have employed a variety of techniques, including the use of expert testimony (whether of the parties' experts or of one appointed by the court), judicial research, and the direct interpretation of foreign materials.[38] Interestingly (but less obviously), English law also offers a range of evidential options. Undeniably foreign law is almost always proved by reference to the evidence of the parties' experts. But English courts have been prepared to employ several other means.[39] They have, for example, construed foreign legislation without expert assistance.[40] And in principle the rules of procedure permit a court to appoint an independent expert in addition to, or instead of, those of the parties.[41]

---

[38] Wright and Miller (n 12) sect 2441.
[40] Ibid 257–62.

[39] Fentiman (n 11) chs VII and VIII.
[41] Ibid 211–18, 232–8.

Secondly, any successful regime for establishing foreign law (whatever its origin) is likely to recognize that the conceptual character of foreign law is not immutable, but depends upon the circumstances. Thus, most legal systems have tended to characterize foreign laws as either facts or laws for all purposes. But the reality may be different. Some issues of foreign law may have a 'legal' character in so far as they resemble questions of domestic law. To treat them as facts (or merely as facts) may be a serious and misleading distortion. It obscures the reality that all laws have a certain common character and that, idiom and convention aside, the basic requirements of rational legal discourse are universal. It ignores the extent to which a court may meaningfully employ its legal expertise in handling questions of foreign law. This is especially so when the laws of a cognate legal system are involved, as perhaps when an English court is required to apply the laws of another common law jurisdiction.[42]

But in other cases there may be little resemblance between foreign law and the *lex fori*, in which case it is understandable that foreign law should be treated as fact. In such cases a court's understanding of foreign law is likely to be hindered (by comparison with its grasp of local law) by unfamiliarity with its cultural context, its underlying principles, and the methods of reasoning and interpretation employed by foreign lawyers.

In this respect it is of particular interest that in American federal practice no attempt is made to classify foreign laws as facts or laws. True, the effect of Federal Rule 44.1 is to abolish the principle that foreign laws are facts.[43] But the effect is to leave it open to the courts to treat questions of foreign law in a fashion appropriate to the circumstances. Less obviously, the English courts have begun to move in a similar direction. In one important case the Court of Appeal recognized that some questions of foreign law can appropriately be treated as legal (where the construction of a statute from another common law jurisdiction was in issue).[44] In another they held that this approach is not always possible (where difficult questions of Italian law were involved).[45]

The perception that not all cases involving foreign law are the same also underlies recent developments in French law.[46] There the distinction is not between issues of fact and law. In French law foreign laws are laws. Instead the approach that a court should adopt is determined by whether or not the rights in dispute are *disponibles*—capable of alienation by the beneficiary.

---

[42] See eg *A–G for New Zealand v Ortiz* [1984] 1 AC 41 (HL) (New Zealand law); *MCC Proceeds Inc v Bishopsgate Investment Trust plc* [1999] CLC 417 (CA) (US law).

[43] Wright and Miller (n 12).

[44] *MCC Proceeds Inc. v Bishopsgate Investment Trust plc* [1999] CLC 417 (CA).

[45] *Morgan Grenfell & Co Ltd v Sace-Speciale per l'Assicurazione* 21 Dec 1999 (unreported) (CA).

[46] See Fauvarque-Cosson ch 1 in this volume; also Fentiman, (n 11) ch IX.

But, to an English lawyer, the distinction mirrors that between fact and law. Where inalienable rights are in question, questions of foreign law are treated in a 'legal' fashion: foreign law must be applied, and it is the court's responsibility to do so. But where the rights are alienable the treatment of foreign law resembles (to common law eyes) the treatment of facts: it is the parties' responsibility to introduce and establish foreign law.

But the most striking recognition that not all questions of foreign law are the same is perhaps to be found in common law systems. Certainly, in English and American law it has been recognized that some questions of foreign law are beyond meaningful proof, for which reason a court should not exercise jurisdiction in such cases.

(b) Declining Jurisdiction over Foreign Law

A second response to the foreign law problem is to exclude from the start difficult or impossible questions of foreign law. At one time English courts simply declined jurisdiction over foreign laws.[47] Modern common law jurisdictions adopt a more calibrated approach. The doctrine of *forum non conveniens* permits a court to stay proceedings where it considers another forum to be the most appropriate court to hear a dispute.[48] Sometimes jurisdiction will be declined on grounds of efficiency, because the proof of foreign law would be unacceptably costly and time-consuming, by comparison with a trial in the relevant foreign court. And sometimes (if rarely) a case will be excluded because the accurate application of foreign law is impossible.[49] The English courts have responded in like fashion when English law would have to be applied in a foreign court. As we have seen, the Court of Appeal has held that the courts of England are better placed to apply English public policy than those of Illinois.[50]

(c) Permitting Party Autonomy

A third response is to leave the parties free to decide for themselves whether or not to plead and prove foreign law.[51] By this means the foreign law problem is made to disappear at the outset. And some would say that any adverse consequences in establishing foreign law may be laid at the parties' door, since the decision to introduce foreign law is theirs. The market-oriented solution has considerable and obvious benefits, and has traditionally been favoured in many common law jurisdictions. It tends not to exist, however, or exists in a severely qualified form, in civil law jurisdictions. In some such systems a court must judge a case on the objectively correct legal

---

[47] Sack (n 1) 381.
[48] Fentiman (n 17) 275.
[49] *The Nile Rhapsody* [1992] 2 Lloyd's Rep 399.
[50] *Du Pont de Nemours v Agnew* [1987] 1 Lloyd's Rep 585 (CA).
[51] See, further, De Boer 'Facultative Choice of Law' (1996) 257 *Recueil des Cours* 227.

basis, which includes applying any foreign law that may govern.[52] Alternatively, there are systems in which the pleading of foreign law is mandatory in so far as the parties are unable to divest themselves of inalienable rights of a 'patrimonial' nature.[53]

(d) Managing Failure in Proof

A fourth strategy is to accept that the proof of foreign law may fail, and design an appropriate response in the event that foreign law is not established.[54] This has attracted less discussion in common law jurisdictions than elsewhere. No doubt this is because the possibility of staying proceedings, and the greater freedom parties enjoy to avoid pleading foreign law, ensures that the problem arises less often. But it may also owe something to the logic of an adversarial approach, in which each party's case depends upon the strength of its own expert's evidence. In such a system, whatever the correctness of the court's findings, it will generally be possible to say that one expert's argument is the more convincing, or one expert's credentials are more impressive. But, as we have seen, an English court may in principle apply English law by default, although this seldom (if ever) appears to happen. More commonly an English court will disregard the expert evidence, and make its own findings based upon any documentary evidence of foreign law relied upon by the experts.[55]

In other jurisdictions a failure to establish foreign law may be more common. This is not because their approach to foreign law is inferior. In systems that regard foreign laws as laws it is perhaps harder to adopt a purely 'evidential' solution to the problem, by declaring that the burden of proving foreign law has not been discharged, or by finding that one expert is better qualified, or gave more compelling testimony, than another. In such systems a number of other solutions have been canvassed, which seek to respect the legal character of foreign law.[56] One possibility is to appeal to comparative law, by seeking an answer based upon the solutions adopted in legal systems related to that of the law in question.[57]

---

[52] As in Germany; Stein and Jonas *Kommentar zur Zivilprozessordnung* (21st edn 1997) vol 3, sect 293.

[53] As in France; see B Fauvarque-Cosson *Libre Disponibilité des droits et conflits de lois* (LGDJ Paris 1996).

[54] Fentiman (n 11) 182 ff.

[55] See eg *Buerger v New York Life Assurance Co* (1927) 96 LJKB 930 (CA); *Bumper Developments Corpn v Commissioner of Police* [1991] 1 WLR 1362 (CA).

[56] Fentiman (n 11) 281–3.

[57] As in Germany: von Bar, *Internationales Privatrecht* (1987–) vol 2, 329; and see Cappelletti 'Mandatory *Ex-Officio* Application of Foreign Law: The Comparative Method as a Solution Where the Foreign Law Cannot Be Ascertained' (1970) 3 CILSA 60.

2. *Partial Solutions*

These are, however, but partial solutions to the foreign law problem, each of which has inevitable limitations. Consider the machinery for establishing foreign law. However varied the range of techniques, however intensive the forensic process, cases may arise such as *The Spirit of Independence* where no mechanism is likely to have worked.

Again, the flaw in the *forum conveniens* route is that it may be more compelling in principle than in practice. Certainly, it may not always be easy to determine in preliminary proceedings how difficult a question of foreign law may be. Or it may not be easy to do so without in effect attempting to prove foreign law in interlocutory proceedings, which itself may be a lengthy, costly, and unsatisfactory process.[58]

Nor is it enough to privatize the problem, and leave it to the parties to decide whether to rely upon foreign law. In some cases such a choice is unreal, as when the very basis of a claim or defence depends upon foreign law. In some cases it may also be inappropriate to allow the parties such freedom. Even in English law, the most voluntarist of systems, the courts have qualified the principle of party autonomy in matters of foreign law. They have come to doubt the appropriateness of assuming in every case that English and foreign law can be the same.[59] And in some cases it is arguable that the relevant rules for choice of law are mandatory, leaving no room for party choice.[60]

Nor is it easy to see how any default rule, for use in hard cases, can offer a true solution to the foreign law problem. Some means to avoid deadlock is clearly required, for a court can scarcely declare a draw. And each of the proffered default rules no doubt supplies the courts with an answer. But they are merely devices to avoid an impasse and secure a result. They are not a means to apply foreign law. Indeed, they are an admission that no solution to the foreign law problem is possible.

IV. THEORETICAL QUESTIONS

As this suggests, there can be no *complete* solution to the foreign law problem, a conclusion that need cause no surprise. Some commentators are therefore drawn to an apocalyptic vision of the proof of foreign law, and of the choice of law process which it supports. They would count the conflicts

---

[58] Fentiman (n 17) 291–3.

[59] See eg *Shaker v Al-Bedrawi* [2002] 4 All ER 835 (CA); see also *Damberg v Damberg* [2001] NSWCA 87.

[60] As perhaps in cases under the 1980 Rome Convention on the Law Applicable to Contractual Obligations; Fentiman (n 11) 80–97.

process a failure, undermined by doubt that one country's courts can truly apply another country's laws.[61]

Presumably none could deny that foreign law can sometimes be applied efficiently and with accuracy. In some cases foreign law is applied without dispute, where the parties admit its content. In others the dispute can be resolved because the evidence in favour of one conclusion is clearly stronger. In others the question resolves itself into little more than a question of statutory construction which a court may resolve with relative ease and confidence of success. Moreover, there are cases, such as *City of Gotha*, in which an English court has answered difficult questions of foreign law with conspicuous success. But the fact that foreign law can be successfully applied offers little comfort to the sceptical. They might suggest that the very existence of cases where the process of proof cannot work (or work effectively) is an indictment of the process. And they might argue that the true nature of the problem is concealed. They would suggest that the risk that the proof of foreign law will fail is always present. They might argue that the very existence of such a risk may deter those with a legitimate claim or defence from pursuing it in court—deterring access to justice by legitimate litigants. Or they might argue that, for those who do proceed, the true nature of the problem will only emerge too late, once the evidence has been heard at considerable expense.

Sceptics might also say that cases where foreign law appears to have been satisfactorily applied are (or are often) an illusion. Hard cases where the evidence is balanced are in their nature those that require of a court uncommon complicity in the thought processes of a foreign lawyer—something which in some cases may be impossible even if the court appears to apply foreign law. Alternatively they are cases in which a court is likely to resolve the difficulty by resorting to strategies that owe nothing to the foreign law. To favour one view of foreign law over another because one expert was better qualified, or more convincing, than the other is not in the end to apply foreign law. Such devices are means to untie a knot in the evidence, not to discern the truth about foreign law.

Such arguments might suggest that the risk of failure in the process of proof is too great. And the risk may seem enough that we must declare the enterprise of proving foreign law a failure—and with it the choice of law process.

---

[61] See Juenger 193 (1995) *Recueil des Cours* 203–5; Hay Lando and Rotunda 'Conflict of Laws as a Technique for Legal Integration' in Cappelletti Seccombe and Weiler (eds) *Integration Through Law* 170; Lando '*Lex Fori in Foro Proprio*' (1995) 2 Maastricht Jl of European and Comp L 359, 367–71.

V. OF RIGHTNESS AND AUTHENTICITY

Such concerns are real. But we should avoid overstating the problem. It is especially important not to expect too much of the proof of foreign law. Certainly, it is easy to have inflated expectations of the proof of foreign law, born in turn of unrealistic expectations about the process of adjudication generally. More precisely, those who suppose that a court in any country is capable of arriving at an objectively correct answer to a question of law are likely to make two further assumptions about the proof of foreign law. They may suspect that the proof of foreign law lacks the objectivity associated with adjudication on questions of local law. And they may conclude that a court whose law is in question is more likely to arrive at a correct solution than a court elsewhere. But this perception rests upon an assumption about the nature of adjudication which most if not all theorists would discount. It rests upon the philosophical notion that in contested cases there can indeed be a 'right' answer to a question of law—whether local or foreign. Of course there may be in undisputed cases. But beyond that most would now accept there can be no single right answer, as distinct from a range of possible, plausible answers.[62]

Jurisprudentially this is trite learning. But it has an important consequence here. It suggests that we cannot expect too much of any process of adjudication—and that we should not expect more of the proof of foreign law than of adjudication in general. But this begs a question. What then can we expect of the process of adjudication, and thus of the proof of foreign law? To deny that the outcome of legal disputes can be correct in any objective sense does not mean that adjudication in hard cases cannot be subjected to standards of correctness. Adjudication in hard cases may not be concerned with the excavation of legal truth. But it must (at least) comply with general standards of rationality, with the requirements of coherence, relevance, and lack of bias; it must be consistent with the substantive principles underlying the area in question and immanent in the legal system itself; and it must employ the conventions of legal method accepted in the system concerned.

Viewed in these terms, whether foreign law can be satisfactorily applied is not a matter of a court's ability to discern 'the truth' about another country's laws. It is a matter of whether it is possible to replicate the foreign process of adjudication, the process appropriate to elucidating the best answer available. The question is not whether, say, an English court can arrive at the right answer under French law; it is whether it is possible to reproduce the conditions under which questions of French law are

---

[62] See, further, Dworkin (n 29) ch 4; Woozley 'No Right Answer' (1979) Philosophical Quarterly 25.

answered in France.[63] What matters is whether adequate information can be provided concerning the substance of the matter in dispute, and (of equal importance) whether it is possible to reproduce the legal method, and habits of thought, employed in the country whose laws are in question. The test is not whether the answer is right; it is whether the process of adjudication is authentic. We cannot expect an English court to arrive at the 'right' answer under French law, any more than we could expect a French court to do so. But we can expect to arrive at an answer that is *true* to French law—an answer *of* French law.

Here the problem suggested by *The Spirit of Independence* is again revealed. As we have seen, the difficulty there concerned not the quality or the quantity of the evidence but the authenticity of the evidential process. Rix J himself was concerned that it was inauthentic to approach the French jurisprudence in an English fashion. And it is far from clear that his preferred method of resolving the evidential conflict—doing the just thing— was in fact how a French court would have proceeded. Indeed, it is possible (even likely) that a French judge would have been able to avoid arriving at the position where the competing views seemed evenly balanced.

This perspective, like *The Spirit of Independence*, also suggests the line that must be drawn between cases in which the application of foreign law is possible and those where it is not. The former category includes those in which the evidence in favour of one solution is compelling. But it also includes at least two situations involving more difficult cases where the evidence is conflicting. In some cases a court may resolve any conflict by appealing either to legal techniques shared with the country whose law is in question—as where an English court is required to apply the law of another common law jurisdiction. In others it may be able to employ ubiquitous standards of sound reasoning—as perhaps in *City of Gotha*, where the idiom was foreign but the issue turned merely on which of two arguments was soundest on its face. By contrast, the latter category comprises (at least) two types of case: those where everything turns on an understanding of underlying legal principles that cannot readily be communicated by evidence; and those where a grasp of distinctive legal methods, or habits of thought, is required.

The difficulty, however, is not to recognize that such a category of hard cases exists. Two questions remain. How can we tell that a case belongs to this category? More precisely, how can we tell before it is too late, before substantial costs are incurred, and before a court is forced to resort to some technical device to resolve the matter? More troubling, what (if anything) can be done when such cases arise? How can we respond to the uncomfortable conclusion that foreign law cannot always be applied? This, for the conflicts lawyer, is the challenge.

---

[63] Fentiman (n 11) 20–1, 308–11.

VI. CONCLUSION

As this suggests, the problems associated with applying foreign law in national courts are profound. And they are more pressing than any that may arise when the courts of one country look to another country's laws out of interest, or for guidance, or to clarify their thinking. For they concern directly the rights and duties of the parties.

As we have seen, these problems are partly technical, partly philosophical, and touch on the very nature of adjudication. They belong to the law of evidence, and to the conflict of laws. But the foreign law problem is important in two particular ways. It raises in acute form the epistemological puzzle at the heart of comparative law: what may we truly know of foreign laws? In the abstract this has an archly academic ring. But it has special resonance in the present context. Doubtless scholars of comparative law can master the laws of other countries. But how can counsel and the courts acquire the familiarity with foreign law necessary to apply it efficiently and fairly in the course of real proceedings?

Above all, perhaps, the problem of applying foreign law begs a question touching the very purpose and possibility of the choice of law process. The conflict of laws takes for granted that the applicable law may be foreign. Yet in some cases a proper understanding of foreign law seems impossible. This does not mean that the proof of foreign law will invariably fail. But it may sometimes fail, and whether it will succeed or not is often hard to discern. What future, then, for the conflict of laws if we cannot—or cannot with confidence—apply foreign law in national courts?

3

Of Transcultural Borrowing, Hybrids, and the Complexity of Legal Knowledge: An Example of Comparative Law Before the French Courts

Horatia Muir Watt

In legal traditions where formalism or the presence of codes has hindered the development of a strong tradition of critical legal studies, the use of comparative law by the courts may serve a salutary 'subversive' purpose,[1] injecting into judicial reasoning those 'outsiders' insights'[2] without which legal conservatism will tend to flourish. Of course, from an academic standpoint, comparative scholarship also fulfils an important epistemological function by providing food for thought about the structuring of legal knowledge;[3] it contributes usefully to the philosophy of law by confronting different representations of the legal system.[4] The legislator, on the other hand, may indulge in wholesale 'legal transplants'[5] from abroad when responding to new social needs or indeed when forging a new national identity.[6] But it is by dissolving hidden factors of path-dependency[7] and challenging deeply rooted preconceptions about legal categories or distinctions

---

[1] P Legrand *Le Droit comparé* coll 'Que sais-je?' (PUF Paris) 100; G Fletcher 'Comparative Law as a Subversive Discipline', (1998) 46 AJCL 683; H Muir Watt, 'La fonction subversive du droit comparé', (200) 52 RIDC 503.

[2] B Markesinis 'The Comparatist', Yearbook of European Law (Oxford OUP 1995) 263; B Markesinis 'The Familiarity of the Unknown' in B Markesinis *Always on the Same Path: Essays on Foreign Law and Comparative Methodology* (Oxford Hart 2001) vol 2.

[3] See G Samuel *Epistemology and Method in Law* (Aldershot Ashgate 2003).

[4] See G Timsit 'L'Ordre juridique comme métaphore' *Droits* (Paris PUF 2001) vol 33, 3; a series of seminars was organized on this theme by the UMR of Comparative Law of Paris (University of Paris I/CNRS), 2001–2, including contributions from Ronald Dworkin, Lord Justice Sedley, Brian Leiter, and Richard Posner, on file with the UMR.

[5] On legal transplants, see A Watson *Legal Tranplants* (Edinburgh 1974).

[6] As is the case, for example, in eastern europe: see eg Cabrillac *Les Codifications* (Paris PUF 2002) 47.

[7] For the use of economic analysis in comparative law, see U Mattei *Comparative Law and Economics* (University of Michigan Press Ann Arbor 1997).

which prevent adaptation and progress[8] that comparative law has the most significant part to play before the courts.

Indeed, looking to foreign models may suggest that divisions and labels that seem inevitable or 'natural' when viewed from a purely 'internal' standpoint are in fact mere constructs, products of history or circumstance that may not, or may no longer be, the fairest nor the most efficient way of dealing with the various social issues they address. Comparison helps put these institutions into perspective, dispelling the myths and deconstructing the metaphors which, having at one time served a useful purpose in the construction of the legal system, then become intellectually cumbersome over time, in modified social and economic conditions.[9] But how far do courts actually contribute to this liberating process in individual cases? Just as comparative scholarship is often felt to be somewhat disconnected from practice, more concerned with designing a sophisticated 'grammar' with which to construct the relationships between legal systems than attentive to practical examples,[10] courts may similarly seem to be largely excluded from the comparative scene. However, while this may well have been true in the past, particularly—once again—in systems where the scope for creative judicial 'borrowing' is traditionally restricted by the presence of the codes and the deductive reasoning they involve, courts appear increasingly ready to use comparative law as a means of breaking free from traditional categories where these hamper the development of fair and efficient solutions in a modified environment.[11] To illustrate this trend, this chapter will focus on a recent development before the French courts in the field of international insolvency.[12] Its particular significance resides not only in the—remarkable—fact that the courts spontaneously referred to foreign practice for guidance in framing new tools to deal with the practical difficulties endemic to this field, but also in the fact that

[8] See V Grosswald Curran 'Dealing in Difference: Comparative Law's Potential for Broadening Legal Perspectives' (1998) 46 AJCL 657.

[9] On the use of images and metaphors in law, see G Samuel (n 3) 188 ff; G Timsit (n 4). Mystification occurs when categories or distinctions are held to be consubstantial to the very existence of the legal system. A good example concerns the private–public law distinction, whose mystifying effects are not limited to the Romanist tradition: see D Kennedy 'The Stages of Decline of the Public/Private Distinction' (1982) 130 U Pa L Rev 1423.

[10] U Mattei and M Reimann 'Introduction: New Directions in Comparative Law' 46 AHJCL 597; Ma Reimann 'The Progress and Failure of Comparative Law in the Second Half of the Twentieth Century' (2002) 50 AJCL 671.

[11] In France the famous *Perruche* affair, relating to the action for wrongful life brought by a child born handicapped after a faulty prenatal diagnosis, illustrates the readiness of courts to look for guidance in comparative study. On this case from a comparative viewpoint, see B Markesinis 'Réflexions d'un comparatiste anglais sur et à partir de l'arrêt *Perruche*' [2001] Rev trim dr civ 77; from an epistemological standpoint, see P Jestaz 'Une Question d'épistémologie (à propos de l'affaire *Perruche*)' [2001] Rev trim dr civ 547.

[12] Cass civ 1ère 19 nov 2002, *Banque Worms* (2002) JCP 10 201 concl Sainte-Rose note Chaillé de Néré; [2003] D 797 note Khairallah.

comparative law was put to constructive use in a sphere usually thought to be the seat of insoluble conceptual differences between civil and common law worlds relating to the very process of adjudication.

The breakthrough consisted in the French courts' having recourse to a form of extraterritorial injunctive relief, directly inspired from the British practice of freezing orders operating *in personam*,[13] and designed to avoid the obstacles that traditional territorial dogma had long put in the way of coherent management of insolvencies involving assets in more than one country.[14] Indeed, the existing state of French law offered no means for a court to prevent the untimely removal or interference with assets situated in a foreign jurisdiction, whether by the insolvent debtor or by an undisciplined creditor. To remedy this deficiency, it was necessary to overcome the absence of any conceptual category, within French law, capable of accommodating measures that operate *in personam* yet affect assets in ways equivalent to provisional measures *in rem*, such as the *saisie-conservatoire*. Introduced by the Court of Appeal of Versailles, the judicial transplant was approved and given theoretical form by the Cour de cassation.

The move took place in the space now occupied by the new EU Insolvency Regulation[15] and might be seen as a mere anticipation of changes specific to that context,[16] in which territorial boundaries are progressively shedding much of their previous significance.[17] But the Cour de cassation's recent decision can credibly be held to contain a normative principle whose import extends far beyond both the specific context of insolvency proceedings and indeed the frontiers of the European Union. To appreciate its significance, the decision itself first requires close scrutiny. Indeed some of the commentaries to which it has given rise have actually ignored the novel appearance of injunctive relief before the French courts[18]—no doubt a credit to the way in which the 'intruder' was made to

---

[13] On the case-law relating to the Mareva injunction, see Dicey and Morris *The Conflict of Laws* (13th edn) vol 1, ch 8, 182.

[14] On the perceived requirements of territoriality in their field, see J-P Rémery *La Faillité internationale* coll 'Que sais-je?' (PUF Paris 1996).

[15] Council's Regulation No 1346/2000 of 29 May 2000, in force since 31 May 2002.

[16] Not infrequently French courts will apply international instruments not yet in force, at least where the applicable law is case-law: see eg Cass civ 1ère, 9 déc 1974 [1975] Rev crit de int priv 504 note Mezger; [1975] JDI 534 note Ponsard, anticipating the entry into force of the Brussels Convention, by conferring automatic recognition on a German judgment cancelling a sale, which would normally have required an exequatur.

[17] Under the Regulation, proceedings opened in the state of the insolvent's principal centre of interests extend automatically, ie with no need for an exequatur, to assets located in other member states (unless ancillary proceedings under the Regulation have been opened there). Outside the Insolvency Regulation, of course, territorial boundaries have lost much of their significance (see the changes brought about in chapter 3 of the Brussels I Regulation on Jurisdiction and Judgments; see, too, the proposed Regulation for a European *titre exécutoire*: COM OJ (2002) 159 final, C–203 E of 27 Aug 2002).

[18] To date, the only commentary to have focused on the injunction is that of Sandrine Chaillé de Néré (2002) 2(10) 201.

appear a natural fit within the borrowing system (A). However, it is enough to recall that the change took place in the shadow of the *Justizkonflikt* apparent within the European Union, between two very different conceptions of the judicial function, to measure the full extent of the novelty involved in a civilian court's extending relief to assets located abroad (B). As is the case with many attempts at legal borrowing, the result is unquestionably a hybrid, differing on many counts from the foreign practice that inspired it and a potential 'irritant'[19] within its new environment (C). This of course is no reason to condemn the attempt itself, if its effects can adequately be absorbed by the receiving legal system. On the contrary, the Cour de cassation's hybrid creature may foreshadow a complex new form of 'post-axiomatic' legal knowledge,[20] which comparative scholarship has done much to catalyse (D).

I. THE TRANSPLANT: EXTRATERRITORIAL INJUNCTIVE RELIEF IN FRENCH
PRIVATE INTERNATIONAL LAW

The case concerned insolvency proceedings initiated in France in respect of a couple of art dealers domiciled in Paris who possessed immovable assets in Spain. In order to save time and money in the general interest of the creditors, the liquidator had been authorized by the *tribunal de commerce* in charge of the proceedings not to ask for an exequatur in Spain; the creditors, who were all French, were clearly expected to refrain from taking individual measures to seize the Spanish assets, despite the fact that the proceedings had not been formally made operative in Spanish territory. However, a French bank, the Banque Worms, which had declared its claim in the French proceedings, nevertheless initiated a *saisie-immobilière* on the insolvents' property in Spain. On an application made on their behalf, the Court of Appeal of Versailles, reversing the judgment of the tribunal, ordered the bank to refrain and desist from all actions and proceedings in Spain, subject to an *astreinte* (that is, a penalty in the form of special damages awarded to the claimant for each day of non-compliance by the defendant).[21] This decision was challenged in turn before the Cour de cassation. Although it was reversed on other, purely procedural, grounds, the Supreme Court expressed clear approval of such an order as a matter of

---

[19] The reference is of course to Gunther Teubner's 'Legal Irritants: Good Faith in British Law or How Unifying Law Ends Up in New Divergences' (1998) 61 MLR 11.

[20] Samuel (n 3) esp 335 ff, suggesting that law may have been moved beyond the 'axiomatic' stage identified by Blanché and symbolized by the great European codes, towards a 'post-axiomatic stage', that sees law as a matter of both symbolic and non-symbolic knowledge—ie knowledge that cannot be reduced to normative propositions (the rule model epistemological thesis), but consists of mental images that operate primarily on facts.

[21] Loi du 9 juillet 1991 (Arts 33 to 37), replacing Loi du 5 juillet 1972.

principle, in the name of the equality of the creditors and the universal vocation of the insolvency proceedings.[22] Rejecting the objections raised by the defendant in relation to the territorial limits of the French courts' jurisdiction to interfere with enforcement procedures abroad, the Cour de cassation stated, in its uniquely laconic style, that 'an injunction addressed to the defendant personally to act or refrain from acting, wherever the assets in question are situated, does not fall foul of such jurisdictional limits, as long as it is awarded by the court with legitimate jurisdiction over the merits'. Read in the light of the conclusions of the Advocate-General Sainte-Rose, which refer to the practice of the English courts, this statement reveals a distinct case of judicial borrowing.

The reason for looking to foreign practice lay in the difficulties to which the strictly territorial reach of insolvency proceedings, under traditional principles of French private international law, regularly gives rise. Indeed, since proceedings opened in a foreign court leave the insolvent debtor entirely free to dispose of assets in the forum state, and the creditors conversely free to arrest them, until an exequatur is obtained in France, there is an obvious incentive for fraud in the period separating the foreign decision and its exequatur: as illustrated in the case under discussion, it is extremely frequent, for instance, that individual creditors—here, the Banque Worms—whose claims are suspended under the foreign insolvency law, seek to take advantage of the lack of extraterritorial effect of the foreign proceedings in the forum state by arresting assets there, to the detriment of the other creditors.

Various attempts to attenuate the undesirable effects of the territorial principle in such instances are visible in the case-law. While still apparently unready to consider that foreign decisions opening insolvency proceedings give rise to immediate and automatic recognition in France, as do other decisions that appoint and vest power in trustees, executors of wills, administrators of companies, etc,[23] the Cour de cassation has nevertheless decided that an exequatur once awarded has retroactive effect in certain circumstances[24] and can therefore invalidate a *saisie* or other provisional measure

---

[22] The universality of insolvency proceedings means that proceedings opened in the forum claim to extend to all of the insolvent's assets, wherever situated (even if, in practice, the extension of the effects of insolvency to foreign territory requires the cooperation of the local sovereign—at least before the advent of the injunction).

[23] The automatic recognition of foreign judgments appointing administrators, trustees or representatives dates back to Cass civ 30 janvier 1912 [1913] Rev crit dr int priv 31, (1916) 1 s 113 note Audinet; [1919] JDI 845. The appointment of a liquidator by a foreign judgment is therefore recognized without any formality; however, since the other effects of the insolvency proceedings require an exequatur, and, in particular, assets in France are not affected until an exequatur has been obtained, the liquidator is powerless both to collect these assets in order to pay the creditors and to prevent the insolvent from disposing of them.

[24] This is an important step since, in theory, a foreign judgment that does not benefit from automatic recognition lacks any legal existence in the eyes of the forum until an exequatur is

obtained in France after the opening of the foreign proceedings but before their effect was formally extended to French territory.[25] However, although such a solution restores equality between creditors to a certain extent, there is obviously no way, absent an international agreement, to ensure similar extension of the effect of forum proceedings in a foreign jurisdiction. This, of course, is where the injunction comes in. By enjoining the creditors, under threat of an *astreinte*, from initiating or pursuing before the Spanish authorities an enforcement procedure relating to the insolvent's assets in Spain, the Court went far in ensuring the 'universal vocation' of the forum proceedings.[26] These were made indirectly effective in Spanish territory, thus bypassing the need for an exequatur in Spain. Here, then, is the essence of injunctive relief in an international context: recourse to relief which acts *in personam* dispenses with the need to seek local enforcement before the authorities of the territory in which the assets are located.

That the inspiration behind this development lies in the deliberate use of comparative law by the Cour de cassation can be fully appreciated only if its decision is read in the light of the conclusions of the Advocate-General. This, in itself, is an important comparative point:[27] the one succinct, impersonal sentence, ostensibly flowing from the Articles of the Code,[28] reveals neither the source of the new solution, its intended scope, nor the full extent of its normative implications; the explanatory material is to be found outside the *arrêt*, in the Advocate-General's conclusions, clearly followed by the Court. These contain a direct reference to a recent comparative study relating to the use by the English courts of freezing orders in an interna-

---

conferred. Conceding that, once the exequatur is obtained, the foreign judgment produces effects as from the date it was handed down is to suggest that it had some form of existence before the exequatur.

[25] Cass civ 1ère, 25 fév 1986 *Kléber* [1987] Rev crit dr int priv 589 note Synvet; (1987) 2 JCP 20776 note Rémery [1988] JDI 425 note Jacquemont; Cass civ 1ère 22 fév 2000 *Transitas* [2000] Rev crit dr int priv 778 note Ancel et Muir Watt; [2000] JDI 107 note Raimon.

[26] See n 21.

[27] M de SO l'E Lasser, 'Judicial Self-Portraits: Judicial Discourse in the French Legal System' (1995) 104 Yale Law Journal 1325; M de SO l'E Lasser 'Lit. Theory Put to the Test: A Comparative Literary Analysis of American Judicial Tests and French Judicial Discourse' 111 Harvard L Rev 689.

[28] Here the texts invoked by Banque Worms in an attempt to have the appellate court's decision overturned were Arts 14 and 15 of the Civil Code. Formally, these texts deal with the international jurisdiction of the French courts, based on the French citizenship of either party. Their relevance here lies in the fact that, being the only texts in the Code relating to jurisdiction, all case-law in this field has sprung from them. In particular, 19th-century cases ruled that French nationality could not provide a legitimate basis for the jurisdiction of the French courts to order measures of enforcement on assets situated abroad. It is to this argument, invoked by Banque Worms, that the Cour de cassation replies here, by stating that injunctive relief *in personam* does not infringe these limits, since it does not involve direct enforcement on assets abroad.

tional context,[29] in which it was shown that there is nothing in French law to prevent recourse to orders *in personam* in order to prevent interference with, or indeed to obtain the return of, assets situated abroad, subject to the dual condition that the injunction is awarded by a court with a legitimate basis for international jurisdiction to do so[30] and does not require the addressee to act illegally under the local law.[31]

The Advocate-General subscribes to this point of view, setting aside objections relating both to the violation of the creditors' individual right of access to justice (Article 6–1 ECHR) and to the violation of Spanish territorial sovereignty. Using, remarkably, terminology that is inhabitual in French law because of the lack of the corresponding substantive categories—or at least, their lack of legal significance—he explains that while a French court may not take action *in rem* over assets located abroad, injunctions *in personam* to act or refrain from acting are entirely acceptable, subject to the requirements of comity described above. Indeed, on the one hand, any restriction on individual creditors' access to justice is already implicit in the collective discipline inherent in the insolvency proceedings, to which French law recognizes a universal vocation; on the other, foreign territorial sovereignty is untouched by a measure that does not claim to operate directly, *in rem*, on foreign territory. Although the outsider—and particularly the common lawyer—may find this proposition unexceptional, it suffices to glance at the hostility expressed in French legal literature with respect to measures with indirect extraterritorial effect to appreciate the extent of the step thus taken.[32] Indeed, it takes place in the shadow of the *Justizkonflikt* opposing two models of adjudication in the common law and civilian worlds.

---

[29] The study to which the Advocate-General refers is that of H Muir Watt 'L'Extraterritorialité des mesures conservatoires *in personam* (à propos de l'arrêt de la Court of Appeal, *Crédit suisse Fides Trust v Cuoghi* du 11 juin 1997)', [1998] Rev crit dr int priv 27. This study broached the possibility of acclimatizing Mareva injunctions in French private international law, and, with particular reference to worldwide injunctions awarded by a court other than the one seized of the merits, called attention to the need to think carefully about the grounds on which jurisdiction to award injunctive relief over assets situated abroad can legitimately be exercised without infringing international comity. The conclusions of the Advocate-General reflect, similarly, a desire to avoid intrusiveness.

[30] Many of the difficulties that arise in the context of the *Justizkonflikt* described below stem from the fact that injunctive relief is awarded by courts exercising jurisdiction on grounds perceived to be inadequate: see eg L Collins 'The Hague Evidence Convention and Discovery: A Serious Misunderstanding?' *Essays in International Litigation and the Conflict of Laws* (Oxford Clarendon Press 1996) 289.

[31] In the case of a 'true conflict', international law—or comity at the very least—would seem to allow the territorial law to prevail (see the demonstration in the cited study, 46–7).

[32] See eg Se Guinchard and T Moussa (eds) *Action, droit et pratique des voies d'exécution* (Paris Daloloz 2001–2), §9946; R Perrot and P Théry *Procédures civiles d'exécution* §39.

II. THE CONTEXT: THE *JUSTIZKONFLIKT*[33]

Beyond the context of insolvency proceedings the French Cour de cassation's decision also provides a significant contribution to the recurrent
debate, fuelled by the House of Lords' prejudicial question to the European
Court of Justice in *Turner v Grovit* [2001] WLR 107 over the availability
of extraterritorial injunctive relief within the scope of the Brussels I
Regulation—whether in the form of anti-suit injunctions in cases of parallel proceedings, or indeed of freezing orders under Article 31 (ex-24
Convention) in relation to assets situated in another Member State. Doubts
as to the compatibility of such relief, awarded for either purpose, with the
principles that dictate the allocation of jurisdiction among Member States,
are clearly linked to the fact that both the architecture and the underlying
values of the Regulation stem directly from the civilian tradition, where the
use of indirect pressure on a litigant to obtain compliance abroad with a
judicial order is perceived as an infringement of international comity. Thus,
from a Continental perspective, or at least so the traditional argument goes,
injunctive relief awarded *in personam* and designed to bring about, albeit
indirectly, effects on foreign assets or proceedings is considered as unduly
intrusive, infringing the monopoly of the foreign State to regulate the functioning of courts and enforcement agencies within its borders. This debate
is clearly linked to profound cultural differences which span the very
conception of the judicial function, affecting not only the existence of
discretion to entertain or stay proceedings, but also the extent to which
courts are perceived to be involved in enforcement process. In such a
context injunctive relief appears very much a misfit.

  The first idea is too well known to warrant a long explanation. Civilian
courts have no discretion over the exercise of their own jurisdiction. *Forum
non conveniens* has thus been banished from the realm of the Brussels
Convention/Regulation[34] in the name both of foreseeability, a value fundamental to a rule-based legal culture, and of the right of access to justice,
which bears a distinct cultural charge in systems in which hard-and-fast
jurisdictional rules are designed to incorporate considerations of conve-
nience and proximity between the court and the *res*, rendering the doctrine
of the 'natural forum' (supposedly) redundant.[35] Similar objections are

---

[33] On the *Justizkonflikt*, particularly in the context of discovery across national frontiers,
see A F Lowenfeld *International Litigation and the Quest for Reasonableness* (Oxford
Clarendon Press 1996) 136.

[34] The question (now pending before the ECJ pursuant to a prejudicial question from the
Court of Appeal of England) remains whether the doctrine of *forum non conveniens* survives
in cases in which the more appropriate forum is situated outside the European Union (see
Andrew Owusu v Nugent B Jackson, Mammee Bay Resorts Ltd 2002 WL 1039653).

[35] See A Bell *Forum Shopping and Venue in Transnational Litigation* (Oxford Hart 2003).

equally relevant in respect of anti-suit injunctions; they explain why, in the present case, the Advocate-General was careful to dispose of the argument raised in the name of the creditors' right of access to justice in Spain.[36] However, in so far as such injunctions involve extraterritorial effects, they appear doubly suspect from a traditional Continental perspective. While *forum non conveniens* may have its civilian partisans, even within the scope of the Brussels Regulation,[37] few are those who would support the use of injunctive relief to interrupt legal proceedings abroad—despite Lord Hobhouse's attempts to mollify opposition in *Turner v Grovit*. Whether or not the award of an injunction is exclusive of any value-judgment upon the foreign court's jurisdiction,[38] and whether or not existing techniques are adequate to deal with situations of parallel litigation,[39] there is a strong feeling that awarding injunctive relief infringes on the foreign State's exclusive right to regulate the working of its courts—and indeed to decide whether its own courts are the instrument of an abuse of process.[40] This perception of injunctive relief as alien to values embedded in the Regulation is linked to a second, less-known, factor, which is the lack of court involvement in the enforcement process in the civilian tradition.[41]

In Continental systems ensuring compliance with judicial decisions is a matter to be left to enforcement agencies. Once the legal position is stated (*juris-dictio*), the court's role is over. Enforcement is in the hands of public agencies, whose field of action is strictly territorial and whose means are similarly restricted to the seizure of assets.[42] The court may for instance declare that X is under a contractual duty to perform a service for Y, but if X refuses to comply, it is then up to Y to apply to an enforcement agency

---

[36] As seen above, the Advocate-General emphasizes the constraints inherent in the insolvency proceedings, which involve the suspension of individual claims; since the forum proceedings have a universal vocation, they must affect individual claims before any court, including foreign courts.

[37] For an excellent comparative approach on this point, see C Chalas *L'Exercice discrétionnaire de la compétence juridictionnelle en droit international privé* (Aix–Marseille PU 2000).

[38] One may indeed wonder whether Lord Hobhouse's reading of precedents on this point is entirely convincing on this point: see Bell (n 35) 176.

[39] In *Turner v Grovit* the *lis pendens* mechanism should arguably have led the Spanish court second seised to relinquish jurisdiction. Either because it was unaware of the prior English proceedings, or because it did not consider the requirements of Art 21 of the Convention on *lis pendens* to be fulfilled, it maintained the parallel proceedings. Hence the anti-suit injunction awarded by the English court first seised.

[40] Under *Overseas Union* the courts of a Member State may not sit in judgment on the jurisdiction of the court of another Member State. One might argue that this also entails leaving it to each court to decide whether its own seisin is abusive.

[41] On this point, see G Cuniberti *Les Mesures conservatoires sur les biens sis à l'étranger* (Paris LGDJ 2000).

[42] For the comparative aspects of enforcement, see W Kennett *The Enforcement of Judgments in Europe* (Oxford 2000); K Kerameus *Enforcement in the International Context* Rec Cours la Haye (1997) vol 264.

to obtain the seizure of X's assets with a view to their public sale, the proceeds of which will allow Y to obtain payment for the value of the service due. The court will no more involve itself in the enforcement process than the agencies whose function it is to carry out the court's order may use any form of constraint other than the various *saisies* laid down in the code of civil procedure. This is true despite the recent introduction into French law of the *injonction de faire*,[43] which can be obtained rapidly, as an inter-locutory measure, from the *juge des référés*, when there is a clear prima facie case showing that the party being enjoined is indeed under a duty to act. However, once such an injunction is awarded, there is no guarantee that it will be carried out. If the claimant returns to court to complain of non-compliance, he may be awarded . . . damages![44] In other words, his ultimate remedy will, once again, take the form of a seizure of assets. The same conclusion applies when the act to be accomplished, for instance, the service in the above example, is to take place abroad. Nothing prevents the court from declaring X to be bound to perform a service for Y, even when the place of performance is in a foreign jurisdiction; but if X ignores the court order, Y's only remedy is to apply to the local enforcement agencies, after having obtained an exequatur, registration, or equivalent formality in the foreign court.[45]

As comparative studies in the sociology of justice show, this separation between the court's function, confined to stating the law from 'on high', and the enforcement process, left to agencies outside the judicial function, raises the sensitive issue of the ineffectivity of judicial decisions.[46] The *injonction de faire* described above was part of an attempt to remedy this discrepancy, under the impulsion of President Drai, whose initiatives designed to increase the efficiency of civil procedure, particularly in intro-ducing measures involving the courts in the enforcement process,[47] might be seen more or less as the counterpart of those contained in Lord Woolf's Report *Access to Justice in England*. Another such attempt is the *astreinte*,

---

[43] See Art 809 §2, Code of Civil Procedure ('injonction de faire' added in 1985).

[44] See Court of Appeals of Paris 10 avr 1990 D1990 IR 121.

[45] This is true even under the Brussels I Regulation. French law allows the beneficiary of a foreign judgment or arbitral award which has not yet acceded to an exequatur to obtain provi-sional or protective measures, on the condition that proceedings with a view to obtain an exequatur are introduced within a month (Art 215 décret 31 juillet 1992).

[46] For a comparative outlook on this point, see A Garapon 'La Culture juridique française au choc de la mondialisation' in *Le Juge et le jugement dans les traditions juridiques européennes* coll 'Droit et Société' (Paris LGDJ 1996), 379; 'La Justice, point aveugle de la théorie politique française?' in *Le Juge entre deux millénaires, Mélanges offertes à Pierre Drai* (Paris Dalloz 2000) 53.

[47] For an overall picture of these initiatives, see the various contributions to *Le Juge entre deux millénaires* (n 46), particularly the preface, by Jean Foyer, portraying the ex-president of the Cour de cassation as a 'modernizer' of the administration of justice. President Drai was responsible for the introduction of the *référé* provision (interim order for payment) in French law.

a penalty for non-compliance actually created by the courts themselves before it received legislative unction in 1972.[48] To date, the *astreinte*, used in the *Banque Worms* case, is probably the closest approximation which exists in French law to the leverage inherent in the sanctions for contempt of court which accompany the award of equitable relief in England. However, if the defendant refuses to pay the *astreinte*, the only remedy left to the claimant is, once again, to apply to an enforcement agency for the seizure of the defendant's assets—supposing that such assets are available within the territory of the forum state. However unsatisfactory this state of affairs may seem, it is clear that extraterritorial injunctive relief, in the form of freezing orders relating to assets abroad, do not appear to 'fit' within the structure of civilian procedural categories, since it involves crossing the dividing line between *jurisdictio* and enforcement.

This is why the 'real connection' (*lien réel*) laid down by the European Court of Justice in the important *Van Uden* case[49] as a prerequisite for the exercise of jurisdiction to award a provisional measure under Article 24 Convention/31 Regulation is naturally understood on the Continent as referring to a territorial link between the court and the assets on which the measure—supposed to operate *in rem*—is to be enforced. According to this understanding of the European Court's ruling, the scope of the derogatory jurisiction under Article 24/31 is restricted to cases where the assets on which such measures are to be enforced (or the evidence to be examined, etc)[50] are located within forum territory. The different reading adopted by Dicey and Morris, according to which 'real' means 'substantial' in this context, so that extraterritorial freezing orders may still be awarded as provisional measures on the basis of Article 24/31,[51] obviously proceeds from a very different cultural approach to civil procedure. While there have been some recent indications that civilian objections to extraterritorial relief are not entirely insuperable—the Dutch courts, for example, have gone as far as awarding so-called 'euro-injunctions' to prevent the violation of industrial property rights in other Member States[52]—the recent step taken by the French Cour de cassation in the *Banque Worms* case undoubtedly

---

[48] See n 21.

[49] ECJ 17 Nov 1998 C–391/95 Rec I-7091 concl Léger.

[50] According to the definition given in the *Reichert II* case (Rec I-2149 concl Gulmann) the measures that fall within the scope of art 24 of the Convention are those that maintain the status quo in order to protect rights pending their final adjudication. They include measures relating to assets, but also judicial measures designed to preserve evidence (see Art 145 French Code of Civil Procedure).

[51] Dicey and Morris (n 13) §8-027, 193.

[52] See too the instance of interim extraterritorial relief awarded by the Italian courts in a case involving an alleged infringement of intellectual property, which gave rise to an interesting conflict under Art 27-3° of the Brussels Convention with a German decision, refusing such relief locally: *Italian Leather v WECO* ECJ 6 June 2002 [2002] Rev crit dr int priv 704 note Muir Watt.

calls into question the constraints usually associated with the requirements of territoriality in an international context.[53] However, in ignoring traditional divisions and mixing established legal categories, such a step must necessarily generate ripple effects within the French legal system.

III. THE CONSEQUENCES: HYBRIDS AND LEGAL IRRITANTS

Indeed, in acclimatizing an alien remedy, the Court has created an intriguing hybrid (one may therefore prefer to talk about the 'glocalization' of a foreign model).[54] The relief provided takes the form, interestingly, of an anti-suit injunction (to refrain from action before the Spanish authorities with a view of obtaining a *saisie-immobilière*), introduced under cover of a freezing order (to refrain from removing the assets, metaphorically, from the scope of the insolvency proceedings). This cover no doubt explains the ease with which the anti-suit injunction has found its way into French law, since, while novel, a freezing order designed to prevent interference with assets is no doubt perceived as potentially far less intrusive on foreign sovereignty than an order to refrain from suit before the foreign courts. As is made clear by the Advocate-General's conclusions, the relief was designed to ensure that the insolvent debtors' Spanish assets remained subject to the collective discipline of the insolvency proceedings in progress in the forum; it so happened, incidentally, that the means used by the undisciplined creditor to immunize those assets from the effects of French proceedings were the various procedural steps required by Spanish law to obtain a *saisie-immobilière*, which therefore needed to be restrained. The fact that the Court understood the anti-suit component of its order as ancillary to the freezing of the assets explains the presence of the phrase 'wherever the assets are situated' in a statement designed to express approval of the Court of Versailles's injunction to the creditor to refrain from suing abroad. It is noteworthy that in its anti-suit component the order was designed to sanction the disloyal behaviour of the bank, which deliberately ignored the collective understanding that the Spanish assets were virtually within the scope of the French proceedings, and was in no way a denial of the jurisdiction of the courts of Spain—which were undoubtedly competent to authorize enforcement measures on Spanish territory. Shades of *Turner v*

---

[53] Henceforth, objections to the use of anti-suit injunctions within the scope of the Convention or Regulation must be drawn from the architecture of the Convention or Regulation, since arguments linked to the characteristics of jurisdiction in the civilian tradition will now be difficult to sustain.

[54] R Robertson 'Glocalization: Time-Space and Homogeneity–Heterogeneity' in Featherstone Lash Robertson *Global Modernities* (London Sage 1995), quoted by Pierre Legrand 'L'Hypothèse de la conquête des continents par le droit américain (ou comment la contingence arrache à la disponibilité)' in *L'Américanisation du droit* APD (2001) vol 45, 37.

Grovit? Whatever the real justification for the anti-suit injunction, it is noteworthy that the *Banque Worms* case expresses a normative principle ('an injunction addressed to the defendant personally to act or refrain from acting, wherever the assets in question are situated, does not fall foul of such jurisdictional limits, as long as it is awarded by the court with legitimate jurisdiction over the merits') that introduces, in one fell swoop, both freezing orders and anti-suit injunctions. On this point, canons of interpretation of French case-law do not mandate restricting the reach of the decision to the underlying facts, but invite discovery of the guiding principle from which the solutions of future cases may be deduced.[55]

But the hybridization does not stop with the unusual combination of two different types of injunction. To the extent that French law has no sanction for non-compliance with court orders equivalent to contempt of court, it obviously cannot re-create injunctive relief exactly as it exists in England. The only means available under French law to ensure enforcement of a judicial order to act or refrain from acting is not a criminal sanction but the *astreinte*, of which the proceeds benefit the claimant directly. As such, the transplant may well prove to be what Teubner has described as a 'legal irritant',[56] with ripple effects within the borrowing system. Indeed, while in this particular instance the result would not necessarily have been untoward in so far as the benefit of the award would have served to increase the funds made available to the creditors collectively, nevertheless, importing injunctive relief by means of the *astreinte* may exacerbate difficulties linked to the use of private penalties in French law. Notwithstanding the unquestionable practical success of the *astreinte*, the French legal system is still uneasy with the punitive function of private damages.[57] A concession to private penalties in the particularly sensitive field of extraterritorial relief may lead to other inroads into traditional values. For instance, can a legal system coherently maintain that punitive damages are contrary to its public policy, while promoting the use of private penalties as leverage to ensure extraterritorial compliance with judicial decisions? A preferable, but no doubt ideologically unrealistic, solution would no doubt be the adoption—by the legislator—of criminal sanctions for non-compliance with judicial decisions, emphasizing

---

[55] On the epistemological implications of this difference in approach between common law and civilian traditions, see P Legrand 'Sens et non-sens d'un code civil européen' [1996] RIDC 779; G Samuel (n 3) ch 3, 95. This article remains the most intellectually stimulating piece in the debate in France over the proposed European civil code, despite being curiously excluded from the assemblage of texts on the subject, edited by the Société de Législation comparée, 2003.

[56] See n 19.

[57] See, for the state of French law on this point, S Carval *La Responsabilité civile dans sa fonction de peine privée* (Paris LGDJ 1995), preface by Geneviève Viney; F Terré P Simler and Y Lequette *Les Obligations* (8th edn Paris Dalloz 2002) §1121 on the doubts generated by the 'shocking and exorbitant' nature of the *astreinte*.

that such a situation involves a contempt of court rather than an issue of compensation for the deprivation of a private right. For the moment, however, in the absence of such a sanction, it is only by 'translating' equitable sanctions for contempt of court into civil damages that the French courts have been able to afford recognition to English Mareva injunctions invoked in France.[58] Once again, court practice demonstrates a willingness to cross traditional conceptual divides.

IV. THE LESSON TO BE LEARNED: COMPARATIVE LAW AND THE SHAPING OF LEGAL KNOWLEDGE

The *Banque Worms* case thus provides ample illustration of the ways in which borrowing can bowl over traditional categories. Henceforth, for example, it is difficult to define exactly what characterizes a measure which operates *in rem*: the state of English law shows that injunctions *in personam* operate in effect to freeze assets located abroad, and can extend their reach to third parties,[59] which are precisely the two features perceived to be of the essence of measures *in rem* in French law. Similarly, the requirements of state sovereignty need to be rethought, since territorial boundaries no longer ensure immunity from outside interference. On this point, the renewal is apparent in other, neighbouring, fields. For example, it is now suggested that a court with a legitimate basis of jurisdiction to judge a case ought to be able to order the production of evidence wherever located;[60] yet the clash of discovery procedures before courts from common law jurisdictions with the civilian conception of a judicial—and territorial—monopoly for collecting evidence is yet another expression of the *Justizkonflikt* discussed above. A third illustration of the blurring of traditional divides concerns the crossing of the separation between the adjudication and enforcement; court involvement in the latter invites reflection on what is really comprised within the judicial function. Significantly, such reflection is already under way in the field of international arbitration, where the issue arises as to whether the arbitral tribunal can award an *astreinte*: the answer

[58] See Court of Appeals of Paris, 5 Oct 2000 and 14 June 2001 [2002] Rev crit dr int priv 704 note Muir Watt. One may wonder why recognition of the Mareva injunction was necessary in any event. It appears that the claimants wished to invoke it as a 'titre exécutoire' enabling them to obtain the arrest of assets in France.

[59] The effect of the freezing order on third parties is subject to the 'Banabaft proviso', which ensures that third parties abroad who are wholly outside the jurisdiction of the English court are not made subject to the contempt powers of that court (see Dicey and Morris (n 3) §8-015, 187). The fact that an injunction awarded *in personam* is liable to affect third parties is the point on which civilian doctrine has the greatest difficulty in accepting the concept of injunctive relief.

[60] A Bucher *Droit international privé suisse* vol 1/1, §570.

depends both on the nature of the *astreinte* and where to draw the limits between adjudication and enforcement.[61] In all these examples civilian courts have been labouring under artificial constraints, which comparative law can help to dissolve, allowing more efficient solutions.

At the same time it is apparent that borrowing gives rise to culturally acclimatized hybrids rather than pure transplants. For instance, after *Banque Worms* French law will hardly abandon its own way of structuring legal relationships around persons and things;[62] the newly created injunctive relief will not replace the old categories, but will constitute a new stratum, an additional factor of complexity of the law. Was this, then, a wise move, given the risk of deforming established concepts and creating new ripple effects? Comfortable or not, one of the most important epistemological lessons to be drawn from the increased circulation of legal models[63] linked to Europeanization and globalization of the law may well be to call attention to the need for structuring legal knowedge in ways capable of 'dealing in complexity'.[64] To accept, for instance, that one and the same measure may concern persons and things at the same time, or may concern both adjudication and enforcement, or may operate extraterritorially and yet not interfere with the territorial sovereignty of the foreign State. In other words, comparative law may have a fundamental contribution to make to the emergence of what Geoffrey Samuel has described as a 'post-axiomatic' or multidimensional scheme of intelligibility, adapted to the increasing interactions of legal systems today. The breakthrough may well be more significant for the civilian tradition, whose greater formalism favours a more dogmatic, monodimensional architecture of legal knowledge than the common law, structurally more adapted to accommodate complexity.[65]

V. CONCLUSION

Under the Insolvency Regulation (No 1346/2000 of 29 May 2000, in force since 31 May 2002) the French bankruptcy would have been immediately effective in Spain, reducing the need for strategies designed to extend its

---

[61] On this debate, see P Théry 'Judex Gladii (des juges et de la contrainte en territoire français)' in *Nouveaux Juges nouveaux pouvoirs: Mélanges en l'honneur de Roger Perrot* (Paris Dalloz 1996) 477.

[62] On the ways in which the civilian codes structure fact situations around persons and things, Samuel (n 3) 149–50.

[63] The terms are those of Rodolfo Sacco *La Comparaison juridique au service de la comparaison du droit* (Paris Economica 1991).

[64] Samuel (n 3) Concluding Remarks, 335.

[65] Ibid. Restitution provides a good comparative illustration of this point. Monodimensional in civilian systems, its existence in English law involves a complex coming-together of various sources and remedies. For an excellent comparative 'map', see G Panagapoulos *Restitution in Private International Law* (Oxford Hart 2000).

reach beyond national frontiers. However, there is nothing in the decision itself, nor in the Advocate-General's conclusions, that restricts the normative content of the decision to the particular context in which it was handed down. Extraterritorial injunctive relief, in the hybrid form which it inevitably takes on within a civilian system, seems here to stay. The next question, which remains unanswered at the date this text is written,[66] is whether its exercise remains compatible with the allocation of jurisdiction within the Brussels Convention/Regulation. Any objection drawn from the civilian tradition that underlies these instruments is of course no longer available.

[66] A month after the hearing in *Turner v Grovit* in May 2003 the European Court's response to the House of Lords' prejudicial question was still awaited. On the considerable difficulties this question raises, see H Muir Watt [2003] Rev crit dr int priv 116.

4

Liaison Magistrates: Their Role in Comparative Law and International Judicial Cooperation

Bernard Rabatel

Until relatively recently it was not common practice for a domestic judge to consult the legislation or the jurisprudence of foreign countries before giving his decision, though he might well have been given the opportunity to find out about the legal system of a foreign country, more or less distant from his own in geographical, cultural, and linguistic terms, during the course of his legal studies.

This interest in foreign law now appears to be one of the elements forming part of the training of young lawyers. The large number of requests for internships received by French embassies confirms this and suggests that future judges may well adopt a different approach from that of their predecessors towards foreign legislation.

The École de la Magistrature, which has ensured the initial and continuing training of French judges for over forty years, has developed programmes with the primary objective of raising awareness of the legal systems of other countries. However, there is a difference between, on the one hand, initiation in the law of other countries and, on the other hand, the concrete and practical use which judges are able to make of such knowledge when they must give judgment in cases where the issues are not confined to the domestic sphere.

The development of Community law and the jurisprudence of the European Court of Human Rights, and the accompanying consequences, have profoundly changed the way in which judges have, up until now, viewed the operation of their legal systems.

Equally, the arrival of the Internet in courts means that judges now have access to the law of foreign jurisdictions by means of a simple click.

Times are changing.

It could therefore be thought that the majority of barriers that discouraged judges from being inspired by, or indeed from borrowing, legal concepts or solutions from their neighbours have fallen. That would, however, be a somewhat premature conclusion. In reality, even with the assistance of technology, obstacles remain and such obstacles go beyond simple questions of linguistics. A desire to resolve a legal problem by comparing solutions already adopted in other jurisdictions can come up against the problems caused by a greater or lesser understanding of the real meaning of foreign legislation and case-law. A lack of knowledge of the local context of a country's laws and jurisprudence can lead to misunderstanding, which does not assist the reasoning of a judge curious to know how a foreign colleague would respond to a question that is similar to the one before him.

For a little over ten years now, judges have been able to receive assistance from certain colleagues if they wish to find out the solution adopted by foreign jurisdictions towards a novel problem. In March 1993 the first appointment of a French judge to a post in the Italian judicial authorities was made, in Rome, with the primary mission of improving mutual judicial assistance between France and Italy. This first appointment was followed by the appointment of another French judge, this time in Holland. Several other posts for so-called 'liaison magistrates' have been created within the judicial authorities in America, Spain, Germany, the United Kingdom, the Czech Republic, Canada, and Morocco. Reciprocal posts for 'liaison magistrates' have been created in France at the Ministry of Justice in Paris. These appointments, made with the common objective of improving, in a general manner, judicial cooperation between countries, have encouraged other countries to embark upon this route. The process was formalized by a Joint Action of the European Union of 22 April 1996.

The activities undertaken by liaison magistrates fall into four broad categories:

- mutual assistance in the sphere of international criminal law;
- mutual assistance in the sphere of civil law;
- comparative law;
- the forging of links between judicial authorities.

I. LIAISON MAGISTRATES AND MUTUAL ASSISTANCE IN MATTERS OF INTERNATIONAL CRIME

Owing to their knowledge of the law and procedure both of their own country and of their host country, liaison magistrates tend to be in a position to remove the principal obstacle which a domestic judge is likely to encounter when he considers that it would be useful to consult the law of another country: misunderstanding created by the real or imagined differences between the legal systems. In the sphere of bilateral cooperation in criminal law an imperfect understanding of another country's legal system can still lead all too often to a form of self-censorship. Thus, for example, a French *juge d'instruction* who wishes to hear evidence from a witness who is abroad or who wishes to collect evidence (bank documents, DNA samples . . .) may well hesitate to send an international letter rogatory, fearing that a response is by no means certain. On the other hand, if such a judge is able to request assistance from a colleague posted in the relevant country, he is able to direct his request, taking into account the requirements particular to the procedure applied in that other country.

An increasingly large number of *juges d'instruction* in France now send to the liaison magistrate, by fax or by email, letters rogatory which they wish to send to the authorities of that country. Their colleague in the foreign post will accordingly be led to clarify certain points, such as the capacity in which a person is to give evidence (as a witness or as a suspect), to provide the evidence required for a search warrant, or to have telephone numbers identified. This advisory, indeed expert, work, carried out prior to the transmission of the request for mutual assistance in the criminal sphere, can pre-empt the need for the foreign authorities to make a request for further information, which would otherwise delay the execution of the letters rogatory. In an urgent case the proximity of the liaison magistrate to his colleagues in the host country enables him to draw their attention to the need to respond to the request for judicial assistance as quickly as possible.

Similarly, liaison magistrates are able to provide information to their foreign colleagues on the requirements of French law and on the rules of procedure applicable in their country of origin. This explanation is rendered easier by their presence in the workplace of their foreign colleagues. Even in the era of the Internet nothing quite compares to a direct exchange, face-to-face, between two people who know each other and meet regularly.

Equally, the judge who has made the request for mutual assistance can, with the help of his colleague posted to the relevant Member State, follow the execution of his request and so will not receive the impression that his request has fallen into a black hole, a reproach heard all too often in the area of cooperation in international crime. Moreover, should difficulties arise in the execution of the request, the judge can swiftly be informed of the reasons for the problem. Such information is particularly useful if one or more of the people being investigated are being held in detention. How often it is heard that a *juge d'instruction* cannot complete his dossier since he is still waiting for the response to his international letters rogatory.

The formation of joint enquiry teams between two or more countries— a form of cooperation which is now indispensable in order to combat more effectively the new types of international organized crime—means that liaison magistrates will increasingly play the role of facilitator and interpreter of legal systems. Even though the rules applicable in a country are often no

more than the specific enunciation of common principles, the intervention
of liaison magistrates means that a rapid response can be provided to the
everyday, practical problems of cooperation: changing the letter of the law
is not enough unless there is also a simultaneous change of mentality.
Mutual assistance must be founded on a great degree of confidence between
operators, based on common standards which guarantee respect for the
rights and liberties of those participating in a criminal trial.

For some ten years now liaison magistrates have thus intervened as real
'legal adapters' between different systems. Since they are integrated within
the workplace of their foreign colleagues, liaison magistrates are also regularly consulted by the judicial authorities of their host country when
members of such authorities have an interest in the legislation, the jurisprudence, or, more generally, the operation of the French legal system.

This role of facilitator beween the procedures of different countries
also encompasses extradition procedures (which are going to undergo
profound change in 2004 with the entry into force of the European arrest
warrant). In 2003 it must be acknowledged that, despite the European
texts which are applicable to the extradition procedures between different
countries of the EU, there remain significant differences between countries. Which should take priority: a request that a suspect be taken into
preventive custody or an extradition request? The answer may differ
according to the country in question. The compilation of a dossier must
also take into account the avenues of appeal available in the country in
question: for example, the opening of a dossier of extradition to the
United Kingdom is directly dependent on habeas corpus appeals and judicial review, exercised against the decisions of the judge sitting at Bow
Street in London and of the executive power (the Home Secretary). The
liaison magistrate must thus play his role of adapter between two systems
which are even further apart.

The same goes for matters concerning the transfer of people who have
been sentenced to imprisonment and who wish to serve their sentence in the
country of which they are a citizen.

II. THE LIAISON MAGISTRATE AND MUTUAL ASSISTANCE IN CIVIL MATTERS

Liaison magistrates also participate in the handling of bilateral cases, such
as those concerning the international abduction of children by a parent (the
Hague Convention of 1980). Liaison magistrates ensure that the two
parties who are claiming custody of the child do not take advantage of the
different legal systems in order either to deprive one of them of the exercise
of their rights as a parent of the child, or to render impossible any amicable agreement: liaison magistrates aim to fill the gaps between the legal

systems that might otherwise present problems to one or other of the parents when they have to make submissions to the foreign judiciary.

Moreover, the recent creation of the European Judicial Network in civil and commercial matters, in which liaison magistrates are included, should contribute to facilitating the execution of judicial decisions from one country to another, preventing parties from 'choosing' their judges.

The implementation of measures to protect those under guardianship increasingly gives rise to the intervention of liaison magistrates as soon as those under guardianship move from one place to another, thus presenting difficulties for the administration of their possessions.

The execution of letters rogatory in civil matters therefore means that the liaison magistrate's sphere of competence is not limited to matters of criminal law.

III. THE LIAISON MAGISTRATE AND COMPARATIVE LAW

An area in which liaison magistrates are increasingly involved is that of the dissemination of foreign law, when a national court is called to pronounce upon a new legal question.

In the absence of any relevant legislative provision or case-law precedent it is tempting, and even advisable, for the domestic judge to try to find out what answer has been given to the question by a foreign legislature or court. This situation can often arise in the sphere of so-called 'social problems'. In France one can cite the legal problems raised by, for example: a couple's use of a surrogate mother; an application for adoption made by a same-sex couple; the case of involuntary manslaughter of a foetus; the principle of whether compensation should be granted to children who are born handicapped, where the mother had been denied the option of abortion owing to a clinical error . . . Each time they have been consulted, liaison magistrates have informed their colleagues of the response, or absence of response, made by the foreign legislature or courts to fundamental questions of this sort which confront our society.

Even in more so-called 'classic' cases, bearing on, for example, the right to respect for private life, liaison magistrates are invited to inform the court of the approach adopted by the courts in their country of origin. Obviously, it is not simply a matter of copying another judge's decision, made in the context of a different legal system. However, the knowledge of the law applicable in another country and of its interpretation by one of that country's judges undoubtedly provides valuable assistance in reaching a decision. Liaison magistrates do not content themselves with simply providing a copy of the relevant judgment, which could prove to be of limited use to a foreign court. Rather, they accompany their response with personal commentary, enriched by their knowledge of the legal system of their host country.

Thus, the era, not so long ago, when it was considered to be an admission of a lack of serious argument for a lawyer to cite foreign legislation or case-law appears to be consigned to history. This can only be welcomed.

At their modest level, liaison magistrates thus participate in the growing convergence of legal cultures.

IV. THE 'RAPPROCHEMENT' OF JUDICIAL AUTHORITIES

Knowledge of the particular characteristics of a foreign legal system can assist in preventing misunderstandings, assuaging anxieties born of ignorance, and facilitating exchanges between those participating in the civil and criminal systems.

Each year internships are organized in order to allow lawyers, judges, or public prosecutors to discover or to deepen their knowledge of the operation of justice in other countries. Evidently in those countries where there are liaison magistrates the latter will intervene directly, both in the setting-up of the internship and in the choice of the programme. Liaison magistrates benefit in this from the valuable assistance provided by organizations that forge links with different legal cultures, such as associations of lawyers, schools, universities, and training institutions. In addition to such institutions, an important role is played by the goodwill shown by many lawyers in welcoming their foreign colleagues and in helping them to get to know their legal system.

Liaison magistrates also participate in the preparation of bilateral negotiations concerning, for example, the implementation of a convention on mutual judicial assistance in criminal matters (such as that signed between France and the United States) with a view to forging links between the positions of the countries in question. During the elaboration of these new texts liaison magistrates are asked to shed light on the difficulties that they have observed in the course of their everyday work, enabling the implementation of concrete and useful solutions.

At the point at which linguistic and textual barriers disappear, the barrier that exists too often in the minds of those participating in the legal systems must also be removed in order to give way to confidence: in their own way liaison magistrates are dedicated to achieving this aim.

PART II
European Law

5

The Use of Comparative Law in A & Others v National Blood Authority[1]

Michael Brooke QC and Ian Forrester QC

I. INTRODUCTION

The editors of this volume have invited two of the claimants' advocates instructed in an important case presenting both comparative law and Community law questions to describe how the case came to judicial attention, and the legal and factual challenges presented by arguing broad principle-driven doctrines before an English court during a trial lasting forty-nine court days. We represented 112 individuals who were infected with hepatitis C as a result of blood transfusions in England. This chapter, written with the consent of the claimants' solicitors, is extended with a Postscript by counsel for the defendant and completed by an Afterword from the trial judge. The claimants were successful, but it was a 'close-run thing'.

The problem of contaminated blood transfusions is not new to medicine or to litigation, especially in the United States. The United Kingdom avoided the excesses of the United States by having a non-commercial blood bank system. The claimants had certainly been injured, but it was questionable whether they had a good cause of action under conventional negligence principles. It is intrinsically difficult to establish liability on the part of a public authority performing a valuable public service. A case based on negligence would need to demonstrate considerable levels of breach of duty. While the HIV Haemophiliac Litigation (HHL)[2] in England was brought to an acceptable conclusion for the plaintiffs infected with HIV from blood products, the difficulty of pursuing such a case in negligence against government departments and agencies raising arguments of immunity and 'non-justiciability' and at the very least challenging the plaintiffs to establish 'Wednesbury negligence'[3] was daunting.

---

[1] *A & Others v NBA* [2001] 3 All ER 289 [2001] Lloyd's Rep Med 187. Hereafter references to the reported judgment will be by paragraph number, thus: para.

[2] Where the plaintiffs' cause of action was negligence.

[3] For non-English lawyers, liability of the public authority by reason of its manifestly gross or unreasonable misconduct.

For the victims of infection with the hepatitis C virus through blood transfusions a case based on Community law appeared more promising, precisely because it was intended to remove the need to prove negligence or knowledge on the part of the blood authorities. However, as of the late 1990s, although the EU Product Liability Directive[4] had been in force for some fifteen years (and had been under discussion for years before that), it had been little commented upon by courts in the UK or indeed elsewhere in the Common Market. The Newcastle solicitors who represented the majority of the potential claimants had already instructed barristers specializing in common law clinical negligence and product liability to review their clients' chances. One was also a member of the Paris Bar, with a network of professional colleagues and professional acquaintances in France and elsewhere. Counsel advised the potential claimants they had a sustainable case under the Consumer Protection Act 1987 (CPA) on the basis that blood infected with hepatitis C virus was defective upon a proper construction of the CPA.

The point being novel and not straightforward, the Legal Aid Board authorized the solicitors to seek a second opinion from further counsel, based in Brussels, a member of a London chambers working with colleagues of different nationalities.

The latter's opinion on the application of the Directive was first sought in 1997. In March 1997 he gave the opinion that it was reasonable to presume that patients and others would expect to receive uncontaminated blood in a transfusion, and would correspondingly regard as 'defective' blood that might infect them with a serious illness. As we will describe further below, the Directive presented a number of questions: would the public at large be entitled to regard as 'defective' a blood transfusion which might transmit hepatitis C, and would the various defences contemplated by the Directive avail the defendant blood authority? On this basis, questions of whether the potential defendants had followed good practice with respect to epidemiological probabilities appeared relevant not so much for whether the blood was defective under the Directive, but rather whether a defence might be available based upon the patient's acceptance of the risk or the defendant's unawareness of the risk. The opinion noted that there were surprisingly few judicial decisions applying the Directive, although there was a large quantity of material commenting on the proposal to have a Directive, the dangers and uncertainties of the Directive, and its implications for domestic product liability law. Particular attention in counsel's opinion was given to the writings of the European Commission official charged with drafting the Directive who from the early 1970s had been

---

[4] Council Directive 85/374/EEC on the approximation of the laws, regulations, and administrative provisions of the Member States concerning liability for defective products.

responsible for shepherding the proposal through the process of inter-governmental and intra-institutional negotiation to a conclusion in the form of the promulgation of Directive 85/374/EEC.

The two leading counsel thus separately reached the conclusion that an action based upon the Directive would indeed have a reasonable prospect of success. A number of supplementary opinions were dispatched, on the strength of which the solicitors were able to persuade the legal aid author-ities in England that the case was maintainable. (The Scottish legal aid authorities apparently rejected a parallel claim for help in Scotland on the grounds that the case was not winnable.)

II. THE MEDICINE

It is necessary to give a brief outline of what the scientific case was about.

Hepatitis is an inflammation of the liver, which can be caused by various viral infections. Once the hepatitis A virus and the hepatitis B virus had been identified in the early 1970s, it was appreciated that post-blood trans-fusion viral hepatitis continued to occur owing to infection with other (as yet unidentified) viruses, and NonA NonB Hepatitis (NANBH) was the description applied to this viral hepatitis. It was particularly noted because people were regularly seen to develop symptoms of hepatitis after receiving blood transfusions. At first there was no direct screening test to identify donors as carrying the virus, but there were practical procedures for exclud-ing blood from donors at increased risk of carrying the virus. These were called 'surrogate' tests, and the most useful one was to carry out a blood test to check the levels of an enzyme produced in the liver (ALT). High levels of ALT in the blood were suggestive that the person might have some abnormality of liver function, and one possible cause for this was that the donor was a carrier of the NANBH virus. This surrogate testing of blood donors had been routine in Germany since the 1960s; it was made routine in the United States in 1986 and in France by 1988. Routine ALT screening of blood donors was considered in the UK but never introduced.

In May 1988 came a breakthrough when the Chiron Corporation of America announced the identification of the hepatitis C virus and the devel-opment of a prototype screening test. The first version of the test (the Ortho Elisa) became commercially available in late 1989 (when a licence for the export of the test from the United States was first obtained) and it was soon used in programmes for the routine screening of blood donors in Japan and in France. In May 1990 the US Food and Drugs Administration (FDA) gave approval for use of this test within the United States and so it went into routine use for screening there, as well as in a number of other countries.

There were concerns about the accuracy of this 'first generation' test, both in regard to its sensitivity (not detecting all it should, ie false negatives) and its specificity (detecting those it should not, ie false positives). A further concern was the lack of a confirmatory or supplementary test to verify positive results and identify some of the false positives. Nevertheless, the relevant Department of Health committee (UK Advisory Committee on Virological Safety of Blood, ACVSB) advised, in principle, as early as November 1989 that the Ortho Elisa should be used for routine screening subject to three conditions.[5] In May 1990 a confirmatory test (RIBA 1) became available. In July and November 1990 the ACVSB recommended that screening of blood donors should be started, subject to the holding of various trials. Second-generation Elisa tests became available by April 1991. Routine screening of blood for hepatitis C was introduced throughout England and Wales on 1 September 1991.

NANBH had been a proxy in the HIV Haemophiliac Litigation (HHL) for the AIDS virus emerging in the 1980s, the argument being that the precautions that could and should by then have been taken against the contamination of blood products with NANBH would also have avoided their contamination with the yet to be identified HIV.[6]

Near the end of the HHL Mr Justice Ognall allowed for the plaintiffs' lawyers acting in the forthcoming Hepatitis Litigation, to use the knowledge acquired when acting in the HHL, particularly resulting from the disclosure provided by the various defendants. In the Hepatitis Litigation NANBH, no longer the proxy, was the target itself.

III. THE ENGLISH LEGAL PRINCIPLES

The Product Liability Directive (1985/374) came into effect on 25 July 1985 after a very lengthy process of drafting, lobbying, discussion, and negotiation, including intergovernmental and parliamentary discussion. The UK[7] implemented the Directive by passing the Consumer Protection Act 1987, which came into effect on 1 March 1988. A claimant's cause of action under the CPA is made out where *Damage* is caused to the *Claimant* by a *Defect* in a *Product* taken[8] to have been *Produced* by the *Defendant*. Section 4(1)(e) of the CPA provides that a defendant may escape liability by showing: 'That the state of scientific and technical knowledge at the relevant time was not such that a producer of products of the same description

---

[5] Satisfactory pilot tests, FDA approval, and availability of a confirmatory test.

[6] The keystone of the argument was the Scottish decision by the House of Lords in *Hughes v Lord Advocate* [1963] AC 837.

[7] One of the early Member States to do so.

[8] That is, the producer or the own brander or the importer or the supplier unable to identify the producer.

as the product in question might be expected to have discovered the defect if it had existed in his products while they were under his control.'

The litigation therefore turned on the rights of patients infected owing to transfusions after 1 March 1988.

Most[9] of the claimants in the Hepatitis Litigation relied on the CPA cause of action, although argument in the litigation essentially focused on the Directive, whose words, by common consent, prevailed in case of doubt, and it is that cause of action which is the subject of Mr Justice Burton's judgment in *A & Others v NBA*.

IV. PREPARATION OF THE CASE

The Directive is framed in the civil law tradition, expressed very tersely with questions of general principle set forth in a few words. The fifty[10] days in court turned on the proper construction[11] of fewer than one hundred words. A respectable case could be made that the reasonable expectation of the public at large should reflect the intrinsic characteristics of transfused blood in a bag: having come from another person's body, it could not fail to contain the qualities of the blood of the donor. It would be strange, the defendants would say, if liability could exist despite the defendants having taken every, or every reasonable, or every practical, precaution against the transmission of contaminated blood. If it were proved that no method (or no sufficiently reliable method) existed of catching infective bags of blood, was the ordinary citizen entitled to hope that the transfusion service would never deliver an infective bag of blood? Could society regard as 'defective' what science could not prevent?

Setting the purpose of the legislation in context would be essential. The preparations fell into different categories: (i) research on German civil law under Article 823 of the Bürgerliches Gesetzbuch (the German Civil Code, BGB) until the adoption of the Directive; (ii) gathering *travaux préparatoires*; (iii) consulting the now retired drafter of the Directive; (iv) research in other EC Member States and in the United States concerning relevant writings and judicial experience; (v) carrying out research at the Max-Planck-Institute; and (vi) collecting all language versions of the legislation and selecting those portions of other authorities in foreign languages that required translation in whole or in part into English.

---

[9] There were a small number relying on clinical negligence.

[10] Forty-nine days trying the case and one day delivering the reserved judgment.

[11] Legal argument as to that proper construction took place on no less than thirteen days in the course of the trial.

1. *German Law*

The Bundesgerichtshof (Germany's supreme civil court, BGH) rendered a series of judgments from 1956 concerning product liability. In each case, undoubted injury was done owing to the failure of a product: the fork of a bicycle broke and injured the rider; a mineral-water bottle exploded, injuring a child; a consignment of vaccine infected a flock of chickens with fowl pest. In each case the supplier said that the product had been manufactured according to the highest possible standards, under the strictest conditions of supervision, and with all due diligence. In the 1956 case the BGH found for the manufacturer, stating that the injury was one of the *Lebensrisiko*, one of the risks of life, and that, without demonstrable fault on the part of the manufacturer, the victim could not be compensated. The victim almost always would lack the capacity to show how the fault had occurred (particularly without a doctrine like *res ipsa loquitur*), and anyway the manufacturer could show it had done all in its power to prevent rogue products from reaching the market. The climate of opinion changed in the late 1960s and early 1970s owing to the Thalidomide tragedy (*Contergan* was its name in Germany), when children were born with unforeseen defects, and was further influenced by the legal consequences of compensating victims of the crash of a Turkish aircraft in Paris in 1974 because of a badly designed cargo-hold door. The BGH decided to reverse its previous positions and found for the claimant in an exploding mineral-water bottle case in 1995. Translations of these judgments (which are by English standards quite brief) were prepared; and copies of the relevant portions of the BGB were compiled both in German and in English translation.

2. Travaux Préparatoires

The Secretary-General of the European Council was requested to furnish copies of the *travaux préparatoires* from the Council's archives pertinent to the drafting, review, modification, and final adoption of the Directive. After some weeks the Secretariat-General supplied a large mass of documents dating back to the earliest days (late 1960s, early 1970s) when notions of a European Directive on product liability were first canvassed. Included were memoranda prepared within the context of a Council of Europe experts' committee, the first working drafts of a possible Directive prepared within the Commission, submissions by a wide range of parties concerning the merits of the draft Directive and, most interestingly, the minutes of the many meetings of the EU Council Working Group at which the proposed Directive moved through its successive stages to final adoption in 1985. Most of the latter documents were in French and indicated the identities and theories of the Member States requesting particular modifications during the drafting process. The *travaux préparatoires* could be relied on, the claimants thought, to demonstrate that most of the arguments to be considered in the litigation had been reviewed and debated extensively during the drafting process; quite how far they would be useful was uncertain.

3. Consulting the Retired Draftsman[12] of the Directive

Commission officials generally rotate between positions every three to five years. The Product Liability Directive was so controversial and so sensitive that the official in question had the rare privilege of seeing it through from initial conception in about 1970 to ultimate adoption by the Council in 1985. He had written an excellent book in German on the subject[13] and was a teacher of law at German universities. He quite relished the opportunity to see how a case concerning the Directive was prepared and was happy to give his personal comments on the history of the Directive, and a statement was framed recording his recollection of its drafting. There was debate between opposing counsel concerning the admissibility of such testimony, since part of it would consist of recording familiar institutional and procedural facts about how directives are drafted, revised, debated, and adopted. Community law (it was said) is a matter for argument, not evidence. The learned doctor could not testify to the proposition that a former Commission official considered the Directive should be interpreted in a particular way, but his insights were plainly useful to a full understanding of the history and the purposes of the Directive. After discussion with the Bench and between counsel, it was agreed that he would not submit testimony and that the procedural history to which he could speak would be adopted as part of the submissions by the claimants on the history of the Directive.

4. Research in Other EC Member States and in the United States Concerning Relevant Writings and Judicial Experience

As already noted, although the implications of the adoption of the Directive had been widely debated, and, indeed, colourfully debated, actual decisions applying the Directive appeared to be rare. Judgments in all civil law countries are brief by comparison with English standards. The reasoning of the French Cour de cassation may be one short sentence, a phenomenon that has so far survived scrutiny by the European Court of Human Rights. There is generally speaking no principle of *stare decisis* in civil law jurisdictions, although the significance of that difference can be exaggerated.

---

[12] Professor Dr Hans Claudius Taschner.
[13] *Produkthaftungsgesetz und EG-Produkthaftungsrichtlinie* (München Beck 1990).

It was therefore decided to research the implementation of the Directive in France, Spain, the Netherlands, Belgium, Italy, and Portugal. Accordingly, friendly members of the Bar in those countries were consulted and requested to report on significant academic writing or judicial decisions concerning the Directive, particularly in the context of medical practice. It turned out that there was a remarkable dearth of judicial authority and a moderate level of academic commentary during the period after the adoption of the Directive. Two cases had reached the European Court, one of which had been decided. One lower court judgment emerged: a district court in the Netherlands made a finding partially favourable to the claimants and partially unfavourable (that the blood was a defective product but that the hospital could not be blamed for having delivered it to the patient, since the defect could not have been screened out). There were a number of French cases reflecting more the distinctive and painful history of contaminated blood in France than the Directive in particular. Apart from the German cases before the Landgericht, Oberlandesgericht, and BGH, referred to above, there were few other judgments of obvious relevance, but the academic commentary was fairly copious, and would in due course be relied upon both in argument and in the judgment. The professional colleagues in other countries were extremely interested and helpful in suggesting lines of approach and relevant sources of academic literature.

Advice on the American experience was sought from an American friend, Professor Shael Herman, who taught at the Tulane University of Louisiana and at the Sorbonne. He synthesized the complex and inconsistent American history of how blood transfusion infection cases have been handled judicially and legislatively.

5. Carrying Out Research at the Max-Planck-Institute

Academic writing is a stronger source of legal authority in the civil law tradition than in England. In the absence of judgments of higher courts (with the notable exception of Germany) it was necessary to review the available literature. For this purpose the best-equipped law library in Europe was the Max-Planck-Institute in Hamburg. The Institute staff were hospitable and welcoming. Works by a number of authors of different nationalities in German, Swedish, Spanish, Italian, Portuguese, and English were consulted. One curiosity was that Belgian authors wrote on German law, German authors wrote on French law, and Australian authors wrote on English and Australian law. The claimants were thus able to produce at least twenty-five books and articles published outside the UK relevant to the fundamental questions presented by the litigation: was blood capable of being regarded as a product? Was it the reasonable expectation of the public that a blood transfusion would not contain hepatitis C virus? Was the public entitled to regard as defective a contaminated transfusion? What was the relevance of the precautions which could in theory be taken or had in fact been taken? Did it make a difference if the unwanted characteristics of the transfused blood were incapable of being eliminated by skill and diligence? What was the relevance of the prescribing doctor's knowledge of the risk of infection? Of what relevance was the so-called 'state-of-the-art defence'? Was the public entitled to have an expectation about the quality of transfused blood, which was technically unattainable in the circumstances?

6. Collecting All Language Versions of the Legislation and Preparing Translations of Other Material

The parties were greatly helped by the fact that the judge having the conduct of the litigation, Mr Justice Burton, was known to speak French comfortably and, as it turned out, other European languages very adequately. It was not necessary to go to the expense of preparing translations of all the material in various foreign languages. This was particularly convenient in regard to French, the language of most of the *travaux préparatoires*. However, translations of the entirety of two of the judgments of the BGH were prepared, as well as translations of the Arnhem district court judgment and Swedish *travaux préparatoires* which accompanied the promulgation in Swedish law of the Directive. The full texts of the academic commentators relied upon were made available and translations prepared of sentences or paragraphs which seemed particularly relevant. (All counsel spoke French, and some spoke moderate German and Italian.)

V. THE REQUEST FOR A REFERENCE IN 1999

In October 1999 the claimants invited the judge to make a preliminary reference to the European Court of Justice on a number of questions as to the true and proper construction to be placed on the Directive. This application was rejected. His order indicated that he felt the request was premature in that it was not yet certain what questions would turn out to be the relevant ones. A year later the trial started before the same judge. By then the scene had been set for a very full comparative analysis of how the Directive should be construed and applied to the facts relating to the claimants' infection through blood transfusions with the hepatitis C virus.

VI. THE NON-ISSUES

Three points of general importance hovered in the wings of the trial but did not in the end arise for decision. They are worth mentioning in passing and may crop up in future cases.

Product. On the generic pleadings the claimants' allegation that blood and *blood products* were 'products' within the meaning of the CPA was not admitted by the defendant. The defendant's position on the pleadings had support from one of the leading academic writers in the field, Professor Jane Stapleton in *Product Liability*,[14] but in the event it was conceded by the time of trial that blood and *blood products* were 'products'.

Producer. The defendant admitted that it was responsible for the liabilities of its predecessors in the National Blood Transfusion Service and the Bio Products Laboratory[15] and in effect accepted that they were the producers within the meaning of the CPA. During the course of the trial it was submitted by the defendant that in approaching the question of the consumer's legitimate expectation as to the safety of blood, the court should put in the defendant's favour the fact that, unlike a purely commercial producer, the defendant had no alternative but to continue supplying blood to hospitals and patients as a service to society. Burton J rejected this argument in paragraph 42 of his judgment: noting that the defendants did not put forward a defence under Article 7(d) 'that the defect is due to compliance of the product with mandatory regulations issued by the public authorities', he concluded that there was no necessary reason why a public authority or a non-profit-making organization should be in any different position from a commercial undertaking if the product is unsafe. He also noted that that was the opinion expressed by the Advocate General (Colomer) in the *Danish Kidney* case.[16] This was before the ECJ gave its judgment in the case[17] on various questions referred to it by the Højesteret (Danish Supreme Court).

---

[14] (London Butterworths 1994). Professor Stapleton is Research Professor, Research School of Social Sciences, Australian National University; Ernest E Smith Professor, University of Texas School of Law; Commonwealth Fellow, British Institute of International and Comparative Law; and Academic Associate, Fountain Court.

[15] The Regional Health Authorities and the Central Blood Laboratories Authority.

[16] *Henning Veedfald v Århus Amstkommune* Case C–203/99, para 27.

[17] Holding that Art 7(c) 'the product was neither manufactured by him for sale or any form of distribution for economic purpose nor manufactured or distributed by him in the course of his business' did not furnish a defence where the defective product is used in the course of a medical service financed entirely from public funds and for which the patient is not required to pay any consideration. The Court also addresses some interesting questions directed to whether the damage suffered in the case (loss of a harvested kidney through contamination prior to transplant into the plaintiff) was within Art 9 of the Directive.

Consumer Protection Act versus Directive. There are significant differences between the wording not merely of Article 7(e) and section 4(1)(e) CPA but also between Article 6 and section 3 in the definition of defect. The differences between Article 7(e) and section 4(1)(e) were considered by the European Court of Justice in the enforcement proceedings brought by the Commission against the UK[18] to challenge the adequacy of the UK's implementation of the Directive. As the pleadings developed, a pattern emerged of the claimants sticking resolutely to the wording of the Directive, while the defendant stuck to the wording of the CPA. By the time of the trial, however, it was accepted on both sides that the dominant provision was the Directive and that in so far as the CPA's wording differed from the wording of the Directive, the CPA should not be construed differently from the Directive. As Burton J said: 'and consequently the practical course was to go straight to the fount, the Directive itself'.[19] The clash of the statutes, feared by the Commission in its challenge to the UK's implementation of the Directive and an issue on our pleadings,[20] did not in fact take place, although a great deal of time was spent analysing *Commission v UK* in at least three language versions.

VII. THE CORE ISSUES

The two fundamental issues were:

(a) Is the infection of blood with hepatitis C virus a defect within the meaning of Article 6?
(b) If so, was the state of scientific and technical knowledge such that the existence of the defect could not be discovered as provided by Article 7(e)?

Article 6(1) provides:

A product is defective when it does not provide the safety which a person is entitled to expect, taking all the circumstances into account, including:

(i) the presentation of the product;
(ii) the use to which it could reasonably be expected that the product would be put;
(iii) the time when the product was put into circulation.

The main points of common ground were:[21]

---

[18] *Commission v UK* Case C–300/95 [1997] All ER (EC) 481.
[19] Para 2.
[20] Despite the terms of section 1(1) CPA, 'This Part [of the Act] shall have effect for the purpose of making such provision as is necessary in order to comply with the product liability Directive and shall be construed accordingly.'
[21] See Para 31, where Burton J lists in detail a number of points of common ground.

(*a*) That liability under the CPA is 'defect-based' not 'fault-based' (Recitals 2 and 6 of the Directive).

(*b*) That the question to be resolved is the degree or level of safety or safeness which persons generally are entitled to expect.

(*c*) The expectation is that of the public at large.

(*d*) The expectation is not the *actual* expectation of persons generally, but what they are *entitled* to expect. 'Legitimate expectation' became the common formulation of the expectation, which was consistent with other language versions of the Directive, eg 'la sécurité à laquelle on peut légitimement s'attendre'.

(*e*) The court decides what the public is entitled to expect.

Against that common background:

(*a*) The claimants' primary case on defect was that:
  (i) The legitimate expectation of people generally throughout the relevant period[22] was that transfused blood would not infect patients with hepatitis C.
  (ii) The conduct of the producer is irrelevant and questions of avoidability of the defect, practicability of its avoidance, and economic feasibility thereof are all irrelevant.

(*b*) The defendant's case on defect was that:
  (i) The risk of infection with hepatitis C was known to the treating doctors, for whom it was a risk worth running for the sake of the patient in need of a transfusion.
  (ii) Avoidability or unavoidability is a circumstance for the purpose of Article 6.
  (iii) The legitimate expectation of people generally was not that blood would be 100 per cent clean but that all legitimately expectable (reasonably available) precautions had been taken.
  (iv) It would therefore be necessary to investigate whether the producers had taken all legitimately expectable steps to avoid the risk of the product being defective.

(*c*) The claimants' fallback case on defect, in consequence, was:
  (i) That the defendant's case is contrary to the intention of the Directive as revealed by the *travaux préparatoires*, the Recitals, and the observations of the Advocate General and the European Court of Justice in *Commission v UK*, requiring as it did an investigation of fault in all but name.
  (ii) That, nevertheless, the investigation required by the defendant's case in fact reveals that throughout the relevant period the

---

[22] From 1 Mar 1988.

producers *had* failed to take all legitimately expectable steps to avoid the risk of the product being defective:

1. From 1 March 1988 in failing to perform routine surrogate testing of blood donors.
2. From 1 January 1990 in failing to perform anti-hepatitis C Elisa testing of blood donations.

Article 7(e) provides: 'The producer shall not be liable as a result of this Directive if he proves . . . that the state of scientific and technical knowledge at the time when he put the product into circulation was not such as to enable the existence of the defect to be discovered.'

(*a*) The defendant's case on Article 7(e) was that in the then state of scientific and technical knowledge, the defect in the particular product could not be discovered, given the shortcomings of both surrogate testing and anti-hepatitis C Elisa first-generation tests. In other words, the defect has to be discoverable in the blood in the bag in question.

(*b*) The claimants' case on Article 7(e) was that the defence is not available once the risk of the product being defective was known (which had been the case since the 1970s), whether or not the defect can be discovered in a particular product. In other words, the existence of the defect in the population of products in general has to be undiscoverable for the defence to arise.

VIII. COMPARATIVE LAW FEATURES OF THE ORAL ARGUMENT

Once the trial began, the European law case was opened by referring to the adoption of the BGB in 1896, and the evolving interpretation of Article 823, which is the basis for establishing liability due to fault under German law. German law in the 1950s and 1960s found against plaintiffs who had unquestionably been injured but were unable to demonstrate fault as against a diligent manufacturer who could show the existence of all possible precautions. Thereafter the law changed, reflecting what English lawyers would call a decision to shift the burden of proof, concluding with the celebrated case of the child injured by the exploding mineral-water bottle. This case concerned a young claimant injured by an exploding mineral-water bottle resulting from a very fine hairline crack, not discovered despite what was found to be a technical and supervisory procedure in the defendant's factory in accordance with the very latest technology. Both the Court of Appeal of Hamm and the BGH had experienced little difficulty in concluding that the bottle was a defective product under Article 6 of the Directive, categorizing the bottle as an *Ausreisser*, a rogue product or sub-standard product. The battlefield in the German courts was Article 7(e), and the young claimant was the victor in the BGH. German law was thus presented as an example of legal evolution in accordance with the principles ultimately espoused by the Product Liability Directive. There was then a very thorough examination of the *travaux préparatoires* over a period of about fifteen years, from which, so argued the claimants, one could observe that many of the arguments advanced by the defendants had been voiced, examined, and not accepted by the drafters of the Directive. The claimants of course had to concede that it was the words of the Directive which should prevail, and that the *travaux préparatoires* could not supply principles which were not present in the adopted text. It was interesting to observe that the *travaux préparatoires* contained submissions from chambers of commerce, memoranda from governments, and reports by successive chairmen of the Council Working Group charged with the responsibility of reaching a consensus among the Member States. The books and articles published by those involved in the drafting process, especially Professor Taschner, were particularly relied on.

The claimants also referred to English and Scottish cases such as *Smedleys v Breed* [1974] AC 839 (the factory produced 3,500,000 cans of peas a year successfully but was convicted when four caterpillars of the same colour, shape, and density as the peas escaped detection in its food preparation processes and were discovered in a can of peas), and *Donoghue v Stevenson* [1932] AC 562 [23] (concerning the alleged snail in the bottle of ginger beer) was invoked as authority for the proposition that what manufacturers claimed was ridiculously severe nonetheless could make good law. There had been two recent English decisions under the CPA,[24] which the trial judge considered. The conclusion of the BGH was echoed[25] (albeit obiter) by Ian Kennedy J in *Richardson*:[26]

This provision [Article 7(e)] is, to my mind, not apt to protect a defendant in the case of a defect of a known character merely because there is no test which is able to reveal its existence in every case.

---

[23] It should be recorded that, despite its absence from the lists of authorities in both the Lloyd's Rep Med and the All ER reports of *A v NBA*, the great case of *Donoghue v Stevenson* was referred to in argument on at least ten occasions. Reading the dissenting speeches in *Donoghue v Stevenson* was a salutary reminder that famous cases were not foregone conclusions; Mrs Donoghue was fortunate in having a dogged solicitor who believed he could change the law.

[24] *Iman Abouzaid v Mothercare (UK) Ltd* (Court of Appeal 21 Dec 2000); *Richardson v LRC Products Ltd* [2000] Lloyd's Rep Med 280, a decision at first instance in respect of a failed condom which Ian Kennedy J held not to be defective.

[25] Ian Kennedy J cleaves to the CPA in the course of his judgment and does not mention the Directive at all. While counsel had referred him to *Commission v UK* and the Art 7(e)/section 4 (1)(e) linguistic discrepancy, he was not apparently referred to the BGH decision.

[26] At 285.

A certain amount of time was devoted to the United States, where the commercialization of the blood industry led to a high incidence of infection and a corresponding number of lawsuits, to which a number of legislatures had reacted by enacting so-called shield laws immunizing blood banks from liability in certain circumstances. Indeed, New Jersey and Illinois judgments were duly cited in the judgment.

An Australian case[27] of toxic[28] oysters was considered, but the wording of the Australian statute's equivalent of Article 7(e) was subtly different, alluding to the discoverability of the defect in 'the action goods'. This, it was held, provided a defence since the presence of hepatitis A virus in any given oyster could not be discovered.

The language of Articles 1, 4, 6, and 7 of the Directive as well as its Recitals were reviewed at length. Of the eleven European Union languages, the judge was the only person who attempted the modern Greek texts, and the Finnish text was not consulted. Most attention was given to the English, French, German, Italian, and Portuguese texts. The Livenote transcribers of the shorthand record of the hearings included linguists[29] who were able to produce accurately typed German, French, Italian, or Spanish in the transcript delivered to the judge and counsel at the end of the day. Emphasis was placed on the fact that the explanatory memoranda adopted by other Member States usually made recitals of certain principles relevant to the construction of the Directive. Much time was also devoted to the opinion of Advocate General Tesauro and the judgment in *Commission v UK*.[30]

IX. THE JUDGMENT

The resolution of these issues as to the true and proper construction of the Directive, having entailed wide-ranging comparative arguments, led to a judgment, which refers to authorities from eight[31] jurisdictions and numerous learned books and papers.[32]

The learned judge directed himself that he should approach the *travaux préparatoires* with caution.[33] Bearing in mind that he should be alive to there being an 'autonomous' or Community meaning or construction for harmonizing pan-European legislation, the judge welcomed the guidance to

---

[27] *Graham Barclay Oysters v Ryan* [2000] FCA 1099.
[28] They were contaminated with the hepatitis A virus.
[29] Assisted by one counsel's polyglot son.
[30] Case C–300/95 [1997] All ER (EC) 481.
[31] England, ECJ, New Jersey, Illinois, Germany, Holland, France, and Australia.
[32] The reader should know that the judgment, even by English standards, is long: as handed down it is 170 pages long containing 284 paragraphs (105 pages in Lloyd's Law Reports, Medical, containing 283 paragraphs).
[33] Para 15.i.

be obtained from considering the official different language versions of the Directive and was tentatively prepared to look at how the Directive had been implemented and judicially applied in other Community countries;[34] a little later in his judgment he shows more enthusiasm for judicial decisions elsewhere in Europe for reasons of both comity and harmony in approaching this piece of common legislation.[35] The judge attached great importance to the Directive's recitals as aids to its construction, listing the significant ones at an early stage.[36]

The judgment makes many citations from the academic literature in respect of both Article 6 and Article 7(e). In part this is because of the dearth of previous judicial decisions, particularly on Article 6, but it also demonstrates a willingness by the judge to adopt a broad and purposive approach to the task of construction that faced him. The judge, in formulating his conclusions on Article 6, underpins them at the outset by reference to European academic literature.[37]

The court decisions that carried most weight with the judge and clearly gave him most assistance were *Commission v UK* and the decision of the BGH in the mineral-water bottle case, both cases directed at Article 7(e) but both offering some assistance on Article 6. It is interesting to observe that the opinion of Advocate General Tesauro (in *Commission v UK*) needed to be consulted in its original Italian to see that at one point he had used the subjunctive, which had not been carried over into the official English translation.[38] The judge took on the task of analysing the BGH's very dense judgment in the mineral-water bottle case and came to the conclusion that 'What the *BGH* was primarily saying is that if the risks are known, unavoidability of the defect in the particular product is no answer.'[39]

Burton J's conclusions on Article 6 may be summarized thus:

(*a*) The words *all the circumstances* are not exclusive; neither are they unlimited. They are not to be subjected to a restricted construction *eiusdem generis* to the specific examples given in Article 6. Having regard to other language versions,[40] in particular the French where 'notamment' (approximately meaning 'notably') is used rather than 'including', the specific examples given in Article 6 are intended to

---

[34] Para 15.ii.   [35] Para 44.   [36] Para 14.   [37] Para 55.
[38] Para 53.i.a.   [39] Para 53.ii.
[40] In Para 34.ii. the judge observes: '[a possibility is] that they ['all circumstances'] are to be construed as the most significant examples of the circumstances. There was some support for this proposition, both by way of some exemplars in European legislation—from which it could be suggested that European draftsmen had considered that the matters actually set out as examples were the ones most worthy of mention—and also by reference to the French language version of Article 6, which used the word, before the list of the circumstances, "notamment", and the German, which used "insbesondere", both of which I take to mean "'in particular" or "'especially"—although other language versions use phraseology more similar to the English "including".'

be the most significant circumstances. *All the circumstances* are to be construed as all *relevant* circumstances.

(b) *Avoidability* (ie the defendant's case on Article 6) is not one of the *circumstances* to be taken into account within article 6.[41] It is not a relevant circumstance, being outwith the purpose of the Directive,[42] which was to relieve consumers not merely of the need to prove fault or negligence but also of the need to show that the producer had taken all legitimately expectable steps. Furthermore, had *avoidability* been relevant, it would have been a significant circumstance departing from the purpose of the Directive and as such would have been mentioned specifically in Article 6.

(c) The first step is to identify the harmful characteristic which caused the injury. The next step is to conclude whether the product is standard or non-standard. If the respect in which it differs from the series includes the harmful characteristic, then for the purpose of Article 6 it is non-standard. The judge preferred this approach to that taken in the United States[43] of categorizing product defects as design, manufacturing, or labelling[44] defects, which approach has commonly been adopted by academic writers. The judge saw[45] no reason to take this approach (he was not invited to do so by either party) and observed both that the Directive made no attempt to categorize defects and that the attempt to fit any particular situation into one of these 'boxes' in fact gave no assistance in carrying out the task of deciding under Article 6 whether the product is defective. Materials in the *travaux préparatoires* deflected the judge from taking the 'risk/utility' approach to defect favoured by the US Second Restatement on Torts (1965).[46] He was encouraged in his course of preferring 'standard/non-standard' as part of the test of defectiveness by the fact that both Italy and Spain by express legislation had provided that non-standard products would automatically be defective within Article 6 of the Directive, an example of implementing legislation in other Community countries feeding the debate.[47]

(d) In the case of non-standard products it will be relevant to compare them with other products on the market and to consider whether the public at large accepted the non-standard nature of the product, but

---

[41] Para 63.

[42] Having regard, in particular, to the recitals of the Directive, Recitals 2 and 6 being most apposite.

[43] See the American Law Institute's Third Restatement of the Law of Torts 1998, Cap 1, section 2, Categories of Product Defect.

[44] Instructions and warnings.

[45] Paras 39–41.   [46] Para 35.i.   [47] Para 36.

that is not the end of the matter as the court has to decide the question what is the *legitimate* expectation as to safety of the product, which may be higher or lower than the public expectation.

(e) If the unsafe product is standard for the purpose of Article 6, then the judge acknowledged that the process may be more difficult,[48] though questions of *avoidability* would remain irrelevant and social acceptability would only arise through knowledge of the unsafeness.[49]

(f) The judge proceeded to hold:
  (i) that blood infected with hepatitis C was non-standard;[50]
  (ii) that the public had not taken it to be socially acceptable for non-standard units of blood to infect patients with hepatitis C,[51] the knowledge of the medical profession being irrelevant to that consideration;[52]
  (iii) that the public at large were entitled to expect that the blood transfused to them would be free from infection;[53]
  (iv) that the blood that infected each of the claimants, was defective for the purpose of Article 6.

(g) Burton J went on to address the defendant's case on defect and, having heard a large body of factual and expert evidence, having made a number of findings of fact, having taken into account:
  (i) all the *circumstances* on the defendant's construction of Article 6,
  (ii) the fact that the precautions of the introduction of surrogate testing and earlier introduction of routine screening were not taken,
  he came to the conclusion[54] that 'such blood so infected on and after 1 March 1988 did not provide the safety which persons generally are entitled to expect.'

Burton J's conclusions[55] on Article 7(e) may be summarized thus:

(a) Article 7(e) derogates from the purpose of the Directive and should be construed strictly for that reason.[56] The judge had already used the very restrictedness of the Article 7(e) defence as an aid to construction when considering Article 6.[57]

(b) The *existence of the defect* means the existence of the generic defect, not the defect in the particular product.[58]

---

[48] Para 73.   [49] Para 65.ii.   [50] Para 73.   [51] Para 65.ii.
[52] Para 80.   [53] Para 80.   [54] Para 173.   [55] Paras 74–7.
[56] Para 75. Note that in the *Danish Kidney* case the ECJ said much the same in relation to Art 7(a) treating it as a given but going through a similar thought process (see para 15 of the judgment).
[57] Para 64.   [58] Para 74.iii.

(c) Article 7(e) protects the producer in respect of the unknown generic defect; its purpose is to protect the producer against liability for the 'inconnu', not to provide a defence in the case of damage caused by a known but undetectable generic defect.[59] In his analysis of Article 7(e) the judge acknowledges the guidance of *Commission v UK* and suggests that his conclusions are in line with the decision of the BGH and the majority of academic writers. When encapsulating the *travaux préparatoires* for the purpose of Article 7(e),[60] the judge records that originally the intention of the Commission was that the Directive should impose liability even for the 'inconnu', meaning the inclusion of liability for true development risks; the outcome of the legislative process was the opposite and became Article 7(e). This was a further reason for concluding as the judge did in respect of Article 7(e): 'Hence it protects the producer in respect of the unknown (*inconnu*).'[61]

(d) Accordingly non-standard products may qualify under Article 7(e); 'However once the problem is *known* by virtue of accessible information, then the non-standard product can no longer qualify for protection under Article 7(e).'[62]

(e) Throughout the relevant period the generic defect of blood sometimes being infected with hepatitis C[63] was well known and the defendant could not therefore establish a defence under Article 7(e).

Burton J also addressed the consequence had the defendant's construction of Article 7(e) been accepted[64] and resolved several causation issues and a number of damages issues. It is not proposed to discuss those matters here.

X. *ENVOI*

Participating as advocates in the case was a great honour. No other European country would devote so much care and resources by so many specialized lawyers to settling a question of product liability for personal injuries. The judge can have handled little else for about six months. The courtroom was filled with medical and legal authorities who came and went. The atmosphere was quiet, orderly, courteous, *confraternelle* and intense, qualities that are not necessarily found in every Member State. The Legal Aid authorities in England are to be commended for making enough money available to permit a good job to be done. As advocates we had the privilege of very thoroughly prepared written pleadings, the loose rein but firm grip of very experienced instructing solicitors, a broad and deep survey

[59] Para 76.
[60] Para 52.
[61] Para 76.
[62] Para 77.
[63] Or NANB.
[64] Paras 181–7.

of the academic literature in at least twelve countries, excellent professional relations with our opponents (throughout the case), and the undistracted attention of an interested and talented member of the judiciary with a gift for languages and an interest in the development of the law.[65] The quality of the judgment, its thoroughness and comprehensiveness, reflect the amount of money and time which the legal system in our country traditionally affords to the resolution of important matters affecting ordinary people. By continental European standards this was luxury justice.

Recently Mr Justice Lightman gave an interesting lecture.[66] Without dissenting from many of his observations (eg about the value of good preparation and pre-trial resources), we respectfully but firmly disagree with his suggestion that a continental European approach to civil litigation would deliver a better *quality* of civil justice than is provided by the systems we enjoy in the UK. We have each of us had the privilege of pleading both in the UK and in its civil law neighbours across the channel. It may be worth concluding by recording some differences. The English tradition used to give greater weight to oral pleading. Written arguments—so-called 'skeletons'—were matchstick-thin, and in the old days were often not used at all. Today, skeletons have become fleshy, and the oral portion has become more focused. But the oral portion is still a highly demanding exchange of views with a well-prepared judge. Counsel expects to be thoroughly cross-examined. That which is not relevant is rebuffed. The judge advances several theories to test the argument.

The French approach is quite different. Commonly the oral argument is heard in total judicial silence: counsel have no inkling whether they are being relevant, persuasive, or tedious. The judgment is usually short, sometimes very short (French Cour de cassation judgments may have one sentence of reasoning). The written pleadings (customarily two for and two against) are pieces of advocacy, more carefully polished than an English skeleton, closely responding to the arguments of the adversary.

We would submit, as our personal and no doubt idiosyncratic conclusion, that the relative weights accorded to written and oral submissions are reversed between England and France. The care given to crafting individual judgments is higher in England than in France and, consequently, a French judgment is 'only' a decision about the case in hand. England takes more care with a single judgment than France, and individual English judgments can be major sources of new legal principle. It is very unlikely that in France

---

[65] And, also in accordance with the traditions of the English Bar, all the barristers and the judge had a dinner together, and the menu for the dinner contained such dubious delicacies as *potage générique, agneau réformé par directive, fromage résolument anglais sans référence aux normes européennes*, capped with *café de l'avenir* (which beverage was named in the—ill-founded—expectation that an appeal was inevitable).

[66] 6th Edward Bramley Memorial Lecture, University of Sheffield.

120 infected patients advancing novel legal theories would have received such a thorough examination of their claims. It is very rare that one first-instance French or Belgian judgment would shape the flow of future legal developments. We can be proud that the English legal system could deliver high quality justice to people of modest means pursuing a case with a difficult legal theory and complex scientific facts.

POSTSCRIPT BY
NICHOLAS UNDERHILL QC[67]

I am grateful to have been given the opportunity to comment briefly on Michael Brooke and Ian Forrester's lucid and fair-minded account of the *Hepatitis C* litigation. I need not argue the toss on the few points where I disagree with their exposition of the issues and the submissions, still less argue whether the decision was correct. The area of interest for readers of this volume is the extensive use made in the course of the trial of comparative law materials. The authors clearly explain how central the use of such materials was to their presentation of the claimants' case. If I had more space, I should be inclined to argue that it does not follow that they were central to the determination of the decisive issues. The parties agreed on most of the points of principle: see the section of the judgment headed 'Common Ground', which contains a valuable summary of the correct approach to the Act.[68] Although the judge referred at some points in that summary to comparative law materials, there was nothing that could not have been clearly derived from the terms of the Directive and the Act themselves. The only fundamental difference of principle as regards Article 6—whether so-called 'avoidability' was a relevant circumstance—was one on which the authorities and academic materials hardly touched.

However, there is no opportunity here to develop this provocative thesis. I will confine myself to drawing attention to three specific points, which may not clearly emerge from the authors' account.

First, the authors write feelingly of the assistance they received from Dr Taschner, the Commission official who had had primary responsibility for the Directive from its genesis through to its final adoption. As they say, it was their original intention to call Dr Taschner as a witness. His witness statement not only gave a factual account of the prolonged gestation of the Directive but also expressed strong views about the intended meaning and effect of the relevant provisions. The defendants opposed the admission of this evidence in principle. In relation to English legislation it would of

---

[67] The defendants' leading counsel.
[68] See para 31, where Burton J lists in detail a number of points of common ground.

course be wholly improper to adduce the evidence of the promoter or the draftsman of a piece of legislation as to what he intended it to mean. The defendants argued that the position should be no different in relation to EU legislation. Indeed the objections here were a fortiori. The genesis of the Directive was bitterly contested. Different Member States took widely different views as to just how strict the new strict liability regime should be. The result is generally acknowledged to have been a political compromise. It would be extremely dangerous for a court to entertain evidence from one of the protagonists in that debate since his intention as to the effect of the Directive could not be taken to represent the eventual (and largely notional) 'collective intention'. Although the authors may be formally correct to say that it was eventually 'agreed' that they would not seek to rely on Dr Taschner's evidence, that agreement was only reached after the judge had made it plain that he accepted the validity of the defendants' objection. The point seems to me important because it is sometimes thought, or assumed, that familiar domestic rules as to the admissibility of evidence can be ignored when 'Euro-issues' are in play. That may be so where the rules are purely local and technical; but where, as here, they reflect legitimate objections of principle, they should apply equally whatever the source of law being relied on.

My second point is not dissimilar. The authors explain that they obtained from the archive of the European Commission a mass of minutes and associated materials showing the formal progress of the draft Directive. These went far beyond the drafts that appeared in the Official Journal and the other formal *travaux préparatoires* that are sometimes relied on. The defendants objected to the admission of these materials—partly because of their sheer untranslated dullness, but also as a matter of principle. The trouble with such materials is that they can give the illusion of completeness but in fact only tell part of the story. In this case, for example, the minutes largely ceased at the crucial moment when the Directive entered the black hole of consideration by the Council of Ministers. It was impossible to find out from them what considerations—if what was no doubt largely a matter of political horse-trading can be so dignified—influenced the final form of the Directive. Again, there was no formal ruling; but the claimants agreed to a short summary of the legislative history based almost wholly on materials from the Official Journal, and virtually none of the minutes were referred to in court. Again, the moral is that the introduction of Euro-issues is not carte blanche for unrestricted reference to the legislative history.

My third point is somewhat different. Our prolonged discussion during the trial of a variety of comparative law materials often left me with the feeling that we were skating—enjoyably and with a fine display of linguistic talent (my own lagging behind that of the claimants' counsel)—on very thin ice. At any point we might fall though the surface and discover ourselves seriously out of our depth. Comparative law materials are not easy to use properly. If they are not in English, they have to be translated: even when translated, unfamiliar terminology, concepts, and procedures have to be explained if basic misunderstandings are to be avoided. There is no expert available to the court, which is accordingly dependent on counsel. In our case Mr Forrester was as fair as he was learned, and when he offered the court a translation of an untranslated passage in an article, or in the parallel text of the Directive, it could be accepted without reserve— though the passage of arms about the significance of the use of the subjunctive in one sentence in the Italian version of the Advocate General's Opinion in *Commission v UK* possibly tested the parties' mutual confidence. But it is dangerous in principle to be thus reliant. Without a sure and impartial guide it is very easy to go astray.

Superficiality is a risk in other ways as well. The claimants' counsel, as they have explained, had done extensive research in the library of the Max-Planck-Institute. The defendants' counsel had in turn had great assistance from Professor Stapleton[69] in mining the very thick seam of product liability law in the United States (and the narrow but rich seam of the *Oysters* litigation in Australia). But it was not realistic to draw the court's attention to any but a very small proportion of this material. Hundreds of pages of copied materials—from both sides—were not in the end deployed. I hope we were intelligently selective. The judge in any event showed himself keenly able to identify points of principle out of a wide variety of disparate materials. But the fact is that English lawyers cannot hope to educate either themselves or the court to a full understanding of the subtleties of foreign legal systems. Comparative law materials are best used to illustrate or illuminate broad points of principle: even the most learned cannot become good German or US lawyers in the space of a single trial.

This postscript is intended as a counter-balance to the main chapter and has accordingly focused on qualifications to the authors' main thesis. But I would not want it to be thought that the comparative law materials deployed in the *Hepatitis C* case were of little value, still less that they were of little interest. Anyone reading Burton J's formidable judgment will see how deeply they penetrated the argument—and also with what vigour counsel and the court debated them.

---

[69] See n 15 above.

AFTERWORD
MR JUSTICE BURTON[70]

A number of reflections occur to me in relation to the *Hepatitis C* litigation, by reference to the need for consideration of comparative law and its relevance to the decision:

1. Although the decisions of foreign courts are, in the English courts, strictly speaking only a part of the evidence, because evidence of foreign law is at English law to be treated as evidence of fact, nevertheless our modern systems now enable us to dispense with any problems with admissibility: hence the cases and the relevant academic works, whether extracts from textbooks, learned treatises, or articles from journals, are collected together and bundled, and, in a long case, delivered to the judge before the trial starts.

2. In this case such 'foreign law' authorities and the academic articles were efficiently copied, indexed, and paginated into files which rendered it easy for me to be able to underline and 'sticker up' with colour-coded tabs (essential in a case such as this where in the end there were not far off a hundred files, including more than ten containing comparative law authorities and written submissions). This could be done both during the process of speed-reading prior to the hearing, before I was fully understanding what all the issues consisted of, and then again during the hearing as they were given more detailed consideration and explanation. I was given some time to read all the documents prior to the trial starting. With the modern system of 'skeletons' (very often, at any rate in a long case, a misnomer for the lengthy written submissions which are delivered) supplied by way of exposition of each party's case, a judge can obtain a relatively informed grasp in advance by reading the submissions with care, and by speed-reading particularly those documents or, in the case of these comparative law questions, authorities and articles which are specifically referred to, or cross-referred to, in the submissions. Not only did we look at authorities from more than a dozen different jurisdictions (cases which became familiar friends, such as the *German Bottle* case[71] and the *Danish Kidney* case),[72] but we considered learned contributions from academic writers from the UK, the United States, Australia, Germany, Italy, and France.

3. The decisions of other national courts in Europe are of course of great interest, but they are normally at best persuasive. However, where they are decisions seeking to construe or enforce the same European Directive, and we all ought together to be aspiring towards a common or 'autonomous' meaning of that Directive, then such comparative study becomes the more

---

[70] The trial judge.   [71] BGH 9 May 1995.   [72] See n 16 above.

essential. Of course, unless and until there is a definitive conclusion by the European Court binding on all the national courts, we may nevertheless each be arriving at our own different result.

4. It is in my experience very rare, short of the House of Lords, for a court to have the opportunity to look at so much foreign law and academic authority as we did in the *Hepatitis C* case. This was not just because of the importance of the case and the time, which had been set aside for the hearing, but I think largely because of the novelty of the issues and arguments, at any rate in an English Court. There has been a considerable jurisprudence developed in the United States which, on analysis, did not appear to be of great assistance in the interpretation of the somewhat differently drafted European Directive, but, that apart, there was little jurisprudence throughout the world, and certainly very little in England and Wales. In attempting to arrive at the correct solutions, an English judge in those circumstances had to look abroad at any rate for his starting point, and the parties gave me that opportunity.

5. The same novelty meant that whereas, on some occasions, in a long case it may be possible, as the proceedings continue, for a judge to be reaching provisional conclusions, or even provisionally drafting parts of his judgment in advance, this was not possible for me. Indeed I had an entirely open mind and was very much swayed first one way and then the other as the argument and evidence continued and developed. This meant that, once the case finished, I was able with a blank sheet of paper to reread not only my notes but, more importantly and more accurately, the transcripts of the forty-nine days of evidence and argument, and in particular to reconsider the bundles, including the comparative law. I was given some five weeks' 'time off' to write the judgment, and I just about managed it in the deadline, working the sort of hours which I had thought I had left behind at the Bar!

6. The full and detailed oral argument was in my view essential both to ensure proper investigation of the issues and to put me in a position to arrive at an informed and reasoned decision. Bad ideas (whether coming from counsel or from the judge) can be tested and discarded. Good ideas can actually emerge in the course of discussion, but in any event can be tested and developed. Misunderstandings can be eliminated. Difficult arguments can be explained and reiterated. The need for oral argument, both in respect of the legal submissions and in due course by reference to the factual disputes, the time necessary for exploration and assimilation of the documents, and above all the need for examination and cross-examination of the considerable number of important witnesses, both factual and expert, meant that it took a great deal of cooperation, hard work, and case management to achieve a situation in which everything that anyone wished said or read was completed in forty-nine days of hearing.

7. It is certainly right that my judgment ended up very much longer—perhaps at least ten times longer—than any of the cases which we had been considering at any rate in European jurisdictions. Perhaps it is right to suggest that the traditional English legal proceedings are a luxury. But it is certainly the case that it is expected of the judge to give full reasons, analysing all the evidence and law before him or her, and in a case such as *Hepatitis C*, by reference to the British system, after a three-month trial, this inevitably meant a long judgment. One of the authors of this chapter, Ian Forrester QC, has told me that in conversation with some European judges he has found them astonished that our judgments are of the length they are, and he says (although I am not sure I believe him!) that they wish they were permitted or encouraged to follow suit. The time when this kind of detailed analysis, giving proper credit to the arguments, both of law and of fact, put before the judge during the course of the hearing, is of particular importance is, naturally, at the ground-breaking stage. *Hepatitis C* was the first case in England and Wales in which any detailed consideration had been given to all the relevant aspects of the European Directive, and there were very full and thorough arguments by very able counsel to be resolved. It may be that the very setting out in detail of my reasoning, which had to be given in the judgment, contributed to a decision not to appeal.

8. Perhaps the most important matter to emphasize, from the judge's point of view, under our system, is of course the fact that our procedure is adversarial. Absent a case in which a judge happens to be familiar with an authority of which none of the parties in front of him had previous knowledge, in which case he would draw it to their attention and give them an opportunity to make submissions on it, the judge depends upon being 'fed' with information and authorities from the various parties in front of him. We are not expected to do our own research, and we do not have any system of researchers or clerks to do any original work for us. It is therefore interesting to me to read in this chapter how it came about that the various documents were collected and put before me. But I made my decision solely on the basis of those documents and authorities. At one stage prior to trial I asked the parties whether they thought it would be a good idea if I were accompanied by an expert assessor (as is now occasionally the case in our courts), who would have no part to play in the decision-making, but could assist the judge in relation to reading and assimilating the documentation, particularly on medical matters. The parties were both strenuously opposed to the idea, and I did not pursue it, because in fact I agreed with them. There is clearly a risk, in the appointment of an assessor, that the judge will find himself delegating either some part of his understanding or possibly some part of his decision-making to someone else: and at least the parties knew who it was that they were in the process of educating and then persuading during the hearing. But the result of this

fact, that it is the judge who is being educated by the parties and not carrying out his own independent research, is that sometimes outsiders do not understand why points are not dealt with by the judge. Indeed such an experience occurred to me in this case. Professor Stapleton, the leading expert in the field of consumer law, to whom reference has been made above,[73] was kind enough to take me out to lunch some months after the judgment and, from her deep understanding of the law, she belaboured me over points that I did not seem to have taken into account. I was able to indicate that, so far as I could see, such points, even if otherwise available to either of the parties on the particular facts, had not in fact been put before me. This means that perhaps the *Hepatitis C* case, notwithstanding that it was not appealed, will not be the last word on the subject.

---

[73] See n 14 above.

6

Some Aspects of the Influence of the European Convention on Human Rights on Domestic Law[1]

Jean-Paul Costa

It would be absolutely impossible to deal with the influence of the European Court of Human Rights[2] on domestic law in a few pages. The subject matter is rich and complex. I'll try simply, drawing on my experience as a judge of the Strasbourg Court, to give you a glimpse of some aspects of that influence.

First of all, there is the *institutional* influence of the Convention on domestic law. The Convention and its Protocols define a series of rights and freedoms. These are more civil and political in nature than social and economic, even if, since the *Airey v Ireland* judgment, 1979, the Court has held that there is no watertight division separating the field covered by the Convention and its Protocols from the social and economic implications of this sphere.

Being an international treaty, the Convention has legally binding effect on the States that have ratified it—presently forty-four States. Article 1 reads: 'the High Contracting Parties shall secure to everyone within their jurisdiction the rights and freedoms defined in Section 1 of this Convention'. In this respect it does not matter that a State is monist, like France or Italy, or dualist, like Sweden or the United Kingdom. The only difference resides in the possibility, or not, to invoke the Convention before the domestic courts in the absence of specific legislation such as the Human Rights Act 1998. The possibility now exists for all individuals to claim before the European Court of Human Rights that their rights set forth in the Convention have been violated by a contracting State. Protocol No 11, which entered into force on 1 November 1998, did away with the declarations of recognition of the right of individual petitions and acceptance of the compulsory jurisdiction of the Court; since that date both elements are automatic and general.

---

[1] The author would like to thank for his valuable assistance in preparing this text Mr Lawrence Early, Deputy Section Registrar at the European Court of Human Rights.
[2] Hereinafter 'the Court'.

Moreover, under Article 46 of the Convention, the high contracting Parties undertake to abide by the final judgment of the Court in any case to which they are parties. Execution is supervised by the Committee of Ministers of the Council of Europe. The execution of a final judgment whereby the Court holds that there has been one or several violation(s) of the Convention implies the payment by the responding State to the injured party of the 'just satisfaction' afforded by the Court, if any. Just satisfaction may include the payment of compensation for pecuniary or non-pecuniary damage as well as costs and expenses. But execution implies other forms of redress, such as *restitutio in integrum* whenever this is possible (for instance, the return to the applicant of his unlawfully confiscated house), and changes in the legislation, regulations, or practice that authorize the breach. It is not infrequent that countries have to modify their domestic law in order to comply with the Court's judgment. For example, both France and the United Kingdom had to adopt legal provisions to ensure the compatibility with the Convention of their systems for intercepting telephone communications. More recently, Turkey modified its legislation, and even the Constitution, in order to adapt the composition of the State Security Courts to the *Incal* judgment; the United Kingdom modified its court martial procedure as a result of *Findlay v UK*; France, following the *Mazurek* judgment, abrogated Article 760 of the Code civil, which, according to the Court, established a discriminatory distinction between adulterine children and legitimate children with regard to inheritance rights.

I would like to draw attention to two matters. First, Article 46 of the Convention gives binding effect to the Court's judgments only as regards the parties themselves; the binding force of a judgment applies *inter partes*, not *erga omnes*. By way of example, France could have drawn the consequences of the *Malone v UK* case by adopting legislation regulating its own system of telephone-tapping; but, not being a party to the case, France preferred to wait, and it was only after the *Huvig and Kruslin v France* cases, which concluded that France had breached Article 8 of the Convention, that a bill was drafted and adopted by the Parliament ensuring compliance with the rulings of the Court. Some people think that Article 46 could be revised in order to give *erga omnes* effect to the judgments. Even if the idea is good, it is not easily applied in practice. Secondly, in various countries, including France, the domestic courts themselves are increasingly drawing conclusions from a finding of a violation of the Convention *before* the intervention of national legislator. This is possible whenever the national Constitution recognizes the superiority of a treaty (such as the Court) over domestic legislation. This is the case with France according to Article 55 of the Constitution. After *Mazurek* civil tribunals in France decided, in analogous cases, not to apply Article 760 of the Code civil, though it was still in force, because it was contrary to the Convention, as interpreted by the Strasbourg Court. The Conseil d'État did the same after a judgment, *Association Ekin*, where the Court found that the banning of the distribution and sale of a book of foreign origin by the Minister of the Interior was in breach of Article 10 of the Convention which guarantees freedom of expression. It is worth noting that, five years before, the Conseil d'État had decided that entrusting such a power to the Minister *was not* contrary to Article 10 . . . This role of national courts is interesting, in the sense that, more and more, they are applying the Convention as part of domestic law. And sometimes they do so even in the absence of pertinent existing case-law of the European Court of Human Rights: in a way, they *anticipate* future case-law, which is a new, and somewhat surprising, phenomenon.

Let me now address the *judicial* influence of the Convention. By this I mean the influence of the Court, in so far as it interprets the Convention and its Protocols in a 'dynamic' way.

I would like to make three points in this connection.

First, the Court (and the Commission before 1999) has *extended* the field of the Convention by giving an extensive interpretation of the 'conventional' rights and freedoms. Either by interpreting broadly the rights themselves, for instance by including the right to a safe environment within the right to respect for private and family life (see, for instance, *Lopez Ostra v Spain*, a 1994 judgment); or by increasing the obligations of the defending States, for instance by imposing on them the so-called 'positive obligations', although the Convention essentially prescribes negative obligations (see *X and Y v the Netherlands* 1985, and many other authorities); or by adding to substantive violations of Articles such as 2 and 3 'procedural violations': this means that in cases of murder, disappearance, or torture, for instance, a State may be responsible, even if its direct responsibility for the facts is not established, if it is found that the authorities failed to conduct an effective investigation or inquiry (see, for example, *Assenov v Bulgaria* 1998, or *Tanrikulu v Turkey* 1999). In a sense, a procedural violation derives from the breach of a positive obligation which, by implication, engages the responsibility of the State.

Secondly, the Court's case-law tends to affirm the principle of *subsidiarity* and leaves to the national authorities space for the exercise of discretion or a margin of appreciation. The Court has repeatedly said that 'it is not within the province of the Court to substitute its own assessment of the facts for that of the national courts' (see *Dombo Beheer v the Netherlands* 1993). Equally, domestic law itself cannot be supervised by the Court *in abstracto*; the Court only checks to see whether, in the particular circumstances of the case, its application has violated, or not, a provision of the Convention. The doctrine of the 'margin of appreciation' goes even further, in so far as the Court has deduced from the subsidiary principle the right of the national authorities (including the legislator, the executive, and the courts) to interpret the notion of necessity, which decides whether interferences with restrictions or limitations on some freedoms guaranteed by the Convention and its Protocols are legitimate. Perhaps the first example of this doctrine is provided by the Court's judgment in *Handyside v UK*, back in 1976. The case dealt with freedom of press. While asserting that national authorities must be given a margin of appreciation, because they are in principle in a better position than an international court to assess the exact requirements and limits of some freedoms, the Court nevertheless takes care not to afford them an unlimited power of appreciation. The result is that the Court's judgments are, generally, delicately balanced: as was said in *Handyside*, 'the domestic margin of appreciation goes hand in hand with a European supervision'—which leaves the problem open, and explains why some authors are critical of the margin of appreciation as being too imprecise and too variable in its application from one field to another. Nevertheless, I must remind you there is no scope for a margin of appreciation when very serious violations of human rights are at issue, such as inhuman or degrading treatment or torture.

Thirdly, the influence on national law of the Convention, as interpreted by the Court's case-law, is in principle a factor, if not of unification, at least of harmonization of European law, by which I mean the law of the various European countries. In the field of procedural rights, such as right to a fair trial, or the right to an effective remedy, there are and there will continue to be a number of important differences between countries. Some of them distinguish between appeal and cassation; others do not. You can find in certain countries prosecutors who are more or less independent from the government. In other countries they do not exist. More and more countries have constitutional courts, but with different competences and procedures. This means that the recourse to a constitutional court does not always constitute a domestic remedy to be exhausted before bringing a case to Strasbourg. In the criminal field, investigation, indictment, and trial are organized quite differently depending on the country.

However, the case-law of the European Court of Human Rights has obliged the States to abide by common requirements, such as an accused's right to silence, the necessity of promptly informing everyone who is arrested of the reasons for his arrest and of the charges against him, judicial control of arrest or detention by a judge or independent magistrate, that detention on remand should not exceed a reasonable length of time, the presumption of innocence, the right of access to a tribunal, respect for the rights of the defence, the independence and impartiality of judges, a fair and public hearing, judgment within a reasonable time. The result is that many European countries—not only the so-called 'new democracies'—have modified, sometimes profoundly, their codes and legislation on civil, criminal, administrative, and other procedures, in order either to avoid condemnation by a judgment of the Court or to ensure compliance with such a judgment. If I take the case of France, important laws were passed recently, for instance the Act of 15 June 2000, reinforcing the presumption of innocence and the rights of victims. These new laws are clearly inspired by the European Court's case-law. There is an apparent paradox here: why and how do very specific national systems succeed in fulfilling their obligations under the Convention, while remaining different from each other? The answer is twofold: first, there have been some rapprochements; I would be less optimistic than Lord Woolf, who, two years ago in Paris, stated that there was no longer an English and a French legal system, but rather a mid-Channel legal system! But of course there's a good deal of truth in what he said. On the other hand, and maybe this is another form of the margin of appreciation, if the States are obliged to have legislation compatible with the requirements of the Convention, they do retain some freedom as regards the ways and means of reaching this objective. This explains why I personally think the Convention is a factor of harmonization rather than of unification.

In conclusion, it seems to me that one of the main goals of the European Court of Human Rights is to set up European standards for the rights and freedoms which the Convention defines. Those standards are minimum standards, since it is clear from Article 53 of the Convention that nothing prevents the contracting States from adopting laws that provide better safeguards for human rights. But, minimum as they are, European standards must be common, to northern and southern Europe, to Western states and Eastern as well. Moreover, the so-called evolutive interpretation provided by the Court is aiming at adapting the Convention to the changing needs and problems of society, and at progressively raising the standards. As the Court recalled in *Christine Goodwin v UK* last year, 'it is in the interests of legal certainty, foreseeability and equality before the law that it should not depart, without good reason, from precedents laid down in previous cases.' But a good reason for doing so is precisely to try progressively to raise the level of protection in the field of human rights in Europe. It cannot be done without a certain amount of boldness and imagination; but it would be badly done by exerting too great a pressure on national law and practices. Therefore, I am convinced that the Court's jurisprudential policy should be to place itself in an intermediary position between judicial activism and judicial self-restraint.

Is it possible to succeed in this way? That is another story . . .

7

European Law and the French Constitutional Council

Olivier Dutheillet de Lamothe

In this chapter, I would like to try to describe the relationship between the French Constitutional Council and European law. The French Constitutional Council is a young institution created in 1958 which exercises a constitutional review of statutes after they have been passed by Parliament but before they are promulgated. This constitutional review, provided for by Article 61 of the Constitution, may be described as preventive and abstract: preventive, as it is exercised before the statute comes into force; abstract, as it is independent of any actual dispute.

At a similar time European law also started to emerge: the European Convention on Human Rights was signed on 4 November 1950 and was complemented by the case-law of the European Court of Human Rights; European Community law appeared in 1957 with the Treaty of Rome followed by secondary community legislation and the European Court of Justice case-law.

I will describe the relationship between this young institution—the Constitutional Council—and this young lady—European law—as the story of a couple. It was an arranged marriage (I). This arranged marriage turned into a divorce (II). This divorce turned itself into a smooth and friendly relationship (III).

I. THE MARRIAGE BETWEEN THE CONSTITUTIONAL COUNCIL AND EUROPEAN LAW WAS SETTLED BY THE CONSTITUTION OF 1958

Two articles of the Constitution of 1958 settled this union. Article 54 of the French Constitution provides for the possibility of constitutional review by the Constitutional Council in order to ensure compatibility of treaties with the Constitution prior to ratification. It states:

If, upon the demand of the President of the Republic, the Prime Minister or the President of one of other House or sixty deputies or sixty senators, the Constitutional Council has ruled that an international agreement contains a clause contrary to the Constitution, the ratification or approval of this international agreement shall not be authorised until the Constitution has been revised.

This procedure guarantees, in principle, that no international agreement will be ratified or approved if it is not in conformity with the Constitution.

Secondly, account must be taken of Article 55 of the Constitution. France is a 'monist' country. This means that, unlike German, Irish, Italian, and UK law, French law does not require treaties to be incorporated by means of specific legislation. On the contrary, treaties become applicable as soon as they have been ratified by the government and published in the 'Journal Officiel' of the French Republic.

According to Article 55 of the Constitution, treaties prevail over statutes. More precisely, Article 55 states that: 'Treaties or agreements duly ratified or approved shall, upon publication, prevail over Acts of Parliament, subject, in regard to each agreement or treaty, to its application by the other party.'

So everything should be for the best in a brave legal new world: European law—whether Community law or the law of the European Convention on Human Rights—prevails over statutes, and the Constitutional Council should ensure that statutes always conform to international law.

But things are not so simple.

II. THE ARRANGED MARRIAGE ENDS IN DIVORCE

The divorce was pronounced by a decision of 15 January 1975 on the Voluntary Interruption of Pregnancy Act. This Act authorizes abortion under specific conditions and the referral claimed that this Act violated the right to life secured by Article 2 of the European Convention on Human Rights.

The Constitutional Council answered that, despite the principle of the primacy of treaties established by Article 55 of the Constitution, it had no jurisdiction to review the conformity of statutes with France's international commitments. 'It is not for the Constitutional Council', the decision says, 'when a referral is made to it under Article 61 of the Constitution, to consider the consistency of a statute with the provisions of a treaty or an international agreement.'[1]

This decision was based on two major arguments. First, a legal argument. Article 61 of the Constitution does not confer on the Constitutional Council a general or specific discretion identical to that of Parliament, but simply empowers it to rule on the constitutionality of statutes referred to it.

---

[1] Décision No 74-54 DC du 15 jan 1975 Recueil, 19.

If the provisions of Article 55 of the Constitution confer upon treaties an authority superior to that of statutes, these provisions neither require nor imply that this principle must be honoured within the framework of constitutional review as provided by Article 61. Secondly, a practical argument. According to the Constitution, the Constitution Council has only one month to take its decision. It would be very difficult to examine in such a short time the conformity of statutes with the considerable number of international commitments by which France is bound. In the case of Community law, it would be impossible for the Constitutional Council to refer to the European Court of Justice for a preliminary ruling in accordance with the former Article 177 (now Article 234) of the European Community Treaty.

In subsequent decisions the Constitutional Council made it clear that, if the review of the rule stated in Article 55 of the Constitution could not be effected within the framework of constitutional review, it had to be effected by other courts.

The Cour de cassation—our supreme court in civil and criminal law—responded very quickly to this invitation. In a judgment given on 24 May 1975, that is, a few months only after the abortion case of the Constitution Council, the Cour de cassation decided that Article 95 of the Treaty of Rome, prohibiting barriers to competition, prevailed over statutory provisions regulating the taxation of imported coffee, even though they had been enacted after the Treaty.[2]

The Conseil d'État—our supreme court in administrative law—which has always been more reluctant to accept the European construction, took much longer, nearly fifteen years more, to recognize the supremacy of treaties over statutes. In a judgment given on 26 October 1989 the Conseil d'État decided that the Treaty of Rome must prevail over a French statute of 1977 concerning the organization of elections to the European Parliament.[3]

Reviewing the conformity of statutes with treaties is now a matter for the ordinary and administrative courts. National courts, from both the administrative and ordinary jurisdictions, no longer hesitate to set aside legislation and regulations, which they deem to be contrary to European law. This kind of question is very frequently raised in particular with respect to Article 6 of the European Convention on Human Rights on the principle of a fair trial.

By not directly securing the primacy of treaties over statutes but leaving it to other courts to achieve that result, the Constitutional Council has opened to those courts a new form of constitutional review.

[2] Chambre mixte 24 mai 1975, *Société des Cafés Jacques Vabre* (Paris Dalloz 1975) 497 concl Touffait.

[3] *Assemblée Plénière* 20 oct 1989 *Nicolo* Recueil, 190, concl Frydman.

Technically, it is not a constitutional review since the ordinary courts are reviewing the 'conventionnalité' of the statute, that is, its compatibility with the international rule. This does not amount to the courts censuring the legislation, of course: it simply means that an international rule can be held, if need be, to prevail over a national rule. But it has very similar effects: the statute cannot be enforced.

And the substance of this international review is very close to a constitutional review if you think about the content of the European Convention of Human Rights enriched by the case-law of the Court of Strasbourg. To avoid any contradiction between the Constitutional Council, the Cour de cassation, and the Conseil d'État, it has been the Constitutional Council's interest, as well as its conviction, to follow very closely the Strasbourg Court's case-law. This is one of the reasons why the divorce between the Constitutional Council and European law turned finally into a smooth and friendly relationship.

III. LIKE MANY MODERN COUPLES, THE CONSTITUTIONAL COUNCIL AND EUROPEAN LAW, EVEN IF DIVORCED, NOW HAVE A VERY SMOOTH AND FRIENDLY RELATIONSHIP

1. European Community Law

As regards European Community law, although the Constitutional Council still refuses to review the compatibility of domestic legislation with European law, it has also contributed to establishing the supremacy of European law.

First, in its constitutional review of treaties, according to Article 54 of the Constitution, the Constitutional Council fully recognizes the specificity of the European construction.

Until the Constitutional law of 1992 the only constitutional basis for the European construction was §15 of the Preamble to the Constitution of 1946 which the Constitution of 1958 refers to. §15 states: 'Subject to reciprocity, France will consent to such limitations of sovereignty as are necessary to the realisation of the defence of peace.'

Oddly enough, the Treaty of Rome of 1957 was not submitted to the Constitutional Council. The first European Treaty to be submitted to the Council was the Treaty signed in Luxembourg on 22 April 1970 modifying certain budgetary provisions of the European Community Treaty.

In its decision of 9 April 1992 on the Maastricht Treaty the Council decided that 'Respect for national sovereignty does not preclude France, acting in accordance with the Preamble to the Constitution of 1946, from concluding international agreements for participation in the establishment or development of a permanent international organisation enjoying legal personality and decision-making powers on the basis of transfers of powers decided by the Member States, subject to reciprocity.' It added, 'However, should an international agreement entered into this way involve a clause conflicting with the Constitution or jeopardising the essential conditions for the exercise of national sovereignty, authorisation to ratify would require prior amendment of the Constitution.' The Council estimated that such was the case for the establishment of a single currency. So, the French Constitution was completed by a new Article, 88-1, which states: 'The Republic is a party to the European Communities and the European Union, consisting of States, which by means of the constitutive treaties have voluntary resolved to exercise some of their powers in common.'

Secondly, in its constitutional review of statutes, according to Article 61 of the Constitution, the Constitutional Council also fully recognizes European law. An early example of this was the decision of 30 December 1977 relating to the provisions of the 1977 Finance Act for recovery of a national levy to regularize the isoglucose market, the levy having been established by a regulation of the Council of the European Communities.

The Members of Parliament who made the referral criticized these provisions because they restricted themselves to making arrangements for collecting a tax, the rate and basis of which had already been determined by a Community regulation; this, they asserted, violated the principle of national sovereignty and the principle of the people's consent to taxation.

After specifying that the levy in question was a Community resource not subject to the rules applying to national taxation, and pointing out that Community regulations are binding and directly applicable under the second paragraph of Article 189 of the Treaty of Rome, the Constitutional Council affirmed in this decision that the distribution of powers operated by the regulation between Community institutions and the national authorities was simply 'the consequence of international commitments entered into by France which fall within Article 55 of the Constitution'.

One more sensitive point, however, is the possibility of indirect constitutional review of secondary Community legislation. There is nothing to prevent statutes that transpose a directive from being referred to the Constitutional Council under Article 61 on the ground that there is an incompatibility between the Community instrument and the French Constitution. In one case, at least, the Constitutional Council reviewed the constitutionality of a statute transposing a directive and decided that some of its provisions did not conform to the Constitution.[4] This kind of control, without asking if the provisions of the statutes were the necessary

---

[4] Decision No 94-348 DC du 3 août 1994 Recueil, 117.

consequences of the directive transposed, is not fully compatible with the primacy of the community law.

It is interesting to note that the European Court of Human Rights adopts the same attitude: the fact that a statute is based, almost word for word, on a Community directive 'does not remove it from the ambit of the Convention of Human Rights'.[5]

2. *European Convention on Human Rights*

As regards the European Convention on Human Rights and the Strasbourg Court case-law, the relationship is still closer and warmer.

There have always been great similarities between the Constitutional Council case-law and the Strasbourg Court case-law. They have had common roots: the Declaration of Human and Civic Rights of 26 August 1789—which the Constitution of 1958 refers to—directly inspired the wording of the European Convention on Human Rights. They use the same judicial techniques: control of proportionality, the balancing of conflicting fundamental rights, the notion of 'national margin of appreciation' left to the Member States by the European Court of Human Rights which directly echoes the 'general discretionary decision-making power' left to the Parliament by the Constitutional Council.

But for the past ten years the case-law of Strasbourg has been followed more and more noticeably by the Constitutional Council. This is clear at four levels. First, the European Court of Human Rights helped to generate new rights. The new rights that the Constitutional Council drew from the general provisions of the Constitution often correspond to those deduced by the European Court of Human Rights. I can quote: 'the right to respect for one's private life', secured by Article 8 of the European Human Rights Convention and deduced by the Council from the principle of liberty; the freedom of marriage, provided for by Article 12 of the European Convention and deduced by the Council from individual freedom; 'the right to lead a normal family life', drawn from the Preamble to the Constitution of 1946, by reference to decisions from the European Court; 'the principle of the dignity of the human person', recognized as a constitutional principle in 1994 by the Constitutional Council in an echo of the decisions of the European Court of Human Rights.

Secondly, the European Convention on Human Rights has notably enriched the French conception of rights. Freedom of speech, 'one of the most precious rights of Man', as stated by the Declaration of 1789, is a good example. Freedom, in our modern information society, does not only mean prohibition of censorship. It also involves access by the public to

---

[5] CEDH 15 nov 1996 *Cantoni v France* Recueil V, 1614.

pluralistic sources of information. This idea, clearly expressed in the Strasbourg Court case-law, such as *Handyside* in 1976,[6] is now part of the Constitutional Council jurisprudence.

Thirdly, the Strasbourg Court case-law has had a major impact on procedures, especially criminal procedures: the Constitutional Council now frequently refers to 'fair trial' implying 'equal rights for both sides', and also to the right of every person to 'an effective remedy'.

Last but not least, in one field, the Strasbourg Court led the Constitutional Council to change its jurisprudence. This regards the retrospective validation of statutory instruments. In 1994 the Constitutional Council ruled that legislative provisions that retrospectively validated the interpretation of contracts between the social security organization and its employees so as to avoid the payment of a bonus were constitutional, given that it allowed the French government to avoid financial risk.

Five years later, in 1999, the European Court of Human Rights held that these provisions were contrary to the requirement of fair process. The Court affirmed 'that while in principle the legislature is not precluded in civil matters from adopting new retrospective provisions to regulate rights arising under existing laws, the principle of the rule of law and the notion of fair trial enshrined in Article 6 preclude any interference by the legislature—other than on compelling grounds of the general interest—with the administration of justice designed to influence the judicial determination of a dispute'.[7]

Only a month later the Constitutional Council, drawing from the conclusions of this decision, modified its jurisprudence. The Council decided that:

The legislature may, where there are adequate grounds of general interest, validate an instrument referred to an administrative Court in order to avert the difficulties that might flow from its annulment, but only on condition that the scope of the validation is strictly defined, given the impact on the review by the relevant Court. The effect of validation may not be to preclude all judicial review of the instrument validated irrespective of the grounds pleaded by the applicants for declaring it illegal, for that would violate the principle of the separation of powers and the right to redress in the Courts conferred by Article 16 of the 1789 Declaration of Human and Civic Rights.[8]

And since these decisions the Constitutional Council follows very closely the Strasbourg case-law in the field of retrospective validation.

In a very brilliant essay[9] in 1952 Claude Lévi-Strauss, a French ethnologist, demonstrated that cultures and civilizations progress only through

---

[6] CEDH,7 déc 1976 *Handyside* série A, no 24.

[7] CEDH 28 oct 1999 *Zielinski, Pradal, Gonzalez and Others v France* Recueil VII, 96.

[8] Décision N. 99-422 DC du 21 déc 1999, 143; Décision No 99-425 DC du 29 déc 1999 Recueil,168.

[9] 'Race et Histoire' Folio Essais.

their confrontation with other cultures and civilizations, whatever the forms of the confrontation: war, migration, trade, cultural exchange. Withdrawn into themselves, they die and disappear, as the examples of Athens and the Roman empire show.

This applies also to legal cultures: I strongly believe that each of our legal cultures—civil law as regards France—will progress through its confrontation with other legal cultures such as common law, whether English common law or American common law, which are very different. In this respect European law is like a melting pot. It is a major drive for change, and it makes the dialogue between judges and academics from different countries and different cultures all the more important.

8

Interlocking Legal Orders or the European Union Variant of E Pluribus Unum

*Koen Lenaerts**

I. INTRODUCTION

Even if an external observer who takes an interest in the case-law of the Court of Justice of the European Communities (hereafter 'Court of Justice') and of the Court of First Instance of the European Communities (CFI) may not at first receive such an impression, 'comparative law' plays a central role in the activities of these courts. This means much more than simply looking at solutions to certain problems provided in the legal orders of the Member States. As a former president of the Court of Justice rightly observed, recourse to comparative law is, for the Court of Justice, essentially a method of interpretation of Community law itself.[1] For the Court of Justice and the CFI (hereafter often referred to together as 'Community judge' or 'Community courts'), it is one among several methods of interpretation of the law (literal, exegetical, historical, or systematic), and it thus constitutes a tool for establishing the law.[2]

Depending on the characteristics of the case, the Community judge may be brought to take a closer look at the legal orders of one, several, or all Member States, at the legal order of third countries,[3] or even at the international legal

---

* All opinions expressed are personal to the author.

[1] J Mertens de Wilmars 'Le Droit comparé dans la jurisprudence de la Cour de justice des Communautés européennes' [1991] Journal des Tribunaux 37.

[2] N Fennelly, 'Legal Interpretation at the European Court of Justice' [1997] Fordham International Law Journal 656–79.

[3] On this issue, see P Pescatore, 'Le Recours, dans la jurisprudence de la Cour de justice des Communautés européennes, à des normes déduites de la comparaison des droits des États membres' [1980] Revue internationale de droit comparé 352; M Hilf 'The Role of Comparative Law in the Jurisprudence of the Court of Justice of the European Communities' in *The Limitation of Human Rights in Comparative Constitutional Law* (Cowansville Les Éditions Yvon Blais 1986) 558; Mertens de Wilmars (n 1) 38; CN Kakouris 'Use of the Comparative Method by the Court of Justice of the European Communities' [1994] Pace International Law Review 282.

order.[4] Comparative law thus stands for a method of examining principles and rules originating in legal orders other than the judge's own. The ultimate objective is always the same, namely, to establish the rule of law in the Community legal order.

In this chapter the different expressions of the methods of comparative law in the activities of the Court of Justice and the CFI are addressed first (II). Then the legal bases, whether general or specific, on which this method rests, as well as the common objective served by its multiple manifestations—in other words, its 'teleology'—are examined (III). Finally, an attempt is made to draw up a typology of the actions taken by the Community courts in order to reach this common objective (IV).

II. THE DIFFERENT EXPRESSIONS OF THE METHODS OF COMPARATIVE LAW IN THE ACTIVITIES OF THE COMMUNITY COURTS

It is striking that the case-law of the Court of Justice and the CFI contains remarkably few express references to comparative law. True, it happens that the Court of Justice and the CFI will refer in their judgments to the 'legal traditions', 'constitutional traditions', 'legal orders', 'legal notions', or 'legal principles' common to 'all' Member States, or, at least, to 'several' Member States. However, one will only exceptionally find traces of an explicit and extensive comparative law study in the case-law of the Community courts. Moreover, clear references to comparative law seem rather to be found in the 'old' judgments delivered at the time when the Community comprised only six Member States.

The *Algera* judgment of 12 July 1957 serves as a perfect illustration.[5] Each applicant in these staff cases sought to obtain the annulment of a decision of the Common Assembly that had withdrawn his or her appointment as an official on the ground that the appointments had been made illegally. The Court of Justice, having found that the Treaty does not lay down the conditions upon which an institution of the Community can lawfully set aside an administrative measure that was invalidly adopted, considered it necessary 'to solve the problem by reference to the rules acknowledged by the legislation, the learned writing and the case-law of the member countries'.[6] Having made a comparative study of the legal traditions of the six Member States, the Court 'accept[ed] the principle of the revocability of illegal measures at least within a reasonable period of time'.[7]

---

[4] On this issue, see P Pescatore 'International Law and Community Law: A Comparative Analysis' [1969] CMLR 177; Hilf (n 3) 558–60; Kakouris (n 3) 271, 272, and 282.

[5] Joined Cases 7/56 and 3/57 to 7/57 *Algera and Others v Common Assembly* [1957] ECR 39.

[6] Ibid 55.   [7] Ibid 56.

The relatively rare judgments of the Court of Justice and the CFI in which comparative law comes to the fore may be said to constitute merely 'the tip of the iceberg'.[8] This is not surprising. As an international institution, the Community judicature is 'naturally' brought to adopt a comparative approach for different reasons: the members of the Court of Justice and the CFI have their roots in different legal cultures,[9] the texts and notions to be interpreted are multilingual,[10] and most of the cases brought before the Community judicature are anchored in a precise national context.[11]

In contrast to the judgments of the Court of Justice, studies of comparative law regularly occur in the Opinions of the Advocates General.[12] Even when the judgment does not refer to the analysis made by the Advocate-General, the latter will often have guided the judges in determining the outcome of the case brought before them.[13] Quite regularly, in the course of the procedure, the Commission will offer, on its own initiative, to the Court of Justice or the CFI an extensive analysis of comparative law. Member States or natural or legal persons that are parties to the proceedings before the Community courts sometimes do the same in order to have a principle of law allegedly common to the Member States recognized by the case-law,[14] or in order to draw the judges' attention to the special characteristics of their national legal system.

By means of a measure of inquiry,[15] the Court of Justice or the CFI may also ask the Commission, in its capacity as a party to the case or as an *amicus curiae* (eg in preliminary rulings proceedings[16]), to communicate to the Court a comparative law study.[17] The Court of Justice has also reopened the oral procedure in cases where this was felt necessary to allow the parties to make observations with respect to the legal traditions of the

---

[8] Pescatore (n 3) 358.

[9] On the influence of the different legal cultures in the case-law of the Court of Justice, see T Koopmans 'The Birth of European Law at the Crossroads of Legal Traditions' [1991] AJCL 500–5.

[10] See Hilf (n 3) 566–7 and the references in pp 61 and 62 nn. See also G van Calster 'The EU's Tower of Babel: The Interpretation by the European Court of Justice of Equally Authentic Texts Drafted in More Than One Official Language' [1997] Yearbook of European Law 363–93.

[11] See eg Case 283/81 *CILFIT* [1982] ECR 3415 paras 16–19.

[12] For examples, see hereafter, throughout the text as well as the particularly important Opinion of Advocate General P Léger in Case C-353/99 P *Council v Hautala* [2001] ECR I-9565, in which the laws of all fifteen Member States relating to the right of access to information held by public authorities are analysed.

[13] See P Pescatore (n 3) 346–7. See eg Opinion of Advocate General J Mischo in Joined Cases 46/87 and 227/88 *Hoechst v Commission* [1989] ECR 2859 paras 49–96 of Opinion.

[14] See eg Case 108/81 *Amylum v Council* [1982] ECR 3107.

[15] Art 45 of the Rules of procedure of the Court of Justice and Art 65 of the Rules of procedure of the CFI.

[16] On these proceedings, see K Lenaerts and D Arts *Procedural Law of the European Union* (London Sweet & Maxwell 1999) 17–55.

[17] See eg Case 155/78 *M v Commission* [1980] ECR 1797.

Member States concerning a problem of particular interest for the case in question.[18] More often, the Court of Justice or the CFI will request their research and documentation service, which is composed of lawyers familiar with the respective national legal systems, to prepare a comparative survey on a particular issue. Such a survey normally highlights the recent trends observed in the case-law and the writings of academics and other commentators in the different Member States. Even if such research rarely emerges directly in the reasoning set forth in the judgment, it nevertheless backs up the decision taken by the Court.

As a result not only of the nature of the cases dealt with by the Court of Justice and the CFI but also of the different nationalities of the judges, each deliberation gives rise to a 'mixing' of mentalities, cultures, and legal constructions. A judgment will thus tend to be the result of 'cross-'contributions of different legal systems and ways of legal reasoning. The origin of these contributions will not always be identified and may sometimes even be unidentifiable.[19] Although the Court of Justice and the CFI—anxious to present Community law as a 'unitary' and autonomous set of rules—might erase in their judgments too visible signs of reasoning based on the comparison of different legal rules, the comparative approach nevertheless permeates the daily activities of the Community judge in many ways. For this reason, some commentators have called the Court of Justice and the CFI a 'laboratory of comparative law'.[20] Others think that in a spirit of cooperation and transparency access to this library of comparative law, which has been gradually developed by the Court of Justice and the CFI with the help of its research and documentation service, should be opened up to the courts of the Member States.[21]

II. LEGAL BASES AND TELEOLOGY OF THE COMPARATIVE LAW METHOD APPLIED BY THE COMMUNITY COURTS

1. *Legal Bases of the Comparative Law Method*

The Community courts can rely on different legal bases—some of them general, others specific—which allow them, or even oblige them, to have recourse to the comparative law method.

---

[18] See Case 155/79 *AM & S v Commission* [1982] ECR 1575 paras 19–22. On this issue, see T Koopmans 'Comparative Law and the Courts' (1996) ICLQ 547–8.

[19] P Pescatore, (n 3) 349; Mertens de Wilmars (n 1) 37.

[20] See Hilf (n 3) 550.

[21] See Y Galmot 'Réflexions sur le recours au droit comparé par la Cour de justice des Communautés européennes' [1990] Revue française de droit administrative 261. See also W Van Gerven 'Taking Article 215 (2) EC Treaty Seriously' in J Beatson and T Tridimas (eds) *New Directions in European Public Law* (Oxford Hart 1998) 45 and 46 n.

Article 220 EC (ex-Article 164 of the EC Treaty), according to which the Court of Justice and the CFI have to 'ensure that in the interpretation and the application of this Treaty the law is observed' is the primary source of legitimization for the Community courts' recourse to the comparative approach. Indeed, in its judgment of 5 March 1996, in the *Brasserie du Pêcheur and Factortame* case, the Court of Justice clearly accepted on that basis the comparative approach as a method of interpretation of Community law. It is for the Court

in pursuance of the task conferred on it by Article [220] of the Treaty of ensuring that in the interpretation and the application of the Treaty the law is observed, to rule . . . in accordance with the generally accepted methods of interpretation, in particular by reference to the fundamental principles of the Community legal system and, where necessary, general principles common to the legal principles of the Member States'.[22]

Comparative law—or, more precisely, the legal traditions, written or unwritten,[23] common to the Member States—thus helps the Court of Justice and the CFI to find the *ius commune*—ie 'the law'—whose observance they are to ensure in the interpretation and application of the Treaty.[24]

The recourse of the Community courts to the comparative law method finds another legal basis in the joint provisions of Articles 6(2) and 46 of the Treaty on European Union (TEU), according to which the Court of Justice and the CFI have jurisdiction, within certain limits, to ensure respect for fundamental rights as they result 'from the constitutional traditions common to the Member States, as general principles of Community law'. In fact, these Treaty provisions take over a principle which was established a long time ago in the case-law of the Community courts. In his Opinion of 2 December 1970 in *Internationale Handelsgesellschaft*[25] Advocate General Dutheillet de Lamothe set out to emphasize the major importance of the 'fundamental principles of national legal systems'[26] for Community law. According to the Advocate General, these principles

contribute to forming that philosophical, political and legal substratum common to the Member States from which through the case-law an unwritten Community law emerges, one of the essential aims of which is precisely to ensure the respect for the fundamental rights of the individual. In that sense, the fundamental principles of the

---

[22] Joined Cases C–46/93 and C–48/93 *Brasserie du Pêcheur and Factortame* [1996] ECR I-1029 para 27 (for the substance of this case, see nn 82–93 below and accompanying text).

[23] See Kakouris (n 3) 273 and 278.

[24] J Schwarze 'Tendances vers un droit administratif commun en Europe' [1993] Revue trimestrielle de droit européen 235–45; K Lenaerts and P van Nuffel *Constitutional Law of the European Union* (London Sweet & Maxwell 1999) 534.

[25] Opinion of Advocate General A Dutheillet de Lamothe in Case 11/70 *Internationale Handelsgesellschaft* [1970] ECR 1125, 1140.

[26] Ibid 1146.

national legal systems contribute to enabling Community law to find in itself the resources necessary for ensuring, where needed, respect for the fundamental rights which form the common heritage of the Member States.[27]

Whilst the Opinion of the Advocate General found a modest reflection only in the *Internationale Handelsgesellschaft* judgment itself,[28] his reasoning was duplicated by the Court of Justice in its later *Nold* judgment of 14 May 1974.[29] In ruling that '[i]n safeguarding [fundamental] rights, [it] is bound to draw inspiration from the constitutional traditions common to the Member States' and that 'it cannot therefore uphold measures which are incompatible with fundamental rights recognized and protected by the Constitutions of those States',[30] the Court of Justice wanted to stress that the Community is embedded in the constitutional current of its Member States so that the protection given to the fundamental rights of the citizen in the different national constitutions constitutes not only a source of inspiration for the Court but even a binding guideline.[31] Concerning the protection of fundamental rights, comparative law has progressively been considered as a reference value in the activities of the Community judge even if it remains complementary to the 'key reference' in the matter, namely the European Convention for the Protection of Human Rights and Fundamental Freedoms (ECHR) which represents a wider range of national legal traditions.[32]

A reference to the comparative law method can also be found in Article 288, second paragraph, EC (ex-Article 215, second paragraph, of the EC Treaty) which states that '[i]n the case of non-contractual liability, the Community shall, in accordance with the general principles common to the laws of the Member States, make good any damage caused by its institutions or by its servants in the performance of their duties'. Even if the analysis of the case-law shows that, until now, the Court of Justice and the CFI have not taken the best advantage of the opportunities offered by this Treaty provision to trace, on the basis of a comparative approach, the foundations of a non-contractual liability regime for the Community institutions,[33] it has certainly to be welcomed that the Court of Justice, applying

---

[27] Ibid 1146–7.

[28] Case 11/70 *Internationale Handelsgesellschaft* [1970] ECR 1125 para 4.

[29] Case 4/73 *Nold v Commission* [1974] ECR 491.

[30] Ibid para 13.

[31] As stated by Pescatore (n 3) 341. In a joint declaration of 5 Apr 1977 (OJ C–103, 1), the European Parliament, the Council, and the Commission have endorsed this case-law in stressing the 'prime importance' they attach to the protection of fundamental rights 'as derived in particular from the constitutions of the Member States and the [European Convention on Human Rights]'.

[32] K Lenaerts 'Fundamental Rights in the European Union' [2000] ELR 578.

[33] Pescatore (n 3) 342–3, and the reference (at 14), to the analysis made by EW Fuss 'Die Allgemeinen Rechtsgrundsätze über die ausservertragliche Haftung der europäischen

by analogy Article 288, second paragraph, EC, developed, on the basis of the general principles common to the national legal systems, the rules governing the liability of the Member States for a breach of Community law.[34]

Finally, the legal basis for applying the comparative law method can also be found outside the Treaty provisions. Thus, Article 44 of the Staff Regulations of the European Investment Bank (EIB) refers to 'general principles common to the laws of the Member States' that have to be respected in the contractual relationship between the EIB and its staff and which can be enforced before the Community judge.[35]

It follows from the foregoing that, in the activities of the Community judge, the comparative approach is a 'quasi-compelling' method of interpretation of Community law, intrinsically linked to the continuous integration process which characterizes the European construction.[36] In its *Algera* judgment,[37] the Court of Justice had already stressed that '[u]nless [it] is to deny justice', it cannot simply find in a particular case that there exists a lacuna in Community law. In such a case the Court seeks to find a solution by reference to the general principles common to the Member States.

2. The Teleology of the Comparative Law Method

Whatever its legal basis, the comparative law method, when applied by the Community judge, is driven by a single leitmotiv, and that is to find through examination of other legal orders the solution that best suits[38] the objectives of the Community—namely, European integration in a 'Community based on the rule of law'[39]—as well as its structure, and that is acceptable to the different national legal orders responsible for implementing Community law. Or, in other words, as Zweigert and Kötz have stated: 'Comparative law is an "école de vérité" which extends and enriches the

---

Gemeinschaften' in *Festschrift für Raschhofer* (Kallmünz Verlag Michael Lassleben 1977), 43–57; Hilf (n 3) 556; Galmot (n 21) 256; Kakouris (n 3) 270–271; van Gerven (n 21) to 46.

[34] *Brasserie du Pêcheur and Factortame* (n 22) paras 28–30 and 41 (see, further, nn 82–93 below and accompanying text).

[35] Case 110/75 *Mills v EIB* [1976] ECR 955 para 25; Case T–192/99 *Dunnett and Others v EIB* Judgment of 6 Mar 2001, not yet reported in ECR.

[36] G Benos 'The Practical Debt of Community Law to Comparative Law' [1984] *Revue hellénique de droit international* 251; Hilf (n 3) 566.

[37] Joined Cases 7/56 and 3/57 to 7/57 *Algera and Others v Common Assembly* [1957] ECR 39, 55.

[38] 'The most appropriate rule' (Kakouris (n 3) 279; U Drobnig 'The Use of Comparative Law by Courts: General Report' in U Drobnig and S van Erp (eds) *The Use of Comparative Law by Courts* (The Hague Kluwer Law International 1999), 7]; 'the solution which best suits', the 'best solution', or the 'optimum standard' (Hilf (n 3) 562 and 563).

[39] Case 294/83 *Les Verts v Parlement* [1986] ECR 1339 para 23.

"supply of solutions" . . . and offers the scholar of critical capacity the opportunity of finding the *"better solution for his time and place"* .[40]

The contribution of the comparative law method to the case-law of the Community courts is not limited to being a source of positive law among other sources of law.[41] It also aims at conferring upon the Community legal order a label of acceptability to the national legal orders. Knowing that the Community legal order and the national legal orders are closely intertwined and even interdependent in that the former can only function properly if the latter are willing to ensure the correct application of Community law, the Court of Justice and the CFI, when they are considering a particular case, will want to avoid 'going too far' and may therefore opt for a solution that is not necessarily the most ambitious, considered from the exclusive angle of Community law, but that has the advantage of being 'compatible' with the traditions of the Member States and of not hurting special sensitivities in certain Member States. The Community judge will thus try to establish 'the middle-line',[42] which has the best chances of 'surviving' the relentless conflicts between the requirements of Community law and the interests of the national systems. In other words, he will seek a solution that does not risk encountering incomprehension or resistance in some Member States, which could undermine the effectiveness and the uniform application of Community law. It can therefore be said that the comparative approach contributes in quite an essential way to guaranteeing the primacy, effectiveness and uniform application of Community law.[43]

Indeed, the national—legislative, executive, or judicial—authorities that have to apply Community law in their respective spheres of competence will only consider that the solutions put forward by the Community judge offer a degree of judicial protection (at least) equivalent to the judicial protection offered by their national legal system,[44] when these solutions find their

[40] K Zweigert and H Kötz *An Introduction to Comparative Law* (Oxford Clarendon Press 1987) vol 1, 12; emphasis added.

[41] CN Kakouris 'L'Utilisation de la méthode comparative par la Cour de justice des Communautés européennes' in Drobnig and van Erp (ed) (n 38) 99.

[42] Term used by Hilf (n 3) 563–4; see also Pescatore (n 3) 356 and 359.

[43] See Van Gerven (n 21) 46–7.

[44] The recent case-law of the Bundesverfassungsgericht (German Constitutional Court) shows that the Community legal order, since it draws its inspiration from the constitutional traditions common to the Member States, is considered to confer upon the individual a high level of judicial protection. Thus, by order of 7 June 2000, the Bundesverfassungsgericht dismissed as inadmissible a reference for a preliminary ruling made by the Administrative Court of Frankfurt am Main concerning the compatibility of a Community scheme relating to the import of bananas with the German Basic Law. When the Administrative court made its referral to the Bundesverfassungsgericht, the Court of Justice had already ruled in its *Atlanta* judgment of 9 Nov 1995 (Case C–466/93 *Atlanta*, [1995] ECR I-3799) that the Community scheme in question was valid. The Bundesverfassungsgericht ruled that a reference for a preliminary ruling concerning the constitutionality of an act of secondary Community legislation is inadmissible if the reasons set forth in the referral do not clearly explain why

roots in the mainstream of the different national legal cultures—'rooting' which is sometimes presented as a necessary counterpart for the partial transfer of sovereignty from the Member States to the Community[45]—and are based on a very precise assessment of the threshold of tolerance in the national legal orders taken as a whole.[46]

Community law, including the case-law of the Court of Justice, no longer affords an acceptable level of protection of fundamental rights.

[45] Benos (n 36) 252.

[46] The case-law concerning the direct effect of Community directives illustrates particularly well the importance the Court of Justice attaches to national sensitivities in its quest to find a Community law solution for a novel issue. In this respect it should be recalled that Art 249 EC (ex-Art 189 of the EC Treaty) makes a distinction between regulations and directives. A regulation is directly applicable in all the Member States. By contrast, a directive is binding, as to the result to be achieved, upon each Member State to which it is addressed, but leaves to the national authorities the choice of form and method. A directive prescribes a time period during which the Member States have to implement its provisions into their national legal orders. In its *Van Duyn* judgment of 4 Dec 1974 (Case 41/74 *Van Duyn* [1974] ECR 1337) the Court of Justice ruled that provisions of a directive that impose a precise and unconditional obligation on the Member States have direct effect in the national legal orders, just like the provisions of a regulation. This case-law was not well received in some legal orders. Thus, in its 'Cohn-Bendit' judgment of 22 Dec 1978 the French Conseil d'État ruled that it follows clearly from Art 249 EC (which constitutes an *acte clair*) that whatever the degree of precision the provisions of a directive may have, such provisions cannot be relied upon before the national courts against an administrative act of a Member State. Aware of the fact that a too ambitious position with respect to the question of direct effect of Community directives could undermine the credibility of its judgments, the Court of Justice later 'specified' its *Van Duyn* case-law. Thus, in its judgment of 5 Apr 1979 in the *Ratti* case (Case 148/78 *Ratti* [1979] ECR 1629) the Court of Justice based the direct effect no longer on a broad interpretation of Art 249 EC but on a general principle of law common to the Member States, namely the principle *nemo auditur qui suam propriam turpitudinem allegat*, or the 'estoppel' principle. On this basis the Court of Justice ruled that a Member State that has not adopted the implementing measures required by a directive in the prescribed period may not rely, as against individuals, on its own failure to respect Art 249 EC. In other words, if, in litigation opposing an individual and a 'failing' Member State, the individual requests the national court not to apply a provision of national law incompatible with the directive, that court must uphold such request if the provision of the directive is unconditional and sufficiently precise. The Court, however, stressed that as long as the period prescribed for the Member States to incorporate the provisions of a directive into their national legal orders has not yet expired, the directive cannot have direct effect. This readjustment of the Court's case-law was confirmed in the *Faccini Dori* judgment of 14 July 1994 (Case C–91/92 *Faccini Dori* [1994] ECR I-3325). In this case the Court of Justice reiterated that the possibility of relying on directives against State entities is based on the binding character of directives under Art 249 EC. The direct effect thus aims at avoiding a Member State taking advantage of its own breach of Community law constituted by the fact that it has failed to implement the directive in its national legal order within the time limit stated. However, in contrast to what Advocate General CO Lenz had proposed in this case, the Court of Justice ruled that, even in such circumstances, directives do not have direct effect as between individuals (horizontal direct effect), such effect being reserved as their distinctive feature to regulations. Without any doubt, the position expressed by many governments against such horizontal direct effect in the course of the proceedings influenced the Court's choice. The Court clearly preferred to play it prudently instead of imposing a solution that would have been more in the interest of Community law but which risked being unacceptable in the Member States. See also the judgment of the Bundesfinanzhof of 16 July 1981 ([1981] Europarecht 442–4), which expresses resistance within the German legal order against the direct effect of tax directives.

Since it permanently draws from legal concepts prevailing in the Member States, Community judge-made law naturally enjoys a great deal of authority in the Member States where it is accepted as an integral part of the national legal order. National courts in their capacity of ordinary courts of Community law[47] and in application of the principle of sincere cooperation enshrined in Article 10 EC (ex-Article 5 of the EC Treaty)[48] ensure the respect of this judge-made law, if need be, setting aside any conflicting rule of national law. In fact, national courts have come to the point of perceiving a violation of Community law as a violation of national law. This occurred in a recent judgment of the Bundesverfassungsgericht (German Constitutional Court) of 9 January 2001 annulling a decision of the Bundesverwaltungsgericht (national court of last instance) for breach of the principle, enshrined in the German Basic Law, according to which each person has the right to see his or her case decided by the court enjoying adjudicatory jurisdiction to that effect as a consequence of a legal provision, *ie* the *gesetzliche Richter*. In this case the Bundesverwaltungsgericht——instead of referring a preliminary question to the Court of Justice, had ruled on its own authority that two EC directives, one of 1986 and one of 1993, concerning the training and free circulation of medical doctors took precedence over another EC directive, of 1976, concerning the equal treatment of men and women. The Bundesverfassungsgericht criticized the fact that the Bundesverwaltungsgericht had based its decision exclusively on criteria of national law and had completely disregarded Community law, in particular the case-law of the Court of Justice. The Bundesverfassungsgericht held that the Bundesverwaltungsgericht had breached its obligation to refer a preliminary question to the Court of Justice enshrined in article 234 EC and, in so doing, had violated the right to the *gesetzliche Richter* enshrined in Article 101 of the German Basic Law. The Bundesverfassungsgericht rightly stated that the principle of equal treatment of men and women is a fundamental principle of Community law and that Community legislation which violates that right is invalid. The protection of fundamental rights would become ineffective and incomplete if the Court of Justice, failing preliminary references, could no longer control the compatibility of Community legislation with the fundamental rights guaranteed by the Community legal order.

---

[47] See, in particular, CN Kakouris 'Do the Member States Possess Judicial Procedural "Autonomy"?' [1997] CMLR 1389–412; Lenaerts and Arts (n 16) 3–4; M Struys 'Le Droit communautaire et l'application des règles procédurales nationales' [2000] Journal des tribunaux, Droit européen 49–53.

[48] This obligation of sincere cooperation imposed on the national authorities (notably judicial authorities) is, in fact, the counterpart of the 'federal loyalty' obligation which the Community authorities have under Art 10 EC vis-à-vis the national legal orders (see order of the Court of Justice of 13 July 1990, in Case C–2/88 Imm *Zwartveld and Others* [1990] ECR I-3365 paras 16–18).

This judgment of the Bundesverfassungsgericht is important for two reasons. First, it confirms that Community law forms an integral part of the German legal order and that the Court of Justice is perceived as forming an integral part of the system of judicial protection organized by the German legal order. Without any doubt the confidence expressed by the Bundesverfassungsgericht towards the Community legal order is to be attributed to the fact that Community law, as far as the protection of fundamental rights is concerned, is embedded in the constitutional traditions common to the Member States. Secondly, the judgment of the Bundesverfassungsgericht makes it apparent that a breach of Community law—in this case the violation of the obligation under Article 234 EC for a national court of last instance to refer a preliminary question to the Court of Justice—is perceived as a breach of national law, namely the violation of the right to the *gesetzliche Richter* enshrined in Article 101 of the German Basic Law. It should be stressed that it was only on the basis of the violation of this provision of the German Basic Law that the Bundesverfassungsgericht had jurisdiction to review the decision of the Bundesverwaltungsgericht. The operational connection between the Community and the German legal orders could hardly have been stronger.

The judgment of the Bundesverfassungsgericht is also remarkable if one takes into account the extreme reticence expressed in the early years by the German legal order, in particular the Bundesverfassungsgericht, with respect to the principle of primacy of Community law.[49] For a very long time, the Bundesverfassungsgericht indeed considered that, as long as the Community legal order lacked a codified catalogue of fundamental rights as clear and explicit as that contained in the German Basic Law,[50] it had jurisdiction to examine the compatibility of a Community measure with the fundamental rights guaranteed by the German Basic Law. The Bundesverfassungsgericht considered itself competent to carry out such judicial review even if the Court of Justice had already ruled, in the context of preliminary proceedings concerning the validity of the Community measure in question, that the measure did not violate any fundamental right. Only after having received assurances, in different judgments of the Court of Justice[51] concerning the importance attached by the Community institutions to the constitutional traditions common to the Member States as a source of protection of fundamental rights, did the Bundesverfassungsgericht change its position. It thus ruled, in a judgment of 22 October 1986,[52] that an additional review from its part of Community legislation in

[49] See, on this subject, K Lenaerts and P van Nuffel (n 24) 518.
[50] See judgment of the Bundesverfassungsgericht of 29 May 1974 (English version (1974) 2, CMLR 540–69; also called 'Solange I' judgment).
[51] See eg Case 44/79 *Hauer* [1979] ECR 3727 para 15.
[52] 'Solange II' judgment (English version (1987) 3 CMLR 225–65.

the light of the fundamental rights guaranteed by the Basic Law was no longer necessary so long as the case-law of the Court of Justice, which takes into account the common values of the Member States, offers a degree of protection equivalent to that which can be found in the German legal order.[53]

IV. TYPOLOGY OF THE DIFFERENT ACTIONS TAKEN BY THE COMMUNITY COURTS APPLYING THE COMPARATIVE LAW METHOD

The analysis of the case-law of the Community courts reveals a constant concern to find through the comparative law method the best solution acceptable throughout the Member States. Faced with a lacuna in the Community legal order (see subsection 1 below), or asked to interpret a notion of Community law (see subsection 2), or else in order to rule on the compatibility of a national legal solution with Community law (see subsection 3), the Community courts will instinctively seek the right balance between the interests of Community law and the acceptability of their ruling to the national legal orders.

1. A Lacuna in the Community Legal Order

When the Community courts examine the pleas raised by the parties in a case, they may find that the legal construction, the rule or principle of law referred to by one of them, has no parallel in the Community legal order. They will then, on the basis of one of the provisions mentioned above make a comparative study of the problem within the different legal orders of the Member States. That analysis may either indicate that national solutions converge (see subsection (*a*) below) or contradict one another (see subsection (*b*)). The courts can also consider that a particular national solution meets the objectives of Community law so well that it should be transposed into the Community legal order (see subsection (*c*)).

(a) Convergence Between National Solutions

The comparative law method may make it clear to the Community courts that the legal orders of the Member States tend to converge with respect to a particular issue in a more or less pronounced way.

---

[53] The Bundesverfassungsgericht confirmed its 'conditional acceptance' of the primacy of Community law in its judgment of 12 Oct 1993 concerning the constitutionality of the Maastricht Treaty (English version of this judgment (1994) 1 CMLR 57–108); see also Lenaerts and van Nuffel (n 24) 519.

Legal Concepts Common to all Member States

When a legal concept or rule proves to be common to all the Member States, the Community courts may, without risking opposition in the national legal orders, promote it to a concept or rule of the Community legal order. Amidst a wealth of case-law the *Köster* judgment may serve as an example.[54] In this judgment the Court of Justice, ruling on a preliminary question concerning the implementation of a Council regulation adopted in the field of the common agricultural policy, based itself on the 'legal concepts recognized in all the Member States'[55] to justify the view that, under the legislative scheme of the Treaty, the Commission may, by virtue of a legislative authorization, adopt legal provisions implementing the basic regulations of the Council.[56]

The recent judgment of the CFI of 6 March 2001 in the *Dunnett* case[57] contains another illustration of how a solution common to the legal systems of all the Member States can serve the advancement of Community law. This case concerned the decision of the EIB to abolish, as from 1 January 1999, the right of employees of the EIB to transfer part of their salary, which was normally paid in Belgian or Luxembourg francs, into another currency at a special conversion rate. During the consultations that had taken place before the adoption of this decision, the human resources department of the EIB had informed employees' representatives that the abolition of the system of special conversion rates was an inevitable consequence of the introduction of the euro. Before the CFI the applicants submitted that the decision to abolish the system of special conversion rates was unlawful because it was adopted without proper consultation of the staff representatives. According to the applicants, the consultation had indeed been based on a false premise. Relying on an analysis of comparative law which had been communicated to the Court by the EIB, the CFI noted that according to 'general principles of labour law common to the Member States of the European Union', an employer can unilaterally withdraw a financial advantage which he has freely granted to his staff on a continuous basis *only* when, before adopting such decision, timely and bona fide consultations with the staff have taken place.[58] In the *Dunnett* case, however, it was clear from the documents before the Court that the EIB itself was aware of the fact that the introduction of the euro did not make the application of the system of special conversion rates impossible.

---

[54] Case 25/70, *Köster* [1970] ECR 1161.

[55] Ibid para 6.

[56] See, in the meantime, Art 202, third indent, EC (ex-Art 145, third indent, of the EC Treaty), introduced into the Treaty by the Single European Act (1986).

[57] Case T–192/99 *Dunnett and Others v EIB* Judgment of 6 Mar 2001, not yet reported in ECR.

[58] Paras 85–90 of the judgment.

Therefore, in presenting to the employees' representatives the abolition of this advantage as the inevitable consequence of the introduction of the single currency, the EIB had not conducted bona fide consultations with its staff, and had thus violated a general principle of labour law common to the Member States. As a result, the CFI annulled the salary statements of the applicants in so far as the system of special conversion rates was no longer applied in them.

The case-law concerning the protection of fundamental rights offers other examples of the same approach. As Advocate General Tizzano stressed in his Opinion in the *BECTU* case, the Preamble of the Charter of Fundamental Rights of the European Union solemnly proclaimed on 7 December 2000 by the European Parliament, the Council, and the Commission also recalls the invaluable contribution of the comparative law method as a source of inspiration for stating fundamental rights.[59] It indeed mentions that '[t]his Charter reaffirms, with due regard for the powers and tasks of the Community and the Union and the principle of subsidiarity, the rights as they result, in particular, from the constitutional traditions and international obligations common to the Member States'.[60]

Strong Convergence Among National Solutions

The convergence of national solutions with respect to a given problem is, of course, not always total. The stronger the convergence, however, the less the risk for the Community courts that the solution they retain by reference to the traditions of the Member States will be rejected by the national legal orders. Where such convergence exists, the Community courts will not hesitate to give preference to the biggest common denominator of the traditions of the Member States, to the highest standard of protection,[61] or to the most performing law,[62] in order to improve the level of judicial protection within the Community. Here again the case-law concerning fundamental rights and general principles of law offers many examples. Indeed, the Community courts have often built upon a core of legal conscience suffi-

---

[59] See Case C–173/99 *BECTU* Opinion of Advocate General A Tizzano of 8 Feb 2001, not yet reported in ECR, paras 26–8. See also Case C–353/99 P *Council v Hautala* Opinion of Advocate General P Léger of 10 July 2001, (n 12) paras 80–3. In order to regard the principle of access to documents as a fundamental right, the Advocate General emphasizes the 'convergence of national laws' which in his view 'constitutes a decisive reason for recognising the existence of a fundamental principle of a right of access to information held by Community institutions' (para 55). Art 42 of the Charter of Fundamental Rights of the European Union merely confirms the existence of such a fundamental right in the Community legal order. In the light of all of this, 'it appears natural to [the Advocate General] to accept that there exists a principle of access to infomation held by the national public authorities and that that principle is such that it would engender an equivalent principle at Community level' (para 59).

[60] See K Lenaerts and E de Smijter 'A "Bill of Rights" for the European Union' [2001] CMLR 273–300.

[61] Pescatore (n 3) 341.   [62] Galmot (n 21) 258.

ciently common to the Member States in order to establish a fundamental right or a general principle of Community law.[63]

The judgment of the Court of Justice in the *Johnston* case can serve as a striking example.[64] In this case the Court had to rule on preliminary questions raised in a dispute between Mrs Johnston and the authority competent for appointing reserve police constables (the Chief Constable) in Northern Ireland. The dispute concerned the refusal of the said authority to renew Mrs Johnston's contract and to give her training in the handling and use of firearms. At that time a high number of police officers were being assassinated in Northern Ireland each year and against this background the Chief Constable had decided no longer to assign to women police operations that required the carrying of firearms. The preliminary questions put to the Court related to the interpretation of Council Directive 76/207/EEC of 9 February 1976 on the implementation of the principle of equal treatment for men and women.[65] In particular, the Court was asked to rule on the compatibility with this Directive of a provision of British law according to which a certificate of the national authorities declaring that the conditions for derogating from the principle of equal treatment for the purpose of protecting the public safety are fulfilled constitutes conclusive evidence and could not be subject to judicial review. After having recalled that Article 6 of the Directive requires Member States to introduce into their internal legal systems the necessary measures to enable all persons who consider themselves wronged by discrimination 'to pursue their claims by judicial process', the Court held that 'the requirement of judicial control stipulated by that Article reflects a general principle of law which underlies the constitutional traditions common to the Member States'.[66] It added that, according to this provision, interpreted in the light of the said general principle, it is for the Member States to ensure effective judicial control as regards compliance with the applicable provisions of Community law and of national legislation intended to give effect to the rights for which the Directive in question provides.[67]

As some commentators have rightly observed,[68] it follows from the *Johnston* judgment that when a fundamental right finds a solid foundation in

---

[63] See Pescatore (n 3) 339–41, 344–6, 352, and 353; Benos (n 36) 248–50; Lenaerts and van Nuffel, (n 24) 534–6 and 539–50.

[64] Case 222/84 *Johnston* [1986] ECR 1651.

[65] OJ L39 40.

[66] *Johnston* (n 64) paras 17 and 18.

[67] Ibid paras 19 and 20. See also FG Jacobs 'Access to Justice as a Fundamental Right in European Law' *Mélanges en hommage à Fernand Schockweiler* (Nomos Verlagsgesellschaft Baden-Baden 1999) 197–212.

[68] See, in particular, Galmot (n 21) 258. For an example in the case-law, see the Opinion of Advocate General P Léger in Case C–353/99 P *Council v Hautala* (n 12) para 119 as to the right of partial access to documents containing some confidential elements.

the constitutional traditions of the Member States, the Community courts will not have scruples about 'attacking' a less performing rule of national law. In other words, the Community courts will not hesitate to opt, in such a case, for a 'levelling up', instead of a 'levelling down', of the judicial protection.

A 'Dominant Idea' in the National Legal Systems: The Example of the Case-Law Concerning the Non-Contractual Liability of Public Authorities
In some cases the Community courts will not find in the national legal systems a sufficient convergence for a solution that can be transposed, as such, into the Community legal order. Divergences between the national legal systems, however, often concern details of the solution given in the different legal orders to a certain legal issue. That does not prevent the Community courts from finding a common denominator or dominant idea through the comparative approach. Guided by such general legal tendency, the courts will mould, in the image of the attitude adopted by the national legal orders, a 'custom-made' Community solution taking into account the priorities of the Community legal order, the objectives of the Treaty, and the particularities of the Community structures and of Community law.

The case-law concerning the non-contractual liability of national and Community public authorities offers the best illustration of this attitude. Even if Article 288, second paragraph, EC imposes on the Community courts the obligation to have recourse to the general principles common to the laws of the Member States, they have so far not elaborated a clear body of rules in the matter. At first sight, one would even be inclined to conclude that the source of inspiration found by the Community courts in the national legal orders amounts to nothing more than the following: in order for a national or a Community public authority to be held liable, one has to demonstrate the existence of illegal behaviour on the part of such an authority, damage, and a causal link between the illegality and the damage.

However, it was on the basis of the comparative law method that the Community courts established in the Community legal order the principle of the non-contractual liability of public authorities for damage caused in the exercise of their normal activities. Furthermore, in the absence of a 'common model', the same method was used to find a dominant tendency in the national legal systems according to which

the[re was a] need to balance the opposing, competing interests at stake: on the one hand, the injured party's interest in obtaining at least financial restitution for the loss or damage he sustained as the result of an activity—in particular legislative activity—of the State; on the other, the State's interest in not having to answer invariably and in any event for loss or damage caused by the activities of its organs in performing the institutional tasks entrusted to them.[69]

[69] Opinion of Advocate General G Tesauro in *Brasserie du Pêcheur and Factortame* (n 22) I-1066 para 12.

In order to avoid the exercise of the legislative power by a public authority being hindered 'by the prospect of applications for damages whenever it ... adopt[s] legislative measures in the public interest which may adversely affect the interests of individuals',[70] the Court held that public authorities should only exceptionally be liable for the damage resulting from the adoption of a normative act. Therefore, it has been observed that in the rare cases where the Court of Justice referred to the general principles common to the laws of the Member States, it has done so not to define the basis, but to trace the limits, of the liability of the public authorities.[71]

A glance at the case-law shows that this balancing—known to all national legal systems—of the obligation to compensate and the concern to safeguard the effectiveness of the exercise of normative power underlies the definition by the Court of Justice and the CFI of the 'Community conditions'[72] for the non-contractual liability of Community and national authorities as a result of infringements of Community law.

This can be illustrated first with the case-law concerning the liability of the Community for damage caused to individuals by normative measures adopted by one of its institutions. In the *Zuckerfabrik Schöppenstedt* case,[73] the Court had to rule on a request made by a German firm to compensate the damage caused by the Community as a result of the adoption by the Council of a regulation concerning the common organization of the sugar market. Following the Opinion of Advocate General K Roemer,[74] it established the principle of non-contractual liability of the Community for normative acts. The Court, however, taking into account the restrictive position taken in the national legal systems with respect to this matter and adapting it to the specificities of Community law, held that

[w]here legislative action involving measures of economic policy is concerned, the Community does not incur non-contractual liability for damage suffered by individuals as a consequence of that action, by virtue of the provisions contained in Article 215, second paragraph, of the Treaty [now article 288, second paragraph,

---

[70] Joined Cases 83 and 94/76, 4, 15, and 40/77 *HNL and Others v Council and Commission* [1978] ECR 1209 para 5. See also *Brasserie du Pêcheur and Factortame* (n 22) para 45, and the Opinion of Advocate-General N Fennelly in Case C–352/98 P *Bergaderm and Goupil v Commission* 2000 [ECR] I-5291, I-5294 para 29.

[71] Pescatore (n 3) 342.

[72] See Opinion of Advocate General G Tesauro in *Brasserie du Pêcheur and Factortame* (n 22) I-1081.

[73] Case 5/71 *Zuckerfabrik Schöppenstedt v Council* [1971] ECR 975.

[74] Opinion of Advocate General K Roemer in Case 5/71 *Zuckerfabrik Schöppenstedt v Council* (n 73) 986, 990. In his Opinion the Advocate General, on the basis of a study of comparative law prepared by the German Max-Planck-Institute, considered it justified to recognize the liability of public authorities resulting from normative activity as a 'part of Community law, because it is widely recognized [in the Member States] and in certain cases even includes formal laws'.

EC], unless a sufficiently flagrant violation of a superior rule of law for the protection of the individual has occurred'.[75]

This common vision of the national legal systems is also present in the case-law of the Court of Justice concerning the liability of Member States for breaches of Community law. Thus in *Francovich*[76] the Court of Justice was asked to rule on the liability of the Italian State for the damages suffered by some individuals as a result of the fact that the Member State in question had failed to implement into its legal order, within the prescribed time-limit, the provisions of a Council directive relating to the protection of employees in the event of insolvency of the employer. In this case the Court of Justice disregarded, as Advocate General J Mischo had suggested in his Opinion, the principle of immunity of the public authorities to which some governments had referred,[77] and established as a principle of Community law the liability of the Member State for loss and damage caused to individuals as a result of breaches of Community law for which the States can be held responsible.[78]

The Advocate General further proposed, after taking into consideration the role played by the general principles common to the laws of the Member States in the limitation of the non-contractual liability of the Community for breaches of Community law, that the liability of Member States for breaches of Community law should be subject to the same conditions as the liability of the Community in like circumstances.[79] In line with this Opinion, the Court of Justice, following the restrictive position it had taken in *Schöppenstedt*,[80] ruled that, where the breach of Community law committed by a Member State takes the form of a failure to take all the measures necessary to achieve the result prescribed by a directive, individuals would be entitled to reparation from the Member State in question where three conditions are met. First, the result prescribed by the directive should entail the grant of rights to individuals; secondly, it should be possible to identify the content of those rights on the basis of the provisions of the directive; and thirdly, there should be a causal link between the breach

---

[75] *Zuckerfabrik Schöppenstedt* judgment (n 73) para 11. In *Brasserie du Pêcheur and Factortame* (n 22) the Court held that the decisive test for considering a breach of Community law sufficiently serious is 'whether the Member State or the Community institution concerned manifestly and gravely disregarded the limits on its discretion' (para 55). See also *Bergaderm and Goupil v Commission* (n 70) para 43. See, on this subject, A Arnull 'Liability for Legislative Acts Under Article 215 (2) EC' in T Henkell and A McDonnell (eds) *The Action for Damages in Community Law* 129–53.

[76] Joined Cases C–6/90 and C–9/90 *Francovich and Others* [1991] ECR I-5357.

[77] Opinion of Advocate General J Mischo in *Francovich* (n 76) I-5370 para 47.

[78] *Francovich* judgment (n 76) paras 35 and 37.

[79] Ibid para 71.

[80] *Zuckerfabrik Schöppenstedt* (n 73).

of the State's obligation and the loss or damage suffered by the individuals concerned.[81] In *Francovich* these conditions were clearly met.

The contribution of the comparative law method is far more visible in the Opinion of Advocate General G Tesauro and in the judgment of the Court of Justice in *Brasserie du Pêcheur and Factortame*.[82] In this case, which concerned the liablity of Member States resulting from a violation of a directly applicable rule of Community law,[83] the Court of Justice held, in a much clearer way than in *Francovich*,[84] that the liability of the State for the damage caused by its acts or omissions to individuals simply expresses—in the same way as the Community liability laid down in Article 288, second paragraph, EC, does—a general principle known to the legal systems of the Member States that an unlawful act or omission gives rise to an obligation to make good the damage caused.[85] It further noted that in many national legal systems the essentials of the rules governing State liability have been developed by the courts.[86] On the basis of this common trend, and disregarding again, just like in *Francovich*, the opposition of certain Member States to the principle that a State could be held liable when acting as a legislator,[87] the Court of Justice, taking into account the superior interests of Community law, established once and for all the principle of liability of the State for loss or damage caused to individuals as a result of breaches of Community law for which it can be held responsible and added that this 'principle holds good for any case in which a Member State breaches Community law, whatever be the organ of the State whose act or omission was responsible for the breach'.[88]

When defining the 'Community criteria' relating to the liability of the 'State legislator' for a breach of Community law, the Court of Justice took into account the fact, which had been stressed by Advocate General G Tesauro in his Opinion,[89] that 'in all the legal traditions liability for legislative activity on the part of the public authorities is limited in various ways'. On the basis of this concept common to the Member States, it ruled that, when a Member State acts—as was the case in *Brasserie du Pêcheur and Factortame*—in a field where it has wide discretion, comparable to that of the Community institutions in implementing Community policies, the conditions under which the Member State may incur liability must be the

---

[81] *Francovich* judgment (n 76) paras 38–46. See, on this subject, DF Waelbroeck 'Treaty Violations and Liability of Member States: The Effect of Francovich Case Law' in Henkell and McDonnell (eds) *The Action for Damages in Community Law* 311–39.

[82] *Brasserie du Pêcheur and Factortame* (n 22), Opinion of Advocate General at I-1066.

[83] For an analysis of this judgment, see in particular W van Gerven (n 21) 36–9.

[84] Cited in n 76.   [85] Ibid para 29.   [86] Ibid para 30.

[87] See, on this issue, Opinion of Advocate General P Léger in Case C-5/94 *Hedley Lomas* [1996] ECR I-2553, I-2556 paras 98–100.

[88] Ibid paras 31 and 32.

[89] (Cited in n 22) para 60.

same as those under which the Community institutions incur liability in a comparable situation. In other words, the Member State will be held liable where a sufficiently serious breach of a superior rule of law which intends to confer rights on individuals is established.[90]

Having placed some limits on the conditions which may 'trigger' State liability, the Court of Justice, guided by a concern inherent in the legal traditions of the Member States to strike a balance between public and private interests, established some rules relating to the obligation of public authorities to make good the loss or damage caused as a result of a breach Community law. Here again the comparative law method adopted by the Advocate General in his Opinion was a source of inspiration for the Court. It specified that reparation for loss or damage caused by an act or an omission of a Member State cannot be made conditional upon a fault having been committed intentionally or by way of negligence by the organ of the State responsible for the breach going beyond that of a sufficiently serious breach of Community law.[91] With respect to the actual extent of the reparation, the Court, again relying on the comparative analysis drawn up by Advocate General G Tesauro, ruled that reparation for loss or damage caused to individuals as a result of breaches of Community law must be commensurate with the loss or damage sustained so as to ensure the effective protection of their rights. In the context of economic or commercial litigation, reparation must therefore cover loss of profit.[92] It added, however, that it was 'a general principle common to the legal systems of the Member States that the injured party showed reasonable diligence in limiting the extent of the loss or damage, or risk having to bear the damage himself'.[93]

This restrictive approach towards the non-contractual liability of public authorities, inspired by the comparative law method, also transpires in the recent case-law of the Court of Justice and the CFI concerning the non-contractual liability of the Community for lawful acts. Thus, in *Dorsch Consult*,[94] the CFI was asked to rule on an application for compensation made by a German consulting company, which claimed to have suffered damage as a result of the adoption by the Council of a regulation preventing trade with Iraq and Kuwait. The CFI, in the absence of a 'dominant idea' in the legal systems of the Member States with respect to this issue, refrained from establishing a principle of Community law according to

---

[90] *Brasserie du Pêcheur and Factortame* (n 22) paras 47–55. In both cases the Court found that such a violation of Community law was established.

[91] Ibid (n 22) para 80.

[92] Ibid paras 82 and 87. For a state of comparative law on these issues, see, eg D Edward and W Robinson 'Is There a Place for Private Law Principles in Community Law?' in Henkell and McDonnell (eds) *The Action for Damages in Community Law* 347.

[93] *Brasserie du Pêcheur and Factortame* (n 22) para 85. See also Opinion of Advocate General G Tesauro (n 22) para 98.

[94] Case T–184/95 *Dorsch Consult v Council and Commission* [1998] ECR II-667.

which public authorities (in this case the Community) could be held liable for damage caused by lawful acts. It held that *in the event* of the principle of Community liability for a lawful act being recognized in Community law, such liability could be incurred only if the damage alleged, if deemed to constitute a 'still subsisting injury', affects a particular circle of economic operators in a disproportionate manner by comparison with others (special damage) and exceeds the limits of the economic risks inherent in operating in the sector concerned (unusual damage), without the legislative measure that gave rise to the alleged damage being justified by a general economic interest.[95] It follows from the reasons set forth in the judgment[96] that this Community solution is drawn directly from the German legal concept of 'exceptional sacrifice' (*Sonderopfer*) and from the Belgian and French legal concept of 'unequal discharge of public burdens'.[97] The CFI tailored these concepts limiting the liability of public authorities for lawful acts in the few Member States where such liability exists, taking into account the particularities of the Community legal order. The approach followed by the CFI was confirmed, upon appeal, by the Court of Justice.[98]

The strictness of the Community case-law with respect to the non-contractual liability of national and Community authorities was considered by some commentators[99] as an attempt by the Community legal order to take back with one hand what it had given away with the other hand. In fact, in adopting a restrictive approach in the matter, the Community courts do nothing else than acknowledge a common idea of the national legal systems according to which a balance must be found between the obligation to compensate which incurs to anyone who causes loss or damage and the need to safeguard the effective exercise of normative power.

Furthermore, the Court of Justice has completed the regime of non-contractual liability of public authorities for normative acts in its judgment of 23 May 1996 in *Hedley Lomas*[100] and, more importantly, in its judgment of 4 July 2000 in *Bergaderm and Goupil*,[101] where it held that when the Member State or Community institution concerned was not called upon to make any legislative choices and had only considerably reduced, or even no, discretion, the mere infringement of Community law may be sufficient

---

[95] Ibid para 80. These conditions were not met in *Dorsch Consult*.

[96] Ibid paras 76–9.

[97] See, in particular, HJ Bronkhorst 'The Valid Legislative Act as a Cause of Liability of the Communities' in Henkell and KcDonnell (eds) *The Action for Damages in Community Law* 155–8.

[98] Case C–237/98 P *Dorsch Consult v Council and Commission* [2000] ECR I-4549. See also K Lenaerts 'Le Tribunal de première instance des Communautés européennes: Regard sur une décennie d'activités et sur l'apport du double degré d'instance au droit communautaire' [2000] Cahiers de droit européen 379 and 380.

[99] Mertens de Wilmars (n 1) 39.

[100] *Hedley Lomas* (n 87).

[101] *Bergaderm and Goupil v Commission* (n 70).

to establish the existence of a sufficiently serious breach.[102] This reflects a dominant idea common to the Member States according to which the strict conditions under which public authorities may incur liability for normative acts give way to a normal liability standard whenever the authorities concerned have little or no discretion in the exercise of their normative powers. Under this standard, liability will be incurred if the applicant proves the existence of a fault or a negligence, that is, any kind of irregularity that a normally prudent and diligent administration would not have committed in like circumstances.[103]

(b) Contradictions Between National Solutions

A comparative analysis of a certain matter may reveal profound contradictions—even as regards the basic principles—between the national legal systems. In such circumstances the Community courts will avoid establishing a Community solution. Indeed, when they are faced with contradictory solutions of national law, the Community courts will prefer not to impose a solution that would not meet sufficient support in some Member States to ensure a uniform and effective application of Community law.

Again, the case-law of the Community courts offers many examples of this situation. In the field of family law the *Grant* judgment deserves special attention.[104] Ms Grant, who had a stable relationship with a female partner, was an employee of a railway company. Her employer had refused to give her the benefit of an advantage (a travel concession for partners) that she would have obtained if she was married or had a stable relationship with a partner of the opposite sex. The Court of Justice was asked to rule whether this decision of Ms Grant's employer was compatible with the principle of equal treatment of men and women as regards remuneration enshrined in Article 119 of the EC Treaty (now Article 141 EC). While in his Opinion Advocate General M Elmer suggested that there was discrimination on the basis of gender,[105] the Court of Justice came to a different conclusion. It first examined the laws of the Member States and found that 'while in some of them cohabitation by two persons of the same sex is treated as equivalent to marriage, although not completely, in most of them it is treated as equivalent to a stable heterosexual relationship outside marriage only with respect to a limited number of rights, or else is not

---

[102] *Hedley Lomas* (n 87) para 28; *Bergaderm and Goupil*, (n 70) para 44. See also Case T–178/98 *Fresh Marine v Commission* [2000] ECR II-3331, under appeal.

[103] See, on this issue, MH van der Woude 'Liability for Administrative Acts Under Article 215 (2) EC' in Henkell and McDonnelle (eds) *The Action for Damages in Community Law* 109–28; and van Gerven (n 21) 42 and 43.

[104] Case C–249/96 *Grant* [1998] ECR I-621.

[105] Opinion of Advocate General M Elmer in *Grant* (n 104) I-623, I-635.

recognised in any particular way'.[106] It then held that 'in the present state of the law within the Community, stable relationships between two persons of the same sex are not regarded as equivalent to marriages or stable relationships outside marriage between persons of opposite sex' and concluded that '[c]onsequently, an employer is not required by Community law to treat the situation of a person who has a stable relationship with a partner of the same sex as equivalent to that of a person who is married to or has a stable relationship outside marriage with a partner of the opposite sex'.[107] The Court deemed it necessary to add that '[i]n those circumstances, it is for the legislature alone to adopt, if appropriate, measures which may affect that position'.[108] The Court, being aware of the fact that certain strongly held views within the Community were not yet ready to accept the equivalence of a homosexual and a heterosexual relationship as a principle of Community law, thus left it to the political authorities to rule on this matter.

(c) Transposition of a National Solution into Community Law

Applying the comparative law method, the Community courts can come to the conclusion that a legal concept or solution known in a particular Member State would best serve the interests of the Community legal order. It therefore happens that such a legal concept or solution is 'imported' in the Community legal order. Thus, the principles of proportionality[109] and protection of legitimate expectations[110]—recognized for many years as principles of Community law—were originally 'borrowed' from the German legal order.[111]

2. The Interpretation of a Concept of Community Law

When dealing with the interpretation of a concept of Community law, the Community courts will very often pay no attention whatsoever to the meaning the same concept may have in the legal systems of the Member States. The case-law indicates that in the name of the autonomous character of Community law the Community courts will, to the greatest extent possible, interpret the concepts of Community law in the light of the rules

---

[106] *Grant* judgment (n 104) para 32.

[107] Ibid (n 104) para 35.

[108] Ibid (n 104) para 36.

[109] Case 11/70 *Internationale Handelsgesellschaft* [1970] ECR 1125. See Koopmans (n 18) 547; J A Usher *General Principles of EC Law* (London Longman 1998) 37–51.

[110] Joined Cases 205 to 215/82 *Deutsche Milchkontor* [1983] ECR 2633. See, in particular, F Belaich 'La Répétition de l'indu en droit communautaire dans la jurisprudence de la Cour de justice des Communautés européennes' [2000] Revue du Marché commun et de l'Union européenne 113–14; see also Usher (n 109) 52–64.

[111] For other examples, see Pescatore (n 3) 346.

of Community law itself and try not to refer to the case-law of a supreme court of a Member State or to the laws of the Member States.[112]

Nevertheless, it does happen that in order to overcome a problem of interpretation the Community courts take a look at the national legal systems. Such an analysis may reveal a solution common to the Member States which will help the courts find an answer to the problem of interpretation (see subsection (*a*) below). The Community courts can also find an excuse in the profound divergences among national interpretations of a given concept in order to establish an autonomous interpretation of Community law (see subsection (*b*)). Finally, through a comparative law analysis, the Community courts may identify the national interpretation which seems most appropriate—given its interest for the realization of the Community's objectives—for 'import' into the Community legal order (see subsection (*c*)).

(a) Common Interpretation in the Member States

The *AM & S* case illustrates perfectly well the contribution of comparative law to the interpretation of an insufficiently precise provision of Community law.[113] The case concerned the respect of the rights of defence in administrative proceedings initiated by the Commission prior to the finding of an infringment of the EC competition rules.[114] The facts of the case were as follows. The Commission suspected that the company AM & S had engaged in anti-competitive practices. It adopted a decision on the basis of Article 14 of Regulation No 17,[115] by which this company was required to produce for examination by officers of the Commission all the documents for which legal privilege was claimed. AM & S sought the annulment of this decision before the Court of Justice. Since Community law itself offered no solution as to how the principle of protection of confidentiality, common to the Member States, was to be interpreted as regards the relationship between a lawyer and his or her client, the Court of Justice made a comparative analysis of the national legal solutions of this problem. Although the principle of the protection of written communications between lawyer and client is generally recognized in the national legal systems, the Court of Justice noted that the scope of this principle and the criteria for its application vary from Member State to Member State.[116] However, it observed that

[a]part from these differences . . . there are to be found in the national laws of the Member States common criteria inasmuch as those laws protect, in similar circum-

---

[112] Mertens de Wilmars (n 1) 38.

[113] *AM & S v Commission* (n 18).

[114] Arts 81 and 82 EC (ex-Arts 85 and 86 of the EC Treaty).

[115] Council Regulation No 17 of 6 Feb 1962. First regulation implementing Arts 85 and 86 (now Arts 81 and 82) of the Treaty [1959–62] OJ Spec Ed 87.

[116] *AM & S*, (n 18) paras 19 and 20.

stances, the confidentiality of written communications between lawyer and client provided that, on the one hand, such communications are made for the purposes and in the interests of the client's rights of defence and, on the other hand, they emanate from independent lawyers, that is to say, lawyers who are not bound to the client by a relationship of employment'.[117]

The Court then concluded that

[v]iewed in that context Regulation No 17 must be interpreted as protecting, in its turn, the confidentiality of written communications between lawyer and client subject to those two conditions, and thus incorporating such elements of that protection as are common to the laws of the Member States'.[118]

Applying these criteria to the case in hand, the Court of Justice did not allow the Commission officials to investigate a series of documents that were considered to be confidential written communications between AM & S and its lawyer.[119]

(b) Divergent National Interpretations as a Pretext for Autonomous Community Interpretation

Often, when the Community courts turn to comparative law in order to find inspiration for the interpretation of a concept of Community law, they will find profound divergences in the interpretation given to the concept in question in the national legal systems. Such a finding may then provide a justification for establishing an autonomous interpretation of the concept in Community law. They will, of course, see to it that this interpretation of Community law reconciles to the greatest extent possible the interests of the Community legal order with the requirement that the Community solution should be 'acceptable' in the member states.

The *Reed* case[120] illustrates this approach of the Community courts. Ms Reed was the partner of a British citizen legally residing in the Netherlands. The Dutch authorities had refused to grant her a residence permit since she was not married to her partner. In this context it should be mentioned that Article 10 of Council Regulation No 1612/68[121] provides that certain members of the 'family' of a worker, including his 'spouse', irrespective of their nationality, 'have the right to install themselves with a worker who is a national of one Member State and who is employed in the territory of another Member State'. In the *Reed* case the Hoge Raad der Nederlanden (Dutch Supreme Court) asked the Court of Justice to rule on the question whether an unmarried partner in a stable relationship should not be assimilated to a

---

[117] Ibid para 21.   [118] Ibid para 22.
[119] See, on this judgment, Galmot (n 21) 256–7.
[120] Case 59/85 *Reed* [1986] ECR 1283.
[121] Council Regulation No 1612/68 of 15 Oct 1968 on freedom of movement for workers within the Community ((1968) OJ Special Edn 475).

'spouse' within the meaning of Article 10 of Regulation No 1612/68. Aware of the fact that—in view of the definition of 'regulations' given in Article 249 EC (ex-Article 189 of the EC Treaty)—its interpretation of the said Article 10 would have effects in all of the Member States, the Court held that 'any interpretation of a legal term on the basis of social developments must take into account the situation in the whole Community, not merely in one Member State'.[122] The Advocate General had already stressed in his Opinion that 'companions can certainly not be treated in the same way as spouses in all Member States in view of the fact that their cultural, social and ethical traditions vary widely in some respects'.[123] The Court of Justice therefore concluded that '[i]n the absence of any indication of a general social development which would justify a broad construction, and in the absence of any indication to the contrary in the regulation, it must be held that the term "spouse" in Article 10 of the Regulation refers to a marital relationship only'.[124]

(c) Import of a National Interpretation into the Community Legal Order

The Community courts will often draw from the richness of the national legal systems when looking for the interpretation of a given concept which suits best the interests of the Community legal order.[125] After having made sure that the interpretation chosen is not likely to meet with serious opposition in the national legal systems unfamiliar with such interpretation, they will not hesitate to 'import' this interpretation in Community law. Thus, for instance, the interpretation the Community courts gave, in the context of actions for annulment, of the concept of 'misuse of power' was largely

---

[122] *Reed* (n 120) para 13.

[123] Opinion of Advocate General CO Lenz in *Reed* (n 120) I-1284, I-1294.

[124] *Reed* (n 120) para 15; see also the judgment of the Court of 31 May 2001 in Joined Cases C–122/99 P and C–125/99 P *D and Sweden v Council* (not yet reported in ECR), in which an appeal lodged against the judgment of the CFI of 28 Jan 1999 in Case T–264/97 *D v Council* [ECR-SC I-A-1 and II-1] was dismissed. The CFI had itself dismissed an action lodged by a Swedish official of the European Community, who had a registered partnership under Swedish law with another Swedish national of the same sex, against the Council decision refusing him the benefit of the household allowance provided for in the Staff Regulations for 'married' officials. The Court of Justice first recalled that 'according to the definition generally accepted by the Member States, the term "marriage" means a union between two persons of the opposite sex' (para 34). It then considered that even if, since 1989, an increasing number of Member States have introduced statutory arrangements granting legal recognition to various forms of union between partners of the same sex or of the opposite sex (such as the registered partnership), such arrangements not previously recognized in law are regarded in the Member States concerned as being distinct from marriage (paras 35 and 36). In such circumstances the Court of Justice concludes that it cannot interpret the Staff Regulations in such a way that legal situations distinct from marriage are treated in the same way as marriage. The intention of the legislature was indeed to grant the benefit only to married couples (para 37).

[125] Mertens de Wilmars (n 1) 39.

influenced by the interpretation of this concept in French administrative law.[126]

3. Judging the Compatibility of a National Provision with the Objectives of the Community

Each time the Court of Justice is asked to rule—in the framework of preliminary proceedings or an infringement action brought against a Member State by the Commission or another Member State—on the compatibility of a provision or 'solution' of national law with the Community legal order, it will adopt a comparative approach. It will indeed have to take a look at the different legal orders concerned as well as their respective priorities and requirements. Taking into account the observations made by the Member State whose law is in issue as well as those submitted by other Member States and the Commission, the Court will 'gauge the temperature' of the national legal systems in order to ascertain the credibility and 'acceptability' of its decision for the whole of the Community.

Through a comparative analysis the Community court can either confirm the compatibility of the national provision with Community law (see subsection (a) below), or set aside a rule of national law which is considered to be incompatible with the requirements of Community law (see subsection (b)), or it can take note of the choice made by the national legal system concerned and confront the latter with the consequences of this choice as regards the Community legal order (see subsection (c)).

(a) Compatibility of a National Provision with Community Law

Asked to rule on a matter revealing an obvious conflict between the interests served by a rule of national law and the requirements of the Community legal order, the Community court may find that the former are nevertheless compatible with the latter. In such case, the comparative law method can be considered as a 'reconciliation process'[127] between Community law and the rules or values enshrined in the internal legal order of the Member State concerned.

The *Eco Swiss* case may serve as a striking example.[128] Benetton had concluded a licensing agreement with Eco Swiss. Benetton terminated the agreement before the end of the period provided for in the contract. The case was brought before arbitrators. The arbitration award ordered

---

[126] See, on this subject, Pescatore (n 3) 354. See also R Dehousse *Comparing National and EC Law: The Problem of the Level of Analysis* Working Paper of the European University Institute, Firenze (1994) 2.

[127] M Darmon 'La Prise en compte des droits fondamentaux par la Cour de justice des Communautés européennes' [1995] Revue de science criminelle et de droit pénal comparé 29.

[128] Case C–126/97 *Eco Swiss* [1999] ECR I-3055.

Benetton to pay damages to Eco Swiss for breach of the licensing agreement. When the parties failed to come to an agreement on the quantum of
the damages, the arbitrators, in a subsequent award, ordered Benetton to
pay Eco Swiss $US23.75 million. Benetton refrained from appealing against
the first award within the prescribed time limit. However, it brought before
a Dutch court proceedings for stay of enforcement of the final arbitration
award. According to Benetton, the licensing agreement violated Article
81 EC (ex-Article 85 of the EC Treaty). The award was therefore said to be
inconsistent with Dutch public policy. The Dutch court referred some
preliminary questions to the Court of Justice. In substance the latter had to
rule on the question whether Community law requires a national court to
refrain from applying a rule of domestic law according to which an arbitration award acquires the force of *res judicata*, if it is not appealed against
within a prescribed time limit. Indeed, in order to examine in the proceedings brought against the final award whether the agreement which the first
award held to be valid in law was nevertheless void under Article 81 EC,
the national court would have had to call into question the first award.

The Court of Justice first held that the three-month time limit, prescribed
by the Dutch rules of procedure, in which an action for annulment of an
arbitration award was to be made 'does not seem excessively short
compared with those prescribed in the legal systems of the other Member
States and does not render excessively difficult or virtually impossible the
exercise of rights conferred by Community law'.[129] It went on to stress that,
upon the expiry of that period, domestic procedural rules that restrict the
possibility of applying for annulment of a subsequent arbitration award
proceeding upon an interim arbitration award which is in the nature of a
final award, because it has become *res judicata*, are justified by the basic
principles of the national judicial system, such as the principle of legal
certainty and acceptance of *res judicata*, which is an expression of that principle.[130] In these circumstances, the Court held that the national court was
not obliged to refrain from applying these domestic procedural rules.[131]

Finding that the time limit prescribed in Dutch law for lodging an
annulment action against an arbitral award was 'normal', the Court of
Justice was anxious not to impose a Community provision that would go
against 'a general principle of law recognized in all the Member States,
namely that "the force of *res judicata* prevents rights confirmed by a judgment of [a court] from being disputed anew" '.[132] It did so, even though the
option chosen entailed a certain reduction of the effectiveness of Article
81 EC.

---

[129] Case C–126/97 *Eco Swiss* [1999] ECR I-3055 para 45.
[130] Ibid para 46.   [131] Ibid, paras 47 and 48.
[132] Opinion of Advocate General A Saggio in Case C–126/97 *Eco Swiss* [1999] ECR I-3055,
I-3057 para 48.

(b) Setting Aside the National Provision Held to be Incompatible with Community Law

It happens that upon a comparative analysis the Community courts set aside a national provision that is held to be incompatible with the objectives and the structure of the Community. This may be illustrated with the *Simmenthal II* case,[133] which is the sequel to *Simmenthal I*.[134] In the latter case the Court of Justice had ruled that the Italian health taxes imposed on the occasion of the importation of meat in Italy were incompatible with Community law. Having regard to this judgment, the Italian court, which had referred the questions to the Court of Justice in *Simmenthal I*, ordered the tax administration to repay the taxes unlawfully charged. The tax administration appealed against this order. It held that, according to the case-law of the Italian Constitutional Court, where there is a conflict between Community law and a subsequent provision of Italian law, the matter must be referred to the Italian Constitutional Court. Indeed, only the Constitutional Court could set aside a provision of Italian law.

Aware of the disadvantages that might arise in a situation where the national court—instead of being able to declare of its own motion that a rule of national law impeding the full force and effect of Community law is inapplicable—was required to raise the issue of constitutionality of the rule in question, the Italian court again addressed a preliminary question to the Court of Justice. It asked whether a rule of national law that is contrary to Community law must be disregarded without awaiting action on the part of the national legislature (repeal) or other constitutional authorities (declaration that the provision is unconstitutional). The Court of Justice found that the case-law of the Italian Constitutional Court was incompatible with the objectives of the Community. It considered incompatible with the requirements that are the very essence of Community law, any provision of a national legal system and any legislative administrative or judicial practice which might impair the effectiveness of Community law by withholding from the national court having jurisdiction to apply such law the power to do everything necessary at the moment of its application to set aside national legislative provisions that might prevent Community rules from having full force and effect.[135] It therefore ruled that a national court which is called upon, within the limits of its jurisdiction, to apply provisions of Community law is under a duty to give full effect to those provisions, even if this implies the setting aside, of its own motion, of a provision of national law.[136] Consequently, it was not necessary for the Italian court to request

---

[133] Case 106/77 *Simmenthal* [1978] ECR 629.
[134] Case 35/76 *Simmenthal* [1976] ECR 1871.
[135] *Simmenthal II* (n 133) para 22.
[136] Ibid para 24.

or await the prior setting aside by legislative or other constitutional means of the provision of Italian law which was incompatible with Community law.[137]

Often—even if, again, this transpires only rarely from the judgment itself—an analysis of comparative law will precede the decision of the Court of Justice to set aside a national provision. The analysis will seek to ensure that the judgment has solid foundations in the national legal traditions. Thus, in *Factortame*[138] the Court of Justice was asked to rule on the compatibility with Community law of a provision of British law that prevented the national court from ordering interim measures in a case where the applicant sought to enforce rights allegedly held under Community law. The Court first referred to its *Simmenthal II* case-law and stressed the need to ensure the effectiveness of directly applicable rules of Community law.[139] According to the Court, it is for the national courts, in application of the principle of cooperation laid down in Article 10 EC, to ensure the legal protection which persons derive from the direct effect of provisions of Community law.[140] The Court then held that the effectiveness of Community law would be impaired if a rule of national law could prevent a court seised of a dispute governed by Community law from granting interim relief in order to ensure the full effectiveness of the judgment to be given on the existence of the rights claimed under Community law.[141] It concluded that a national court which, in a case before it concerning Community law, considers that the sole obstacle that precludes it from granting interim relief is a rule of national law must set aside that rule.[142]

Even if this does not come to the surface in the judgment, the analysis of comparative law contained in the Opinion of Advocate General G Tesauro certainly assured the Court of Justice of the rightness of the solution to set aside the application of the contested British measure. It follows indeed from this analysis that there exists 'in all the legal systems of the Member States (the Danish system constitutes a partial exception), however diverse may be the forms and requirements connected with the duration of the proceedings . . . provision for the interim protection of rights denied under a lower ranking provision but claimed on the basis of a provision of a higher order'.[143]

---

[137] *Simmenthal II* (n 133) para 24.
[138] Case C–213/89, *Factortame and Others* [1990] ECR I-2433.
[139] Ibid para 18.
[140] Ibid para 19.
[141] Ibid paras 18–21.   [142] Ibid para 23.
[143] Opinion of Advocate General G Tesauro in *Factortame* (n 138) I-2450 para 23 of Opinion.

(c) The Community Court Accepts the Choice Made by the National Legal System but Confronts the Latter with the Consequences of this Choice with Regard to the Requirements of the Community Legal Order

It must hardly be recalled that vast areas of law have, until now, not been subject to any legislative coordination or harmonization on a European level. When a preliminary question is referred to the Court of Justice regarding a matter which is thus left to the autonomy of the Member States, the Court will first endeavour to define the choice made by the national legal order concerned. It will then confront this choice with the requirements of the Community legal order. While fully respecting the autonomy of the national legal order in the matter, the Community court will oblige this national order to bear the responsibility for the consequences of the choice made as regards the respect for Community law.

The area of procedural law illustrates this peculiar variant of the comparative law method in the activities of the Court of Justice. The authors of the Treaty did not set up special Community courts in the Member States which would have exclusive jurisdiction to apply Community law. Instead, they opted for a system where the national courts would be the ordinary courts of the Community legal order.[144] Very soon the case-law of the Court of Justice enshrined the principle of procedural autonomy according to which it is for each Member State to designate the competent courts and to lay down the procedural rules governing actions for safeguarding rights that individuals derive from the direct effect of Community law.[145] The principle of procedural autonomy is, however, limited by two requirements of Community law, namely the procedural rules applicable to actions under Community law may not be less favourable than those governing similar domestic actions (principle of equivalence) and they may not render virtually impossible or excessively difficult the exercise of rights conferred by Community law (principle of effectiveness).[146]

The case-law concerning the question of whether a national court can be obliged to raise of its own motion a plea regarding a violation of Community law demonstrates that the Court of Justice prefers, in the context of the relative procedural autonomy of the Member States, not to impose a uniform rule that would hurt the sensitivities of the Member States which are unfamiliar with such particular rule of procedural law (even if such uniform rule would certainly serve the effectiveness of Community law). While respecting the

[144] Struys (n 47) 49.

[145] See eg Case 33/76 *Rewe* [1976] ECR 1989, and Case 45/76 *Comet* [1976] ECR 2043.

[146] See case-law referred to by Struys (n 47) 50. With respect to the difficulties of putting these principles into operation, see M Hoskins 'Tilting the Balance: Supremacy and National Procedural Rules' (1996) ELR 365–77.

choice made by the Member States on this procedural matter, the Court of Justice nevertheless demands from the Member States on the basis of their duty of sincere cooperation under Article 10 EC that they bear, within 'the limits of the acceptable', the consequences of their choice as regards the fundamental requirements of Community law.

This flows from the *Van Schijndel and Van Veen* cases,[147] in which two Dutch physiotherapists contested the legality of a Dutch statute on compulsory participation in an occupational pension scheme. The applicants, however, in their proceedings before the national court, had not raised the issue of the compatibility of the Dutch statute with the competition rules of the EC Treaty. Before the Hoge Raad der Nederlanden they invoked for the first time the alleged incompatibility with the competition rules of the EC Treaty and they contended that the inferior court should have raised the issue 'if necessary of its own motion'.[148] The Hoge Raad der Nederlanden addressed some preliminary questions to the Court of Justice. It first wanted to know whether a national court should apply of its own motion the competition rules of the EC Treaty even where the party to the proceedings with an interest in application of those provisions had not relied upon them. Secondly, if the first question had to be answered in the affirmative, the Hoge Raad der Nederlanden wanted to know whether that answer also applies if in so doing the court would have to abandon the passive role assigned to it under national law, since it would be required to go beyond the ambit of the dispute defined by the parties and/or to rely on facts and circumstances other than those on which the party with an interest in application of those provisions relies in order to substantiate his claim.

The Court of Justice held that where, by virtue of domestic law, national courts must raise of their own motion points of law based on binding domestic rules which have not been raised by the parties, such an obligation also exists where binding Community rules are concerned, such as the competition rules of the EC Treaty.[149] Referring to Article 10 EC, the Court of Justice added that the position is the same if domestic law confers on national courts a discretion to apply of their own motion binding rules of law.[150] So it concluded that, in proceedings concerning civil rights and obligations freely entered into by the parties, it is for the national court to apply the competition rules of the EC Treaty even when the party with an interest in application of those provisions has not relied on them, where domestic law allows such application.[151] After having found that under the Dutch legal order the national judge has the right to raise a plea of law of his own motion, the Community judge, on the basis of the principle of

---

[147] Joined Cases C–430/93 and C–431/93 *Van Schijndel and Van Veen* [1995] ECR I-4705.
[148] Ibid para 10.   [149] Ibid para 13.
[150] Ibid para 14.   [151] Ibid para 15.

sincere cooperation laid down in Article 10 EC and the effectiveness of Community law, transformed this right into a duty as far as pleas based on a violation of the competition rules of the EC Treaty are concerned.

The Court of Justice, however, added that the principle that in civil proceedings a court must or may raise points of its own motion is limited by the obligation for it to keep to the subject matter of the dispute and to base its decision on the facts placed before it.[152] The Court stressed that this limitation is justified by the principle that it is for the parties to take the initiative in a civil suit and that the court is empowered to act of its own motion only in exceptional cases where the public interest requires its intervention. According to the Court of Justice, that principle 'reflects conceptions prevailing in most of the Member States as to the relations between the State and the individual; it safeguards the right of the defence; and it ensures proper conduct of proceedings by, in particular, protecting them from the delays inherent in examination of new pleas'.[153] The Court of Justice therefore concluded that Community law does not require national courts to raise of their own motion an issue concerning the breach of provisions of Community law where examination of that issue would oblige them to abandon the passive role assigned to them by going beyond the ambit of the dispute defined by the parties themselves and relying on facts and circumstances other than those on which the party with an interest in application of those provisions bases his claim.[154]

This second part of the judgment reveals that the Court of Justice—while seeking to impose on the Member States the responsibility to bear the full consequences in terms of Community law of the choices made by virtue of the principle of procedural autonomy—will always seek not to impose requirements on the national legal systems that would certainly serve the effectiveness of Community law but which would come into conflict with legal conceptions of public policy common to most Member States and which would eventually undermine the 'acceptability' of the Community solution in the national legal systems.

In its judgment of 24 October 1996 in *Kraaijeveld and Others*[155] the Court of Justice seemed to adopt a more daring position in the matter. In this case the Court of Justice was asked to rule on the question of whether a national court is obliged to assess of its own motion the compatibility of a national measure with a European directive. The Court of Justice held that, where under national law a court must or may raise of its own motion pleas in law based on binding national rules which have not been put forward by the parties, it must, for matters within its jurisdiction, examine of its own motion whether the legislative or administrative authorities of

---

[152] Ibid para 20.   [153] Ibid para 21.   [154] Ibid para 22.
[155] Case C–72/95 *Kraaijeveld and Others* [1996] ECR I-5403.

the Member State have remained within the limits of their discretion under the provisions of the directive concerned, and take account thereof when examining the action for annulment brought against the national measures implementing the directive.[156] As certain commentators correctly underlined,[157] the Court of Justice thus gave the impression that the national court had a duty to raise pleas concerning the violation of Community law of its own motion irrespective of the question whether the public interest required such intervention.

It flows, however, from the judgment of the Court of Justice of 1 June 1999 in the *Eco Swiss* case[158] that the Court intends to safeguard the equilibrium, defined in *Van Schijndel and Van Veen*,[159] between the obligation for the Member States to bear the consequences of their choice of procedural law concerning the power of the judge to raise a plea of law of his own motion and the concern to respect the common tendency in the national legal systems according to which a judge can only exceptionally act of his own motion where the public interest so requires. In *Eco Swiss* the Court of Justice was asked to rule on the somewhat different question whether a national court to which application is made for annulment of an arbitration award must grant such an application where, in its view, that award is in fact contrary to Article 81 EC. The national court in question could under its domestic procedural rules grant such an application only on a limited number of grounds, one of them being inconsistency with public policy, which, according to the applicable national law, is not generally to be invoked on the sole ground that, because of the terms or the enforcement of an arbitration award, effect will not be given to a prohibition laid down by domestic competition law. After having considered that it is in the interest of efficient arbitration proceedings that review of arbitration awards should be limited in scope and that annulment of, or refusal to recognize, an award should be possible only in exceptional circumstances,[160] the Court ruled that the fundamental character of Article 81 EC for the accomplishment of the tasks entrusted to the Community justifies that a national court, which under its domestic rules of procedure must grant an application for annulment of an arbitration award where such an application is founded on failure to observe national rules of public policy, must also grant such an application where it is founded on failure to comply with the prohibition laid down in Article 81(1) EC.[161]

In this judgment one can thus perceive the intention of the Court of Justice of limiting the duty of national courts to raise pleas of law on their

---

[156] Case C–72/95 *Kraaijeveld and Others* [1996] ECR I-5403 para 60.

[157] See Struys (n 47) 50; E Szyszczak and J Delicostopoulos 'Intrusions into National Procedural Autonomy: The French Paradigm' [1997] ELR 141–9.

[158] *Eco Swiss*, cited in n 132 above.   [159] Cited in n 147.

[160] Ibid para 35.   [161] Ibid paras 36 and 37.

own motion to cases where there is a breach of a provision of Community law considered to be of a level equivalent to an internal legal provision of public policy. This judgment also shows that the concern of the Court of Justice to see to it that the Member States bear the consequences of their internal choices of procedural law in order to further the objectives of Community law is not limited to the question whether a court is required to raise a plea of law of its own motion, but also covers other matters such as the competence of the court to annul arbitral awards.

V. CONCLUDING REMARKS

Situated at the crossroads of different, yet closely intertwined, legal cultures, the Community judicature is by nature a 'comparative' institution. In its daily activities it is permeated with the values of the surrounding legal systems. The comparative approach is a very important tool for the Community courts to interpret Community law. The Community judicature can apply this approach either for its own use in direct proceedings brought before it or for the benefit of the national courts within the context of preliminary proceedings.

Whether the comparative law method is used to confront rules of national law or to compare the Community legal order and one or more other legal orders (whether national or international), it is always inspired by the same objective: to uphold the rule of law in the Community legal order, as prescribed in Article 220 EC. Its purpose is not just to fill lacunae in the Community construction, but rather, after having carefully 'taken the pulse' of the national legal systems, to find the *best solution in the 'middle-line' or compromise solution*, which should enjoy credibility and acceptability in the Member States and which will ensure the effectiveness of Community law. Depending on the circumstances, this solution—which is the fruit of a subtle putting into balance of the interests of the evolution of the Community and the acceptability of this evolution in the domestic legal orders—can take the form of a principle, a fundamental right, an interpretation or a construction of Community law based on a legal concept sufficiently common to the Member States. The *solution in the 'middle-line'* can also be of another kind. In the absence of a *fundus communis*, the Community courts can develop an autonomous Community solution where they find contradictions in the national legal systems, or may import into the Community legal order a 'proven' national solution, or else may impose on a national legal order the obligation, within acceptable limits, to bear the 'consequences of Community law' of its own internal choices.

The comparative approach thus also becomes an exercise in 'psycho-diplomacy' for the Community courts. These courts are constantly divided between the concern 'not to give up' when confronting national divergences and that of respecting, in the interests of the 'acceptability' of Community law in the domestic legal orders, the national sensitivities and the differences that exist in the legal conceptions and constitutional traditions of the Member States and which, at the same time, constitute the richness of the legal heritage of the Community. This exercise, while very delicate, is of the utmost importance since it makes the national legal orders have confidence in the Community legal order, as the evolution of the case-law of the German Bundesverfassungsgericht illustrates.

The preceding considerations show that the European Union, which centrally rests on the Community legal order, has its own variant of *E pluribus unum*, that is, a set of interlocking legal orders showing mutual respect for each other based on equivalent levels of judicial protection of the rule of law. That constitutes the common platform for the legal underpinnings of European integration, a *ius commune* built with the bricks of the comparative law method.

9

The Comparative Method in Judgments of the European Court of Human Rights: Reference Back to National Law*

Paul Mahoney

I. NATURAL PLACE OF THE COMPARATIVE METHOD IN THE INTERPRETATION OF THE EUROPEAN CONVENTION ON HUMAN RIGHTS

The starting point of principle of this chapter is that the comparative method is inherent in the European Convention on Human Rights (ECHR) system of protection;[1] and the conclusion on looking at the case-law of the European Court of Human Rights[2] is that comparative references to national law, although somewhat lapidary, are the expression of a coherent doctrine rather than just piecemeal.[3] A few words will also be said, incidentally, about comparative references to other sources of international law.

The ECHR establishes a two-way bridge between international law and national law: in one direction flows the international obligation for the contracting States to make their national legal orders compatible with specified common standards; in the other direction the inspiration and continuing source of those standards on the whole derive from principles already recognized under the domestic law of all democratic countries. Not surprisingly

---

* This chapter is an updated version of an article published in *The Role of Comparative Law in the Emergence of European Law* (Swiss Institute of Comparative Law 2000). Any views expressed in it are personal.

[1] This is a thesis developed as long ago as 1980 by Walter Ganshof van der Meersch, one of the pioneering judges of the Court: WJ Ganshof van der Meersch 'Reliance, in the Case-Law of the European Court of Human Rights, on the Domestic Law of the States' (1980) 1 Human Rights Law Journal 13, 15–16.

[2] As from 1 Nov 1988, by virtue of Protocol No 11 to the ECHR, there has been a single European Court of Human Rights, replacing the two former semi-permanent enforcement bodies, namely the former Court and the European Commission of Human Rights. In ths chapter the term 'Court' is frequently used as a shorthand for both the Commission and the Court since the case-law principles discussed were developed jointly by both institutions. For ease of reference, however, only judgments by the former Court have been cited.

[3] This chapter takes up some ideas previously expressed in P Mahoney 'Judicial Activism and Judicial Self-Restraint in the European Court of Human Rights: Two Sides of the Same Coin' (1990) 11 Human Rights Law Journal 57.

therefore, when it comes to interpreting and applying the ECHR in particular instances, argument is often adduced from a comparison of national
legislations. The place of comparative law in the ECHR interpretative
process is all the more natural because of certain characteristics of the
ECHR as a regional human rights treaty that are not always found in other
international instruments such as commercial or military treaties.

First, the ECHR, like most other international or national instruments
protecting human rights, frequently uses general, inconclusively worded
formulations that necessarily call for 'fleshing out' through interpretation.
Standards setting an obligation of result and leaving a choice as to means
of implementation rather than detailed rules imposing uniform solutions
tend to be used. To use the words of one commentator, speaking of the
Canadian Charter of Rights and Freedoms: 'many of these rights . . .
contain little or no substantive criteria; they resemble blank slates on which
the judiciary can scrawl the imagery of their choice'.[4] The broad, open-
textured wording of the ECHR and the attendant need for interpretation
confer on the judges of the Strasbourg Court an active role as lawmaker.
But it is not law-making in a vacuum: the comparative method—in the
sense of having regard to the national law of democratic societies and, in
particular, the societies of the European States making up the ECHR
community—is one of the interpretative tools used by the Court for fixing,
in specific contexts, the concrete content of the indeterminate standards
enunciated in the ECHR.

Comparative reference to the growing corpus of human rights law in the
international and supranational fields likewise represents a persuasive, if
not binding, source of interpretative assistance. As the last president of the
former Strasbourg Court, Professor Rudolf Bernhardt, has written,
although regional international human rights treaties such as the ECHR
may express regional convictions and values better than universal texts can
do and thus often secure a better protection of the individual, 'other international texts and decisions should at least be considered as part of the
material to be included in any solid comparative research'.[5] This present
chapter will not delve too deeply into the comparative method as applied to
sources of international law, its main focus being on the relationship
between the interpretation of ECHR law and references back to national
law. The short point is that the ECHR is above all about 'law in society';
and, for the Strasbourg Court when seeking to give meaning to inconclusively worded concepts in particular circumstances, 'society' is to be under-

[4] P Monaghan *Politics and the Constitution: The Charter, Federation and Supreme Court
of Canada* (1987) 53.
[5] R Bernhardt 'Comparative Law in the Interpretation and Application of the European
Convention on Human Rights' in S Busuttil (ed) *Mainly Human Rights: Studies in Honour of
JJ Cremona* (1999), 33–40, 36.

stood as comprising not just the ECHR contracting States taken individually or collectively for the purposes of each case but also, more broadly, the international community in its various components for example, in appropriate instances the Council of Europe, the European Union, the United Nations family of organizations, the International Labour Organization, and so on.[6] Even international instruments in specialized areas such as trade union freedom, data protection, children born out of wedlock, and bioethics may be relevant in so far as such texts may be regarded as sub-legislation regulating specific aspects of the more general human rights legislated for in the regional *loi-cadre*—framework law—that is the ECHR.

Secondly, and a main reason why comparative law in its 'national' aspect is, potentially at least, such a significant interpretative tool, the enforcement machinery set up under the ECHR is subsidiary to national systems of protection of human rights.[7] Although inherent in the ECHR, such subsidiarity is also flagged in the declaratory terms of Article 1,[8] which make it clear that the primary responsibility for securing the guaranteed rights within the domestic legal order is laid on the national authorities. This subsidiary character is reflected in recourse to a comparative approach in the context of the principles of interpretation that the Strasbourg enforcement bodies have developed, in particular the doctrines of autonomous concepts, evolutive interpretation, and the margin of appreciation. This approach involves deriving legitimacy for a chosen meaning on the basis of a comparison of national legislations. Let us look a little more closely at these principles of interpretation.

II. AUTONOMOUS CONCEPTS IN THE ECHR

Many clauses in the ECHR refer back to concepts that are part and parcel of the legal systems of the contracting states: 'liberty', 'detention', 'arrest', 'criminal charge', 'criminal offence', 'conviction', 'court', 'fair hearing',

---

[6] A similar point, albeit not directly in relation to the comparative method, was made in *Al Adsani v United Kingdom* ECHR 2001-XI §55, where the Court held that the grant by the English courts of sovereign immunity to a defendant State in respect of a civil claim for damages for alleged torture committted outside England did not amount to an unjustified restriction on the applicant's access to court (Art 6 §1 ECHR): 'The [ECHR] . . . cannot be interpreted in a vacuum. The Court must be mindful of the [ECHR's] special character as a human rights treaty, and it must also take the relevant rules of international law into account . . . The [ECHR] should so far as possible be interpreted in harmony with other rules of international law of which it forms part . . .'.

[7] See H Petzold 'The Convention and the Principle of Subsidiarity' in R St J Macdonald, F Matscher and H Petzold (eds) *The European System for Protection of Human Rights* (1993) 41–62.

[8] Art 1 ECHR reads 'The High Contracting Parties shall secure to everyone within their jurisdiction the rights and freedoms defined in Section I of this Convention.'

'presumption of innocence', to take notions found in the two main provisions in the ECHR dealing with the administration of justice at national level, namely Articles 5 and 6 which respectively guarantee the right to liberty and the right to a fair trial. The safeguards in Article 6 are triggered in the criminal sphere, for example, when it can be said that a 'criminal charge' has been laid. But national definitions of 'criminal charge' differ. If the text of Article 6 were taken to be a simple reference back to the national law of each State, without more, then the degree of protection afforded by the ECHR to individuals would vary from country to country. In order to avoid inequality of treatment and to ensure the universality of the international standard, an 'autonomous' meaning, the same for all countries, is therefore given to such concepts. Legislations of all the contracting States making up the ECHR community are not, however, without importance in determining this autonomous meaning: they provide one of the sources for deducing the common core of the concept, although this is not always made explicit in the judgments.[9] The existence of what has been termed 'common European ground' is thus a powerful influencing factor in the interpretative process of identifying a unifying 'autonomous' meaning.

To give an example, the autonomous concept of 'civil rights and obligations' for the purposes of Article 6 ECHR has been held not to encompass the service relationship between civil servants and the State largely because of the traditional public policy regulation of this relationship in the legal order of the contracting States. The judgment in *Pellegrin v France* (1999) explained the reasons for this limitation as follows:

As the Court has noted in previous cases, in the law of many member States of the Council of Europe there is a basic distinction between civil servants and employees governed by private law. This has led the Court to hold that 'disputes relating to the recruitment, careers and termination of service of civil servants are as a general rule outside the scope of Article 6 §1'. . .[10]

The Court then went on to adopt an autonomous interpretation of the notion of 'civil service', aligning itself with the position taken in the European Union, notably by the European Commission and the Court of Justice of the European Communities, in what it took to be a comparable context.[11] One may or may not approve of the result in terms of the level

---

[9] See *König v Germany* 28 June 1979 Series A vol 27 §89, for a rare, although somewhat elliptic, dictum: 'In the exercise of its supervisory functions [in the context of determining the autonomous meaning of the concept of "civil rights and obligations" in Article 6 §1 ECHR in relation to the legal system of the respondent State], the Court must also take account of . . . the national legal systems of the other Contracting States'. The other factors which the *König* judgment said had to be taken account were 'the substantive content and effects of the right—and not its legal classification—under the domestic law of the State concerned' and 'the object and purpose of the [ECHR]'.

[10] [GC] ECHR 1999–VIII §59.   [11] Ibid §§63–7.

of human rights protection thereby afforded—civil service disputes being excluded from the ambit of Article 6 §1 and the right to a fair trial—but one can see that the Court was endeavouring to give a legitimate basis for its interpretation by taking judicial notice of its surrounding legal environments, namely the national legal orders and the European Union legal order.

III. EVOLUTIVE INTERPRETATION

A number of the safeguards laid down in the ECHR are linked to societal conditions, attitudes, and values. As a result they are not static but are capable of evolution with time. New and perhaps unforeseen threats to individual liberty will arise because of new phenomena. In order to ensure effective protection of human rights 'in our time', the Strasbourg Court has opted for seeking the current meaning of the inconclusive terms and concepts found in the text. The core of a given right may well be stable but its contours will vary with each generation.

In *Tyrer v United Kingdom* (1978) the Court affirmed for the first time that 'the [ECHR] is a living instrument which . . . must be interpreted in the light of the present-day conditions'. In holding a sentence of birching imposed on an adolescent in the Isle of Man to be 'degrading punishment' outlawed by Article 3 ECHR, the Court '[could not] but be influenced by the developments and commonly accepted standards in penal policy of the Member States of the Council of Europe in this field'.[12] The justification for an evolutive interpretation, changing the content of a guaranteed right from what it was in 1950 when originally formulated, is thus also largely dependent on the existence of 'common European ground'.

This approach was confirmed in *Marckx v Belgium* (1979),[13] where the unfavourable legal position in Belgium of unmarried mothers and children born out of wedlock, as compared with married mothers and legitimate children, was held to violate the right to respect for family life and to be discriminatory (Articles 8 and 14 ECHR). Notice was taken of the fact that the domestic law of the great majority of the Member States of the Council of Europe had evolved and was continuing to evolve, in company with relevant international agreements, towards greater equality of treatment in the area under consideration.

International developments on their own may provide sufficient attestation of evolution of societal attitudes in the domain under consideration, even in the absence of 'common European ground' at national level. In

[12] 25 Apr 1978 Series A vol 26 §31.
[13] 13 June 1979 Series A vol 31.

three successive cases in 1986, 1990, and 1998 the Strasbourg Court held that the inability of post-operated transsexuals to obtain a new birth certificate showing their new sex did not give rise to a violation of the United Kingdom's positive obligation under the ECHR to ensure, through its legislation, effective respect for their private life.[14] All three judgments noted that, despite developments in some countries, in 1998 as in 1986 there was little common ground in legislative practice between the contracting States.[15] These judgments were overruled last year, and a violation found, in the case of *Christine Goodwin v UK*. The Court looked at the legal position within and, significantly, outside European states (Canada, South Africa, Australia, New Zealand, United States) and at international texts. It 'attache[d] less importance to the lack of evidence of a common European approach to the resolution of the legal and practical problems posed, than to the clear and uncontested evidence of a continuing international trend in favour not only of increased social acceptance of transsexuals but of legal recognition of the new sexual identity of post-operative transsexuals'.[16]

The role of comparative law in arguing against an evolutive or progressive interpretation—that is, against an interpretative extension of the reach of the ECHR—is neatly illustrated by a 1999 judgment by the new Court. The case (*V v United Kingdom*)—again a British case—concerned the criminal trial in public of two 11-year-old boys for the horrific killing of a younger child. One of the issues was whether the attribution of criminal responsibility in respect of acts committed when the applicant boys were only 10 years old could, in itself, give rise to a violation of the prohibition of inhuman and degrading treatment (Article 3 ECHR). No common standard could be discerned in the legal systems of the contracting States, and the age of 10, although on the low side in the comparative table, could not be said to be so young as to differ disproportionately from the age limit followed by other European States.[17] The Court was not therefore prepared to accept the reading of Article 3 advocated by the applicants.

---

[14] *Rees v United Kingdom* 17 Oct 1986 Series A vol 106; *Cossey v United Kingdom* 27 Sept 1990, Series A vol 184; *Sheffield and Horsham v United Kingdom* 30 July 1998, Reports 1998–V 2012.

[15] Loc cit §§57–8.

[16] [GC] ECHR 2002–VI §§84–5.

[17] [GC] ECHR 1999–IX §§72–4. It is worth quoting the relevant passage in full, since it represents one of the rare instances where the Court gives some details of the comparative survey that it has relied on: '[In determining this issue, the Court] has had regard to the principle ... that, since the Convention is a living instrument, it is legitimate when deciding whether a certain measure is acceptable under one of its provisions to take account of the standards prevailing amongst the [M]ember States of the Council of Europe ... In this connection, the Court observes that, at the present time, there is not yet a commonly accepted minimum age for the imposition of criminal responsibility in Europe. While most of the Contracting States have adopted an age-limit which is higher than that in force in England and Wales, other States, such as Cyprus, Ireland, Liechtenstein and Switzerland, attribute criminal responsibil-

At the other end of the age scale, in the case of *Papon v France*,[18] in which the incarceration of the elderly was likewise challenged under Article 3 as being inhuman and degrading, the Court concluded after a comparative review of the penal policy in many European jurisdictions that old age was no bar to pre-trial detention or to imprisonment.

There are limits on the extent to which social developments as embodied in national legislations, even if the subject of a large consensus across Europe, can lead through evolutive interpretation as such to a change in the content of the ECHR. In particular, evolutive interpretation does not permit the creation of new rights or freedoms not already protected by the text. This the Court said in the 1986 case of *Johnston and Others v Ireland* when holding that a right to divorce could not be derived from Article 12 ECHR, which guarantees the right to marry, despite the fact that Ireland was practically alone in Europe in not permitting dissolution of marriage.[19] The creation of wholly new rights is a function left to the contracting States through amendment of the treaty.

That said, even though evolutive interpretation may be excluded in such circumstances, amendment of the Treaty may conceivably be effected, not only in the classic manner in the form of negotiated amending protocols, but also by State practice subsequent to the adoption of the Treaty as evidenced by a change in the legislative face of Europe. This was seemingly admitted in *Soering v United Kingdom* (1989).[20] The subject of complaint in *Soering* was the decision by the British authorities to extradite the applicant, a German national, to the United States to face trial on a capital charge of murder. The Court held that a violation of the prohibition of inhuman and degrading treatment or punishment (Article 3 ECHR) would occur—that is, a potential violation—if the applicant were extradited because he would run a real risk of exposure to the 'death-row phenomenon' (a lengthy, stressful wait on death-row before being executed). Before arriving at this finding, the Court examined as a preliminary point whether Article 3 could be interpreted as generally prohibiting the death penalty. At first sight this is an interpretation rendered impossible by the text of the right-to-life clause in the ECHR (Article 2) which in its first paragraph

ity from a younger age. Moreover, no clear tendency can be ascertained from examination of the relevant international texts and instruments . . . The Court does not consider that there is at this stage any clear common standard amongst the [M]ember States of the Council of Europe as to the minimum age of criminal responsibility. Even if England and Wales is among the few European jurisdictions to retain a low age of criminal responsibility, the age of ten cannot be said to be so young as to differ disproportionately from the age-limit followed by other European States. The Court concludes that the attribution of criminal responsibility to the applicant does not in itself give rise to a breach of Article 3 of the Convention.'

[18] *Papon v France* (No 1) (dec) no 64666/01 ECHR 2001–VI.
[19] 18 Dec 1986 Series A vol 112 §§53–4.
[20] 7 July 1989 Series A vol 161.

explicitly permits capital punishment. However, Amnesty International, which had intervened in the proceedings as a third party, argued that the evolving standards in Europe regarding the existence and use of the death penalty required that the death penalty should, in 1989, be considered as inhuman and degrading punishment within the meaning of Article 3. The Court noted that what Amnesty International described as 'the virtual consensus in Western European legal systems that the death penalty is ... no longer consistent with regional standards of justice' was reflected in Protocol No 6 to the Convention, which provides for the abolition of the death penalty in time of peace. What effect did these 'marked changes' on both the national and international level have on the evident intention of the drafters of the ECHR in 1950 when expressly permitting the death penalty in the right-to-life clause? The Court's reply was as follows:

Subsequent practice in national penal policy, in the form of a generalised abolition of capital punishment, could be taken as establishing the agreement of the Contracting States to abrogate the exception provided for under Article 2 §1 and hence to remove a textual limit on the scope for evolutive interpretation of Article 3. However, Protocol No. 6, as a subsequent written agreement, shows that the intention of the Contracting Parties as recently as 1983 was to adopt the normal method of amendment of the text in order to introduce a new obligation to abolish capital punishment in time of peace and, what is more, to do so by an optional instrument allowing each State to choose the moment when to undertake such an engagement. In these conditions, notwithstanding the special character of the Convention ... Article 3 cannot be interpreted as generally prohibiting the death penalty.[21]

This is tantamount to saying that intervening consensus in national legislations and practices may not only operate to fix the content of variable ECHR concepts, as in *Tyrer* and *Marckx*, but also constitute evidence of an outright revision of the text agreed on by the contracting States. Amnesty International invoked the comparative method in a bold attempt to persuade the Court not merely to interpret evolutively but to go so far as to amend the text by deleting a clause that had come to be at variance with 'regional standards of justice'. The Court would appear to have had much sympathy with the Amnesty International view on the unacceptability of capital punishment in modern-day Europe. Reading between the lines, the Amnesty argument would have stood a good chance of being accepted but for the existence of Protocol No 6. To date *Soering* remains an isolated authority for this sort of reasoning, but it does open an intriguing window for the future: the comparative method as an indicator of State practice establishing the agreement of the parties to amend or revise the text of the ECHR.

[21] Loc cit §§101–3.

IV. MARGIN OF APPRECIATION[22]

In some cases the Strasbourg Court has declined to interfere with a measure taken by a national authority even though on the facts it would not necessarily have arrived at the same conclusion. These are the cases where the national lawmaker has been recognized as enjoying a 'margin of appreciation' (that is, a discretionary power) to regulate generally the exercise of the asserted ECHR right, which margin the national executive authority or court did not exceed in its determination of the particular case. The ECHR, like national constitutions safeguarding basic rights, disables democratic discretion in certain domains. But within the disabling limits placed by the ECHR the democratic discretion of the national authorities of the contracting States to regulate the way of life of their citizens remains intact.

In areas where there is a legitimate range of opinion in democratic society, the inference is that the drafters intended to leave a discretionary power to the national authorities to regulate the exercise of the ECHR right in accordance with normal democratic processes. In *Handyside v United Kingdom* (1976), where the main issue was whether an interference with freedom of expression (Article 10 ECHR) as a result of the complainant's conviction for obscene publication was justified as being 'necessary in a democratic society . . . for the protection of morals', the Strasbourg Court said:

[I]t is not possible to find in the domestic law of the various Contracting States a uniform European conception of morals. The view taken by their respective laws of the requirements of morals varies from time to time and from place to place, especially in our era which is characterised by a rapid and far-reaching evolution of opinions on the subject. By reason of their direct and continuous contact with the vital forces of their countries, State authorities are in principle in a better position than the international judge to give an opinion on the exact content of the [requirements of morals] . . . Consequently, Article 10 §2 leaves to the Contracting States a margin of appreciation . . .[23]

'Precisely the same said cannot be said of the far more objective notion of [the maintenance of] the "authority" of the judiciary'—one of the other legitimate aims justifying restrictions on free speech—the Court concluded when finding a violation in a subsequent case in relation to a prior restraint on publication ordered by the national courts under a law proscribing 'trial by newspaper': 'The domestic law and practice of the Contracting States reveal a fairly substantial measure of common ground in this area. . . .

---

[22] See the series of articles in (1998) 19 Human Rights Law Journal 1–36 under the title 'The Doctrine of the Margin of Appreciation Under the European Convention on Human Rights: Its Legitimacy in Theory and Application in Practice'.
[23] 7 Dec1976 Series A vol 24 §§48–9.

Accordingly, here a more extensive European supervision corresponds to a less discretionary power of appreciation.'[24]

In *Dudgeon v United Kingdom* (1981) the Court relied on an evolutive interpretation to hold that the criminal laws in Northern Ireland that had the effect of outlawing male homosexual practices between consenting adults in private fell foul of the right to respect for private life (Article 8 ECHR).[25] Although *Dudgeon*, like *Handyside*, was concerned with protection of morals, the margin of appreciation was held to be a narrow one since the interference by the State was not in the public sphere but with an intimate aspect of private life. In addition, the Court was able to identify common European ground on the issue: legislative consensus among the majority of the Convention countries, towards decriminalization of consensual adult homosexual conduct in private, signalled a common change in fundamental societal values in this sphere. A similar technique—of relying on a change in the legislative face of Europe—has been followed in subsequent judgments holding that certain restrictions or sanctions imposed on individuals because of their homosexuality could no longer be regarded as justified under the ECHR: see the British cases brought by homosexuals discharged from the armed forces following intrusive investigations and the Austrian application directed against the maintenance of a higher age of consent for male homosexual acts than for heterosexual and female homosexual acts.[26] In contrast, in *Fretté v France* (2002) the 'indisputable' absence of common ground between the laws of the contracting States as regards the possibility or not for homosexual single persons to adopt children was indicative of a wide margin of appreciation.[27]

Similarly, in *Rasmussen v Denmark* (1984)[28] lack of legislative consensus was fatal to a father who challenged as discriminatory (Article 14 ECHR) the fact that under Danish law, in order to bring proceedings to contest the paternity of a child born in wedlock, time limits were laid down for the husband but not for the mother. The Court explained the underlying principle as follows: 'The scope of the margin of appreciation will vary according to the circumstances, the subject-matter and its background; in this respect one of the relevant factors may be the existence or non-existence of common ground between the laws of the Contracting States . . .'.[29] Examination of the contracting States' legislation regarding paternity proceedings showed that there was no such common ground and that in

---

[24] *Sunday Times v United Kingdom (No 1)* (merits), 26 Apr 1979 Series A vol 30 §59.

[25] *Dudgeon.*

[26] *Smith and Grady v United Kingdom* ECHR 1999–VI §104; *L and V v Austria*, to be reported in ECHR 2003 §§47, 50.

[27] ECHR 2002–I, §§40–41. The judgment contains the memorable phrase: 'Adoption means 'providing a child with a family, not a family with a child' . . .'(§42).

[28] 28 Nov 1984 Series A vol 87.

[29] Ibid §§40–1.

1984 in most of them the position of the mother and that of the husband were regulated in different ways. That being so, the Danish authorities were not found to have overstepped their margin of appreciation in treating the putative father differently from the mother.[30] In colloquial terms one could say: they had not stepped out of line because, when the impugned measures were taken, there was no common line.

But of course a situation of disparity may evolve with time towards one of consensus. In *Mazurek v France* (2002), where a distinction between adulterine children and children born in wedlock with regard to inheritance rights was held to be discriminatory (Article 14 ECHR taken together with Article 1 of Protocol No 1), the reliance placed by the respondent government on the *Rasmussen* judgment was dismissed as 'not convincing, since the factual and temporal circumstances have now changed'.[31] Without offering any detail, the Court 'note[d], contrary to the Government's assertions . . . a distinct tendency in favour of eradicating discrimination against adulterine children. It [could] not ignore such a tendency in its necessarily dynamic interpretation of the relevant provisions of the Convention.'

In sum, room for legitimate difference of approach from country to country on a human rights issue can be deduced both from the nature of the matter and usually from a disparity in the legislative practices of the contracting (and other democratic) States. Conversely, legislative consensus among the majority of States will usually, but not always (as in the Irish divorce case), signal a reduced area of discretion for States that are out of line.

V. LEGITIMACY OF THE COMPARATIVE METHOD

The mission of the Strasbourg Court often involves ruling on the compatibility of the laws and practices of a contracting State with the requirements of the ECHR. It might therefore be asked whether, in order to accomplish that mission of international judicial control, it is at all legitimate to rely on a comparative reference back to national legislations. Can it be that the

---

[30] The judgment in the 1997 case of *X, Y and Z v United Kingdom* Reports 1997-II §44, where the grievance was the refusal under British law to register a post-operative transsexual (female to male) as the father of a child born to his female partner by artificial insemination by a donor—was explicit in linking lack of legislative consensus with the existence of a broad margin of appreciation: 'Since the issues in this case,'—the granting of parental rights to transsexuals and regulation of the social relationship between a child conceived by artificial insemination and the person who performs the role of father—'touch on areas where there is little common ground amongst the [M]member States of the Council of Europe and, generally speaking, the law appears to be in a transitional stage, the respondent State must be afforded a wide margin of appreciation'.

[31] ECHR 2000–II §52.

Court's adjudicative responsibility to state the higher international ECHR law in relation to a given national law is conditioned by the factual content of the sum of national legislations? How can the ECHR govern national law if it is itself led by or dependent on national law? The Canadian commentator cited above rejects the suggestion that the reference to 'free and democratic societies' in section 1 of the Canadian Charter directs judges to engage in a comparative inquiry: 'The [resultant] analysis would be largely descriptive rather than overtly normative. The reasoning attempts to leap from the fact that a state of affairs exists to the inference that this state of affairs is justified. . . . Constitutional argument is normative; it is about what ought to be, not about what is.'[32]

The first point to be made in response to that critique is that the reference to the comparative situation in ECHR judgments is as an evidentiary indication—for example, of a material change in attitudes and values in contemporary European democratic society—not as a determinative legal criterion of liability. The comparative method is not on its own decisive of the content of an ECHR right in the sense either of consistently tying it down to the lowest common denominator in State practice or of imposing on the contracting States as a whole the optimal human rights solution adopted in the most progressive countries. The inherent limits of comparative law as a method for obtaining a universal vision of a given area of law—national rules cannot simply be compared in isolation but have above all to be understood in their local context, in relation to the national legal system concerned and their operation in practice[33]—should prevent its being given any such determinative effect. The comparative method in the ECHR system serves as an evidentiary accompaniment or supporting factor for other interpretative considerations that point to a given meaning.

Secondly, comparative reference back to national law is a means of seeking to identify the present-day contours of the shared European legal principles that inspired the relevant ECHR standard in the first place. The ECHR contributes to the Council of Europe's aim of promoting European unity,[34] in that it establishes an international legal community sharing 'a common heritage of legal traditions, ideals, freedom and the rule of law', to use the words of the ECHR Preamble. As one Continental commentator has put it, the ongoing effect of the ECHR is to create a 'véritable ordre public européen' in the sphere of human rights.[35] In English terms, one would

[32] Monaghan, (n 4) 54–5.

[33] See, eg, C Kropholler 'Comparative Law, Function and Methods' in R Bernhardt (ed) *Encyclopaedia of Public International Law* vol 2, 702 cited in Bernhardt (n 5).

[34] Art 1 of the Statute of the Council of Europe.

[35] W Ganshof van der Meersch 'Réflexions sur les restrictions à l'exercice des droits de l'homme dans la jurisprudence de la Cour européenne de Strasbourg' in R Bernhardt (ed), *Völkerrecht als Rechtsordnung internationale Gerichtsarbeit. Festschrift für Hermann Mosler* (1983). See also Ganshof van der Meersch (n 1) 15.

speak of a European common law of human rights. The ECHR can be taken as creating a more or less homogeneous European legal community with a common ethos in human rights matters. Seen in this way, although engendered by the United Nations Universal Declaration of Human Rights of 1948, the ECHR also represents, legally speaking, the synthesis of the human rights guarantees enacted in the national legislations of the contracting European States. What more natural then, in order to interpret the ECHR in our time, than to obtain an updated synthesis? Of course there is no absolute identity between ECHR law and the sum of the legislations of each contracting State. But since the ECHR is a kind of fusion of national constitutional principles safeguarding human rights in Europe, having regard to the common character—or lack of it—of those legislations is surely legitimate when interpreting the ECHR.

As far as the 'activist' judicial law-making exercise involved in evolutive interpretation is concerned, the anchoring of an evolved meaning to empiral evidence, namely the perceivable changes in the legislative patterns of the contracting States, is a counter to the argument that the Strasbourg judges are trespassing into the Treaty-amendment domain of the contracting States or are simply relying on their own personal sense of justice to make new law. As I have written in another context:

It is probably not enough simply to say that the legitimacy of the judge's decision depends upon the accuracy of the judge's perception of the common will. In order to reduce to a minimum the inevitable element of the judge's looking at society's values through his or her own spectacles, there should be some methodology or evidence upon which the judge can base the stated perception of the common will. The evolving standards in the [ECHR] should be informed by empirical evidence and should not simply be plucked from the sky by the judge.

This recourse to objective evidence the European Court has sought to achieve primarily by means of a comparative approach. As we have seen, in *Marckx* and *Dudgeon* the Court relied on the developments that had occurred in the legislations of the Contracting States in order to discern a unifying pattern of progress which the respondent State had not followed: a common will was discernible on the face of the laws of the community of States adhering to the [ECHR]. In the absence of a degree of consensus as evidenced by a comparative study, there would be a greater risk of the European Court's straying beyond the bounds of its legitimacy were it to impose a progressive interpretation.[36]

As with any legal source, the same comparative law material may well lead different judges to differing conclusions. The judgment delivered in *Odievre v France*, which concerns the entitlement that women have under French law to give birth anonymously ('sous X') if they wish, provides an illustrative example. This case pitted the competing interests of, on the one hand,

[36] Mahoney (n 3) 73–4.

a child given into public care at birth by her mother to have access to information about her origins and, on the other, the mother to keep her identity as the child's mother secret. The Court held, by a majority of ten to seven, that the French system which gave the mother of a child born 'sous X' a right of veto to prevent any disclosure did not amount to a denial of the right to respect of the child's private life (Article 8 ECHR). The majority relied on 'the diversity of practice to be found among the legal systems and traditions [of the contracting States]' so as to conclude that 'the States must be afforded a margin of appreciation' when deciding which particular measures to adopt in order to balance the competing interests.[37] The minority disputed firstly the majority's analysis of comparative law: the minority rather saw a consensus against the French approach, an 'accepted practice in the vast majority of countries' not recognizing an absolute right for the mother to keep her identity secret. Interestingly the minority then went on to castigate the majority for failing to refer to 'the various international instruments that play a decisive role in achieving a consensus and which seek to achieve a balance between competing rights in individual cases'— such as the 1989 International Convention on the Rights of the Child, the 1993 Hague Convention on Protection of Children and Cooperation in respect of Intercountry Adoption, and a Recommendation of 2000 from the Council of Europe's Parliamentary Assembly.[38]

VI. INJECTION OF COMPARATIVE LAW ANALYSIS INTO THE STRASBOURG COURT'S REASONING

A former president of the Strasbourg Court has observed that 'a comparison [of legislative practice throughout the contracting States] is guaranteed at least to some degree by the fact that human-rights organs are usually composed of lawyers from different legal orders, and their different legal experience and knowledge contribute to a measure of comparative analysis'.[39] Nevertheless, the Court itself is not well equipped to carry out detailed comparative law surveys as a matter of course in every suitable case. On the most basic level, the Registry of the Court simply does not have—or, does rather, not yet have—the resources to staff a proper research unit or to provide adequate library facilities with comparative materials. This is why it is in the interests of applicants, particularly in class actions brought on behalf of a whole category of citizens in society, to adduce suffi-

---

[37] *Odièvre v France* [GC], to be published in ECHR 2003 §47.
[38] Loc cit; minority opinion §§12–16.
[39] R Bernhardt 'Thoughts on the Interpretation of Human Rights Treaties' in F Matscher. and H Petzold (eds) *Protecting Human Rights: The European Dimension. Studies in Honour of Gérard Wiarda* (1988) 65, 65–6. See also Bernhardt (n 5)35.

cient evidence not only in respect of the actual operation in the respondent country of some impugned law or practice but also in respect of the comparative position. One should also note the significant contribution made in this respect by 'third parties', primarily non-governmental organizations, intervening under Article 36 §2 ECHR. If only because of the comparative law analyses that third parties regularly put before the Court, the institution of intervention in ECHR proceedings has proved over the years to be extremely useful. A recent illustration of this being the case of *Nikula v Finland* (2002), where the Court took note of the comparative survey compiled by the intervenor, Interights, when holding that the criminal conviction of a lawyer for critical remarks made during a trial violated freedom of expression (Article 10 ECHR).[40]

To use the word 'analysis' in relation to the references to comparative law that one finds in the Strasbourg Court's judgments themselves is perhaps a little exaggerated. Such references are more often than not rather rudimentary. Usually there is no more than one sentence to the effect that examination of the legislations of the contracting States does or does not display 'common European ground'. In the past commentators have criticized the Court for deciding on the basis of superficial or even misleading comparisons of national legal systems. I could well sympathize with the likely feeling of professional comparative lawyers that if something is to be done it should be done properly and not with such broad-brush generality. But we are again back to the problem of the resources that would be necessary to enable a full and reasoned recourse to comparative law in all appropriate cases.

Apart from this somewhat underdeveloped reliance on comparative law in the judgments themselves, the comparative method also has an invisible role in the interpretative process of the ECHR. I do not think I am breaching my duty of confidentiality as an official of the Court to reveal that often, although a brief comparative survey has been before the judges, it is not referred to at all in the judgment. This is because the survey, in the general picture it presents of the contemporary 'standards of justice' (to use the words of Amnesty International in *Soering*) obtaining in the ECHR community in relation to a given problem, does no more than confirm an interpretation already arrived at by the Court on the basis of other considerations.

VII. CONCLUSION

Although it is perhaps a case of butter being spread on bread extremely

---

[40] ECHR 2002–II §§25, 50.

thinly, the case-law of the Strasbourg Court can be seen to display a coherent and consistent approach to recourse to comparative references back to national law. If one accepts the thesis of the ECHR as creating a constantly evolving common law of human rights for Europe derived from shared values and fundamental legal principles, the natural place of the comparative method—in its national aspect—in the ECHR interpretative process of fixing the concrete content of inconclusively worded human rights standards, notably in identifying the presence or absence of common European ground, is evident, at least in theory.

Up until now, mainly for material reasons, that theoretically influential role has not been fully developed, but with the advent of the transfrontier information revolution, with access to national law data banks via the Internet, there is greater scope for exploiting the potential of the comparative method. As an apt conclusion regarding the situation in practice, one can probably do no better than cite the 'simple statement' with which the last president of the former Strasbourg Court, Professor Bernhardt, summarized his own thoughts on the subject: 'More comparative-law research is needed for the interpretation and application of the [ECHR], in spite of the fact that comparative-law considerations constitute only one element in a complex lawmaking process.'[41]

---

[41] Bernhardt (n 5) 39.

PART III

Comparative Law Before Administrative Courts

10

The Use of Comparative Law Before the French Administrative Law Courts

Roger Errera

This chapter will be divided into three sections:

- Section I will present a few general remarks on administrative law and comparative law;
- Section II will provide some information on the place of foreign and comparative law in the publications of the Conseil d'État;
- Section III will contain an overview on the use of comparative law in the decisions of the Conseil d'État and of other French administrative courts.

I. ADMINISTRATIVE LAW AND COMPARATIVE LAW: SOME REFLECTIONS

If we try to assess the place of comparative law in administrative law, one question arises: is there something special about administrative law that might explain why comparative law does not play, in this area, so far, the same role it plays in private law? A few remarks might be in order here.

Many authors (such as Kötz and Zweigert, J Schwarze, R David, and J Bell) explain this lesser role by two facts:

- Administrative law is, in all systems, a much more recent development than private law.
- Practical need for comparative law is less important here than in respect of private law.

That is true. But there is more to it, and three observations might also be useful. The first is an historical one. Exercises in comparative law began very early: when in Germany, Robert von Mohl published, in 1858, his *History of the Sciences of the State,* he devoted nearly 100 pages to French administrative law. Less than forty years later another German author, Otto Mayer, wrote his *Theorie des französischen Verwaltungsrechts.*[1]

---

[1] *Theorie des französischen Verwaltungsrechts. Mit einer Einleitung von Athanasios Gromitsaris* (Strasbourg 1886).

Immediately after its creation in 1869 the Société française de législation comparée heard reports on the reform of the civil service in the United States, and the English law of public works. Laferrière, Duguit, Hauriou, Carré de Malberg and Jèze, the founding fathers of French public law, were very well acquainted with German law. Dicey was translated into French and published in a series edited by Jèze.[2]

The second observation is as follows. During the second half of the nine-teenth century and indeed until at least the Second World War, comparative law was the domain more of law professors than that of the judges and related, it seems, more to legislation than to the case-law, generally speak-ing. Let us not forget that administrative law has nowhere produced the equivalent of the Code civil or of the German BGB, and has long been, and still is mainly, a judge-made law.

The third observation relates to the nature, the very fabric, of adminis-trative law. It relates to the structures of the state and its relationship with its citizens, as shown by the exploration of the meaning of such concepts as those of

- devolution/decentralization/federalism;
- status of civil servants;
- *service public*;
- remedies.

When we compare today, for example English, German, and French admin-istrative law, we cannot properly understand and explain them without introducing a number of non-legal notions: historical, political, ideological, and social, ie the fundamental elements of legal cultures.

II. FOREIGN AND COMPARATIVE LAW IN THE PUBLICATIONS OF THE CONSEIL D'ÉTAT

In addition to its decisions, published in the annual Recueil,[3] the Conseil d'État publishes under its own imprint two kinds of documents. The first is its public annual Report.[4] It contains a review of its activities (both judicial and consultative), of the case-law of the other administrative courts and tribunals and, in addition, a study on a particular theme. The latter was, in

---

[2] See R Errera 'Dicey and French Administrative Law: A Missed Encounter' [1985] Public Law 695.

[3] *Recueil des décisions du Conseil d'État statuant au contentieux, du Tribunal des conflits, des arrêts, des cours administratives d'appel et des jugements des tribunaux administratifs* (Paris Dalloz).

[4] Before 1991 the Report was contained in the yearly *Études et documents du Conseil d'État*, created in 1947. The annual Report has existed since 1963.

the 2001 Report, independent administrative authorities.[5] The second one is composed of special reports on a given subject, undertaken by the Conseil.[6] Both publications contain studies on foreign law and practice as well as comparisons between French and foreign law, by foreign and French contributors.[7] The subjects treated vary from current developments in judicial review in a given country to more specialized monographs.

III. THE USE OF COMPARATIVE LAW IN RECENT DECISIONS OF THE CONSEIL D'ÉTAT AND OTHER ADMINISTRATIVE COURTS

There are several methods to assess the use of comparative law by a given system of courts. One theme would be here an in-depth study of some of the key tools, or instruments of judicial review, showing the influence of other legal systems.

This is what Mr Letourneur, a senior member of the Conseil d'État, began to do in a 1969 essay. He quoted two examples. First, mentioning the use and scope of the general principles of law and especially one of them, *audi alteram partem*, he said that one of its sources could well be what is called in this country the principles of natural justice. The second example is the following one. Commenting on the scope of scrutiny of administrative action by administrative courts, especially when the administration enjoys a degree of discretion, he said that 'what is called in the case law of the Conseil d'État *"erreur manifeste d'appréciation"* (maybe a very distant relative of "unreasonableness"), used since 1961, resembles cases in which the Tribunal fédéral Suisse (Swiss Supreme court) quashed administrative acts on the ground of their arbitrariness'.

However, to detect and assess the existence and the scope of such a use of comparative law would not be easy. The decisions of French administrative courts do not, as a rule, quote other court decisions unless they have to, eg the European Court of Justice's decisions, or ordinary courts' or administrative courts' decisions carrying with them *res judicata* authority. The relevant information can be found, however, in the conclusions of the Commissaire du Gouvernement, frequently published either in the Recueil

---

[5] Other studies were on legal certainty, EC law, decentralization, public services, transparency and secrecy, equality, the law of health, the general interest.

[6] eg *Statut et protection de l'enfant* (La Documentation française (Paris 1991); *Régler autrement les conflits: Conciliation, transaction, arbitrage en matière administrative* (La Documentation française 1993); *Les Pouvoirs de l'administration dans le domaine des sanctions* (La Documentation française 1995); *La Responsabilité pénale des agents publics en cas d'infractions pénales non-intentionnelles* (La Documentaton française 1996; *La Norme internationale en droit français* (La Documentation française 2000).

[7] See their detailed contents in the Annex.

Lebon or in legal journals.[8] What follows is the result of the study of such conclusions, most of them published during the past ten years.

Foreign and comparative law appears to have been mentioned by the Commissaires du Gouvernement in cases relating to four main fields:

- liability;
- aliens' law;
- civil liberties;
- relationship between domestic and international law.

1. Liability

One of the first, if not the first, mention and use of comparative law in the field of liability occurred in 1895. An employee of a State arsenal had been injured and was disabled. There was no fault on either side. In view of his status he was not entitled to a pension. He asked the Ministry of Defence for compensation. He received a small sum as a form of *ex gratia* payment, the Ministry denying liability. He then asked the Conseil d'État for an increase in damages. The Conseil had to determine the legal basis, in the circumstances, of the liability of the State. The Commissaire du Gouvernement, M Romieu, a great name in the history of French administrative law, examined three issues in his conclusions:

- What is, in civil law, the extent of the employer's liability towards the employees in case of an accident?
- What would be the result if the case-law of the civil courts were to be applied to the instant case?
- Should civil law rules apply to the state when workers are employed by it in a public service?

He studied the case-law relating to articles 1382, 1384, and 1170 of the Civil Code and quoted the case-law from Belgium and Luxembourg. He concluded that civil law did not apply and that the State should be held liable, even in the absence of fault. He based his conclusions on the fact that this was a 'service public', on general principles of law, and on fairness. The sum to which the plaintiff was entitled was increased.[9]

Secondly, in another case, the Strasbourg Administrative Court had to decide in 1994 whether the principle of *confiance légitime* (a cousin of legitimate expectations) should apply to the behaviour of the administration and be the basis of its liability in cases of violation. The case related to an

---

[8] Eg Revue française de droit administratif (RFDA), Actualité juridique—Droit administratif (AJDA); Revue du droit public (RDP); Dalloz (D); La Semaine juridique (JCP), etc.

[9] CE 21 June 1895, *Cames* 509 concl Romieu; (1896) 3) D 65 concl Romieu; (1897) 3 S 33 concl Romieu, note Hauriou. See also the comments on the case in *Les Grands Arrêts de la jurisprudence administrative* (14th edn Paris Dalloz 2003) N. 6, 39.

unjustifiably sudden change of regulations. The Commissaire du Gouvernement mentioned, in his conclusions, the law of Germany (*Vertrauensschutz*), Luxembourg, and, of course, the European Court of Justice's case-law. In his view the principle of *confiance légitime* was an application of the general principle of legal certainty. The court followed him, in a very well-reasoned decision.[10] In an article published later the *rapporteur* also mentioned German and Dutch law, among others.[11] The Strasbourg Court decision was not upheld on appeal by the Nancy Administrative Court of Appeal and by the Conseil d'État. To this day the principle of *confiance légitime* applies only in cases relating to EC law.[12] The Conseil Constitutionnel held later that such a principle had no constitutional standing.[13]

Thirdly, the extent of the liability of the State for negligent supervision of banks was the subject of a 2001 decision.[14] The Commissaire du Gouvernement quoted extensively the US, UK, and German law and practices. The Conseil maintained its previous case-law subordinating such a liability to the existence of a grave fault ('faute lourde').[15]

Finally, in medical liability cases—an important and at times a spectacular part of the case-law of the Conseil d'État as well of the Cour de cassation—have also been an occasion for Commissaires du Gouvernement to use comparative law in their conclusions. Here are two recent illustrations:

1. In 1997 the Conseil d'État had to decide the following case: a pregnant woman asked to have an amniocentesis in order to obtain the result of a examination of the foetus cells. The examination did not reveal any anomaly. She then gave birth to a child suffering from Down's Syndrome. The parents asked the administrative courts to compensate their loss. They also acted on behalf of the child. The Conseil d'État held that the hospital had committed a fault in failing to inform the parents that the results of the aforementioned examination could be subject to a significant margin of

---

[10] Tribunal administratif de Strasbourg 8 Dec 1994 *Enterprise Freymuth c Ministre de l'Environnement* AJDA 1995 555 concl Pommier; commented by R Errera [1995] PL 657.

[11] M Heers, 'La Sécurité juridique au droit administratif français: Vers une consécration du principe de confiance légitime?' RFDA 1995 963.

[12] See Conseil d'État 5 Mar 1999 *Rouquette et autres*, 37 concl Maugüé RFDA 1999 357; note D de Béchillon and Terreyre, 372.

[13] CC 30 Dec 1996 No 96-385 Recueil CC 141; CC 7 Nov 1997 No 97-391 OJ 11 Nov 1997 16390.

[14] CE 30 Nov 2001 *Ministre de l'Économie, des Finances et de l'Industrie v Kechichian et al* Les Petites Affiches 7 Feb 2002 No 28 concl Seban; AJDA 2002 136.

[15] See, on this topic, D Fairgrieve and K Belloir 'Liability of the French State for Negligent Supervision of Banks' (1999) 10 European Business Law Review 17. See also M Andenas and D Fairgrieve 'Misfeasance in Public Office, Governmental Liability and European Influences' 51 ICLQ 2002 757 and in D Fairgrieve, M Andenas, and J Bell (eds) *Tort Liability of Public Authorities in Comparative Perspective* (London BIICL 2002).

error.[16] The mother had asked for an amniocentesis while expressing her wish to avoid the birth of an abnormal child, which was a risk given her age (42). She was led, thus, to conclude that her child would be a normal one.

The behaviour of the hospital led the mother not to ask for another amniocentesis, which could have led to a lawful abortion. Such fault was held to be the direct cause of the parents' loss. The Conseil d'État thus held the hospital responsible and ordered it to pay damages to the parents during the life of the child. In her conclusions the Commissaire du Gouvernement quoted the English and American case-law on wrongful life.

2. What should doctors do when a hospital patient refuses to undergo treatment necessary for his survival? Is the hospital liable if they perform the treatment without his consent? Mrs S's case, decided by the Conseil d'État in 2001, was as follows. Her husband, a Jehovah's Witness, was admitted in a critical state to a hospital. He had earlier explicitly refused, under any circumstance, to have a blood transfusion. While in bed he reiterated this refusal. When his condition worsened, the doctors nevertheless performed a blood transfusion. He died. His widow asked the courts for the compensation of her husband's moral loss. On appeal, the Conseil d'État held that, in view of S's medical condition, the physicians attending him had chosen, their only aim being to save him, to perform an act that was both indispensable for his survival and in proportion with his state. Notwithstanding the obligation to respect the patient's will, they did not commit a fault leading to the liability of the Paris Hospitals Administration. His widow's claim was rejected before both the Paris Administrative Court[17] and the Conseil d'État.[18] The two Commissaires du Gouvernement quoted English, US, and Canadian case-law. So did some of the commentators.[19] Another similar case was also decided by the Conseil d'État, but it was not a liability case and there was no Commissaire du Gouvernement.[20]

In contrast, on two earlier occasions concerning the important issues of medical liability, that of the state arising from infected blood transfusions[21]

---

[16] CE 14 Feb 1997 *Centre Hospitalier régional de Nice*, commented by R Errera [1997] PL 349, concl Pécresse; RFDA 1997 374 concl Pécresse and note Mathieu; AJDA 1997 430 note Chauvaux–Girardot; JCP 1997 II 22828, note Moreau; RDP 1997 113, notes Waline and Auby.

[17] Paris Administrative Court of Appeal 9 June 1998 *Mme S* RFDA 1998 1231 concl Heers; Les Petites Affiches 23 Apr 1999 No 81, 10 note Memeteau; D 1999 227 note Pellissier.

[18] CE 26 Oct 2001 *S*; AJDA 2002 259 note Deguergue; RFDA 2002 155 note de Béchillon; RTDC 2002 484; Droit de la famille 2002 53 note Frier; Les Petites Affiches 15 Jan 2002 No 11, 18 note Clement; PL 2002 comment by R Errera 579.

[19] Eg Memeteau and Pellissier (n 17).

[20] CE 16 Aug 2002 *Mme F*; see PL 2002 comments by R Errera and *Gazette du Palais* 15–17 Sept 2002 Nos 258–60 note Pausier.

[21] CE 9 Apr 1999 MD, 111, conc. Legal; D 1993 312; RFDA 1993 583; JCP 1993 344 note Maugüé and Touvet.

and that of hospitals on no-fault liability in certain cases,[22] the Commissaire du Gouvernement did not use comparative law.

2. Aliens' Law

Several extradition cases have led the Commissaires du Gouvernement to quote and use comparative law in their conclusions in respect of three issues.

First, the law and practice of other European countries when extradition is requested by a State in cases when the death penalty applies to the offence.[23] The Commissaire du Gouvernement quoted German, Italian, Austrian, Danish, Swiss, and English law and practice.

Secondly, the standing of a foreign government to ask the Conseil d'État to quash a refusal of extradition.[24] The relevant foreign law and practice was mentioned.

Thirdly, the law and practice in California in relation to the death penalty were also mentioned by the Commissaire du Gouvernement in another extradition case.[25]

Finally, in a refugee case the Commissaire du Gouvernement used foreign law on the granting of refugee status to the family of the refugee.[26]

3. Civil Liberties

Civil liberties seem to be a field that lends itself readily to the use of comparative law, as shown by a number of examples.

In a case concerning media law and decided in 1999[27] the Conseil d'État had to decide whether a 1977 statute prohibiting the publication of electoral polls two weeks before an election was consistent with Article 10 of the European Convention of Human Rights. The answer was in the affirmative. The Commissaire du Gouvernement quoted the law of a number of European countries (Portugal, Germany, Italy, Greece, Ireland, Austria, The Netherlands, Denmark, and Britain).

---

[22] CE 9 Apr 1993 *Bianchi*, 127 concl Daël; RFDA 1993 573; JCP 1993 II 22061 note Moreau; RDP 1993 1099 note Paillet; commented by R Errera [1993] PL 537.

[23] CE 15 Oct 1993 *Mme Aylor*, 283 concl Vigouroux; RFDA 1993 1166; AJDA 1993 848; commented by R Errera [1994] PL 137.

[24] *Royaume–Uni. de Grande-Bretagne et d'Irlande du Nord et gouverneur de la Colonie royale de Hong Kong* CE 15 Oct 1993, 268 concl Vigouroux; RFDA 1993 1179; RUDH 1994 217; commented by R Errera [1994] PL 139.

[25] CE 6 Nov 2000 *Nivette* concl de Silva RFDA 2001 103.

[26] CE 2 Dec 1994 *Mme Agyepong*, 523 concl Denis-Linton; RFDA 1995 86; commented by R Errera [1995] PL 182.

[27] CE 2 June 1999 *Meyet*, 161; LPA 8 June 1999 No 113 11 concl Bonichot; AJDA 1999 560 note Raynaud and Fombeur; LPA 11 Oct 1999 No 202, 10 note Desfougères.

The issue of human dignity, a notion of constitutional standing under French law, was central to an important case decided in 1995.[28] The Commissaire du Gouvernement mentioned US law.

Judicial review of disciplinary measures taken against prisoners and military personnel was affirmed by the Conseil d'État in 1995.[29] The Commissaire du Gouvernement quoted English and German law.

The legal status of the Jehovah's Witnesses Association, in particular its right to receive donations was the issue at stake in a 1985 case.[30] The Commissaire du Gouvernement quoted American law.

Important issues of bioethics decided in the 1990s led the Commissaire du Gouvernement to discuss and use foreign law. First, in a 1990 decision, the issue was the compatibility of the 1975 French statute allowing abortion under certain conditions with Article 6 of the International Covenant on Civil and Political Rights and Article 2 of the European Convention for the Protection of Human Rights and Fundamental Freedoms concerning the right to life.[31] The Commissaire du Gouvernement examined the constitutional case-law in Germany, the United States, Austria, Italy, Norway, Portugal, Spain, and Canada. The answer was in the affirmative, in view of the contents of the statute. Secondly, a case decided in 1993 raised important issues relating to experiments performed on a dead patient by a physician without any scientific necessity and previous consent. The disciplinary measures taken against him were upheld.[32] The Commissaire du Gouvernement quoted international medical and legal literature on the criteria of death.

4. *The Relationship Between Domestic and International Law*

In three cases decided in the 1990s comparative law was explored in the conclusions of the Commissaire du Gouvernement.

The first one related to the role of international custom. The Conseil d'État held that, unlike treaties under Article 55 of the Constitution, inter-

---

[28] CE 27 Oct 1995 *Commune de Morsang sur Orge*, 372 concl Frydman; commented by R Errera [1996] PL 166. RFDA 1995.1204; D 1995. 878 note Lebreton; LPP 24 Jan, 1996, 28 note Rouault; JCP 1996 II 123, note Ronault; AJDA 1995 878 note Stahl and Chauvaux.

[29] CE 17 Feb 1995 *Hardouin; Marie*, 82, concl Frydman; RFDA 1995.353; commented by R Errera [1995] PL 331. AJDA 1995 379 note Touvet and Stahl; D 1995 381 note Belloubet-Frier; JCP 1995 II 22426 note Lascombe and Bernard; RDP 1995 1338 note Gohin; LPA 28 Apr 1995, 11 note Vlachos; 9 June 1995, 16 note Nguyen Van Tuong.

[30] CE 1 Feb 1985 *Association Chrétienne les Témoins de Jéhovah de France*, 22; RDP 1986 483 concl Delon note Robert; RFDA 1985 566 note Soler Couteaux.

[31] CE 21 Dec 1990 *Confédération Nationale des Associations Familiales Catholiques et autres*, 368 concl Stirn; RFDA 1990 1065; AJDA 1991 91, note CM FD and YA.

[32] CE 2 July 1993 *Milhaud*, 194 concl Kessler; RFDA 1993 1002; Droit sanitaire et social 1994 52; AJDA 530 note Maugüé and Touvet; JCP 1993 II 22133 note Genod; D 1994 74 note Peyrical; commented by R Errera [1994] PL 140.

national custom did not take precedence over statutes.[33] The Commissaire du Gouvernement quoted the law and practice in the United States and in other European countries.

In 1990 the Conseil d'État decided to abandon its previous practice under which, whenever a question of interpretation of a treaty arose, the matter was referred to the Ministry of Foreign Affairs, the views of which were followed.[34] Subsequently, the European Court of Human Rights found that practice incompatible with Article 6(1) of the Convention.[35]

In 1998 the Conseil d'État had to decide whether judicial review could occur in respect of the decisions of the competent authorities under Article 53 of the French Constitution, under which the treaties listed in that Article can be ratified or approved only by a statute and come into force only after such approval and ratification. The answer was in the affirmative. The Commissaire du Gouvernement mentioned the German and Italian constitutional case-law, which allows the Constitutional court to declare a treaty unconstitutional and quoted monographs analysing the law of these countries.

Comparative law has thus been used by the administrative courts in a variety of spheres. On the other hand, it would seem that foreign and comparative law plays very little or no part at all in areas such as tax law, civil service law, planning, and public procurement.

IV. CONCLUSION

A few words to conclude. The first point is that the European perspective is paramount. In view of the European Court of Human Rights and of the ECJ, of the profound influence of their case-law and of the use of comparative law both in Luxembourg and in Strasbourg, which is the subject of other chapters in this book,[36] it can be safely said that they are an important, if an indirect, source of influence of comparative law for French administrative courts. Moreover, the transformation of the Brussels I and II Conventions into EC regulations, together with the case-law of the European Court of Justice on the Brussels Conventions, will lead domestic courts to enforce more easily foreign judgments in civil and commercial matters leading them to be more and more familiar with foreign law.

---

[33] CE 6 June 1997 *Aquarone*, 206 concl Bachelier; RFDA 1997 1068; AJDA 1997 570 note Chauvaux and Girardot; JCP 1997 II 22945 note Teboul; RGDIP 1997 1954 note Alland; LPA 6 Feb, 1998, 18; JDI 1998 93 note Châmes; commented by R Errera [1997] PL 560.

[34] CE 29 June 1990 *GISTI*, 171 concl Abraham; RFDA 1990 923 note Lachaume; RDP 1990 1579 note Sabiani; JDI. 1990 965 note Julien-Laferrière; JCP 1990 II 21579 note Tercinet; D 1990. 560, note Sabourin; RCDIP 1991.61, note Lagarde.

[35] 24 Nov 1994 *Beaumartin v France*.

[36] Cf Lenaerts and Mahoney Chs 8 and 9.

Secondly, it might be too early, if not presumptuous, to assess which areas of administrative law will be those more influenced by the use of comparative law. I do not think to be much off the mark if I mention the scope of judicial review, the liability of the administration, the scope of legal certainty, civil liberties, and the role of international law. International meetings and comparative studies in these areas would be most welcome.

Inside the EU today the words 'cross-fertilization', 'harmonization of legislation', and '*ius commune*' are widely used by lawyers wherever they meet and discuss issues of comparative law. Whether this is the dawn of a new legal culture remains to be seen, but a new approach, a new frame of mind, is perceptible. Professor P Legrand wrote some time ago: 'L'Europe [est] devenue un paradis pour le comparatiste.'[37] Whether the judges, and especially administrative law judges, have a small plot of their own in that paradise, or whether they still linger in purgatory, is an open question.

ANNEX

As regards the annual Reports since 1991:

1991 Report. The study on legal certainty ('La sécurité juridique') mentions English law (p 17). The Report contains essays by J Bell 'Actualité du droit administratif au Royaume-Uni' 309; S Flogaïtis, 'Le Développement du droit administratif en Grèce' 321; GH Kemper 'Le Pouvoir du juge dans le contentieux administratif allemand' 329; H Mora Osejo 'La Juridiction du contentieux administratif en Colombie' 341.

1992 Report. The study on EC law mentions civil service law in other countries (pp 59 and 63). The Report contains essays by F Delpérée 'Le droit administratif en Belgique' 349; A Photiou 'La Juridiction administrative et le contrôle de la légalité des actes administratifs à Chypre' 363; H Mora Osejo 'Quelques aspects de la jurisprudence du Conseil d'État colombien en 1992' 369; S Flogaïtis, ' Systèmes de Sécurité sociales et Constitution hellénique' 375; J Bell 'Actualité du droit administratif au Royaume-Uni en 1992' 383.

1993 Report. The study on decentralization and legal order does not mention foreign countries. The Report contains essays by P. Pierry Arrau 'Le Contentieux administratif au Chili' 467; A Gil Roblès 'Le Respect de la égalité pour les autorités locales en Espagne: Le role du Défenseur du peuple' 475; G Bermann and P Lindseth 'L'Évolution du droit administratif américain' 483; J Bell 'Actualité du droit administratif au Royaume-Uni' 495; V Toumanov 'Russie: L'ancien et le nouveau dans le contrôle de la légalité des actes de l'Etat' 507; E Palm 'Décentralisation et ordre juridique en Suède' 517.

---

[37] P Legrand 'Comparer' in *Le Droit comparé aujourd'hui et demain* (Centre français de droit comparé Paris 1996), 24. In fact Legrand criticizes and even derides the view according to which, inside the EU, Europe would be a paradise for comparatists, in view of the interpretations between domestic and EU law.

1994 Report. The study 'Public Services: Decline or Renewal?' mentions the law in other European countries in the text (at 51, 91, 104 ff) as well as US law (at 91) and in the Annexe (at 130 ff). The Report contains essays by G Bermann and P Lindseth 'Réflexions sur le droit administratif aux États-Unis' 515; S Cassese 'La justice administrative en Italie: Perspective de réformes' 545; D Gebara-Khoury 'Le Contróle juridictionnel de l'administration au Liban' 553; B Knapp 'Quelques problèmes de la juridiction administrative en Suisse' 577; and J Bell 'Actualité du droit administratif au Royaume-Uni' 561.

1995 Report. The study 'Transparency and Secrecy' does not mention foreign law, which is to be regretted. The Report contains essays by J Bell 'Actualité du droit administratif au Royaume-Uni' 552; F Delpérée 'La Constitution et le Conseil d'État en Belgique' 573; GH Kemper 'Droit de la défense et "rechtichliches Gehör" devant l'administration et les tribunaux administratifs allemands' 591; P Effendie Lotulung 'Le Développement du contentieux administratif en matière fiscale en Indonésie', 601; A Mokry 'Juridictions administratives en République Tchèque' 605.

1996 Report. The study on the principle of equality mentions US law (at 69, 70; see nn 178, 201, 202, 205; at 109 n 345), quoting such authors as M Walzer, R Dworkin, and J Rawls, and German law (at 88 n 261 and at 92 n 278). It contains essays by L Favoreu 'Principe d'égalité et représentation politique des femmes: La France et les exemples étrangers' 395; O Jouanjan 'L'Égalité dans la jurisprudence constitutionnelle allemande' 411; F Delpérée 'L'Égalité en droit public belge' 431; T Font i Llovet 'La Conception et l'application du principe d'égalité en Espagne' 441; A Pizzorusso 'le Principe d'égalité dans la doctrine et la jurisprudence italienne' 451.

1998 Report. The study on the law of health does not mention foreign law. The Report contains an essay by M Rosenfeld 'L'Aide au suicide en droit américain' 379.

1999 Report. The study on the general interest does not mention foreign law. The Report does not contain essays on foreign law.

2000 Report. The study on the law of associations mentions foreign law (at 256, 261, 265 ff). The Report does not include essays on foreign law.

2001 Report The study on administrative independent authorities mentions foreign law (at 270–2, 281–4). The Report includes essays, on the same topic, by J Bell 401 and M Bentancor-Rodriguez 411.

11

The Use of Comparative Law Before the Italian Public Law Courts

Aldo Sandulli

I. THE RELEVANCE OF COMPARATIVE LAW DURING A
DECISION'S PREPARATION AND THE DIFFICULTIES OF
EVALUATING ITS ROLE CONCRETELY

What part does comparative law play in the Italian public law courts? This is a question that is not easy to answer. How important for Licurgus were the journeys to Crete, Asia, and Egypt documented by Plutarch? Or the study of the laws in the other Greek cities for Solon, *kállista nomothetēsai* ('author of the finest laws')? It is difficult to establish the boundaries between exogenous contributions and an endogenous capacity for creation.

What is certain is that foreign models have always had a part in the construction of national legal systems. Such systems thrive on comparisons between analogies and differences. They evolve through a process of cross-fertilization, forming conceptual models on a comparative basis by drawing analogies but also by noting contrasts.

The evolution of the English and French models provides the most significant example of this process. It has been demonstrated that these two European legal archetypes (considered irreconcilable on account of the idealization and radicalization effected by Dicey and Hauriou) have developed through a process of reciprocal contamination and transplantation. This has brought them so close to one another and has made the borderline between common law and civil law so difficult to identify that one wonders whether it is more a case of convergence in different contexts or one of differences in similar contexts.

Returning to the original question, comparative law appears to have had a significant influence on the Italian public law courts in the past and to be even more relevant today.

The problem that anyone studying this subject faces is the difficulty of documenting this role concretely. This is because recourse to comparative law for the purposes of reaching a decision has a conditioning effect both on the judge's preliminary investigation and hearing, but it does not always have (indeed, only very rarely has) an express impact on the decision. It is not rendered explicit in the text of the judgment and frequently remains hovering just out of sight. Sometimes, therefore, it has a decisive influence because it constitutes the element inspiring the decision but is one that nevertheless remains shadowy—in the realm of the unsaid—and must be traced by inductive reasoning.

Then there is the fact that very frequently the influence comparative law exerts is a derived one, having passed through the filter of the legislator or legal theory. The present analysis is obviously only concerned with the second category.

This chapter is divided into three sections. Section II takes a brief look at the links with organizations through which the Italian public law courts build relations with corresponding European bodies for the purpose of discovering new solutions to common problems. Section III proposes to highlight comparative law's historical relevance to the administrative judge's goal of developing both principles of administration and forms of judicial protection for the citizen vis-à-vis the administration. Section IV examines the considerable opening to comparative law brought about recently by the increasing relevance of Community law. Such analysis will include examples of the influence comparative law has exercised on the national administrative judge's work and certain conclusions will be drawn.

II. THE LINKS WITH ORGANIZATIONS THROUGH WHICH COMPARATIVE LAW MAY SURFACE IN THE ITALIAN PUBLIC LAW COURTS

The increasing relevance the Italian public law courts attach to comparative law may also be deduced from their close links with other organizations and the frequent cultural exchanges that they arrange with the corresponding courts in other European countries.

The Italian Constitutional Court runs a Research Unit which has an office specially dedicated to in-depth studies in the field of comparative constitutional law. Through this office the Court studies other models of constitutional justice and the solutions adopted in other countries in relation to the main common problems. An example of the careful monitoring of other systems can be found in the five volumes developed in September and October 1992 on the principle of reasonableness, following which the Constitutional Court carried out an even more penetrating examination of the reasonableness of legislation. Furthermore, the Court hosts judges from superior appellate jurisdictions in other countries and foreign university lecturers in public law for periods of research and cultural exchange.

The Council of State, the supreme organ of administrative justice, is equally active at the level of international relations. The need for a knowledge of the other systems of administrative justice is evidenced by the fact that it was precisely the Italian Council of State which promoted the foundation of the Association of the Councils of State and Supreme Administrative Jurisdictions of the European union, approximately fifteen years ago. The organizations belonging to the association meet every two years to discuss methods they have discovered for solving common problems and those concerning the application of Community law in the Member States, in particular. For example, at the end of a meeting taking place at the beginning of the 1990s, a decalogue of the principles common to the various systems of administrative justice was developed. Moreover, Italian administrative judges maintain relations of a scientific nature with their French, Spanish, and German counterparts through special associations that periodically organize bilateral conferences.

This intense activity aimed at learning about other experiences and comparing them with their own reality demonstrates how, at least recently, the Italian public law courts have opened up to models from other countries. It does not demonstrate, however, that the migration of ideas has resulted in comparative law operating a concrete influence, since that can only be demonstrated by analysing decisions of the courts. It is thus on such an analysis that we must dwell.

To such an end I will focus on the administrative judge's activity, since it seems most interesting to reconstruct the historical developments that have accompanied the evolution of administrative justice. There are two reasons for this.

On the one hand, contrary to Jean Rivero's assertions (that administrative laws are more open than other laws to syncretisms and a certain type of ecumenism that transcends nations and closed systems), Italian administrative law has always been considered the branch of the law least lending itself to comparison on account of its typically national stamp. Administrative judges' receptiveness to comparative law thus assumes a particular significance.

The other reason is that even if the Constitutional Court's function (as the constitutional check on the legality of laws) has made it more constantly open to the influence of comparative law, this attention appears much less explicitly in its decisions. As I said earlier, through its Research Unit the Court carries out careful comparative studies on the most important issues. The problem is that the results of these studies very rarely appear in the text of a judgment, even if they end up influencing the decision (sometimes quite significantly). This is by virtue of a clear choice made by the Constitutional Court aimed at claiming full decisional autonomy while bearing the sum total of the solutions offered by comparative law fully in mind.

III. DEVELOPMENTS IN ITALIAN PUBLIC LAW SINCE JUDGES HAVE
STARTED DRAWING LEGAL COMPARISONS

Legal theory and the Orlandian school,[1] in particular, have played a fundamental part in the construction of Italian administrative law. It must, however, be recognized that the general principles of administration and judicial protection of the citizen vis-à-vis the administration have been established in Italy precisely by virtue of the influence comparative law has had on administrative courts' decisions.

Among the fields to choose from, the judicial protection of citizens' rights and liberties must doubtless be pinpointed. In contrast to the developments in substantive law (in relation to which reasoning followed domestic lines for long periods), a greater interest in comparative law has marked the methods employed in the field of judicial safeguards against oppressive state practices. Activity dedicated to developing suitable procedural safeguards is characterized by a widespread communality of problems constituting a fertile ground of inquiry for comparative law. Thus, at least under this profile, comparative law seems to have had a not indifferent role as regards the activities of the national public law courts and the administrative judge in particular.

At the end of the nineteenth century (the Council of State's Fourth Division, covering litigation, was founded in 1889) administrative court decisions were heavily conditioned by two influences. On the one hand, they were affected by German legal theory (particularly by Otto Mayer's theses, which had made their appearance in Italy primarily through Vittorio Emanuele Orlando's studies) and, consequently, by a Hegelian metaphysical concept of the State. On the other, the French model of judicial protection and, in particular, its typical and original character inherited from the French Conseil d'État (the creative force of praetorian decisions developing rules and principles by integrating and completing a positive datum) also left its mark.

In this context, the interpretation of the ground of review of abuse of power constitutes a decisive step forward for constructing principles of administration. Following the guidance of the French experience, Italian administrative judges have understood abuse of power as a *détournement de pouvoir*, ie as a misuse of power rather than an overflow or excess (from the French *empiément de pouvoir*), which is how the legislator appears to have understood it. The consequences for the limits of administrative judicial review have been extremely important, since judges have found themselves able to carry out judicial review of the exercise of discretionary

---

[1] Vittorio Emanuele Orlando (1860–1952) and his students, Santi Romano (1875–1946), Federico Cammeo (1872–1940), and Oreste Ranelletti (1868–1956), above all.

power. It is from this initial orientation, inspired by the experience of the Conseil d'État, that the more than century-old evolution of judicial review descends. Even if the Italian Council of State distanced itself right from the beginning of the twentieth century from the route taken by its French counterpart, it preserved and still preserves the French model's original inspiration as part of its own genetic heritage.

During the middle decades of the twentieth century the decisions of the courts saw comparative references lessen as they evolved along autonomous lines of development. At the height of the Fascist period and during the 1930s in particular, the courts' decisions became the administrative system's centre of gravity for two main reasons. On the one hand, they carried out the task of counterbalancing the administration by protecting the sphere safeguarding citizens' rights and, on the other, they substituted legal theory in the role of constructing administrative law. During the second post-war period, as the law reacquired its supremacy in the wake of Kelsen's theories, the return to normativism and to an Enlightenment faith in legislation (conceived as the pre-eminent source of law) reduced the judge's role to that of executing legislation. Thus, from 1920 to 1980 a distancing, or rather, a gradual isolation, of Italian administrative courts' decisions may be recorded in relation to the lines of development in corresponding European courts. During this period Italian judges followed autarchic courses that were not influenced externally if not through isolated studies of legal theory in foreign models which gradually found their way into the orientation of the courts' decisions. In this respect we must remember the contribution made by one of the greatest twentieth-century Italian administrative lawyers, Massimo Severo Giannini. His work has allowed an understanding of how fundamental it was to see national administrative law in a comparative light.

During the 1980s Italian administrative courts' decisions maintained a closed attitude despite the fact that Community law was acquiring increasing importance. If first instance judges (the Regional Administrative Court in Lombardy, in particular) demonstrated a greater sensitivity towards the *acquis communautaire*, the Council of State was extremely wary of opening the national system's doors to Community law. Suffice it to say that the Council of State made its first Preliminary Reference to the European Court of Justice in 1991. A sudden change of trend occurred at the beginning of the 1990s when the Council of State first recognized, with the *Fratelli Costanzo* case,[2] the direct effect of Community legislation at a national level and subsequently gradually took the Court of Justice's guidelines into account.

---

[2] Council of State Vth Section 6 Apr 1991 No 452 in G Pasquini and A Sandulli (eds) *Le grandi decisioni del Consiglio di Stato* (Milano Giuffrè 2001) 571.

The close tie established between the Court of Justice and national administrative judges in recent years has fuelled a renewed interest in comparative law on the part of Italian judges. As is known, the Court of Justice has developed a series of legal principles, drawing its inspiration from the 'better law' criterion, ie by choosing from among the solutions accepted in each member state the one considered most appropriate and compatible with the Community system.

Community law has, moreover, revealed itself to be an exceptional point of convergence for common law and civil law models. If, in fact, the comparative perspective for continental European legal systems was, if anything, oriented towards the Franco-German dimension during the middle period of the twentieth century, it has also turned in the direction of common law models in recent years. The mutual exchange has led the civil law systems to attach less importance to the authority of unilateral legal regimes and the common law systems to attribute increasing importance to the fact that administrative action is carried out in pursuit of the public interest.

Increasing reciprocal contamination between models of administration has led to the assertion that 'the domestic approach to administrative law that went unopposed during the last century appears inadequate today, in the face of trends differing in origin and nature but converging univocally upon meeting points between the major systems that allow significant merits for comparison'.[3]

Cases in which principles and institutions deriving from other European countries have been introduced into the national system through judges' pronouncements have clearly multiplied during the last decade. This is primarily by virtue of the process of European integration and the greater attention legal theory has paid to foreign systems.

Thus, through the vehicular function of Community law and the filter of legal theory, national administrative judges have reopened the doors to comparative law. They have done this, however, in a manner that is one stage removed, only using comparative law directly in very rare circumstances.

With the aim of demonstrating this last statement, it appears appropriate to look at some of the examples considered to be most significant for the purposes of the present investigation.

IV. SOME EXAMPLES OF HOW THE ITALIAN ADMINISTRATIVE
COURTS HAVE USED COMPARATIVE LAW

The process of cross-breeding between legal systems can occur through

---

[3] MP Chiti 'Diritto amministrativo comparato' in *Digesto: Discipline pubblicistiche* (Torino Utet 1990) vol 5, 206.

court decisions in one of three ways: through the direct or indirect influence of Community law, through the spread of knowledge via legal theory, or following a transplant deriving from an autonomous urge on the part of the courts. The first two possibilities occur more frequently.

There are cases in which a principle or institution developed in other European systems has made its appearance in Italy through the 'better law' filter applied by Community judges. An all but analogous analysis goes for the vehicular function of the European Court of Human Rights and the influence of its decisions on national decisions, in both the constitutional and the administrative courts.

The principle of proportionality constitutes the most significant example for the Italian system. As is known, such principle had its birth in Germany (*Verhältnismässigkeitsprinzip*), spreading first to the other German-speaking systems and then to France (*contrôle de la proportionnalité de l'acte*), before being acknowledged finally by the European Court of Justice. The process of Community integration has acted in such a way that, through Community judges' decisions, the principle has been applied by national judges in countries where it still had not been recognized as a general legal principle. England and Italy are two such countries.

The Italian and English stories are very similar, despite the differences between their judicial review systems. In both orders the introduction of the principle of proportionality has led to a far more extensive judicial review of the exercise of discretionary power than in the past.

The evolutionary process leading to the principle's recognition has been long and tortuous for both legal systems. The argument by which the courts and a branch of legal theory excluded the application of the principle of proportionality from domestic law for more than a decade is also common to both: judges meddling with the executive's exercise of discretionary power would lead to the judiciary taking the place of public authorities in choosing the solutions to be adopted.

Both in Italy and in England, before the supervisory jurisdiction introduced by proportionality, judicial review of administrative action was limited to verifying the reasonableness of the action. The latter implies a qualitative assessment inherent in balancing the interests involved. Proportionality, as is known, requires the administration to adopt the solution that is appropriate and commensurate and causes the least possible sacrifice of interests simultaneously present. In such a way, judicial review has been extended to a quantitative examination of the right measure of administrative power exercised by public authorities.

Italian administrative judges' definitive recognition of the principle of proportionality is very recent. It dates to just three years ago. There had already been pronouncements that had applied the principle either expressly or, more frequently, implicitly. But it was in the *SEA Aeroporti di*

Milano case[4] that the Council of State, adopting an orientation expressed by the Regional Administrative Court in Lombardy, weighed up respect for the principle of proportionality as far as suitability, necessity, and proportionality in the strict sense were concerned. This it did under the guidance of methods developed by the German public law courts and assimilated by the European Court of Justice. The principle was then applied to so many decisions of the courts (one meriting mention is that made in the *Enel Trade* case)[5] that it may now be considered a fully acknowledged general principle of administrative law.

There are numerous cases where comparative law has made an impact through the filter of Community law. Some of the most important ones are to be noted for the way they have introduced the notion of bodies governed by public law into the Italian order when applying Community legislation.

As is known, the requirements outlined by Community law for identifying a body governed by public law have been formulated by mingling elements of Community law with components typical of the French legal system.[6] In particular, the requirement of 'needs of a general interest of a non-industrial and non-commercial nature' is derived from the combination of the concept of 'needs of a general interest' (which has a European circulation) and that of 'an industrial and commercial nature', which is typical of the French system. Only if one interprets the second part of the phrase as bearing the typical meaning applied in France after the Second World War is it possible to understand that only the legal persons operating in the direct interests of the collective whole, without seeking profit, can be deemed a body governed by public law.

From among the pronouncements made by Italian administrative judges regarding bodies governed by public law, the case of the *Casa Religiosa della Compagnia di Gesù*[7] merits a mention. Here a private ecclesiastical body that had received public funding to restore a work of art was held to be subject to the public law rules governing public tenders.

In other cases it is the filtering action of legal theory, rather than Community influence, that has been decisive.

The *Enel Trade* case just quoted and the earlier *Spirito* case[8] represent

---

[4] Council of State VIth Section 1 Apr 2000 No 1885 [2000] Rivista italiana di diritto pubblico comunitario 439.

[5] Council of State VIth Section 1 Oct 2002 No 5156 <http://www.giustizia_amministra-tiva.it>.

[6] See, in particular, the *arrêt Monpeurt*, Conseil d'État, 31 july 1942 [1942] Recueil J 138. See also C Eisenmann 'L'arrêt Monpeurt: Légende et réalité' in *Études en l'honneur d'Achille Mestre* (Paris) 221 ff.

[7] Council of State Vth Section 7 June 1999 No 295 [1999] Giornale di diritto amministrativo 1057.

[8] Council of State IVth Section 9 Apr 1999 No 601 [1999] Giornale di diritto amministrativo 1179.

valid examples both of the Council of State's different sensitivity towards comparative law and of the fact that very often the latter's influence is of a derived rather than a direct nature.

The two judgments are significant for our purposes because they make use of indeterminate legal concepts (*umbestimmte Rechtsbegriffe*) likewise developed from German law in order to solve an issue regarding the degree to which the actions of the Italian Antitrust Authority are challengeable. More precisely, the Council of State has established (in the *Enel Trade* case) that complex technical assessments (ie those where the moment of technical assessment and a careful consideration of the public interest appear fused and blurred) involve the evaluation of a series of factual elements that are the fruit of inexact and debatable sciences (of a prevalently economic nature). These, it has held, may be used to define indeterminate legal concepts (such as, in the case in point, those of the relevant market, a dominant position, and anti-competitive agreements). This leads to the impossibility of effecting a 'strong' judicial review of complex technical assessments processed by the Antitrust Authority: only a 'weak' judicial review is possible, with the judge ending up substituting the Authority's debatable assessment with his own, equally debatable one. On the other hand the possibility of carrying out judicial review (albeit a weak one) of complex assessments has been recognized as important because it allows a distinction to be drawn between technical discretionary power (reviewable within certain parameters) and the administrative merits which, entailing an examination of opportuneness, are never reviewable.

The arrival of these ideas from the German legal system is attributable not to trends in court decisions, however, but rather to studies carried out by academics during the last twenty years and to a book written in 1995 by Daria de Pretis, in particular.[9] This work faced the issue and solved it precisely through an analysis of the German experience.

As I said earlier, it is only very rarely that an administrative judge has direct recourse to comparative law.

The *Borrelli* case[10] offers us a significant example. Here the Council of State was analysing the provisions that introduced exclusive jurisdiction for administrative judges in relation to public utilities (Article 33 of Legislative Decree No 80/1998, reproduced with slight amendments as Article 7 of Law No 205/2000, reforming administrative trial procedure). It interpreted such law as introducing into the national legal system the criterion of jurisdictional allocation adopted in the French order and based on the concept of '*service public*'. As a consequence, the legislator would have employed a

---

[9] D de Pretis *Valutazioni amministrative e discrezionalità tecnica* (Padova Cedam 1995).

[10] Council of State adunanza plenaria 30th Mar 2000 No 1 [2002] Giornale di diritto amministrativo 576.

broader notion of 'public utility service' than hitherto recognized in the Italian order: therefore, the provision would refer directly to the use the French order makes of the concept rather than those other uses already applied within the Italian system. Recourse to the French concept of *service public* is instrumentally useful to the administrative judge for asserting his own exclusive jurisdiction over all activity carried out in pursuit of the collective interest and exercised through channels that do not constitute public authorities, ie without making use of *puissance publique*. Therefore, rather than the legal nature of the person or entity initiating the act, it is the activity (of whatever type) linked to the protection of collective interests that assumes significance, whether it is carried out by public or private persons. In this sense, one could also state that the choice was dictated by a desire to draw inspiration from the German model by attributing to the administrative judge all cases involving administration (understood in the Community—and therefore broad—sense of the term). Thus, the administrative judge's plenary jurisdiction has seen its boundaries greatly expand at the expense of the ordinary judge, who, not without reason, has demonstrated perplexity at the administrative judge's interpretation of the legislation.[11] The concept of *service public* has therefore brought about a genuine regulation of the jurisdictional boundary lines between ordinary judges and administrative ones. The point of particular interest in the case in question is that reference was made to a concept of *service public* that, by now, differs from that currently in force in France, finding its theoretical reference in the works of Léon Duguit and Gaston Jèze as well as Charles Eisenmann's subsequent studies.[12] In this way, whereas in France the general allocation of jurisdiction has been substituted by an allocation based on *blocs de compétence* precisely by virtue of a crisis regarding the concept of *service public*, in Italy a genuine general jurisdictional allocation has been introduced in the guise of a *bloc de compétence*.

V. CONCLUSIONS

A somewhat contradictory overall picture results from what I have been saying. On the one hand, one can still perceive a sort of cultural gap that is revealed in judges' and barristers' lack of familiarity in handling concrete issues in the light of general principles, seeking possible solutions by referring to institutions existing in other legal systems. The leaning is still

---

[11] Corte di Cassazione sezioni unite 30 Mar 2000 No 72 [2000] *Corriere giuridico* 592. See also Corte di Cassazione sezioni unite 12 Nov 2001 No 14032.

[12] L Duguit *Transformations du droit public* (Paris Colin 1913); G Jèze *Principes généraux du droit administrative* (3rd edn Paris 1925); C Eisenmann *Cours de droit administratif* vol 1 *Cours de 1951–1952* (Paris LGDJ 1982) 21 ff.

towards a hand-made, domestic product. The Italian barrister well knows that a judge remains more impressed by the citation of one of his own precedents than by a reference to a case decided in another legal system.

On the other hand, there is no doubt that the number of enlightened judges looking with great interest over the domestic hedge is increasing. This is due, in great part, to the process of cross-breeding determined by the direct and indirect influence of Community law.

The acknowledgement of foreign experiences through the mediation of both the said law and the decisions of the Court of Justice and the European Court of Human Rights has allowed a corpus of fundamental principles that are common to the various European orders to be identified. This is a phenomenon that is in expansion and now irreversible.

However, it is the influence of Community law rather than the use of comparative law that one perceives in such cases. When comparative law penetrates the national system through the filter of Community law, the former ends up remaining in the background while the latter takes the lime-light. Essentially, a sort of innovation takes place by which the principle or institution becomes part of the national system not so much as an expression of foreign law as a source of Community law.

There is no doubt, in any case, that the Italian public law courts' use of comparative law is becoming increasingly important even if the latter's role often remains hidden. The Constitutional Court has been using comparative law steadily for some time now, even if its judgments do not reveal the complex in-depth studies made of other countries' experiences. Administrative court decisions, traditionally anchored to a domestic approach, are increasingly expressly applying principles and institutions from other legal systems.

On the other hand, the cases examined earlier constitute examples of inter-family comparison, concerning the French system in the majority of cases or, at most, the German one. It could therefore seem that, in accordance with Pierre Legrand's famous comments on *la mentalité*, the Italian courts look at civil law regimes only in rare cases and never at all at common law ones.

In reality, there are evolutionary tendencies of a more general nature that are moving towards a point of convergence for systems. These are the expression not only of judges' orientations but also of those of the legislator and academic opinion, and they constitute the foundations of the slow but steady changes in course made by legal systems.

The most significant of these tendencies concerns the gradual spread of a hybrid (public–private) law following, on the one hand, the privatization of public corporations and, on the other, private law's penetration of public law in the civil law countries and an awareness of the split between public law and private law in the common law countries. With regard to the affirmation of such general trends, the national courts are called to make their contribution, often by applying Community and national sources of law. Thus, in this case too, there is a mediated comparative influence, with the trend in courts' decisions acting not as a driving force but as the application of a positive datum.

Nevertheless, the transformations currently under way thanks to the spread of hybrid law represent a favourable opportunity for the Italian public law courts further to open up the system of judicial protection to the stimulus of comparative law.

And yet the administrative reforms occurring in Italy during the last fifteen years seem to be proceeding precisely in this direction: from Law No 241/1990, on administrative procedure (which has apparently narrowed the gap between the administration and the citizen and has favoured the spread of contracts in pursuit of the public interest), to Law No 205/2000, on administrative court proceedings, introducing 'unlimited jurisdiction' proceedings and giving the administrative judge the power to protect citizens by awarding compensation for damage.[13]

Here, too, one can perceive how the civil law and common law models are drawing closer together as they rediscover the basis of a common feeling. In the era of Dicey and Hauriou the questions asked related to what constituted the most effective form of judicial protection: an *annullamento* (an order similar to that of *certiorari*), typical of administrative law, or damages, typical of private law. The fact that the Italian administrative judge has been vested with the authority to make both types of order is symptomatic of the unstoppable process of convergence the two legal models are undergoing.

An example of this may be found in some of the recent judgments of the Regional Administrative Court in Lombardy. Interpreting the new law governing administrative court procedure in an evolutionary sense, these judgments enforced performance in relation to the administration by obliging the latter to perform an act defined by the judge. This in the wake of all that has been hoped for by legal theory (and by Mario Nigro and Fabio Merusi, in particular[14]) and along the lines of the German *Verpflichtungsklage* in the Continental orders and of judicial review's prerogative remedy of mandatory order in the Anglo-Saxon ones.

---

[13] Administrative judges' powers were previously limited to making orders quashing administrative actions. It was therefore formerly necessary to bring a second, separate action for damages which would be heard by an ordinary judge.

[14] Nigro 'L'esecuzione delle sentenze di condanna della pubblica amministrazione' in G Miele (ed) *La giustizia amministrativa* (Neri Pozza Vicenza 1968) 167 ff; F Merusi 'Verso un'azione di adempimento?', in *Scritti in onore di Giovanni Miele* (Milano Giuffrè 1979) 337; id '*L'ingiustizia' amministrativa in Italia*' in [1988] Rassegna parlamentare 15–16.

BIBLIOGRAPHY

Bell, JS 'Mechanisms for Cross-Fertilisation of Administrative Law in Europe' in J Beatson and T Tridimas (eds) *New Directions in European Public Law* (Oxford Hart Publishing 1998).

Caranta, R *Giustizia amministrativa e diritto comunitario* (Napoli Jovene 1992).

Cassese, S 'Problemi delle ideologie dei giudici' (1969) 2 Rivista trimestrale di diritto e procedura civile 139.

—— 'Lo studio comparato del diritto amministrativo in Italia' [1989] Rivista trimestrale di diritto pubblico 678.

—— 'Grandezza e insuccessi del giudice amministrativo italiano', in *Scritti in onore di Giuseppe Guarino* (Padova Cedam 1998) vol 1.

—— 'La costruzione del diritto amministrativo', in Cassese (ed) *Trattato di diritto amministrativo: Diritto amministrativo generale* (Milago Giuffrè 2000) vol 1.

—— 'Il Consiglio di Stato come creatore di diritto e come amministratore' in G Pasquini and A Sandulli (eds) *Le grandi decisioni del Consiglio di Stato* (Giuffrè, 2001).

Chiti, MP 'Diritto amministrativo comparato', in *Digesto: Discipline pubblicistiche* (Torino Utet 1990) vol 5.

—— 'I signori del diritto comunitario: la Corte di giustizia e lo sviluppo del diritto amministrativo europeo' [1991] Rivista trimestrale di diritto pubblico 796.

D'Alberti, M *Diritto amministrativo comparato: Trasformazioni dei sistemi amministrativi in Francia, Gran Bretagna, Stati Uniti e Italia* (Bologna Il Mulino 1992).

—— and Pajno A 'Il giudice amministrativo tra tutela giurisdizionale e creazione giurisprudenziale' in M Bessone (ed) *Diritto giurisprudenziale* (Torino Giappichelli 1996).

De Pretis, D *Valutazione amministrativa e discrezionalità tecnica* (Padove Cedam 1995).

Gorla, G 'Diritto comparato' in *Enciclopedia del diritto* (Milano Giuffrè 1964) vol 12.

—— 'Diritto comparato e diritto comune europeo* (Milano Giuffrè 1981).

—— 'Diritto comparato e diritto straniero', in *Enciclopedia giuridica* (Roma Treccani 1989) vol 11.

Koopmans, T 'Comparative Law and the Courts' [1996] ICLQ 545.

Legrand, P 'Comparer' [1996] Revue international de droit compare 279 et seq.

—— 'European Legal Systems Are Not Converging' [1996] ICLQ 52.

Merryman, JH 'The Italian Style III: Interpretation' (1966) 18(3) Stanford L Rev 605.

Merusi, F 'Sullo sviluppo giurisprudenziale del diritto amministrativo italiano', in *Legge, giudici, politica: Le esperienze italiana ed inglese a confronto* (Milano Giuffrè 1983).

Pizzorusso, A 'La comparazione giuridica e il diritto pubblico', in *L'apporto della comparazione alla scienza giuridica* (Milano Giuffré 1980).

—— *Corso di diritto comparato* (Milano Giuffrè 1983).

Sacco, R *Introduzione al diritto comparato* (Torino Giappichelli 1990) vol 4.

Sordi, B '*Uno sguardo all'Europa: Il legislatore del 1889 di fronte ai modelli continentali di giustizia amministrativa*' in Consiglio di Stato *Studi per il centenario della Quarta sexione* (Roma Ipzs 1989).

Torchia, L 'Diritto amministrativo nazionale e diritto comunitario: Sviluppi recenti del processo di ibridazione' [1997] *Rivista italiana di diritto pubblico comunitario* 845.

PART IV

Comparative Law Before General Courts

12

The Use of Comparative Law Before the French Private Law Courts

Guy Canivet

I. INTRODUCTION

As globalization increasingly exposes us to problems that transcend national boundaries and legal systems, it seems that the importance of the judiciary is clearly increasing. In our advanced democracies there is a general demand for judicial intervention to solve serious social problems. In whichever legal system he belongs, be it common law or civil law, one of the judge's main roles is to adapt the law to the evolutions of society. The great changes of our times take the form, as we all know, of a vertiginous scientific and technological progress and of the speeding-up of trade globalization. All these phenomena deeply call into question the economic, social, and cultural equilibrium of a country and challenge its system of values.[1]

The specific role of the judge is to accompany these changes by laying down the framework inside which they will produce their effects. There clearly is a bipolarity in the exercise of the judicial function. A first pole of fluidity is represented by scientific and technological progress. This pole is matched by a second pole of stability, represented by society's foundational values. The judge is always guided by the protection of social values. His task is to create constantly a bridge between the law and the values of the society in which he lives, both with the means of his own legal culture and with the aid of comparative law.

In this chapter, I would like to argue that the use of comparative law is essential to the fulfilment of a supreme court's role in a modern democracy. I will use the example of the court I am heading, the French Cour de cassation, which is the supreme court on civil and criminal affairs in my country. In Section II I will try to lay down the theoretical framework that can help us account for and assess a supreme court's role in the preservation of social values in an ever-changing world. In

---

[1] See generally W Twining *Globalisation and Legal Theory* (London Butterworths 2000).

Section III I will try to analyse the importance of comparative law in this enterprise by giving some examples from the Cour de cassation's practice. My working hypothesis is that comparative law is not ornamental, a favorite pastime for Olympian judges isolated in their ivory tower; on the contrary, it is becoming more and more important, both for the resolution of conflicts and for the protection of democratic values by the judiciary.

II. THE PROTECTION OF SOCIAL VALUES BY A SUPREME COURT

As we all know, the opening of the courtroom to scientific progress and innovation is one of the main factors of development of new case-law. New trends in scientific evidence, like genetic expertise, inevitably widen the horizon of the judge by inducing creative legal reasoning.[2] But this reasoning cannot do without legal protection and adjustment of social values. For it is obvious that globalization increasingly exposes the judge to systems of thought and to cultures that transcend national borders. And since the judge assumes an ever widening role in the resolution of social conflicts, he is destined to tackle head-on the legal problems spurred by the process of globalization. Even though the task is novel, he has all the prerequisites of success.

The French private law judge is no longer—if he ever really was—considered as the 'mouth that produces the words of the law' (in the famous words of Montesquieu).[3] He is commissioned to adjust the law to the values of his society. In this task he might find of use his own legal culture, of course, but also comparative law. Anyway, local and foreign legal cultures constantly interact. The judge must, by necessity, maintain the coherence and integrity of a full-blown legal system by relentlessly referring to the abiding features of his own law and legal culture. But no legal culture is exclusively inward-looking; it can favour, at least in the long run, the emergence of a common law for a specified legal region without denying, for that reason, national identities and traditions.

The law does not just regulate social relations. It also reflects widely shared social values. The judge understands his society's law as a coherent ensemble that evolves together with a social reality in perpetual motion. This

---

[2] This point was first made by a great American judge, Benjamin Cardozo. See his famous lecture *The Nature of the Judicial Process* (New Haven Conn Yale University Press 1921) and also BN Cardozo *The Paradoxes of Legal Science* (1928, Westport Conn Greenwood Press 1970) 10–11.

[3] Charles de Secondat, baron de Montesquieu *The Spirit of Laws* introd, notes, and apps DW Carrithers (1750 Berkeley University of California Press 1977) 209.

is clearly the case in common law countries. Their legal systems encapsulate several centuries of flexible responsiveness of the law to social changes. But this is also the case in civil law countries like mine, where the courts complete and give meaning to legislative changes through their work of interpretation.

How does the judge preserve widely shared values by assimilating social changes? The judge's work cannot be conceived under the model of revolution or of discontinuity. Every judgment must maintain the normative coherence of his legal system by implementing its fundamental values. The courts of a country, especially the high courts, must integrate every judicial decision in a narrative that gives voice to its legal traditions. Every judge must, in a sense, contribute to the 'chain novel' of law that is constantly being written, according to the celebrated analogy of legal philosopher Ronald Dworkin.[4]

The judge cannot but strive after a certain consistency and constancy of the law, hostile to any disruption or jolt. The basis of justification for his action is not political will, which is an essentially capricious thing, but argumentative transparency and honesty. The judge is not permitted to propel transformations on his own instigation. In common law countries this idea takes the form of the rule of *stare decisis*, which requires that all distinctions of a judicial precedent be expressly founded on a convincing argument.[5] In civil law countries like France, this idea is mostly expressed as the requirement that every reversal in case-law follow a change in the spirit of legislation. Even in the domains where transformations are speedy (like bioethics), the structure of the fundamental principles and values the judge has to protect always gives a certain stability to legal change.[6]

Other factors play also a role in this tendency towards a more evolutionary than revolutionary change in case-law. The judge never has the initiative of change; he inevitably depends on the petition submitting a case to the court. Thus, the judge does not have the means of promoting a political agenda, since the changes in law he can induce are, after all, limited and interstitial. Only the political branches can master the mass of data that is necessary to global decision-making and can mobilize

---

[4] R Dworkin *Law's Empire* (Cambridge Mass Belknap Press 1986) 229.

[5] See generally R Cross and JW Harris, *Precedent in English Law* (4th edn Oxford Clarendon Press 1991) and N MacCormick and RS Summers (eds), *Interpreting Precedents: A Comparative Study* (Brookfield Vt Aldershot 1997).

[6] On the judge's role as collaborator of the legislator in statutory interpretation, see generally WD Popkin *Statutes in Court: The History and Theory of Statutory Interpretation* (Durham NC 1999). Professor William N Eskridge Jr exposes powerfully the idea of a hermeneutic back-and-forth process between social values and statutory law in his book *Dynamic Statutory Interpretation* (Cambridge Mass Harvard University Press 1994).

institutions in order to obtain desired results.[7] Lastly, even judicial interpretations that are creative and dynamic are always dependent on the
perception and the legitimate expectations of the legal community and of
the public at large. The settled expectations and the reliance of jurists
and of citizens who read judicial opinions do not permit the judge to
overstep his boundaries in the name of experimentation or of innovative
interpretation. Judges dispose of a legitimacy capital they should not
manage in the short run.[8]

One can resumé the preceding developments by saying that a main task
of a supreme court is to stabilize legal norms by seeking consistency and by
implementing incremental changes in the law. Two concepts are instrumental in the judge's effort to maintain this pole of stability: 'fundamental principles' and 'human rights'. These concepts provide the ground for judicial
innovation—including the use of comparative law—because they express
the principles of political morality that underlie the law and tie it down to
societal values.[9]

Fundamental principles—or foundational values—of law underlie and
justify the legal rules of a given society. Without their 'gravitational force'
(according to Dworkin's expression)[10] legal rules would be atomized and
would coagulate in a heap of precepts lacking any internal coherence.
Fundamental principles are the reason why the texture of the law is open
but by no means discontinuous.[11] They are the normative background
against which legal texts will be interpreted and enforced. In other words,
fundamental principles give meaning and restrain at the same time any legal

---

[7] These data are so-called 'legislative facts' that are gathered and processed on a wide scale
by the legislative branch in order to invent a new policy or to reshape an institution; they are
to be distinguished from 'adjudicative facts', which are the facts necessary for the resolution
of a concrete case or controversy before a court. On this distinction, see eg KL Karst
'Legislative Facts in Constitutional Litigation' (1960) Supreme Court Rev 75 and HP
Monagha, 'Constitutional Fact Review' (1985) 85 Columbia L Rev 229.

[8] American sociology of law has been insisting on this point; see G Rosenberg *The Hollow
Hope: Can Courts Bring About Social Change?* (University of Chicago Press 1991). Cf MDA
Freeman 'Standards of Adjudication, Judicial Law-Making and Prospective Overruling' (1973)
26 Current Legal Problems 166, 181: 'To understand the judicial role and apprise the legitimacy of judicial creativity one must explore the shared expectations which define the role of
the judge.'

[9] For the notion of 'public values' expounded by the law, see CR Sunstein *The Partial
Constitution* (Cambridge Mass Harvard University Press 1993). The legal philosopher Ronald
Dworkin uses the term 'political morality' to express the same idea; see R Dworkin *Taking
Rights Seriously* (Duckworth London 1977) and *A Matter of Principle* (Cambridge Mass
Harvard University Press 1985).

[10] Dworkin 1977 (n 9) 26–7. William Eskridge builds on that notion by writing that 'public
values have a gravitational force that varies according to their source . . . and the degree of our
historical and contemporary commitment to these values' (WN Eskridge Jr 'Public Values in
Statutory Interpretation' (1989) 137 U Pa L Rev 1007, 1018).

[11] On the 'open texture of the law', see HLA Hart *The Concept of Law* (Oxford Clarendon
Press 1961) 121–32.

change, because they attach positive law to a certain number of values that shape the public morality of a country. Thus, any influence comparative law has on national practice is necessarily mediated by the domestic legal system's fundamental principles.

For our purposes, it is important to acknowledge at this point the dual nature of fundamental legal principles. Fundamental principles are at the same time aspirational[12] and instrumental; they express the objectives of a legal system and the means that system uses to achieve them. A fundamental principle such as due process of law (or adjudicative fairness), for example, simultaneously expresses an ideal of society and a body of technical legal rules apt to approximate to this ideal. Thus, any comparison of a domestic legal system or institution with a foreign one necessarily passes through the filter of the fundamental principles of the former.[13] Moreover, fundamental principles run the whole spectrum from grand principles (such as substantive justice or fair treatment) to social standards of behaviour (such as the 'reasonable man' or the 'good faith' standards in tort and contract law, respectively). They thus help us place the legal concepts or institutions we want to compare at the proper level of generality, which is not always the same between differing legal systems.[14]

Human rights made a staggering appearance on the scene in the wake of the Second World War. They were integrated in the post-war constitutions and undoubtedly became the horizon of Western democracies.[15] Respect for human rights nowadays condition every economic or social policy. The dynamic character of human rights is the result of the fact that they sometimes put a brake on, and sometimes accelerate, changes. If we take the example of human dignity, which is the matrix of all human rights, one cannot but acknowledge its role as a double-edged knife: sometimes, for example as regards human cloning, human dignity is used as the last moral bastion against possible transgressions of the human species' intrinsic qualities; sometimes, for example as regards the rights of the disabled, human

---

[12] The expression is Lon Fuller's; see LL Fuller *The Morality of Law* (New Haven Conn Yale University Press 1964) 5–19, 41–4.

[13] As I will try to show in Sect III.

[14] It is only by understanding the functionality of a principle in a given legal system that we can assess the similarity between two principles of a different pedigree. Thus, a comparative law research permits us to understand that the principles of 'good faith' in civil law systems and of 'reasonableness' in common law systems share the same function; cf R Brownsword NJ Hird and G Howells (eds) *Good Faith in Contract: Concept and Context* (Brookfield Vt Aldershot 1999) with American Law Institute *Restatement (Second) of Contract* (American Law Institute Publishers St. Paul, Minn 1981). §204 (Washington, DC 17 May 1979).

[15] See L Henki *The Age of Rights* (New York Columbia University Press 1990) and CR Epp *The Rights Revolution: Lawyers, Activists, and Supreme Courts in Comparative Perspective* (University of Chicago Press 1998).

dignity is used as a catalyst for consciousness-raising and for acceptance of the problem by the society.[16]

Accordingly, fundamental principles of law and human rights partake in the reception and assimilation of worldwide legal changes by judges, by stepping sometimes on the accelerator, sometimes on the brake. In any case, they give judges a normative structure without which there can be no opening up of legal systems to foreign influences. In front of an increasing large tendency to harmonize or unify individual legal systems, French private law judges remain sensitive to those cultural differences that are characteristic of their legal traditions. But these traditions, entrenched as they may be, are surely not impermeable to other perspectives or other methods of reasoning.[17]

That is the reason why a reflection on the accommodation of foreign concepts and institutions by a legal system—in short, a reflection on comparative law—is in order. If we look at the development of comparative law, we will see that some of the most important advances have resulted from 'cross-fertilization' between different legal systems, and that comparison enables the existence of 'a strong measure of objective neutrality and critical self-assessment'.[18] The increasing consciousness by national legislators of the value of comparative law has materialized, for instance, in the creation of the English and Scottish Law Commissions. These bodies inquire into the function of legal principles and the framework within which they operate.[19] To do this, they try to ascertain whether a specific legal rule or institution has been successful in achieving what it has set out to do. The point I want to make in Section III is based on that idea. In brief,

---

[16] The literature on the principle of human dignity and bioethics has, as is well known, acquired very big dimensions, even though this principle became central to the common law legal cultures only quite recently. To the contrary, the recent history of tyranny in a country like Germany permanently shaped its legal culture; suffice it to observe that the German Constitution starts by recognizing the inalienable character of human dignity. See notably MJ Meyer and WA Parent (eds) *The Constitution of Rights: Human Dignity and American Values* (Ithaca NY Cornell University Press 1992) and EJ Eberl, *Dignity and Liberty: Constitutional Visions in Germany and the United States* (Westport Con Praeger 2002). In French, see notably B Maurer *Le Principe de respect de la dignité humaine et la Convention européenne des droits de l'homme* preface Frédéric Sudre (Paris La Documentation française 1999).

[17] One should be mindful that there is a doctrinal controversy on whether legal systems actually converge or not. Professor Basil Markesinis, for instance, thinks that there is no doubt that a convergence is taking place (see Bl Markesinis (ed) *The Gradual Convergence* (Oxford Clarendon Press 1994)), whereas Professor Pierre Legrand is of the opinion that legal cultures do not really converge, even though contingent legal rules do tend to become uniform in some areas of law (P Legrand 'European Legal Systems Are Not Converging' (1996) 45 ICLQ 59).

[18] P de Cruz *Comparative Law in a Changing World* (1995 London Cavendish Publishing 1999) 17.

[19] The two Law Commissions are the children of the British Law Commissions Act, Section 3(1)(f), enacted in 1965.

I will try to show that the utility of comparative law research by a domestic supreme court lies not so much in empirical comparison between rules as in the inspiration from the *interpretative methodology* foreign supreme courts use in order to ascertain whether a rule has successfully fulfilled its function.

III. THE IMPORTANCE OF COMPARATIVE LAW IN THE PRACTICE OF THE COUR DE CASSATION

The status of comparative law varies according to the specific traditions of each legal culture. There are cultures that are more hospitable to foreign law and others that are more provincial. The Supreme Court of Canada, for instance, is particularly open to legal experiences stemming from other countries, especially Anglophone common law countries. On the other hand, the Supreme Court of the United States is more reticent about this type of argument, even though some recent decisions[20] show a certain opening up because of their discussion of the international parameters of certain controversial issues.[21]

In France the Cour de cassation is structurally inhibited because of its traditional style of writing, which makes no mention of precedents in the body of the decision that refer to foreign law.[22] A hasty reader of the Court's case-law would reach the conclusion that comparative law is of no significance whatsoever and that the Court lacks judicial techniques to incorporate foreign legal sources. This is certainly not true, as I will try to show in this section. But first, let me elaborate on the importance of comparative law for a supreme court judge's task to preserve social values in a changing world.[23]

---

[20] Notably *Atkins v Virginia* 536 US 304 (2002) on the death penalty, and *Lawrence v Texas* (26 June 2003) on sodomy laws, where Justice Kennedy's opinion for the Court explicitly mentioned the 1981 European Court of Human Rights case *Dudgeon v United Kingdom*.

[21] A retired judge of the Supreme Court of Canada, Claire L'Heureux-Dubé, criticizes the United States Supreme Court's provincialism in her article 'The Importance of Dialogue: Globalization, the Rehnquist Court and Human Rights' in MH Belsky (ed) *The Rehnquist Court: A Retrospective* (New York Oxford University Press 2002) 234. Paradoxically, the US Supreme Court's relative closure to international and comparative law does not deter foreign courts from being inspired by that court's interpretation of the US Constitution; see eg A Lester 'The Overseas Trade in the American Bill of Rights' (1988) 88 Columbia L Rev 537.

[22] On the French Cour de cassation's style of judicial writing, see M de SO-l'E Lasser 'Judicial (Self-)Portraits: Judicial Discourse in the French Legal System' (1995) 104 Yale LJ 1325.

[23] The use of comparative law by the courts is discussed in Uh Drobnig and S van Erp (eds) *The Use of Comparative Law by Courts* 14th International Congress of Comparative Law Athens 1997 (The Hague Kluwer Law International 1999) and by Professor HP Glenn in two important recent works: *Legal Traditions of the World: Sustainable Diversity in Law* (Oxford University Press 2000) and 'Comparative Law and Legal Practice: On Removing the Borders' (2001) 75 Tulane L Rev 977.

What are the uses a national judge can make of comparative law? We can start by stating the obvious, that is that comparison with other legal cultures unquestionably enlarges the judge's horizon. Comparative law multiplies the available viewpoints and interpretative options. With globalization, different national institutions are increasingly called to treat the same kinds of legal problem. Therefore, to the extent that similarities exist between legal values, the judge can better fulfil his role because of the enhancement of his stock of possibilities. But at a deeper level we can see that many fundamental principles underpinning a legal system are common between democratic societies. It is only natural that legal comparison can reveal those options by bringing them out into the open.[24]

The structure of comparison is always more complicated than a simple lining up of rules or institutions coming from different countries. We should not simply compare individual legal solutions on this or that problem; we should also examine the failures and successes of these solutions vis-à-vis the fundamental principles of the legal system in question. In other words, comparative law is always useful for the local judge because it makes him understand the coherence between a judicial precedent and a body of fundamental principles that underlie a legal system. Thus, the judge will be better equipped to perform this work of harmonization in his own legal system.

If two legal systems share basic cultural features, it should be possible to use comparative law as a source of inspiration for the judge's task of interpreting written law. The judge can learn a lot from foreign constitutions or statutes about the aims pursued by another legal system and about the arrangement of legal means with a view to obtaining these aims.[25] Once more, the utility of the comparison does not consist so much in the alignment of concrete legal solutions as in the interpretative methodology, that is, in the way a legal culture approaches a problem and arranges the means it has at its disposal in order to resolve it. The judge will not be so much influenced by concrete legal solutions found in another legal system; he will be mostly influenced by this hermeneutic back-and-forth between the specific or general goals of a legal rule or institution and the practical solu-

---

[24] This distinction is inspired by the fundamental distinction between 'microcomparison' (comparison between topics or institutions of two or more legal systems) and 'macrocomparison' (comparison between two or more entire legal systems) made by K Zweigert and H Kötz *Introduction to Comparative Law* trans T Weir (2nd edn Oxford Clarendon Press 1987) vol 1, 4–5, who draw on M Rheinstein 'Comparative Law: Its Functions, Methods, and Usages' (1968) 22 Arkansas L Rev and Bar Association J 415.

[25] For a discussion of the range of comparative law methodologies in the constitutional law context, see M Tushnet 'The Possibilities of Comparative Constitutional Law' (1999) 108 Yale LJ 1225, and more recently VC Jackson and M Tushnet (eds) *Defining the Field of Comparative Constitutional Law* foreword WH Rehnquist (Oxford Praeger 2002).

tions that foreign judges have conceived in order to pursue those goals. The judge will, in the end, be inspired more by the mechanisms of interpretative decoding he will find in a legal culture that is not his own than by ready-made solutions he can easily discover by simply consulting legal text-books.[26]

The interpretative inspiration from comparative law can easily be ascertained from the Cour de cassation's application of international law, especially of the European Convention for the Protection of Human Rights and Fundamental Freedoms (ECHR) of 4 November 1950. Like any other court in Europe, the Cour de cassation is bound to apply this supranational law, which has a binding force superior to French domestic law.[27] The Court achieves this by referring to the respective case-law and methods of this supranational legal order.[28] It thus continuously incorporates in the French legal order legal principles rooted in a different legal system. Since the ECHR enshrines basic democratic and liberal values that the French legal order shares, it is only natural that the country's supreme civil and criminal court will be heavily influenced in its own case-law by the interpretative methodology of the Strasbourg judges. In short, the normative overlap between two integrated legal orders (such as the French legal order and the ECHR or the European Community law) obviously stimulates a comparative law reasoning on the part of the domestic judge.

Hence, the Cour de cassation has by now become familiarized with the comparative law methodology via its normative commitment to the European legal order. We must not be oblivious to the fact that European legal integration, together with the first signs of an emergent European legal culture, not only results from authoritarian black-letter unification, but also involves gradual internalization of common values by each of the national legal systems. At least as far as European Community law and the law of the European Convention on Human Rights are concerned, harmonization is not necessarily the result of imposed uniformity.[29] It is not always the

---

[26] In an important article Professor George P Fletcher explores the implications of this interpretative function of comparative law; see his 'Comparative Law as a Subversive Discipline' (1998) 46 AJCL 683.

[27] According to Art 55 of the French Constitution of 1958.

[28] There are many examples of the Cour de cassation's referring openly to the case-law of the European Court of Human Rights; see eg the decisions Cour de cassation Chambre commerciale *Rey c directeur général des Impôts* [2002] *Bulletin civil* IV No 124, 113, and *Barbet, Ruth et Société Auchan c Conseil National de l'Ordre des Pharmaciens* Chambre criminelle 10 Jan 2001 (unpub). These references are quite impressive if we keep in mind the French courts' traditional refusal to cite judicial precedents in their decisions.

[29] This is obvious enough from the European Court of Human Rights (*en banc*) case *Open Door and Dublin Well Woman v Ireland* of 29 Oct 1992. In that case the Strasbourg Court declared contrary to the ECHR a ban on advertisement and counselling for Irish women who wished to travel abroad to have an abortion (which remains illegal in their country). There was no effort by the Court to enact a unified substantive law on abortion rights throughout the

impact of European law on the content of given national rules that is important. Harmonization may also—albeit more exceptionally—be the effect of
a spontaneous, incremental growth towards common perspectives and
standpoints. It is important for French judges to discover signs evidencing
the progressive development of a specifically European way of looking at
things. This certainly is the point where comparative law is most useful.

However, even if European human rights law does not open up a space
for legal uniformity, the dynamics of the European Convention on Human
Rights is such that citizens and judges in States that share more or less similar cultures and enjoy a similar level of economic development are less and
less prone to accept that situations raising the same issues of fact yield
different results because of the difference in the legal rules to be applied.
There is a trend towards, one might even say a strong demand for, compatible solutions being reached, regardless of the differences in the underlying
applicable rules of law. This is true, for example, in the field of privacy law.
The recent *Fretté v France* case,[30] in which the European Court of Human
Rights declared that the denial by the French legislation of the right of
homosexuals to adopt children does not contravene the Convention, cast
lawyers and public opinion into disarray. One can legitimately ask what
justifies the existence here of different legal rules between countries having
common cultural values and recognizing the concept of human dignity as
pre-eminent.

This example shows that, in European countries at least, the judiciary
needs to follow a step-by-step approach in order to develop a specifically
European legal culture in at least some highly important moral issues that
are treated by law. The first thing a domestic supreme court like the Cour
de cassation will need to do is to discover the solutions given by other
supreme courts to hard cases. In the French judicial system, which conceives
of justice as a 'public service', no court can address itself to a legal expert
or 'special master' for the ascertainment of a legal solution, since the determination of questions of a legal nature cannot be delegated to a third
party.[31] Interestingly, this procedural impossibility opened up the way to a
new technique akin to the *amicus curiæ* in the common law legal systems.[32]

Member States of the ECHR; rather, the effort of the Court was to balance the individuals'
right to information with the national States' value system, and it did this by applying the
'proportionality' standard, which proved fatal to the Irish legislation.

[30] *Fretté v France* case of the European Court of Human Rights (3rd section) 26 May 2002.

[31] The possibility of appointing special masters is, on the contrary, specifically provided for
in the United States; see Federal Rule of Civil Procedure 53(b).

[32] On the *amicus curiae* in common law countries, see the report by AB Aikman ME Elsner
and FG Miller *Friends of the Court: Lawyers as Supplemental Judicial Resources* (National
Center for State Courts Williamsburg Va 1987), as well as the recent monograph by IR Brodie
Friends of the Court: The Privileging of Interest Group Litigants in Canada (Albany State
University of New York Press 2002).

The Cour de cassation has twice resorted to this technique. It asked the French Comparative Law Institute to issue a research report, the first time regarding a case of wrongful birth,[33] and the second time regarding the possible conviction for manslaughter of a person who had caused a miscarriage in a car accident he was responsible for.[34] These reports were then notified to the parties and to the *Ministère public* (the public prosecutor's office at the Cour de cassation) for use in their briefs before the Court. In those two cases the research undertaken was not limited to technical aspects of foreign positive law, but included an analysis of the legal, economic, and cultural context inside which similar cases were decided by judges in the foreign countries in question. The admittance of comprehensive and relevant studies enabled the Cour de cassation to open up its deliberations to comparative legal methodology.

Even though this trend is gaining importance in the Cour de cassation's practice, it is by no means a novel one. We must not forget that, like their common law colleagues, civil law judges and lawyers have always worked within a transnational judicial culture.[35] Supreme courts in common law jurisdictions enjoy a long tradition of working with reference to the English legal system and to the case-law of its senior courts. It is, therefore, for them quite natural to base their decisions on common law precedents and to be attentive to the evolution of the common law in each of the systems that partake of the same working methods, judicial precedents, legal sources, and legal practices. Consequently, it is not infrequent for the supreme courts of English-speaking countries to make explicit references in their opinions to one another's case-law.[36] This link is easier to make, of course, because judicial opinions stem from the same origin in the common law and are written in the same language. There is also easy access to the case reports of the Anglophone countries' supreme courts, so that judicial opinions are readily accessed, read, and adapted to the domestic stream of precedents.

---

[33] The famous case *Perruche* of the Cour de cassation, Assemblée plénièr, 17 Nov 2000 (2001) Dalloz 332 note Denis Mazeaud and Patrice Jourdain.

[34] *Procureur général près la cour d'appel de Metz* case of the Cour de cassation, Assemblée plénière 29 June 2001 (2001) Dalloz 2916 (2001), note Yves Mayaud.

[35] Professor Slaughter has recently argued forcefully for the existence of a 'transjudicial communication'; see inter alia A-M Slaughter 'Judicial Globalization' (2000) 40 Virginia J Intl Law 1103 and 'A Typology of Transjudicial Communication' (1994) 20 University of Richmond L Rev 99.

[36] Of course, this does not mean that there is an uncritical acceptance of each and any precedent coming from a foreign Anglo-American supreme court. The best example, in that regard, is the attitude Canadian courts have towards US case-law: 'While it is natural and even desirable for Canadian courts to refer to American constitutional jurisprudence in seeking to elucidate the meaning of Charter guarantees that have counterparts in the United States Constitution, they should be wary of drawing too ready a parallel between constitutions born to different countries in different ages and in very different circumstances' (*Rahey v The Queen* [1987] 1 SCR 588, 639).

Civil law countries, even though they do not share this common historical and linguistic background that cements their belonging to a common
legal culture, did face a similar movement in the beginning of the nineteenth
century. But the particularity of this movement is that it revolved around
the historical phenomenon of codification. With the enactment of the
Napoleon Civil Code in 1804 and its adoption by many States during the
nineteenth century, a host of countries engaged in a common interpretation
of this Code, as expounded by their courts. Of course, this trend came to
an end long ago with the abandonment of these first French-inspired Civil
Codes, which had been revised or overhauled, or had undergone such
changes that common references became irrelevant.

If we take the example of two neighbouring countries that share many
historical and cultural traditions, namely France and Belgium, we can still
observe—albeit rarely—cross-references to judicial decisions of their
respective Cours de cassation. Of course, since (as we saw) these courts
never cite precedents in their decisions, it is difficult to ascertain the real
influence which they no doubt still exert on one another. By now the main
instrument of exchange of information on landmark decisions between
French-speaking jurisdictions is the Cour de cassation's annual Report.[37] As
for the French-speaking African countries, which still have legal systems
inherited from the French one, reference to the case-law of the French Cour
de cassation is not surprising.[38]

These remnants of a common legal space revolving around the splendour
of the French Civil Code undoubtedly formed the background against
which legal transplants were performed and comparative law methodology
made its way through the French courts and legal academy. But, since this
common space was fuelled more by the French empire's political power or
prestige and less by the efficiency of the French 'legal product', the radiance
of the French civil law culture slowly began to wane in the twentieth
century, accustoming our national courts to a rather provincial state of
mind. Even today, after the European Community and European Human
Rights legal revolutions fundamentally altered the balance of power
between national and supranational legal institutions, French law is quite
reticent about opening up the judicial forum to foreign law. We can see this
in the conflict of laws area, whose rules command the French courts to
apply foreign law. Taking into account—or maybe under the pretext of—
the difficulty of knowing the applicable foreign law with reasonable
certainty, recent Cour de cassation case-law has limited the cases in which

---

[37] The latest French Cour de cassation annual Report is on civil liability (Cour de cassation
Rapport 2002 *La responsabilité* (Paris La Documentation française 2003).
[38] Reports of African supreme court decisions are gathered since 1891 in a review called
Penant: Revue de droit des pays d'Afrique.

there is an obligation for the lower courts to apply foreign law when no party has raised the conflict of law issue.[39]

This deference of French courts, and first of all of the Cour de cassation, to the self-sufficiency of national law is by now obsolete, owing to the fantastic strike force of European law. Even though there is no mention of foreign or international law, or of comparative methodology of law, in the body of the Cour de cassation's decisions, there is theoretical work to be done on the importance comparative law has in the conclusions and reports that frame and clarify the decisions of the Cour de cassation. These conclusions and reports are not, technically speaking, a part of the judicial decision having a *res judicata* effect; but they *are* a part of the pertinent legal materials lawyers can consult, especially on the Internet,[40] in order to understand the case-law. In the year 2003 the opening of the Cour de cassation, and of French private law courts in general, to comparative law considerations is no longer a scandal.

[39] See eg Cour de cassation Chambre sociale *Application moderne des plastiques AMP v Cremades* (1992) Bulletin civil V No 593 374.

[40] The Cour de cassation's web site has put on line several 'internal documents', such as conclusions or reports accompanying important cases that have been decided by the Court; see <http://www.courdecassation.fr>.

13

Foreign Law in International Legal Practice

Guido Alpa

I. FOREIGN LAW IN THE ITALIAN LEGAL CULTURE: FASHIONS AND MODELS FROM THE NINETEENTH CENTURY TO THE PRESENT.

In Italian legal culture the expression 'foreign law' has quite a restricted meaning, inasmuch as it refers to the law in force in other countries necessarily applied by the courts by virtue of the rules on the conflict of laws, or to the law chosen by agreement of the parties to govern the relationship installed between them.[1] However, according to the teachings of one of the most eminent Italian scholars of comparative law, Rodolfo Sacco,[2] the expression may be used in a wider meaning, which considers not only the statutory rules applied, but also the other 'legal formants', namely 'doctrine' (legal literature) and case-law. From this perspective we are to take into consideration the cultural models, the legal institutes, and the judgments coming from foreign experiences which are used by individuals or by the courts in the solution of domestic legal problems.

In this wider meaning the use of foreign law in Italy is the subject of a very rich history, still awaiting its narrator.[3] To summarize, this history can

---

[1] The same perspective is adopted by U Drobnig 'The Use of Comparative Law by Courts', General Report in U Drobnig and S van Erp (eds) *The Use of Comparative Law by Courts* 14th International Congress of Comparative Law Athens 1997 (The Hague Kluwer Law International 1999) 6.

But what is striking is the use of foreign models to solve domestic cases: see B Markesinis 'Reading Through a Foreign Judgment', in P Cane and J Stapleton (eds) *Essays in Celebration of John Fleming* (Oxford 1998) 261 ff.

[2] R Sacco and A Gambaro *Sistemi giuridici comparati* (Torino 1996) 6 f.; G Alpa (ed) *Corso di sistemi giuridici comparati* (Torino) 10.

[3] G Gorla had studied the use of *lex alii loci* in the Middle Ages (*ius commune Europeum*): see id 'Il ricorso alla legge di un "luogo vicino" nell'ambito del diritto comune europeo'(1973) 5 Foro italiano 89 ff. For further details, see P Grossi *L'ordine giuridico medievale* (Rome 1998) *passim*.

Roman law is still mentioned in Italian decisions, but only *exornatione gratia* (G Micali 'Il diritto romano nella giurisprudenza della Corte suprema di cassazione' (1993) 4 Giurisprudenza italiana 489 ff), while, accordingo to the Spanish Civil Code, Roman law is the basis for interpreting the law through general principles.

be subdivided into five periods: (1) the first period comprises the whole of the nineteenth century, (2) the second, the first half of the twentieth, (3) the third, the period that spans roughly two decades (from 1950 to 1970), (4) the fourth relates to the following two decades, from 1970 to 1990, and (5) the fifth, the last years of the twentieth century. Each subdivision into periods is arbitrary and each period cannot be assumed as a monolith in which a sole and consistent approach took hold; however, taking a bird's-eye view of the formation of law in Italy, certain hues—which correspond to the periods previously mentioned—appear prevalent, thereby lending scientific credibility to this temporal subdivision.[4]

1. The first period evinces a preponderant influence of French law, which reverberates over the entire formants of our legal system, encompassing the statutory formant, legal literature, and the decisions of the courts.

As regards the statutory formant, the Code Napoléon constituted at first the law imposed by the general's armies in the provinces conquered from the Piedmontese, from the Austrians, the Lorraines, and the Bourbons; after the fall of Napoleon his model of Civil Code is transplanted in several of the states into which Italy was divided (the Civil Code of the Kingdom of Two Sicilies, the Civil Code of the Duchy of Parma, the Civil Code of the Kingdom of Sardinia or 'Albertine Code') and is subsequently chosen as the model for the first Civil Code of unified Italy, which was born in 1865.

As for the legal literature formant, the École de l'Exégèse (School of Exegesis) becomes the method for analysis and application of universal law, so much so that the majority of the treatises and manuals of French law are first translated and then imitated by Italian legal writers. More than 600 of these works were translated over the century, which sees the coming into being of the Italian Scuola dell'Esegesi, which holds that only the statutory State-enacted law is law, and that the legal writer's work is limited to an analytical commentary of the provisions of the same.

With reference to the law formant, given the proximity of French law and Italian law, the judgments of the Cour de cassation and of the French tribunals are quoted by the legal writers and employed by the judges with largesse, without regard for the fact that they have been rendered by foreign judges: French law is not considered by Italian jurists as a 'foreign' law, belonging to a *ius alienum*, that is, to the system of a different State and applied by judges belonging to the administration of a foreign State.

---

[4] Unfortunately the literature in English language about this proceeding is very poor: see among other, M Bellomo *The Common Legal Past of Europe (1000–1800)* (Washington 1995); for new comments, see P Grossi *La scienza giuridica in Italia nell'Ottocento* (Milano 2000); G Alpa *La cultura delle regole:. Storia del diritto civile italiano* (Rome 2000).

2. The second period demonstrates a repudiation of the Scuola dell'Esegesi and the triumph of the Pandectist model, the historical School of Germanic origin, introduced in Italy by the scholars of Roman law. Even Roman law was not considered then, as it is not today, a 'foreign' law in a proper sense: it is the primary source not only of the Italian legal language, but also of many of the principles governing natural persons, property, contracts, torts, and the remedies thereto. Roman law is so widely diffused among the roots of our own legal culture that it constitutes, to this very day, a fundamental subject of study for trainee lawyers, is often quoted in decisions of the courts, and is studied in a 'current' dimension, almost as if it were not a body of rules and principles to be historically placed in the context of its bimillennial evolution but a corpus of rules still in force.

The decision to move from French culture to Pandectist culture was not simply the product of a fashion, but rather was born of a perception at the end of the nineteenth century and the beginning of the twentieth that it was necessary: the intenion was to reconstruct dogmatically Italian civil law, and consequently the method for studying it. Savigny, Arndts, Dernburg and Windscheid, among others, peep out from the bookshelves of lawyers, are top of the list in courses on civil law, and constitute the staple diet of jurists and therefore of judges, who, having received a Pandectist training, flaunt it in their judgments. So much so that a jurist of those times, Biagio Brugi, a famous author, renowned scholar of Roman and private law, and editor of one of the manuals of institutions of private law most widely studied by generations of students,[5] could truly state, in a lecture given in 1919, that 'perhaps no influence was ever felt in Italy by foreign scientists that can be compared with that of the Germans in our day and age'. His was not a simple reckoning: it was a *cri de cœur* aimed at fostering awareness among Italian jurists of the bimillennial history to which they were heir, and which he now saw as being crushed in the books copied from the German jurists, and an attempt to restore to these studies their original Italian model. It was also an invitation not to disregard the other aids of foreign legal science: the Italians, he suggested, 'may indeed look as far afield as English *common law* (in which our own authors are often still quoted) and to the decisions of North American Courts, which are in certain points inimitable'.[6]

Brugi's invitation was to remain unheeded: the influence of German culture was to remain unaltered up to the formulation of the new Civil Code in 1942, and further still for several more decades. However, in one of the surprising turns of legal history, at the end of the 1920, an extraordinary event took place as a result of the cosmopolitan climate pervading

[5] B Brugi *Istituzioni di diritto civile* (Milano 1915).
[6] B Brugi 'I danni dell'imitazione straniera nella nostra giurisprudenza' in *Atti della R Accademia Lucchese di Scienze* Lettere ed Arti (1919) vol 36, 7.

continental Europe at the time. In 1927 a bilateral commission officially installed by Italy and France drafted a uniform Code of Obligations. This initiative was due to another great jurist, a scholar of Roman and private law, Vittorio Scialoja, and to the Frenchman François Larnaude. Jurists from other countries, such as Belgium, Romania, Greece, and Canada, took part in the early stager of the initiative but the Code was finally restricted to the two founding nations.[7]

The purpose of the Projet de Code des Obligations et des Contrats, consisting of 739 Articles, drafted in the two languages by the scholars of the 'sister nations', was to 'create, with the consensus of all their strengths united, a body of laws which, within each of the two States, would represent that most perfect regime of law which legal science wished for and legal practice required'.

With the changing political balance, at the end of the 1930s, the German influence made itself felt again, but the scholars of comparative law continued to study the models of common law, taking into account not only principles unheard of in Italy, such as trusts, but also company law.

3. After the introduction of the new Civil Code, which incorporated commercial law in a unified whole, from the 1950s onward, we may detect Italian jurists shutting out foreign experiences: everyone was busy understanding, commenting on, and interpreting the new text, and references to comparison or to foreign laws become quite rare, both in legal literature and in court rulings.[8]

The most notable exception is that of Gino Gorla, who as early as 1955 published a prodigious treatise on contracts in which, in addition to the historical perspective, a comparative approach is adopted which relied on cases: reference to cases, then as today, became a way to discover in other practices, particularly common law, the similarities, convergences, and more useful practical solutions.[9] We too can pride ourselves (as can the United Kingdom today), thanks to the works of Basil Markesinis, on scholars who are more concerned to study what unites us than what divides, 'convergences' rather than 'divergences', and the formulas that can be adapted to practical cases rather than erudite musings which are an end in themselves: scholars, in other words, who are animated by a desire that research, should produce not a sterile form of culture but immediately functional, practical solutions.[10]

---

[7] Commissione Reale per la Riforma dei codici/Commission Francaise d'Etudes de l'Union Legislative entre les Nations aliees et Amies *Progetto di Codice delle Obbligazioni e dei Contratti, Testo definitivo approvato a Parigi nell'ottobre 1927–anno VI* (Rome 1928).

[8] Alpa (n 4).   [9] G Gorla *Il contratto* (Milano 1955).

[10] This is the *leitmotiv* through the essays collected by B Markesinis (ed) *The Gradual Convergence: Foreign Ideas, Foreign Influences, and English Law on the Eve of the 21st Century* (Oxford Hart 1994).

4. The fourth period is the most lively, and to this I shall devote more time: it includes the influences recorded in decisions of the courts, from cases and from the other sources of foreign law, the influences of legal practice from other countries, in particular from the United States, and the deployment of remedies derived from those experiences.

5. The current period shows, in addition to the tendencies that developed during the fourth period, the rise of the law of the European Union, and therefore the necessary circulation of the models of the Member States of the Union, which are merged in the regulations, directives, and the very language used by the European legislator and by the Court of Justice of the European Community.

II. EXAMPLES OF FOREIGN MODELS USED BY ITALIAN COURTS

Foreign judgments (or legal rules) are still rarely used as models by Italian judges. Usually it is the lawyers who use these foreign elements in their defences, and the judges, if they take them into account, make use of them in their reasoning. But recourse to foreign models is left not only to the culture of the lawyer or the judge, but also to the extent that the citation may be instrumental in bringing about a favourable decision in a dispute. However, it cannot be said that the use of comparative law is an everyday working method for the Italian lawyer, and while many cases have been decided taking foreign models into account, the judge may not reveal the sources of his reasoning or expressly quote them. If we hold some of these cases up to the light, however, we can surely note the influence of foreign practice. Here are some examples.

1. Privacy

One of the first Italian cases in which the problem arose of safeguarding the right to privacy[11] relates to the tenor Caruso, whose family life during childhood was depicted in the film *Leggenda di una voc* ('Legend of a Voice'). Certain sequences showed scenes of violence committed by his father, and Caruso himself was portrayed as a short-tempered, heavy-drinking man of dubious morality. To uphold Caruso's right to obtain compensation on the basis of tort law, the judges asked the question whether there should be protection for a general right 'to confidentiality or privacy', denoted in Anglo-Saxon court rulings as a 'right of privacy'. The judges' reply (we are in the mid-1950s) was negative. Their reasoning was

[11] G Alpa 'The Protection of Privacy in Italian Law' in B Markesinis (ed) *Protecting Privacy* (Oxford Hart 1999) 105 ff.

formalistic, the judges having found only rules aimed at safeguarding the use of a person's name or image, or the person's decorum or reputation, but not privacy per se. Therefore, the judges concluded that

in our legal system there is no right to privacy, but only individual subjective rights of the person are acknowledged and protected, in different ways; therefore, it is not forbidden to communicate, either privately or publicly, events, especially if imaginary, of another person's life, when knowledge of the same has not been obtained by means unlawful in themselves, or which impose an obligation of secrecy.[12]

Gradually, however, the right of privacy made its way through the Italian courts: this time through the utilization of the European Convention on Human Rights and Fundamental Freedoms signed in Rome on 4th November 1950 and ratified in Italy with Statute No 848 of 4 August 1955. The Convention, whose Article 8 sets forth that 'every person has the right to the respect of his/her private and family life, home and correspondence', is quoted as the basis for the decision that upheld, both on appeal and in the Court of Cassation, the right to damages of the family of Claretta Petacci, the unfortunate lover of Benito Mussolini, who had been executed alongside him, trying to shield him with her own body. In this case it was a book, in which Claretta Petacci's personality was described pejoratively, that prompted the family to claim their right of privacy, and the judges upheld this, despite the fact that the injured party was deceased.[13]

2. *Taking*

Although no cases, nor the relevant legal theory of German origin, were expressly mentioned, in a landmark decision regarding the regulation of ownership the Constitutional Court held that the legislator cannot, without compensation, restrict the powers of an owner on a thing beyond the limits 'naturally attached to the right of ownership' such as they are acknowledged at the current time. The case concerned the owners of land situated at the centre of Palermo which was under a zoning ordinance that prohibited building. The town plan was compliant with the zoning law, which envisaged no compensation for zoning ordinances or encumbrances that restricted the rights of the owners. The court applied—as was immediately pointed out by specialist on the subject—the German concept of *Einzelakttheorie*, according to which an individual right, particularly the right of ownership, must be considered as a sphere on the surface of which the legislator can carve, that is, can impose restrictions on the owner without compensation; but when restrictions carve into the essential nucleus,

---

[12] Tribunale di Roma 14 Sept 1953 (1954) Foro italiano 115.
[13] Corte di Cassazione 22 Dec 1956 No 4487 (1957) 1 Foro italiano 877.

and reach into the 'vital core' of the right, the loss imposed on the owner must be compensated.[14]

3. Leasing

Leasing contracts first made their appearance in Italian courts, according to the records, only in 1972. A small tribunal in the province of Pavia, which is full of small businesses run by able and tireless entrepreneurs, had to solve the question of whether machinery given by a lessor to the lessee for the manufacture of shoes should be considered the property of the lessor or of the lessee. The contract utilized was a leasing contract, unknown until then in Italian experience, where, according to tradition, use of a thing can be the subject of a contract of rental or of sale, or of a contract creating property rights. The tribunal instead referred to commercial practice—without considering the context within which this type of contract had been used—in order to adopt it in our own system using the principle of freedom of contract.[15]

4. Liability for Prospectuses

Even for the presentation to the public of financial products, in the absence of statutes that would be enacted only in 1983, and then more widely in 1991, the judges—in this case the judges of the Tribunal and of the Appeals Court of the town of Milan, which is the main financial centre of the country—relied on foreign practice, in particular that of England and the United States. They did not choose to cite any cases, but simply proceeded to follow their reasoning. On this occasion a prospectus was prepared by the issuer to favour the underwriting of debenture securities by investors; the issuer was the client of the American Express Bank, subsequently American Service Bank spa, which was in charge of the placement of securities on the Italian market. It had invited its clients to underwrite the debentures and assured them that the issuer was in an economically sound position; the investment, however, proved disastrous, because a few months later the issuer went bankrupt. In the first instance the bank was not held liable because the judge ascertained that there was no contract of guarantee with clients.[16] On appeal, however, the bank was held liable in tort, because it had circulated groundless information on the economic soundness of the issuer. In defining the limits of liability, the judges referred to liability for (misrepresentation in) prospectuses, which is well known to common lawyers.

---

[14] Corte costituzionale 29 May 1968 No 55 (1968) 1 Foro italiano 1365.
[15] Tribunale di Vigevano 14 Dec 1972 (1973) 2 Banca e bors, 287.
[16] Tribunale di Milano 11 Jan 1988 (1988) 2 Giurisprudenza commerciale (1988) 2 585.

5. *Nervous Shock*

In the Italian legal system there has been great discussion about the extent and classification of personal injury. In addition to physical injury and so-called moral injury (which corresponds to the 'pain and suffering' of common law) a different type of injury, consisting of injury to health (so-called 'biological damage'), has been ascertained. Purely psychiatric damage due to nervous shock produced by an accident had never been taken into consideration as a legally relevant injury. However, the Constitutional Court, taking into account English practice, specified as *obiter dictum*, in a case in which the issue was whether compensation was due to the relatives of the victim, that such psychiatric injury, if caused by fault (negligence) or wilful damage, gives rise to compensation. The author of the judgment was one of the most noteworthy scholars of private law, Luigi Mengoni, a former professor at the Catholic University in Milan, subsequently appointed to the Court. The judgment states that liability for nervous shock must be tied to fault; it cannot be strict liability. On the other hand, the English courts, which admit this principle, in order to avoid arbitrariness, and so as not to risk burdening insurance companies with an excessive amount of claims, make the distinction between whether the claimant suffered shock as an actual witness at the time of the accident, or if he was told of the event far away from the scene of the accident, upholding the claim in the first instance but rejecting it in the second.[17]

6. *Italian Trust*

The last example considers trusts, a typical institute of equity, originally only available in the systems of English descent, and subsequently also introduced, with different legal configurations, and on the basis of special statutes, in countries of different legal traditions. Trusts were the subject of the Hague Convention of 1 July 1985), rendered executive in Italy by Statute No 364 of 16 October 1989, which entered into force on 1 January 1992. The Convention deals with the applicable law, but contains certain provisions which give the definition of 'Trust', for the purpose of extending the rules to all the types of this category, in the various forms in which the signing countries acknowledge the existence of the same. It is without doubt, in the Italian legal system, that a trust established abroad with a foreign trustee relating to property located in Italy is valid, even if the sett-lor is an Italian citizen. Italian citizens who intend to set up a trust mostly use foreign legal systems, mainly the rules applicable in Jersey, but also those applicable in Ireland. This choice is preferable for succession

---

[17] Corte costituzionale 27 Oct 1994 No 372 (1994) 1 Foro italiano 3297.

purposes, for fiscal reasons, and for reasons of confidentiality, but also because the purposes achieved through the establishment of a trust are not equally available using the principles of civil law, such as fiduciary contracts, fiduciary nomination, or registration. Usually the following transaction takes place: the property is registered in the name of an Italian company, whose quotas or shares are in turn registered in the name of a foreign trustee.

After the approval, ratification, and entering into force even in Italy of the Hague Convention, the problem arose as to whether it was possible to set up a trust, obviously governed by a foreign law, with an Italian trustee. Because the Convention contained provisions on the definition of 'trusts' it introduced into Italy rules of substantive law; trusts (in their structure at equity) governed by a foreign law would now be fully compatible with Italian law, but only under condition that the trustee be a foreigner.

Decisions of the courts, though extremely rare, are divided.

The first case considered compulsory purchases, promoted in Sardinia, in the 1950s, in order to enact agrarian reform. The land subject to compulsory purchase had been set up in trust by an English national, by will and testament. The expropriating body had instituted proceedings against the surviving spouse, designated as the trustee, and not against their children, designated in the will as 'beneficiaries'. The Tribunal of Oristano, a town on the island, had acknowledged the validity of a trust set up abroad on property located abroad, but had deemed incompatible with Italian law (in particular with the principles of so-called 'public policy') the institute of trust when it consisted of property located in Italy as this would have been in contrast with the so-called *numerus clausus* of property rights. The basic point of the ruling was the idea that, in trust, ownership is split between *cestui que* trust and the trustee, and that this gives rise, therefore, to a form of property right which is not compatible with the wholeness of the right of ownership envisaged in the Italian Civil Code. For the judges, therefore, the choice was between considering as owners either the surviving spouse or the children. By holding that the surviving spouse, as trustee, had only apparent title to the property, with powers to dispose of the same, but only in accordance with the aims of the trust, the Tribunal decided that the children had right of ownership, and therefore they should have been the recipients of the expropriation procedures, which, thus, had not been effected properly.[18]

The second case regarded a trust set up by an English national on property situated in Italy; the executor trustee had applied to the Italian judge (of the Tribunal of Casale Monferrato, a small town in the northern region of Piedmont) for authorization to sell the property; the judge, maintaining that

[18] Tribunale di Oristano 15 Mar 1956 (1956) 1 Foro italiano 1020.

the trust in question was similar to a fiduciary agreement *cum amico* under civil law, refused authorization, holding that it was not necessary as the fiduciary agent was already the owner of the property, albeit on a fiduciary basis.[19]

The third case regarded a trust set up in Jersey by Italian nationals. The plaintiff trustee was the settlor's wife, an Italian citizen, who held the property (that is, the shares in two companies) in the interest of the beneficiaries, her children and her husband, the settlor himself. Having deposited the shares to take part in the annual general meetings of the two companies, the directors of the companies then refused to return them to her. She had therefore acted to reacquire possession of the shares; the directors had objected, claiming that 'trusts' were not recognized in our own legal system, and that the trustee (who had been replaced in the meantime) could not claim any right to the shares. The judge ruled in favour of the plaintiff, without however discussing the nature of 'trusts' and their compatibility with the Italian legal system (which, according to the majority of authors, in the case at hand should have been ruled out as the trustee was Italian); the judge based his ruling on the provisions relating to actions for recovery, which are based on the factual relationship with the property, such as possession[20] rather than on the title to the property.

III.   USE OF *ANSTALT* FROM LIECHTENSTEIN

For the purpose of tax savings, to invest capital abroad, and for reasons of confidentiality, wide use has been made of the institute of *Anstalt*, a typical device of the law of Liechtenstein. It is similar to a foundation set up by a sole subject; it has legal personality and is considered by the Italian judges as a legal person existing under foreign law, recognized in Italy in the same way as our legal system recognizes other foreign legal entities. Under the laws of Liechtenstein, the necessary officers of the company are the founder and the administrator, while the assembly and the statutory auditors are not strictly required. The administrator may dispose of the estate and may promote actions to safeguard it. The general provisions of law (article 16) and the Brussells Convention of 28 February 1968 (article. 1) are applied.

The first doubts that had been expressed by the Italian judges (in particular the Tribunal of Milan)[21] have been settled, and the Court of Cassation has upheld the legitimacy of *Anstalt*s even if set up by founders who remain anonymous.[22]

---

[19] Tribunale di Casale Monferrato 13 Apr 1984 (decree) (1984) 1 Giurisprudenza italiana 2, 754.   [20] Pretura di Roma 8 July 1999 (order), unpub.
[21] Tribunale di Milan, 11 Jan 1979 (1980) Rivista di diritto internazionale 523.
[22] Corte di Cassazion, 21 Jan1 985 No 198.

IV. THE FOREIGN MODELS UTILISED IN ITALIAN CONTRACTUAL PRACTICE.

In Italian contractual practice it is rare for the parties, if they are both Italian, to choose a foreign law to govern the contract. On the other hand, there are numerous institutes, types of contract, negotiating practices, and remedies that have been imported from foreign practice, especially from English or US common law, to govern economic relations. Here are a few examples.

Many types of contract have been accepted in our legal system by virtue of the principle of freedom of contract. These—as opposed to those in other countries, such as France—have retained their original names: for instance, leasing contracts, factoring, franchising, merchandising, project financing, joint ventures, contracts regarding the use of information and data transmission technologies, and so forth. As with all contracts defined as 'atypical', as they are not among those categories regulated by the Civil Code or by statutes, they are governed by the contractual clauses negotiated between the parties. The judge's control is twofold: on the one hand, he verifies if they are worthy of protection under the Italian legal system, that is, if the interests and the objectives they pursue are lawful and economically useful; on the other hand, in the event that a contract should fail to make adequate provision for all contingencies, the judge proceeds to modify it, taking into account the reference legal types. For instance, in the case of a leasing contract, reference is made either to conditional sale agreements (with retention of title) or to rental contracts; for joint ventures, reference is made to association in participation etc.

As for negotiating practices, the use of side-letters is frequent, as is the use of letters of intent and letters of guarantee. Above all, for certain complex economic transactions, such as the sale of shareholdings, the technique adopted in the United States is followed: a due diligence research is made, a first agreement is reached (closing), and then the parties proceed to the definitive contract.

Even as regards remedies, reference has been made to the practices of common law, to better attain the interests of the parties: after some hesitation, the so-called 'autonomous contract of guarantee' has been accepted (configured at common law as bid bonds, etc.).

But it should be pointed out that even among Italian parties the use of US standard contract forms, drafted in English, is often preferred.

Even if the contracts are complex, and therefore more articulate than the average contract utilized in Italy, we never arrive at the detailed regulation of US contracts, consisting often of weighty files, in which every conceivable event is taken into account and provided for.

In international Commercial Contracts the Italian parties, when with a
foreign counter-party, normally refer to the principles of *lex mercatoria*, or
to the principles developed by the Institute for the Unification of Law
(Unidroit), with Head Office in Rome rather than choose a foreign law.

1. Lex Mercatoria

The same observations can be made about *lex mercatoria*—by which the
Italian merchants of medieval times set great store[23]—as were made in
relation to Roman law: it is not considered to be a foreign law since it is
considered part of Italian legal history. While the Italian judges have no
difficulty in acknowledging it as a body of rules of conduct appraisable as
widely used in the mercantile 'societas', problems may arise in relation to
making arbitration awards based upon it. The question is intertwined with
the issue of international arbitration, which is not the subject of this chapter.

It is worth recalling one of the few instances in which Italian judges have
dealt with *lex mercatoria*.

The case concerned a contract entered into between an Italian and a
German company containing an arbitration clause which referred the settle-
ment of disputes to the Refined Sugar Association of London, which applies
the principles of *lex mercatoria*. The award was not reasoned, in accordance with the practices of the Association. As the parties were citizens of
two countries (Germany and Italy) which had signed the Geneva
Convention of 21 April 1961 on International Commercial Arbitration, the
Italian party (non-prevailing) claimed that the award was null and void on
the basis that the Geneva Convention envisages that, where either party
requests that the award be reasoned, prior to the rendering of the decision
the award must be so reasoned (Article 8). The German company had
defended itself, claiming that the Association belonged to a country (the
United Kingdom) which had not signed the Convention, and therefore the
award was valid.

The Court of Cassation gave a very elaborate ruling in which it upheld
the claim of the Italian party. The reasoning for this sets it apart from the
notion of *lex mercatoria*; it went on to specify that *lex mercatoria* lacks
sovereignty because the mercantile 'societas' has no boundaries, but it does
not have the enforceability of sovereign systems. Having, therefore, to
refer to a legal system in order to render the arbitrators' decisions enforce-

---

[23] P Grossi (n 3).

able, the Court of Cassation deemed it appropriate to apply the Geneva Convention, claiming that it has a more modern approach than that of New York. The decision is justified in the sense that where parties are citizens of countries that are signatories to the Convention, the Convention 'must be considered as recalled by implied reference in the contractual stipulations between entrepreneurs belonging to ratifying States of the same'.[24]

2. *The Principles of Unidroit*

The principles of Unidroit represent a veritable melting-pot of models from widely varying practices, but above all they represent a fortunate attempt to merge the principles of civil law, common law, and *lex mercatoria*.[25] They cover the upholding of freedom of contract, and propose clear and simple rules that consider the binding force of contracts, the principle of good faith and reasonableness, the formation, interpretation, and execution of contract, in addition to rules on non-performance and damages. From the viewpoint of Italian practice, of particular relevance are the rules relating to situations of hardship.

In all systems rules are established, either expressly or construed from judicial or legal theory interpretation, regarding the eventuality that performance may become frustrated. In the Italian experience we can point out two occurrences: that in which frustration was extraordinary and unforeseeable, which carries with it the consequence of termination of the contract (Article 1467); and that in which the frustrating circumstances were foreseeable but not actually envisaged by the parties. In this case one has to ascertain the possibility of applying the theory of so-called 'presupposition', which, together with the bona fides clause, with 'causa' of the contract, and with the negotiating basis (that is, with the assignment of advantages and risks), may entail the termination of the contract.

In international trade there is a trend, as emphasized many times, towards keeping the contract alive. Therefore, the general rule according to which the parties are compelled to carry out their respective obligations, even if performance of these obligations has become more onerous (article 6.2.1), is tempered by the principle of hardship.

The features of this principle are outlined in Article 6.2, where they are identified as follows: frustration must be dependent on a risk not accepted in the contract, on external circumstances, which must not be ascribable to the party which invokes the same, and must have supervened or, if

---

[24] Corte di Cassazione 8 Feb 1982 No 72 (1982) 1 Foro italiano 2285.
[25] J Bonell *An International Restatemene of Contract Law: The Unidroit Principles of International Commercial Contracts* (Irvington NY 1994).

precedent, must not have been known or recognizable by the party who invokes them.

The effect of hardship clauses is directed at keeping the relationship alive. Therefore, the opportunity is given to the party invoking the hardship clauses to reopen negotiations without hindrance and without suspension of the performance due under the agreement.

Should negotiations fail, the interested party may apply to the judge (in our case to the arbitrator).

Here lies another opportunity for intervention, an opportunity which in countries of codified law is totally ignored and indeed is strenuously opposed: the judge, in fact, may—beyond the ruling of termination of the contract, which is the customary conclusion—'adapt the contract with the aim of re-establishing the balance between performances' (Article 6.2.3).

What is really extraordinary for civil lawyers is to accept the power of the judge to rewrite the contract on behalf of the parties, in contrast with the principle of sanctity of contract'. But the aim of the principles is precisely to rescue the economic transaction and to render it feasible in accordance with the supervening risks.

VI. THE RULES OF THE COMMON MARKET OF THE EUROPEAN UNION

Community law cannot be considered a 'foreign law', because it is one of the sources of the legal systems of the Member States. However, both regulations and directives tend to create uniform rules for the internal market. These rules are created originally by the organs of the Community but can be traced back to the models coming from the individual countries of the Community. They are effective in the 'strong' models (the French, German, and English models), which are often adapted to the new exigencies; to those stronger models the weaker models (from a political and economic viewpoint) adapt.[26] Thus it was, for instance, for the Directive on 'unfair clauses in consumer contracts', for the Directive on consumer credit, for the Directives on banks and insurance companies, and, above all, for the rules on competition.

It is important to emphasize that from the complex of directives on the subject matter of contracts, special rules can be singled out that tend to become general: take, for example, the use of the form of contract to protect the weaker party; the ban on the abuse of bargaining (contracting)

---

[26] See B Markesinis 'Learning from Europe and Learning in Europe' in B Markesinis *Foreign Law and Comparative Methodology: A Subject and a Thesis* (Oxford Hart 1997) 163 ff and id 'Our Debt to Europe: Past, Present and Future' in B Markesinis *The Clifford Chance Millennium Lectures: The Coming Together of the Common Law and the Civil Law* (Oxford Hart 2000) 37 ff.

power; the rules on prior and subsequent information in the stipulation of contracts; and the principle of good faith which is now at the basis of any type of contract.

VII. SOME TENTATIVE CONCLUSIONS

In rethinking the use of comparative law before the Italian civil courts we may point out some caveats concerning the use of comparative law by not only national judges but also those within the European milieu. If we consider this phenomenon from a very general perspective, we may make the following points.

1. Comparative law is perceived in a narrow, typically Eurocentric fashion, patterns of judgments are chosen from those legal systems that are more accessible for reasons of language, prestige, or tradition: in Italian eyes these legal systems fall into a very limited range (the French and German systems, with that of England still perceived as a very distant planet).

2. Eurocentrism is not a dangerous attitude, and is not a means by which to reduce the potential of the comparative method: rather, this attitude is to be welcomed because it is more efficient in the process of harmonization of European private law, and it is developing almost 'naturally' thanks to the active role assumed by European institutions in drafting so many directives concerning contract law and consumer law. Enacting EC directives, the national legislators are forced to accept notions, concepts, definitions, general principles, general 'standards' and general 'clauses' that are typical of other jurisdictions; the transplantation of these legal elements plays an active role in the apparent creeping convergence between systems.

3. In addition, the enormous efforts made by the European Court of Justice in interpreting EC law lead to a common method of interpreting statutes and the underlying institutions of private law.

4. Comparative law should be considered not from a static but from a dynamic viewpoint: comparison of written texts does not reflect the real situation of a foreign legal system, because the 'living law' (*diritto vivente*) is enriched by the case-law. In codified systems some fields of law are almost wholly built on judicial rules that fill the gap between the needs of a complex society and the abstract texts conceived in previous times; this experience is common to the German, French, and Italian systems, for example in tort law.

5. Reality is often different from the original ideas to which the lawyer is attached: many lawyers praise the divergences among legal systems, but reality leads to convergence. The most striking example is that of the recent reform of the Book of Obligations of the German Civil Code, which has

been shaped in accordance with the 'Principles of European Contract Law' drafted by the Lando Commission.

6. Comparative law is sometimes grounded in ideological prejudices: for example, Roman law is not considered as it should be (ie the changing body of rules of an extinct empire), and is not described from a historical perspective, taking into account all the modifications, misinterpretations, and adjustments made by canon law, medieval law, the German 'reception', amalgamation with customary law, national adaptations, and so on. Rather, it is sometimes considered as a modern and living legal system, complete with all the abstractions and dogmas that were the by-product of the geometrical Roman law system created by the Pandectists.

7. The citation of foreign judgments is carried out by extracting the case-law from its original context, without any consideration of the legal principles that underlie the solution achieved.

8. By way of a broad conclusion, the quotation of foreign judgments cannot be classified as a comparative law experiment. Judges are not required to write a treatise on doctrinal thought; they are simply asked to justify the solution envisaged in search of a better conclusion to their task. When a satisfying solution cannot be found (mainly in hard cases) in domestic case-law, it is wise to look at other experiences, and possibly to find the way out abroad.

14

Comparative Law Before the Spanish Courts

Joaquín Martín Canivell

When I was asked to write a chapter on the situation relating to comparative law before the Spanish courts, my understanding was that it required a description of the present situation of this legal branch in the practice of the courts. However, my chapter would be barely comprehensible without an introduction describing the historical, political, and legal evolution that has determined the current situation, and without an explanation of the organization and functions of the courts at the present time.

From the end of the Middle Ages the kingdoms which a little later united to become Spain began a process of differentiation from the rest of European countries. Although sharing a similar kind of absolutist political system with France and England, in Spain the Catholic orthodoxy was fiercely maintained. Meanwhile the wealth obtained from the American continent, under Spanish rule in great part, was spent in ruinous enterprises and spread among the population a general dislike of working as a normal way of life. This, and also other less important causes led the country into an isolation, especially of an ideological character, that lasted until the last decades of the twentieth century. The early nineteenth century saw a divergence in the views and feelings of Spaniards which led to what has been named the two Spains. One strand was traditional, opposed to any innovation arriving from what was called, derisively, advanced Europe, keeping stubbornly to the ancient traditions and beliefs and refusing to accept the most minimal modernization. The other craved the adoption into the political and social aspects of national life of innovations which were common in other countries but which were so difficult even to become aware of owing to harsh government restrictions on travel abroad and the import of books and papers, always suspected of being dangerous to the moral health and safety of the country. Needless to say, most of the time those who fell into the first category imposed their rule on the country, with short periods of liberal government that did not survive long enough to change the social views of many people. The final lasting imposition of the traditionally minded led to a civil war, in 1936–9, which was followed by nearly forty years of dictatorship, which ended, fortunately bloodlessly, in 1975. During this last period, with many eminent intellectuals expatriated and under an extremely reactionary regime, the possibility of any interest in what could be going on abroad was minimal, with the sole exception, in the last fifteen years of the dictatorship, of a timid opening up in economic matters. The judicial system was among the most retrograde, which accounts for the lack of access to the courts of comparative law subjects as arguments used in the presentation of cases and in decisions. However, it must be added that remnants of foreign legal doctrine, introduced during the earlier short progressive period, were still taught at the law schools and, to a lesser extent, applied in court decisions in so far as they were not considered 'dangerous'.

The current judicial organization in Spain was adopted in the second half of the nineteenth century, following the French pattern. Very few modifications have been introduced during the more than one hundred years since its establishment. Many courts in rural areas have been suppressed, and many more have been created in the cities, and the number of judges has been increased in recent years.[1] Female judges account for over half the overall number today, although until twenty-five years ago women were not admitted to the profession. Aspiring judges are required to pass a competitive public examination (only one in every twenty or more aspirants is admitted). To hold a bachelor's degree in law is the only requirement for this examination, in which the candidates have to prove knowledge of over 300 legal subjects. After a two-year course at the Judiciary School in Barcelona, the aspirants become judges at the lower level (Civil first instance and/or 'Juge d'instruction'). Judges are included in a roster and promoted mostly according to seniority. Some specialist judges may advance through examinations on the special subjects they are later asked to deal with. Criminal cases and civil appeals are decided by three member courts, and sometimes by five member courts. There is a superior court in each of the seventeen autonomous regions in the country, and at the top is the Supreme Court, which encompasses several chambers.[2]

Decisions are adopted primarily in consideration of legal provisions, completed, in practice rather infrequently, by custom and the general principles of law. Theoretically previous judicial decisions are not binding, although the Civil Code establishes that the repeated doctrine of the Supreme Court will complete the juridical order, and, if the Constitution establishes that judges are only subject to the requirements of law, in very recent laws[3] the doctrine or jurisprudence of the Supreme Court, when

---

[1] 1,085 fifty years ago; over 4,000 today.

[2] Civil, Criminal, Administrative, Labour and Military.

[3] Administrative jurisdiction 1998 and Procedural Civil Code 2000.

resolving 'in the interest of law', becomes a binding precedent. In fact for many years the cassation system practised mainly in civil and criminal cases, has determined the existence of jurisprudence followed by all the lower courts. It should be pointed out that in the reasoning expressed in judicial decisions, articles and paragraphs of laws and statutes are specifically cited as well as the dates and content of previous relevant decisions of the Supreme Court, but in practice the names and titles of doctrinal publications on the subject are never cited. This makes it rather difficult to trace the doctrinal influences on the criteria adopted by the judges in their decision-making process. Thus, only the Supreme Court supplies precedents that may be cited in the decisions of judges, and consequently, this is the most important device for introducing innovative theories and solutions into the output of the judiciary system as a whole so as to determine a unified jurisprudence. Nevertheless, the situation is not very satisfactory. To begin with, the justices composing this Court, although numerous (more than eighty, assisted by approximately twenty-five others, most of them retired judges of the same Court, who are kept on as 'emeriti', doing the same kind and amount of work that they did before retiring), find it difficult to cope with their schedules. This is understandable if we consider their output of over 10,000 decisions a year, which means an average of more than ninety decisions by each judge—in fact most of them have to write more than one hundred decisions a year, because one chamber (military cases) takes on far fewer cases than the average. The judges also have to study more than double the number of cases because most are adjudicated by three-judge panels, and a few by five judges or more. Considerable delays in the decision-making process are common, and the average delay for the resolution of cases is more than a year. The inevitable result is a rather high level of difficulty in accomplishing the desirable end of unifying the jurisprudence, although general meetings of each chamber are frequently held with the aim of agreeing on similar solutions for similar cases. Voices have begun to be heard suggesting changes in the functions of the Supreme Court with the purpose of enabling it to perform in more depth its task of unifying jurisprudence. With this aim in mind, the caseload of the Court would be reduced to the resolution of cases that may have unique aspects needing particularly new solutions, leaving other courts to decide the simpler cases. But this possible reform has not yet reached the project level, and has attracted much criticism, because the few cases that would be decided by the Supreme Court might work to the detriment of unification, and because this same aim could interfere with the independence of the judges, who might be compelled to accept solutions sanctioned in the Supreme Court in cases when the just solution may be different.

This situation means that dedicating much time to profound and extensive study, including consulting national and foreign books and legal reviews, demands a considerable amount of extra work from the already busy members of the Supreme Court. But there are many who try to maintain this level of activity. Some of them have previously been law professors, but the great majority simply feel that they have to keep an eye on legal publications and the decisions adopted in other countries.

The judicial doctrine based in comparative law in Spain presents some common characteristics:

1. Its authors tend to be individual judges especially interested in searching for solutions to legal problems in other juridical systems. Some of them become known, even before arriving at the Supreme Court, by their studies and publications on legal subjects. In fact their works on legal matters may contribute to their later appointment to this court. As I have already said, some of them have devoted a substantial part of their professional lives to teaching law.
2. The jurisprudence based on comparative law is applied on a case-by-case basis. The acceptance of foreign law and doctrine on most occasions is determined by the need to solve concrete problematical cases that lack adequate solutions in Spanish law.
3. In most cases the adoption of the comparative law solution is not taken as it is offered originally, but is modified in such a form as to adapt it to Spanish specificities and requirements.
4. Any judicial decision taken since the present Constitution came into existence considers, whenever relevant, the rights constitutionally guaranteed. Any final judicial decision may be submitted to the jurisdiction of the Constitutional Court by any concerned person applying for a remedy called 'amparo' (perhaps best translated as 'protection'). Therefore, any application of norms or doctrine of comparative law in judicial decisions may be subject to examination about its compatibility with constitutional rights.

I would now like to review some cases where comparative law has influenced judiciary decisions. In the field of administrative law practically no traces of Anglo-Saxon or Italian law can be found. The fact that most administrative law professors have studied either in France or in Germany may account for the prevalence of these two countries' norms and doctrines in judicial decisions on administrative matters. In the special case in which secret documents of the CESID (Spanish army intelligence service) were handed to a criminal court, decided by the Third Chamber (Administrative) of the Supreme Court in 1997 composed of all its thirty-three members, primary consideration was given to the constitutional theme of protection of accused persons by allowing disclosure of official secret documents to be used as defence proof, as opposed to national security and international prestige. However only in some of the concurring opinions are foreign law references to be found, as usual without explicit mention of the sources.

In the civil law field there are more varied influences. Some have been well established for quite a few years, as is the case of the abuse of law theory, which appeared in the decision of a former president of the Supreme Court and civil law professor in 1944, and is derived from the German doctrine. It has been received in legal texts like the Civil Code (Article 7) and it is frequently applied in relation to the *pacta sunt servanda* clause and to the general elements of contracts. In some cases, there exist curious errors relating to the origins of some doctrines or theories. For example, the objective imputation theory, already mentioned in Spain in a few sentences from 1928, resulted, without any real foreign influence, solely from the need for solutions, and later overlapped with elements from the German doctrine, or the practice of disclosure of the inside core of corporations, erroneously believed to be of German origin, while in fact it must be traced to English precedent dating from the late nineteenth century, although it has appeared in Spanish courts via the German understanding of the English precedent. In other, more recent, cases the influences derive from English or American sources. Such is the case of the rights to good reputation of corporations, for which a doctrinal article published in 1996 (personality rights of English corporations) was very likely a fundamental influence on a recent decision pronounced by the First Chamber of the Supreme Court (Civil) on 4 April 2002. In deciding cases on medical malpractice the First Chamber has resorted repeatedly to American precedents. Punitive damages, so popular in the United States, while rejected by the Civil Chamber under this name, are frequently found in its jurisprudence under the concept of moral damages with an evident punitive purpose.

Criminal law was much influenced by German penal theory in the 1920s, above all on the subject known as the elements of the crime and its characters: action, legal penal type, against juridical provisions and culpability. Concepts such as the control of behaviour or the situation of a person as warranting protection against the commission of some delinquent activity, used as a means of finding out if responsible participation in delinquency exists, have found their way into criminal adjudication practice at all levels, after their introduction into the jurisprudence of the Second Chamber (Penal Matters) of the Supreme Court. This is also the case for the doctrine of the indivisibility of imputation charges made in a single process, which has been received from Italian doctrine. Very recently the Second Chamber of the Supreme Court has adopted the suffering of undue dilatory tactics as an analogical alleviating cause for the accused and condemned person, originally created in German penal doctrine and practice. At present there is under deliberation by this same chamber a case, initiated at request of the Nobel peace prizewinner Rigoberta Menchú, in which the admission of a crime committed by governmental agencies is being discussed, taking into consideration comparative law sources.

An increase in the resort by the Spanish courts to foreign legal doctrines and norms may be expected in the near future. As I have already stated, in recent years references in the sentences pronounced by the Supreme Court to such doctrines and norms have been expressed more frequently, and in what seems to indicate a change in the decision-drafting practices, further information on the sources has been offered, which assuredly will be helpful in its role as guide to jurisprudence.

15

Comparative Legal Reasoning and the Courts: A View from the Americas

H Patrick Glenn

It has been axiomatic in Western legal theory in recent centuries that comparative law has little or no place before the courts and is not a source of law. This view is closely associated with legal positivism and the concept of a self-sufficient national legal system. Comparative law did play a fundamental role in the construction of national legal systems from, say, the sixteenth century. There was in Europe, from that point, a massive process of mining of Roman, customary, canonical, and other sources of law, in both civil and common law traditions, for purposes of construction of national law.[1] Codification and the emergence of the notion of *stare decisis* marked the end of this process, since they both signalled a turning away from residual or supplementary sources of law and an exclusivist concentration on current sources of state law. In some continental jurisdictions, such as Prussia, Spain, Switzerland, and Italy, citation of non-state sources of law was prohibited by formal enactment.

Comparative law thus achieved some initial prominence as a resource for the construction of State law. This process of construction being largely completed in the nineteenth century, comparative law then assumed a further or auxiliary role, once again in support of State law. It could thus provide advice in the ongoing process of improvement of State law, acting as a kind of scientific filter for foreign experience, absorbing and translating it for whatever purpose judged acceptable by local law-making institutions. As well, State legal systems having developed in multiple form, comparative law could undertake the scientific function of taxonomic ordering of these State forms of law, conferring further legitimacy upon them by categorizing them in accordance with various mega-criteria for legal identification.[2] State sources of law being presumed complete,

---

[1] See generally HP Glenn 'The Nationalist Heritage' in P Legrand and R Munday *Comparative Legal Studies: Traditions and Transitions* (Cambridge CUP 2003); W Wijffels, 'Arthur Duck et le *ius commune* européen' (1990) Re. d'histoire des Facultés de droit 193 (notably for the influence of English civilians on English law); and for French law J-L Thireau 'Le Comparatisme et la naissance du droit français', Rev d'histoire des Facultés de droit 153.

[2] On this taxonomic function of comparative law the fullest justification is the three-volume treatise of L Constantinesco *Traité de droit comparé* (Paris LGDJ 1972–83).

however, there could be no use in principle of comparative law before the courts, since this would directly challenge the presumption of exclusivity of State sources. Further, there could be no resort to transnational or general principles of law, demonstrated though comparative reasoning, for trans-border cases, and the assignation of such cases to one or another national legal system became the basic premiss of private international law.[3] This general theory was remarkably successful in Europe and comparative legal reasoning in large measure disappeared from the courts, retaining some minor visibility only in the common law tradition where English courts would, on occasion, refer to extraterritorial common law authority. In both the civil and common law worlds of Europe, however, comparative legal reasoning was not a direct source of law. It could be only a source of law-making, channelled through local institutions.

Twentieth-century legal positivism very much reinforced this marginal role for comparative legal reasoning, in teaching that legal systems existed as matters of fact. Hart described his work both as analytical and as 'descriptive' of existing municipal legal systems.[4] For him, a legal system would exist once two minimal conditions were met, those of general public obedience and, as well, acceptance by the officials of the system of its rules of recognition and change.[5] Since legal systems simply existed, occupying a given space, it followed that they were incompatible with other legal systems, in that same space. Hart spoke of each of them having 'a certain kind of *supremacy* within its territory and *independence* of other systems'.[6] Joseph Raz has explained that '[a]ll legal systems . . . are potentially incompatible at least to a certain extent. Since all legal systems claim to be supreme with respect to their subject-community, none can acknowledge any claims to supremacy over the same community which may be made by another legal system.'[7] There would thus be an inherent presumption that a system should not be in the business of giving effect to laws other than its own. It would be, in principle, 'undesirable and an unstable situation' for a community to practice two legal systems.[8] Moreover, since legal systems simply exist, with no necessary normative justifications, they in principle can tell us nothing about when they should yield to, or adopt, as a result of comparative reasoning, rules drawn from another legal order or tradition. Legal systems are large, and silent, seen from without.

Today there are major doubts, however, both about the existence and about the completeness of legal systems. In some areas of the world States,

---

[3] For the presumption of completeness of State law as the philosophical foundation of private international law, see H Batiffol *Aspects philosophiques du droit international privé* (Paris 1956) at 16, 24.

[4] HLA Hart *The Concept of Law* (2nd edn (Oxford Clarendon Press 1994) p v.

[5] Ibid 116.   [6] Ibid 24.

[7] J Raz, *The Authority of Law: Essays on Law and Morality* (Oxford Clarendon Press 1979) 119.   [8] Ibid 118.

and their legal systems, are said to have 'failed', and there is doubt about what might replace them.[9] Even where States appear well established, the range of contemporary problems is such that existing legal systems appear inevitably inadequate. The apparent contemporary inadequacy of national legal systems has led Professor Bucher of Switzerland to conclude that tradition must be recognized as a source of law, and that external sources of law are an inherent element of tradition.[10] In France the Court of cassation is increasingly relying on 'general principles of law' as justification for its decisions, and less on posited, national texts.[11] One book has recently been published on the use of comparative law by courts[12] and the present volume adds further reflection to the theme. These legal developments are complemented by those in contemporary philosophy, where it is said that the distinction between fact and value, upon which legal systems are based, has now collapsed.[13]

There is therefore renewed interest in European legal theory in the use of comparative law before the courts. To be more precise, there is renewed interest in comparative legal reasoning before the courts, since comparative law, in its static, taxonomic dimension, is not that which is now being urged. It is rather a more dynamic process of comparative legal reasoning which has become relevant, in which local law and foreign models are assessed against one another, for purposes of application in a given case. From the perspective of European legal theory, this may be seen as a recent development, the return of pre-nineteenth-century judicial practice, but it is also the case, as the experience of the Americas shows in general, that it represents a process which has never disappeared from legal practice before the courts. The practice has not been well represented by Western legal theory, which has devoted its attention almost exclusively to the construction of State law over the last four centuries, but its theoretical interest is now becoming evident once again. New forms of transnational law and 'transgovernmentalism' are now emerging, and comparative legal reasoning is an essential element in these processes.[14]

---

[9] See N Lante Wallace-Bruce 'Of Collapsed, Dysfunctional and Disoriented States: Challenges to International Law' (2000) 47 Neth Intl L Rev 3; R Gordon 'Saving Failed States: Sometimes a Neocolonialist Notion' (1997) 12 Am U J Intl L & Policy 903.

[10] E Bucher 'Rechtsüberlieferung und heutiges Recht' [2000] ZeuP 394.

[11] J-P Gridel 'La Cour de cassation française et les principes généraux du droit privé' (2002) 1 D 228.

[12] U Drobnig and S van Erp (eds) *The Use of Comparative Law by Courts* (The Hague Kluwer Law International 1999).

[13] See H Putnam *The Collapse of the Fact/Value Dichotomy* (Cambridge Mass Harvard University Press 2002).

[14] HP Glenn 'A Transnational Concept of Law' in P Cane and M Tushnet (eds) *Oxford Handbook of Legal Studies* (Oxford University Press 2003) 839; A-M Slaughter 'Judicial Globalization' (2000) 40 Virginia J Intl L 1103.

The Americas are, however, a large and legally diverse geographic area. They have never been the object of a single *ius commune*, or common law, and they are not now, and are unlikely ever to be, the object of overarching political or judicial authorities such as those that exist in the European Union. Neither NAFTA nor MERCOSUR presently entail such institutions, and the Free Trade Agreement of the Americas, should it come into effect as proposed in 2005, will not bring about their creation. Nor do the free trade areas of the Americas imply any formal programme of harmonization of law, such that there remains ample occasion for genuinely comparative reflection on the basis of ongoing national diversity. The Americas are different, moreover, from Europe, in that they represent a much larger number of private law jurisdictions, but much less linguistic diversity. In NAFTA alone there are some ninety-nine private law jurisdictions, and this number would increase to approximately 130 in the projected Free Trade Agreement of the Americas. Cross-border communication is facilitated, however, by the existence of four major official legal languages (English, French, Spanish, Portuguese) of transborder or transnational dimensions.

It is possible to identify a variety of attitudes to comparative legal reasoning in the Americas, notably those that prevail with respect to aboriginal or chthonic peoples, and also those that prevail among the European legal traditions received in the Americas. Further attention should be given, moreover, to the methods of comparative legal reasoning in the context of American free trade areas.

I. COMPARATIVE LEGAL REASONING AND ABORIGINAL LAW

A number of European legal traditions have been received in the Americas, but it is constant throughout all American territories that adjustment to those traditions has been necessary in light of the existence of pre-existing aboriginal or chthonic law. The existence of the law of the first peoples of America is widely recognized in national constitutions and national legislation, and has become the object of major litigation in many jurisdictions. In Latin America there has been a major, and recent, movement towards entrenchment of indigenous law and legal institutions in the most recent constitutions.[15] There have also been major recent efforts of theoretical conceptualization of indigenous law.[16] This formal anchoring of non-written

---

[15] See generally W Assies G van der Haar and A Hoekema *The Challenge of Diversity: Indigenous Peoples and Reform of the State in Latin America* (Amsterdam Thela Thesis 2000).

[16] Eg C Durand Alcántara M Sámano Rentería and G Gómez González *Hacia una fundamentación teórica de la costumbre jurídica india* (Chaping Plaza y Valdés 2000); and for historical dimensions of Maya, Aztec law, O Cruz Barney *Historia del derecho en México* (Mexico Oxford University Press 1999) 3 ff.

indigenous law in basic texts of State law effectively removes objection to its proof and application before State tribunals, and there must be corresponding adjustment to second-order State rules of sources and proof of law. In the United States of America the fundamental concept is that of 'tribal sovereignty,' indicating a fundamental, irreducible core of application of tribal law, though there is ongoing and vigorous debate over the interpretation given to this concept, notably by the United States Supreme Court.[17] In Canada Article 25 of the Canadian Charter of Rights and Liberties provides that the guarantees of the Charter do not abrogate or derogate from 'aboriginal, treaty or other rights and freedoms' pertaining to aboriginal populations. From the nineteenth century, in both the United States and Canada, there has been ongoing litigation on the extent of aboriginal land claims, rooted in aboriginal law, and major decisions of the Supreme Courts of both countries have addressed the issue.

In dealing with all claims rooted in aboriginal law, State courts must be open to effective means of its proof, usually in oral form, by community members or by anthropological experts, and must come to terms with law radically different from State law. This is most evident in land claims, where a notion of a communal usufructary interest is said to underlie aboriginal title, but it is also the case in other areas of law. Adoption, for example, is highly informal in Inuit communities in the Canadian Arctic, but has been accepted by state courts as appropriate for the needs of children in a severe climate. The reasoning in all of these types of cases is comparative, since the institutions of a *lex non scripta* must first be understood, by lawyers and judges not initially familiar with them, and then it must be decided whether the institutions are recognizable by State courts. The extent of divergence from state law is relevant to this inquiry, as is the suitability of the particular institution for the circumstances in which it is invoked. It is also comparative *legal* reasoning, since the view that such unwritten law is not law, or that it is too imprecise for cognizance to be taken of it by a State court, or that it is incommensurable with State law, has now been effectively repudiated throughout the Americas.

II. COMPARATIVE LEGAL REASONING AND EUROPEAN LEGAL TRADITIONS

It is possible to identify a number of zones of law in the Americas, according to the European legal traditions that have been received. Latin America

---

[17] See eg *Nevada v Hicks* 121 S Ct 2304 (tribal jurisdiction over non-members); *Arizona Department of Revenue v Blaze Construction Co* 526 US 32 (1999) (State jurisdiction over tribes); D Getches 'Conquering the Cultural Frontier: The New Subjectivism of the Supreme Court in Indian Law' (1996) 84 Cal L Rev 1573.

has thus been characterized by a large process of reception of Spanish law, adjusted to local circumstance (*il derecho indiano.*) The common law of England has been received into a number of Caribbean Commonwealth jurisdictions as well as into the Canadian common law provinces.

French civil law has been received in diverse measure in Quebec and Louisiana. The United States of America has undergone a complex process of reception first of English common law and then a later, nineteenth-century process of adoption of major institutions of Continental civil law.[18] There are different forms and levels of comparative legal reasoning in each of these zones of law, according to the traditions received. More generally, however, it is the case that all manifestations of European-derived law in the Americas result from a process of transborder transferral of law, originally in the circumstances of colonialism. Thus, while today almost all American jurisdictions are politically independent, and have been so in some cases for hundreds of years, law has not been thought of in exclusively national terms for much of the history of the countries or jurisdictions concerned. American judicial practice has had as its primary historical concern the adjustment of European legal models, or common laws, to American circumstances. The process is one of comparative legal reasoning. Exclusivist concepts of State law have thus had less influence in the Americas than in Europe, and Western, State-centred legal theory is only partially relevant to legal and judicial practice. There are particular and different manifestations of this general phenomenon.

In Latin America it is the Spanish variant of the civilian, Continental tradition that has been received, largely in the form of the *Siete Partidas* but also subsequently in the form of the *derecho indiano*. Since much of this law was in the form of classic texts, in the case of the *Siete Partidas* going back to the thirteenth century, doctrinal exposition of it was fundamental to its ongoing adaptation and application. Comparative legal reasoning thus took place and takes place today within the cadre of this particular, ongoing, hispanic *ius commune*, and according to its traditional sources. The style of judgment in Latin America is generally discursive, and Latin American judges thus cite non-legislative sources of law, including Roman law and European legal authors. This may not be a frequent practice but it certainly does occur and there is no objection to it, as a form of comparative legal reasoning.[19] It is also the case that opinions of local legal authors may be presented to the court, as expert opinions, and these may involve extensive citing of foreign

[18] See A von Mehren *The US Legal System: Between the Common Law and Civil Law Legal Traditions* (Centro di studi e ricerche di diritto comparato straniero Rome 2000).
[19] See, for Mexican examples, WL Butte, '*Stare decisis*, Doctrine, and Jurisprudence in Mexico and Elsewhere' in J Dainow (ed) *The Role of Judicial Decisions and Doctrine in Civil Law and in Mixed Jurisdictions* (Baton Rouge Louisiana State University Press 1974) 311.

material, usually in doctrinal form.[20] In matters of public or constitutional law, US law may also be cited, given the importance of the US model in the development of Latin American constitutional law. There appears to have been no instance in Latin America of formal prohibition of citing of foreign authors, as occurred in Spain, and the ongoing use of extraterritorial sources of comparative legal reasoning prevailed even over strongly territorialist legal and political attitudes, which largely precluded application of foreign law in private international cases (the Calvo clause and doctrine).

In the Commonwealth jurisdictions of the Americas the common law has never been seen as a purely national product. Reception statutes typically set a date of reception for English law during colonial times, but the entire process of reception depended on local judicial appreciation of whether metropolitan legislation and case-law were 'suitable' for circumstances overseas.[21] The process was widespread and involved a constant comparative evaluation of potentially receivable law. Results varied widely through the Commonwealth. Moreover, case-law subsequent to the stipulated date of reception was considered capable of ongoing reception, as persuasive authority, since the common law was not seen as a positive, systemic construction, but rather as a form of ongoing judicial dialogue on what the law should be. The judges acted, and continue to act, according to what has recently been described as the 'philosophy of the common law'.[22] The judicial dialogue could obviously take place across the borders of political authority, in whatever form it took. In this environment notions of national *stare decisis*, when they emerged in the nineteenth century, could obtain only a tenuous place. Given the contemporary decline of *stare decisis*, under the avalanche of decisions, the search for legal principle across borders is now once again well under way, in fields as diverse as human rights, intellectual property, and commercial law. Studies of citation patterns in Canada show widespread use of extra-jurisdictional case-law, drawn largely from the Commonwealth and the US but extending also on occasion to civil law jurisdictions.[23] Judges also participate in transnational judicial meetings and now exchange legal information through electronic means of communication. They are coming to be recognized as a transnational 'epistemic community'.[24]

---

[20] See eg the opinion of Professor da Silva Pereira, citing Roman law, Troplong, Savatier, Josserand (France), Ruggiero and Marci (Italy), Rossel and Mentra (Switzerland), in K Karst and KS Rosenn *Law and Development in Latin America* (Berkeley University of California Press 1975) 7.

[21] See generally HP Glenn 'Persuasive Authority' (1987) 32 McGill LJ 261, 271–73.

[22] G Posterma 'Philosophy of the Common Law' in J Coleman and S Shapiro (eds) *The Oxford Handbook of Jurisprudence and Philosophy of Law* (Oxford University Press 2002) 588.

[23] See HP Glenn 'The Common Law in Canada' (1995) 74 Can Bar Rev 261, 286–8 with references.

[24] A-M Slaughter 'A Typology of Transjudicial Communication' (1994) 29 U Richmond L Rev 99.

In the North American civil law outposts of Quebec and Louisiana there is further diversity in the method and extent of comparative legal reasoning. In both jurisdictions the methods of the common law have been adopted in matters of court structures and jurisdiction (notably in matters of administrative law), procedure, and styles of judgment. Judgments are therefore discursive, as everywhere in the Americas, and judges are able to record the comparative legal reasoning which they engage in. There is perhaps more of this in public law than in private law, since the surrounding jurisdictions share the same public law tradition. In private law matters, where the law is civilian in origin, there are two recognizable directions to the comparison. The first is towards the original metropolitan jurisdictions, France in the case of Quebec and France and Spain in the case of Louisiana. It is the legal writing of the European countries that is now looked to as a source of possible inspiration, and the ongoing linguistic commonality between France and Quebec has greatly facilitated this process.[25] It is sometimes said to be less vigorous in Louisiana.[26] The other direction of comparison is towards the common law jurisdictions of North America, and this has occurred with varying degrees of tension. There have been varying forms of reification of the civil and common laws, and calls for their ongoing integrity and resistance to influence, but the judicial practice of comparison has been issue-specific and resistant to large-scale generalization.

The United States of America went through a period of intense comparative legal reasoning in the nineteenth century, the process very much paralleling the mining of Roman and other sources that preceded national legal closures in Europe.[27] The process was one of constructive borrowing or comparison, for purposes of national law-making. Much civil law thinking was thereby incorporated into US law, notably through the great treatises of Story and Kent. As in Europe, the process of comparative legal reasoning declined thereafter, though it has never disappeared entirely. Studies of case citation patterns show a steady decline of citation of out-of-State and foreign cases from the later decades of the nineteenth century through the twentieth century.[28] By 1970 the California Supreme Court was citing other State courts and foreign courts in only 10 per cent of its citations.[29]

---

[25] P-G Jobin 'Les réactions de la doctrine à la création du droit civil québécois par les juges: Le début d'une affaire de famille ' (1980) 21 C de D 257; HP Glenn 'La Cour suprême du Canada et la tradition du droit civil' (2001) 80 Can Bar Rev 151.

[26] T Yiannopoulos 'Louisiana Civil Law: A Lost Cause?' (1980) Tul L Rev 830, but see at 845, 846 ('solutions reached in civil law jurisdictions, especially France, are always pertinent and frequently persuasive').   [27] Above, text accompanying n 1.

[28] LM Friedmann et al 'State Supreme Courts: A Century of Style and Citation' (1981) 33 Stan L Rev 773.

[29] JH Merryman 'Toward a Theory of Citations: An Empirical Study of the Citation Pattern of the California Supreme Court in 1950, 1960, and 1970' (1977) 50 Cal L Rev 381, notably at 394–400.

The notion of Anglo-American law was still alive, though not in the best of health. More recently, however, a US commentator has concluded that there is 'increasing use of foreign law' in US courts, at least in connection with transborder cases, that there is ongoing use of Spanish law in matrimonial property and water rights cases in a number of southern States, and that 'episodic' comparison occurs in judicial practice elsewhere.[30] Perhaps more significantly, there is now a major debate within the US judiciary as to the need and appropriateness of acknowledging and using foreign sources of law. The United States Supreme Court has been divided on the issue, though a majority judgment has now cited European authority.[31] There have also been calls by State judges for increased use of enlightening foreign material.[32] As elsewhere, this process appears driven by the intractable nature of many problems now appearing before the courts and increasing communication, at a transnational level, among judges.

Comparative legal reasoning has also appeared in judicial practice in the Americas with respect to immigrant and minority populations, since personal laws are often invoked by members of such populations as justification for conduct before the courts. Here the question is whether implanted European legal traditions will cede in some measure before non-European ones. The answer is that they will, in some measure, though the practice falls short of recognition of personal laws. The comparative legal reasoning which takes place in such cases is designated as the process of 'reasonable accommodation' of personal law or so-called cultural practices,[33] or the recognition, in criminal matters, of a so-called 'cultural defence'.[34]

III. COMPARATIVE LEGAL REASONING IN THE CONTEXT OF FREE TRADE

Free trade areas are now multiplying throughout the Americas and it is possible that they will all be replaced by a single free trade area with the coming into force, in 2005 or later, of a Free Trade Agreement of the

---

[30] D Clark 'The Use of Comparative Law by American Courts I' (1994) 42 AJCL (Supp) 23, 23, 24, 40; see also A Levasseur 'The Use of Comparative Law by American Courts II' (1994) 42 AJCL (Supp) 41 (on what would be a decline in influence in the US of Continental law).

[31] *Laurence v Texas* 539 US (2003), the dissenting judgment of Scalia J referring to the citations as 'meaningless' and 'dangerous' dicta. Compare the earlier remarks of Breyer J in *Printz v United States* 521 US 898 (1997) 970–1 with those of Scalia J at 935.

[32] See SS Abrahamson and MJ Fischer 'All the World's a Courtroom: Judging in the New Millennium' (1997) 26 Hofstra L Rev 273.

[33] J Woehrling 'L'Obligation d'accommodement raisonnable et l'adaptation de la société à la diversité religieuse' (1998) 43 McGill LJ 325 with references.

[34] See A Dundes Renteln *The Cultural Defense* (New York Oxford University Press forthcoming).

Americas. Comparative legal reasoning plays an important role in free trade areas, for a number of reasons. First, it is unlikely that the free trade area would have come into being without a great deal of comparative legal reasoning already having been undertaken, in the intensifying legal relations that preceded the formal conclusion of the free trade agreement. In this sense, the emergence of a free trade area can be seen as the culmination of a process as much as the beginning of a process.[35] Secondly, the coming into force of a free trade agreement has a major effect on the volume of transborder transactions and transborder litigation. This inevitably intensifies cross-border legal relations and it is possible to identify a major process of unilateral adjustment of national law to accommodate the new circumstances of the free trade area. Free trade has a kind of informal slipstream effect on national law and national legal institutions. Adjustment to national law takes place as a result of comparative evaluation of national law against other laws in the free trade area and the needs of participants in the free trade.[36] The comparative law which is here identifiable may be seen in some measure, however, as comparative law of the constructive type, a means of informing and facilitating the reform of national law by national institutions. In the practice of free trade, however, there is a much more active process of comparative legal reasoning, which occurs in legal practice generally as well as before the courts.

In the North American free trade context there are two features of the process of comparative legal reasoning which are worthy of mention. The first is the development of transborder law firms, which now exist in trans-state or transprovincial form in all of the NAFTA countries and which are now beginning to develop across national borders. The transborder law firm generates a more intense and sophisticated form of comparative legal reasoning than has been previously known. It straddles political boundaries, may survey and choose among jurisdictional laws according to criteria and expertise from within its own structures, and may function in any number of jurisdictions with its own, locally qualified resources. The situation is very different from the historical one in which single practitioners

[35] On pre-NAFTA processes of convergence in North America, see V Loungnarath 'L'Intégration juridique dans la zone ALENA: Un chantier axé sur les processus' (2001) 61 R du Barreau 1, 15; and on the phenomenon generally, D Trubek Y Dezalay R Buchanan and J Davis 'Global Restructuring and the Law: Studies of the Internationalization of Legal Fields and the Creation of Transnational Arenas' (1994) 44 Case W Res L Rev 407, 466. To say that convergence facilitates the creation of free trade areas is not to say, however, that it is irreversible, or that it eliminates major elements of diversity. See the following discussion in the text.

[36] See, for this process in the context of NAFTA, HP Glenn 'Conflicting Laws in a Common Market? The NAFTA Experiment' (2001) 76 Chicago–Kent L Rev 1789–1819; HP Glenn 'North America as a Medieval Legal Construction' (2002) 2 (1) Global Jurist Art 1 (<http://www.bepress.com>) and in M Bussani and U Mattei (eds) *The Common Core of European Private Law* (The Hague Kluwer Law International 2003) 49.

would have contact with foreign law only through the medium of rules of private international law and formal opinions from foreign colleagues or academic institutions. Transborder law firms thrive in large measure on their ability to engage in comparative legal reasoning, and it has been said that in matters of contemporary transnational commercial law it is 'practising lawyers who are making the running'.[37] Where a case is litigated is thus much more the result of comparative legal reasoning than has historically been the case.

The second feature of relevant practice before the courts in the Americas is the absence of any rule, or the absence of any enforced rule, to the effect that rules of private international law are applicable in a mandatory way (*d'office, von Amts wegen*) by the judge. The contrary rule, that judges are obliged to apply conflicts rules to any transborder case and eventually to apply the designated law, exists in a number of European countries. It is the result of an apparently laudable attempt to offset the local bias of exclusivist national legal theory by ensuring that foreign States are treated on an equal footing with the State of the litigation. It is a highly unsuitable rule for a free trade area, however, since it creates a presumption that differences in national laws must be treated as conflicts of laws (in spite of results which may frequently be similar) and subjects all transborder litigation to an expensive and time-consuming second-order process of court-directed choice of law. The absence of such a rule in the Americas means that parties are able to bury formal differences of laws and litigate according to the *lex fori* if they agree that it is appropriate to do so. The presumption is one of harmony rather than of conflict, though the presumption may be reversed by either party pleading foreign law if they feel it is necessary to their case. The result is productive of comparative legal reasoning, since appreciation of foreign law cannot be left to the court and an eventual opinion by an institute specializing in foreign law, but must rather be the object of immediate appreciation and evaluation by litigants and their counsel. This active process of comparative legal reasoning, combined with a presumption of harmony of laws, means that there is no movement towards formal harmonization of laws in the Americas.[38] Given generalized knowledge of different laws, legal and judicial practice is perfectly capable of facilitating the functioning of a free trade area through a process of conciliation of laws. Comparative legal reasoning is fundamental to this process.

[37] R Goode 'International Restatements and National Law' in W Swadling and G Jones (eds) *The Search for Principle: Essays in Honour of Lord Goff of Chieveley* (Oxford University Press) 45, 57.

[38] See HP Glenn 'Harmony of Laws in the Americas' (2003) 34 Inter-American L Rev 223.

16

Comparative Law Before the Dutch Courts

AS Hartkamp

In this chapter, I shall discuss if, and to what extent, the Dutch Supreme Court of the Netherlands (Hoge Raad) uses comparative law in its decisions relating to private law.[1] I use the concept of comparative law in a broad sense, meaning that the court takes its decision only after comparing Dutch law with at least one foreign legal system.

To begin with and for clarity's sake I want to make two preliminary remarks on the external aspects of the decisions of the Dutch Supreme Court.

The first relates to their style. The style may be situated somewhere in between the French and the German tradition. They are neither as brief and laconic as the decisions of the French Cour de cassation,[2] nor as lengthy and discursive as the decisions of the German Bundesgerichtshof. Normally (subject to only a very few exceptions) there is no discussion of arguments pro and contra the solution adopted by the Court and there is no discussion of or reference to opinions expressed by legal authors or by lower courts. The same is true for comparative law considerations: they are rare.

My second remark is that one reason for their being relatively brief is that they are preceded by and effectively based on the 'conclusions' of the procureur-general or advocates-general. These conclusions are advisory opinions in which the facts of the case are set out, followed by an (often extensive) discussion of all legal aspects of the case, with references to relevant statutory provisions, case-law, and scholarly opinion. In these opinions also comparative reflections may be found. These conclusions are published together with the decision of the court and the court often refers to them,

---

[1] See, for previous discussions of this topic, HU Jessurun d'Oliveira *Rechterlijke rechtsvorming en rechtsvergelijking* (Rede Ned Ver v Rechtsvergelijking 1976) Publicaties No 24 (1977); L Strikwerda and IR de Jong *Rechtsvergelijking en rechtsvinding in burgerlijke zaken* (Ars Aequi 1994) 20 ff; T Koopmans 'Comparative Law and the Courts' (1996) 45 ICLQ 545–57; Sjef van Erp 'The Use of the Comparative Law Method by the Judiciary: Dutch National Report' in *The Use of Comparative Law by Courts* 14th International Congress of Comparative Law Athens 1997 (The Hague Kluwer Law International 1999) 235 ff.

[2] The Dutch Supreme Court is a court of cassation in the French tradition.

both for factual information (eg relating to the parliamentary history of a statute) and for arguments underlying the decision.

A court may be under a duty to enter into a study of foreign law, in which case the use of foreign law could be called non-voluntary.[3] The best-known example of this use of foreign law is where (national[4] or international)[5] private law prescribes a national court to decide a case according to foreign law. In the Netherlands this is of course a frequent phenomenon—but only in judgments of lower courts. For historical reasons that cannot be discussed here, according to statute these decisions—as far as they apply to foreign law—cannot be reviewed by the Supreme Court.[6] For this reason I will not discuss this type of case here.

Another reason to pass over them in silence is that they do not reflect comparative law in the sense indicated above. However, it must be noted that this may be different, eg, where a court is permitted by its rules of private international law to decide a case according to the legal system (ie one of several potentially applicable systems) which it considers to offer the best solution to the case under consideration (*favor*-principle).[7]

There is also non-voluntary use of foreign law where an international convention instructs the court that 'in the interpretation and application of the provisions of this Convention, regard is to be had to its international character and to the need to promote uniformity (. . .) in international trade'.[8] Such a clause 'compels the courts to develop their jurisprudence in company with the courts of other countries'.[9] Again, strictly speaking this is not comparative law, but it entails study of legal documents from foreign countries and in foreign languages; and full understanding of those materials sometimes requires an insight in the legal systems involved.[10]

Where the interpretation of statutory provisions based on international conventions (or, for example, in the European Union, directives of the Council of Ministers) is concerned, the situation will be practically identical.

The situation is different where the Court is dealing with the construction of statutory provisions of purely national private law, notably the Dutch Civil Code. It is here that the courts are free to decide if and to what

---

[3] See van Erp (n 1) 235.

[4] Either a Dutch statute or a rule of unwritten private international law developed in case-law or in legal doctrine.   [5] Eg the 1980 Rome Convention.

[6] Art 79 para 1 litt b Wet RO (Wet op de rechterlijke organisatie, ie the statute relating to the organization of the court system). As far as they apply foreign law: the 'conflict rule', which indicates the applicable law, is a 'normal' rule of Dutch law, which may be reviewed by the Supreme Court.   [7] Strikwerda and de Jong (n 1) 20.

[8] Eg Art 7 para 1 CISG.

[9] J Honnold *Uniform Law of International Sales Under the 1980 United Nations Convention* (1991) 142 ff citing Lord Scarman.

[10] See, for examples, Strikwerda and de Jong (n 1) 23. More recent cases are HR 10 Nov 1995 [1996] NJ (Nederlandse Jurisprudentie) 177; HR 9 Feb 1996 [1996] NJ 667; HR 17 Apr 1998 [1998] NJ 602; HR 30 Nov 2001 [2002] NJ 143; HR 19 Apr 2002 [2002] NJ 412.

extent they are willing to accept foreign inspiration as a source for their interpretation of the law. Here two further distinctions can be drawn.

1. The question may arise whether, in a given case, a court has relied on comparative materials in order to *find* a solution to the problem they are faced with, or whether it refers to foreign law in order to *justify* a solution arrived at on different grounds, for example on the basis of their interpretation of national law.[11] Theoretically this is an interesting divide, but in the Netherlands the Supreme Court does not inform the reader what has been the exact nature of the foreign law influence on the decision and for an outsider that nature is often difficult to ascertain.

2. Does it make any difference whether the provision that is subject to interpretation has a purely national origin or whether it has been taken from a foreign legal system? In the Netherlands we are accustomed to this latter situation because the old Civil Code was, to a large extent, a copy of the French Civil Code and the new Civil Code is based on extensive comparative studies which have left many visible traces in the Code.[12] Under the old Code (and especially in the nineteenth century) it was customary for the courts and for legal authors to study developments in French law, but these developments were not considered in any way binding for Dutch courts. In fact Dutch law has in many respects developed in a direction different from French law.[13] Under the new Code, which only entered into force in 1992, there is not yet a firm practice in this respect but it is not to be expected that the course of things will be different. So the answer to the question is yes and no: 'yes' in the sense that a foreign background invites more readily the consideration of foreign law, but 'no' in the sense that the courts will not find themselves in any way obliged to interpret a provision in the Dutch Code according to the meaning in the foreign legal system from which it has been derived.[14]

Finally, the answer to the initial question: does the Dutch Supreme Court voluntarily practice comparative law when interpreting provisions of Dutch law? The answer to this question is clearly yes, but it must be added immediately that it is only rarely admitted by the court in the sense that the judgment contains an explicit reference to foreign law. Three cases may be distinguished.

1. In the first case neither the judgement nor the advisory opinion of the procureur-general or advocate-general contains any reference to foreign

---

[11] See, for this distinction, Koopmans (n 1) 550.

[12] See AS Hartkamp 'Statutory Law Making: The New Civil Code of the Netherlands' in *Towards Universal Laws: Trends in National, European and International Lawmaking* (Uppsala 22–6 Mar 1995), De lege, Juridiska Fakulteten i Uppsala, Arsbok, Argang 5, 1995, 151 ff.

[13] EM Meijers 'Uitlegging en toepassing in Nederland van aan den Code Civil ontleende wetsvoorschriften' in *Verzamelde Privaatrechtelijke Opstellen* vol i 45 ff.

[14] Cf Asser-Vranken *Algemeen Deel* (1995) Nos 211 and 212.

law, but, nevertheless it is clear or at any rate highly probable that the decision of the court is based on comparative law reflections. Dutch case-law presents several important examples of this phenomenon.[15]

2. The judgement is silent on foreign law, but the advisory opinion of the procureur-general or advocate-general discusses aspects of foreign law. This often happens, in particular when new problems have to be solved. In these cases it is obvious that the court takes these considerations into account. This amounts to 'making use of comparative law' in the broad sense indicated above (n 1), even if the court does not follow a foreign law solution. An example is the DES decision, to which Lord Bingham referred in the *Fairchild* case.[16]

3. The court itself refers to foreign law. As I said, these cases are very rare. The first examples date from the middle of the twentieth century and were concerned with the interpretation of a Dutch provision on private international law[17] and with the law of damages.[18] In the latter one it was held that the damages that could be recovered in the case of a traffic accident included those for what was called 'non-pecuniary harm'. The Court said that this solution was in accordance with legislation or case-law in neighbouring countries. The Court could base itself on the advisory opinion of the procureur-general, in which the state of foreign law was extensively explained. After the 1940s I have only been able to find three other cases, one in the law of insurance[19] and two in the law of damages.[20]

The conclusion is that the Dutch Supreme Court is quite willing to consider comparative law. In this sense it operates in the same way as the legislator of the new Civil Code, and this approach is also perfectly

[15] Eg HR 25 May 1928 [1928] NJ 1688 ('Normzwecklehre', cf §823 para 2 BGB), HR 5 May 1950 [1951] NJ 1 (acquisition in good faith a *non domino*, cf §932 BGB), HR 30 Jan 1959 [1959] NJ 548 (sources of obligation, cf art 1173 Cod civ it). In the 1950 case it was clear that the Court based its decision on the German example, because it decided a dispute in Dutch legal doctrine in which the French and German solutions of the problem had been amply discussed.

[16] HR 9 Oct 1992 [1994] NJ 535, discussed by AS Hartkamp and MMM Tillema, *Mass torts* Netherlands Reports to the 14th International Congress of Comparative Law Athens 1994 (1995) 51–69 and by Koopmans (n 1) 551 ff, Lord Bingham in *Fairchild v Glenhaven Funeral Services* [2002] 3 WLR para 29, 115. Other examples (after Strikwerda and de Jong (n 1) 25) are: HR 3 Nov 1995 [1998] NJ 380; HR 16 Jan 1998 [1999] NJ 284; HR 19 June 1998 [1999] NJ 533; HR 28 May 1999 [1999] NJ 564; HR 1 Feb 2002 [2002] NJ 122; HR 22 Feb 2002 [2002] NJ 240; HR Sept 2002 [2002] NJ 240. Most of these cases are concerned with damages in cases of physical injury.

[17] HR 2 Apr 1942 [1942] NJ 468 (10 AB). See also HR 1 Feb 1985 [1985] NJ 698 and HR 24 Oct 1997 [1999] NJ 316.

[18] HR 21 May 1943 [1944] NJ 455.

[19] HR 13 Dec 1991 [1992] NJ 316.

[20] HR 21 Feb 1997 [1999] NJ 145 (wrongful birth); HR 28 Apr 2000 [2000] NJ 430. In HR 8 July 1992 [1992] NJ 714 the Court ruled that in assessing the amount of non-pecuniary damages lower courts are allowed to take into account developments in other legal systems, which, however, cannot be decisive.

compatible with a long-standing tradition in Dutch legal literature. However, the number of cases where this inspiration is openly admitted in the judgments is small. In view of the heavy workload of the Court,[21] it is essential that the procureur-general and the advocates-general in their advisory opinions provide the Court with the necessary information about foreign law. In the light of developments in present-day Europe with its 'gradual convergence' of private law systems, comparative law before the Court and in the judgments of the Court will become increasingly important.

---

[21] In the Netherlands there is no such thing as a 'leave to appeal' system and the Civil Senate of the Supreme Court does not have the assistance of law clerks.

17

Comparing Human Rights Jurisdictions

Sydney Kentridge

This chapter diverges from what I would think of as 'pure' judicial review into that corner of public law that concerns human rights. And it deals with the uses of comparative law in human rights jurisprudence.

One may ask at the outset why the use of comparative law in human rights cases should differ from its use in other branches of law. The use of comparative materials as a judicial technique in private law contexts, especially by the House of Lords, has become well established. Indeed, the House of Lords now expects counsel to produce relevant comparative material, at least from other common law jurisdictions. To take one striking example, earlier this year the House of Lords was faced with a difficult problem in the proof of causation in personal injury claims involving multiple but unconnected and sometimes unidentified wrongdoers. The Law Lords in their judgments examined the various solutions to the problem proposed by courts, statutes, or jurists in France, Germany, Greece, the Netherlands, Norway, Australia, Canada, and California, and by the Roman jurists Julian and Ulpian. The foreign comparisons informed the court of possible solutions to the problem, equally of the difficulties which might attend any solution.[1]

The same advantages naturally apply to the use of comparative human rights jurisprudence. But I believe that comparison with other jurisdictions is particularly appropriate in relation to human rights, for three main reasons. The first is the close family relationship between modern domestic bills or charters of rights. The common ancestor is the Universal Declaration of Human Rights with descent through such instruments as the European Convention for the Protection of Human Rights and Fundamental Freedoms and the International Covenant on Civil and Political Rights. The Universal Declaration itself had drawn heavily on the rights provisions in the Constitution of the United States. There have also been other easily discernible borrowings—thus South Africa's Constitution took from Canada the two-stage process of adjudication of alleged infringements of rights, and took from Germany the emphasis on human dignity as a fundamental right.

---

[1] *Fairchild v Glenhaven Funeral Services Ltd* [2002] 3 WLR 89.

Secondly, the use of comparative materials is virtually mandated in countries like the United Kingdom that have introduced a justiciable bill of rights for the first time and have few if any precedents in their own courts.

Many of the concepts found in a bill of rights are broadly stated, eg the right to life, or to freedom from cruel or inhuman punishment. It is not easy to find judicial standards by which to assess the reach of these rights, and the dangers of an entirely subjective approach to what is essentially a value judgment is obvious. As an American judge once warned, a constitution does not mean whatever we want it to mean. So my third reason for saying that comparative jurisprudence is particularly appropriate to human rights adjudication is that it enables the judge to test his or her value-judgment against the judgments of other judges who have grappled with similar provisions. These comparisons must be particularly helpful when considering provisions such as those in Articles 9, 10, and 11 of the European Convention, which permit limitations on the rights stated provided that they are 'necessary in a democratic society'. It is surely sensible to inquire whether other democratic societies have found the limitations in issue to be necessary.

Let me now give you an example of the comparative method in practice. I take a South Africa case, the first one heard by the new South African Constitutional Court, a court of eleven judges.

The case was *The State v Makwanyane*.[2] The issue was the constitutionality of the death penalty for murder in light of the new Bill of Rights. In the Bill of Rights one finds that there is a right to life, a right to dignity, a right not to be subjected to cruel or inhuman punishment—all subject to limitation to the extent justifiable in an open and democratic society based on freedom and equality. The Constitution itself said nothing explicitly about the death penalty. Naturally, the starting point was a consideration of the concepts themselves. But the Court had put before it by counsel a mass of treaties, constitutions, judgments, academic writings, and statistics from many parts of the world. How were these to be used? Some constitutions explicitly accept the death penalty (the United States, India): others expressly prohibit it (Germany, Namibia). In nearly all countries where the death penalty had been abrogated, that had been done by Parliament, not by judicial decision (an exception was Hungary). The largest body of caselaw was to be found in the United States. In some cases State death penalty statutes had been struck down because they resulted in the infliction of the death penalty in an arbitrary, unequal, and often racially weighted manner. But persistent majorities in the Supreme Court of the United States had held that the death penalty could not in itself be regarded as a cruel and unusual

---

[2] (1995) 6 BCLR 665. (BCLR = Butterworths Constitutional Law Reports, a series covering South Africa, Zimbabwe, and Namibia.)

punishment under the United States Constitution. How did the Constitutional Court deal with this mass of conflicting authority? The judgments—eleven of them—are not easily summarized. In essence, the Court found that the death penalty was not compatible with the recognition of the dignity and worth of the individual which underlay the new Constitution. It negated the right to life and the right to dignity and was in itself cruel and inhuman. Most of the judgments dealt in some detail with the American cases. The judges noted that the US Constitution expressly recognized the existence of capital punishment; but they were more impressed by the fact that distinguished dissenting judges in the US Supreme Court, in particular Brennan J, had nonetheless felt driven to take another view, holding that the concept of human dignity, although not mentioned in the US Constitution, was at the core of the constitutional prohibition of cruel and unusual punishment. In Brennan J's words (*Gregg v Georgia*):[3] 'The fatal constitutional infirmity in the punishment of death is that it treats members of the human race as non-humans . . . [It is] thus inconsistent with the fundamental premise of the clause that even the vilest criminal remains a human being possessed of common human dignity.'

The South African judges noted that the Supreme Courts of California and Massachusetts had struck down the death penalty in those States. They were also impressed by the fact that Blackmun J, who had in earlier cases in the Supreme Court upheld the death penalty, had eventually stated (now in dissent) that it was impossible to eliminate the factors of discrimination and arbitrariness in its application, and that it could no longer be constitutionally justified.[4] They also observed that distinguished American judges (albeit also in dissent) had held that the death penalty now had to be measured against standards of humanity and decency which had evolved since the far-off time when the US Constitution had been framed. Some weight was also placed on a Canadian and a European Court of Human Rights judgment on extradition of murderers to the United States, and on judgments of the Privy Council and of the Supreme Court of Zimbabwe on the cruelty of what had been called the 'death-row phenomenon'. One of the judges also referred to a number of judgments of the German Federal Constitutional Court.

On the second-stage inquiry, namely whether the death penalty, although an infringement of the enumerated rights, could be justifiable in a democratic society, the Court considered a mass of statistical and other evidence from many countries in addition to South Africa (sometimes dignified with the description 'a Brandeis brief'), cited to prove either that capital punishment was or was not a real deterrent to would-be murderers. Not surprisingly, the Court found the evidence inconclusive. Finally, it held that the

---

[3] 428 US 153 (1976) 230.   [4] *Collins v Collins* 114 SCt 1127 (1994) 1130–1.

Attorney-General had failed to show that the death penalty was justifiable in a democratic society.

As I have said, there were eleven judgments (one I confess was mine), but what I would commend to anyone interested in the handling of comparative law materials is the main judgment of the President of the Court, Justice Arthur Chaskalson. It shows an impressive mastery of the variegated materials, an appreciation of the important differences between various bills of rights, and above all an appreciation of the differing legal, historical, and social backgrounds to the decisions of foreign courts. It cannot be praised too highly, as an example of the use of comparative law at its most sensitive.

And yet there are questions. The South African Court was very much alive to the danger of assuming that a constitution is whatever a judge would like it to mean. But one cannot avoid some feeling of unease. In using comparative materials the freedom to select is virtually unfettered. None of the foreign judgments referred to was binding on the court. The judges were able to choose freely between the conflicting views of, say, Brennan J and Scalia J. It was open to them to approve the judgment of the Hungarian Court and to distinguish or disapprove the judgment in a contrary sense of the Supreme Court of Tanzania. As to what was or was not justifiable in a democratic society, the judges attached great weight to the abolition of capital punishment during the twentieth century in most democratic countries. But that entailed rejecting as a source of guidance the practices of the two great democracies of the United States and India.

I must cite here, as I did in my concurring judgment, what Scalia J once said on the subject of the evolving standards of humanity and decency: 'The risk of assessing evolving standards is that it is all too easy to believe that evolution has culminated in one's own views.'[5] I believe that the South African Court avoided that pitfall (at least the other ten judges did), but it is an ever present danger when the freedom exists to follow congenial authorities and reject inconvenient ones.

Professor Christopher McCrudden of Oxford has written, with more learning and sophistication than I can muster, on the problematical aspects of the use of judgments from other countries as so-called persuasive authorities.[6] Some critics have said that foreign authorities which may at the will of the judge be used or ignored are, when cited, no more than confirmation of the judge's opinion rather than a force that shapes that opinion. The term 'cherry-picking' has been used. And it has been suggested that so-called foreign authority is no more than a source of comfort for the judge who has to make a difficult or controversial decision.

[5] *Thomson v Oklahoma* 487 US 815 (1988) 865.
[6] C McCrudden 'A Common Law of Human Rights?' (2000) 20 OJLS (2000) 499.

It is well known that the United States Supreme Court does not find it necessary to seek comfort in foreign authority.

In *Thompson v Oklahoma*,[7] a case before the US Supreme Court in 1988, in which a majority held that the death penalty for murderers younger than 16 years was unconstitutional, Stevens J noted that the law or practice of most Western democracies did not countenance the execution of juveniles.

His dissenting colleague, Justice Scalia, rebuked him. He said that the Court was only concerned with the United States Constitution: 'the views of other nations, however enlightened the Justices of this Court may think them to be, cannot be imposed upon American through the Constitution.' But in a country without the benefit, or the burden, of 200 years of constitutional jurisprudence that is hardly a useful approach. On the contrary, and despite the dangers to which I have referred, I have no doubt that comparative human rights jurisprudence, carefully used, is at least informative, is in general enriching, and at best can be inspiring.

One of the constantly recurring questions wherever a constitution or bill of rights protects the presumption of innocence in criminal trials is the constitutionality of reverse onus provisions in criminal statutes. Nowhere, as far as I know, is it held that all reverse onus provisions must be struck down as infringements of the presumption of innocence. The individual's right must be balanced against the needs of society. But how is the balance to be struck? It is hard to believe that any court coming new to this problem would not be assisted by the analysis developed by the Supreme Court of Canada.

The Supreme Court of Canada has held that a reverse onus provision prima facie offends against the presumption if it permits a conviction despite a reasonable doubt as to the guilt of the accused. If that infringement is to be justified, it must survive a rigorous testing. In an oversimplified summary, the objective of the reverse onus provision must be of sufficiently pressing public concern to warrant overriding a constitutionally protected right. If the existence of such an objective has been established, the means chosen to achieve it must pass a proportionality test: first there must be a rational connection between the reverse onus provision and the objective; secondly the provision must impair the basic right as little as possible; and thirdly the infringement of the basic right should be proportional to the objective.[8]

The Privy Council in an appeal from Hong Kong[9] pointed out that the Hong Kong Bill of Rights, unlike the Canadian Charter of Rights and

---

[7] Above, n 5.
[8] See eg *R v Oakes* (1886) 26 DLR (4th) 200, *R v Whyte* (1988) 51 DLR (4th) 481, *R v Downey* (1992) 90 DLR 449
[9] *A-G, Hong Kong v Lee Kwong-kut* [1993] AC 951.

Freedoms, did not provide for a two-stage examination of alleged infringements of rights, and considered that in most cases all that was needed in
relation to a reverse onus provision was a general balancing of the interests
of the individual and society. In my respectful opinion the open-ended
impressionistic balancing exercise of that sort tends to miss the emphasis on
the importance of the primary right and the heavy onus of justification
which emerge from the Canadian analysis—an analysis generally adopted
now by the South African courts. A less rigorous balancing tends to give
undue emphasis to the seriousness and prevalence of the crime in question.

The Privy Council said, in the Hong Kong appeal, 'In a case where there
is real difficulty . . . regard can be had to the approach now developed by
the Canadian courts.'[10] I would respectfully agree, with the rider that in my
experience all these cases are cases of real difficulty.

More recently, Lord Steyn in the House of Lords[11] has attempted to curb
a too easy justification of the transfer of the burden of legal proof by reference to the more rigid analyses of the Canadian Supreme Court and the
South African Constitutional Court. I do not think that his use of foreign
authority could be described as a mere comfort blanket. Lord Steyn quoted
at length a passage from an eloquent[12] judgment of Sachs J in the South
African Constitutional Court on the dangers inherent in the less than rigorous individual versus society exercise mode of balancing recommended in
the Hong Kong appeal. I should like to quote it too:

There is a paradox at the heart of all criminal procedure, in that the more serious the crime and the greater the public interest in securing convictions of the
guilty, the more important do constitutional protections of the accused become.
The starting point of any balancing inquiry where constitutional rights are
concerned must be that the public interest in ensuring that innocent people are
not convicted and subjected to ignominy and heavy sentences, massively
outweighs the public interest in ensuring that a particular criminal is brought to
book . . . Hence the presumption of innocence, which serves not only to protect
a particular individual on trial, but to maintain public confidence in the endur-
ing integrity and security of the legal system. Reference to the prevalence and
severity of a certain crime therefore does not add anything new or special to the
balancing exercise. The perniciousness of the offence is one of the givens, against
which the presumption of innocence is pitted from the beginning, not a new
element to be put into the scales as part of the justificatory balancing exercise. If
this were not so, the ubiquity and ugliness argument could be used in relation to
murder, rape, car-jacking, housebreaking, drug-smuggling, corruption . . . the list
is unfortunately almost endless, and nothing would be left of the presumption of
innocence, save, perhaps, for its relic status as a doughty defender of rights in the
most trivial cases.[13]

---

[10] Per Lord Woolf at 967.   [11] In *R v Lambert* [2002] 2 AC 545.
[12] The description is Lord Steyn's.   [13] *State v Coetzee* (1997) 4 BCLR 437 para 220.

You will understand why I said that at its best comparative human rights jurisprudence can be inspiring.

I also said earlier that the use of material from other jurisdictions could be enriching. Let me illustrate that with a contrary example.

In *Dudgeon v The UK*[14] the applicant had complained to the European Court of Human Rights (ECHR) that under the laws of Northern Ireland the police had entered his house and questioned him about his homosexual activities—activities conducted in private but for which he was liable to prosecution under the laws of Northern Ireland. The ECHR in a fully and carefully reasoned judgment had held that the Northern Ireland legislation constituted an unjustifiable interference with the applicant's right to respect for his private life and thus infringed article 8 of the European Convention. Some years later in *Bowers v Hardwick*[15] on virtually the same facts and the same domestic law, the issue came before the US Supreme Court in an appeal from Georgia. The majority in a divided court held that the equivalent Georgian legislation was *not* unconstitutional. For the majority, in Justice White's succinct opinion, the Constitution simply did not create a right to engage in homosexual sodomy. That was the end of it. Blackmun J for the dissenters was equally terse. He said that civilized man's most valued right was the right to be let alone. In the words of a caustic American commentator,[16] on the theory that two clichés are better than one, Blackmun J added that a man's house was his castle. The *Dudgeon* case was not mentioned by either majority or dissenters, nor, it seems, by counsel.

The same commentator, Mary Ann Glendon, said of these judgments:[17]

Regardless of how one views the outcome of *Bowers v Hardwick*, it is hard to avoid a sense that the opinion writers in that case did not do justice to the gravity and complexity of the matter before them. This is not to insist that the result in *Bowers* was 'wrong' and certainly not that *Dudgeon* was 'authority' that American judges should have followed. The Supreme Court justices, however, and perhaps more especially plaintiff's counsel, did ignore a valuable (and readily available) resource. Crosslighting from other cultural and political contexts cannot solve American problems, but it can illuminate them ... The six *Dudgeon* opinions ... contained ideas and information that could have focussed issues, enlarged perspectives, improved the quality of reasoning, and ultimately helped to place our Court's decision—whichever way it went—on a sounder and more persuasive footing.[18]

I also remarked earlier that comparative human rights law must be used carefully: that was a statement of the obvious. Care is needed because bills of right are not all the same, notwithstanding the strong family resemblances. One must always start with one's own text. Nor can differences in

---

[14] (1982) 4 EHRR 149.
[15] 478 US 186 (1986).
[16] MA Glendon *Rights Talk* (New York Free Press 1993) 151.
[17] Ibid 152.
[18] The issue is expected to be revisited by the US Supreme Court.

legal and social background be ignored. That is why, to take one instance, courts of the Commonwealth have rightly been reluctant to follow American First Amendment authority in freedom of speech cases.

It is appropriate, in ending, to quote Justice Kriegler of the South African Constitutional Court, in a judgment on freedom of speech and its limitation in cases of the form of contempt of court, known by its archaic name of 'scandalizing the court'. The Constitutional Court rejected an invitation to apply the 'clear and present danger' test formulated by the United States Supreme Court:[19]

The fundamental reason why the test evolved under the First Amendment cannot lock on to our crime of scandalising the court, is because our Constitution ranks the right to freedom of expression differently. With us it is not a pre-eminent freedom ranking above all others. It is not even an unqualified right. The First Amendment declaims an unequivocal and sweeping commandment; section 16(1), the corresponding provision in our Constitution, is wholly different in style and significantly different in content. It is carefully worded, enumerating specific instances of the freedom and is immediately followed by a number of material limitations in the succeeding subsection. Moreover, the Constitution . . . proclaims three conjoined, reciprocal and covalent values to be foundational to the Republic: human dignity, equality and freedom. With us the right to freedom of expression cannot be said automatically to trump the right to human dignity. The right to dignity is at least as worthy of protection as is the right to freedom of expression. How these two rights are to be balanced, in principle and in any particular set of circumstances, is not a question that can or should be addressed here. What is clear though and must be stated, is that freedom of expression does not enjoy superior status in our law.[20]

You may think that type of constitutional analysis will ensure that there is more to comparative human rights law than mere cherry-picking.

[19] See *Bridges v California* 314 US 252 (1941).
[20] Kriegler J in *State v Mamabolo* (2001) 5 BCLR 449, 469–70 (para 41).

18

Comparative Civil Procedure Before Austrian Courts

Paul Oberhammer

I

Comparative civil procedure can be relevant for national courts in two respects. On the one hand, courts can apply comparative law (without being formally obliged to do so) as a method of interpretation taking into account not only national, but also foreign, sources. On the other hand, there are, of course, also constellations where the application of foreign civil procedural law is legally necessary: The generally known principle of *lex fori*, whereby although national courts might have to apply foreign substantive law they always have to apply domestic procedural law, is in reality only a rule of thumb for the uninformed; in fact a procedural law of conflicts is currently evolving in many countries (often without this being clearly recognized).[1] The focus of this chapter is on the first of these two issues.[2] However, in the first place[3] I will briefly deal, by way of an example, with the difficulties existing in Austria, even if Austrian courts were strictly obliged to ascertain the content of foreign procedural law.

II

In two recent decisions the Austrian Oberste Gerichtshof (Highest Court of Justice) had to decide whether a plaintiff, which had its registered office in New York (and did not have the nationality of a Member State of the European Union), had to pay security for costs for pursuing an action in Austria. A central condition for the decision was, in each case, the question of whether an Austrian judgment, ordering a losing plaintiff to reimburse the defendant's costs, would be enforceable in New York.

[1] Cf from a German point of view Schack *Internationales Zivilverfahrensrecht* (3rd edn 2002) 16 ff. [2] Cf Sect III ff. [3] Cf Sect II below.

In a decision passed in 1997[4] the Oberste Gerichtshof initially dealt with the statutes applicable in the State of New York in quite a lot of detail. On this basis the court then came to the 'interim conclusion' that an Austrian costs decision would be enforceable in New York. The comments on common law which followed on from this may—to put it cautiously—appear somewhat strange to a lawyer from a common law jurisdiction: apart from the relevant foreign country's legislation, its practice must (according to the Oberste Gerichtshof) also not be ignored; this is, of course, still true. However, the Oberste Gerichtshof then remarks, 'It is precisely in legal systems which are strongly characterised by judge-made law—like Anglo-American law—that it must also be considered whether enforcement is very probable under the other State's case-law.' There follows the remarkable attempt to explain the nature of common law in three sentences:

The origin of US law is also common law, a case-law developed in medieval times by English courts, which is not based upon broad legal principles but upon legal axioms developed by judges out of numerous decisions. A decision made by a judge can become a precedent case for all following, similar cases provided the facts are similar to the facts of the precedent case. The specificity of a case is therefore important.

Against the background of this 'common law in a nutshell' one would like to think that the Oberste Gerichtshof would therefore only analyse the case-law relevant to New York. However, this is not precisely the case. Instead common law's 'specificity of a case' is then used as an argument in order to qualify the 'interim conclusion' mentioned before arrived at on the basis of American statutory law. In brief and spelled out, the Oberste Gerichtshof means nothing other than—because of the existence of case-law in Anglo-American law—one cannot rely on the existing statutes there being applied! The court then uses this as an opportunity to engage in speculation about the grounds upon which the New York courts could perhaps refuse to enforce an Austrian costs decision. It is strongly emphasized that—because of the 'sacred' 'American rule' in the United States, whereby the other side's litigation costs do not have to be reimbursed as a matter of principle—one could not reject out of hand the objection that a New York court 'could refuse to enforce an Austrian judgment on costs despite the above-described legal situation.' This decision has correctly been criticized, not only because the content of foreign law was completely inadequately ascertained (as was previously the case in similar cases), but also particularly because the speculation by the Oberste Gerichtshof that American courts might refuse to enforce Austrian cost decisions because of the 'American rule' can be refuted by, of all things, relevant American case-law.[5]

---

[4] SZ 70/86 = ZfRV 1997, 167.
[5] Czernich 'Die Ausländerprozesskostensicherheit nach §57 ZPO', [1998] ÖJZ 254 ff; cf also id 'Österreichisch–Amerikanisches Zivilprozessrecht' [2002] JBl 629 ff.

The Oberste Gerichtshof has clearly taken this criticism seriously and commented in a subsequent decision from 2001 that the author of the criticism 'correctly stated that the question of whether a decision by an Austrian civil court on the reimbursement of costs can be enforced in the USA requires careful examination'.[6] In Austria (as in Germany, for instance) the application of foreign law is not subject to the principle of *iura novit curia*; rather, evidence can be heard on it pursuant to section 271 of the Austrian Code of Civil Procedure (*Zivilprozessordnung*).[7] In German practice, lawyers at the universities and other academic research institutions frequently prepare opinions in such cases about the applicable foreign law.[8] In the decision just mentioned (in which the Oberste Gerichtshof directed the court at lower instance to collect information about the content of the relevant New York law), there is a noteworthy final comment: the Oberste Gerichtshof advises the lower courts that the Max-Planck Institute for Foreign and International Private Law in Hamburg or the Swiss Institute for Comparative Law in Lausanne can give information about foreign law which was 'beyond all controversy, superior, quick and at a reasonable price'. The court presumably means; no one in Austria can. I would not like to add anything further to this sad, but (save for a few exceptions) correct finding about the state of academic comparative law in Austria.

III

Quite a lot has already been said and written about—as Zweigert called it—'comparative law as a universal method of interpretation'.[9] Indeed it is nothing new for courts to look for and find new arguments in foreign legal systems.[10] Naturally, this is particularly often the case in closely related legal systems, where the courts often do not even consciously think of such an approach being a method involving comparative law; thus, for instance, Austrian decisions contain countless references to German decisions and

---

[6] Oberste Rückstellungskommission beim Obersten Gerichtshof 28 Nov 2001 Rkv 1/01 (unpub).

[7] Cf Rechberger in Rechberger (ed) *Kommentar zur ZPO* (2nd edn 2000) commentary to sect 271.

[8] On this practice, cf Schack *Internationales Zivilverfahrensrecht* 276 ff.

[9] K Zweigert 'Rechtsvergleichung als universale Interpretationsmethode' (1949–5a) 15 RabelsZ 5.

[10] Cf eg(on German case-law) Aubin 'Die rechtsvergleichende Interpretation autonom-internen Rechts in der deutschen Rechtsprechung' (1970) 34 RabelsZ 458; Dölle 'Der Beitrag der Rechtsvergleichung zum deutschen Recht' in *Hundert Jahre deutsches Rechtsleben: Festschrift zum hundertjährigen Bestehen des deutschen Juristentages II* (1960) 19 ff; for Switzerland, Spiro 'Über den Gerichtsgebrauch zum allgemeinen Teil des revidierten Obligationenrechts' (1948); for Austria F Bydlinski *Juristische Methodenlehre und Rechtsbegriff* (2nd edn 1991) 385 ff.

literature and, in some cases, German court rulings have even been absorbed
en bloc. For example, the Oberste Gerichtshof noted in a leading decision in
1991 verbatim 'that the rules on capital-replacing shareholder loans developed
under German law'—ie the rules whereby a loan granted by a shareholder to
the company when the company is in a crisis may not be treated as a loan, but
as equity, in any subsequent insolvency proceedings—'are also to be applied
under Austrian law'.[11] Here, although Austrian courts hardly notice it in these
and similar cases, comparative law is, of course, being applied as a method for
the court to make its findings. Especially in the context of commercial and
corporate law, but sometimes also in relation to civil procedure, the relationship which Austrian law has to German law is, of course, so strong that
Austrian judgments frequently refer to German literature or German decisions
without even making it clear that the source is in fact a foreign source (which
sometimes even leads to mistakes because courts and also academic authors
forget to take into account that statutory law in Germany *is* indeed different
from the Austrian one). One reason for this is—as might be the case with similar connections within common law—the common legal development in
Austria and Germany over a long period of time, which has led to the legal
systems being very similar and naturally the fact that there is no language
barrier between these two countries.[12] Another reason is that, from an
Austrian point of view, it would also be very uneconomic to ignore German
discussions on similar legal problems. After all, Germany's population is
roughly ten times greater than Austria's, which makes it highly probable that
a legal problem which has not yet been resolved in Austria has already been
the subject of court decisions or academic treatment in Germany. This aspect
may also be a reason (though perhaps not the only reason) why, in contrast,
Austrian developments are hardly noticed in Germany.[13] A lot more could be
said about the relation between Austria and Germany, which is indeed a
complex one (from the Austrian perspective) not only, but also, in the field of
law.[14] However, this 'special relation' is not the main subject of this chapter.

IV

While in such cases comparative law is applied rather pragmatically and intu-
itively as a method for a court to make its findings, there are also decisions in

---

[11] SZ 64/53.

[12] The factor of the common German language must, however, not be overestimated; Swiss
sources are almost never cited in Austria.

[13] Schlosser 'Die lange deutsche Reise in die prozessuale Moderne' (1991) JZ 603 even
states that almost a principle of 'Austriaca non leguntur' is applied in Germany.

[14] See in this context eg the interesting study by Kramer 'Der Einfluss des BGB auf das
schweizerische und österreichische Privatrecht' (2000) 200 (AcP) 365 ff.

which the desire for European legal unification is stated as a reason for using comparative law for the purposes of argumentation. This notion has become particularly important in Austria in the area of procedural law. An early example, also known in continental Europe,[15] of such a 'pro-European' comparative law approach by courts is the English decision in the case *Rasu Maritima v Pertambangan*; in that case Lord Denning justified the English courts' development of the Mareva injunction by referring to the fact that such a remedy was widely known in continental Europe, which is why England should also take this approach: 'By doing so we should be fulfilling one of the requirements of the Treaty of Rome, that is the harmonisation of the laws of the member countries.'[16]

From the point of view of common law it may come as a surprise that there is also judge-made law based on similar notions in a civil law jurisdiction such as Austria. Of course one must not underestimate the practical significance of judges developing the law, especially in the German *Rechtskreis*: it is not the notion of judges developing the law which is new here; rather it is, on the one hand, the 'internationalized approach' and, on the other hand, the fact that this has become particularly important in procedural law, for the Austrian courts (like the German courts) are traditionally significantly more reticent in matters of procedural law than in matters of substantive law.

A decision of the Austrian Oberste Gerichtshof in 1997[17] provides a particularly vivid example of this new development. In Austrian law it was disputed for decades (in both court decisions and academic writing) whether judgments in civil cases also had the effects of a judgment on an intervening third party or a party summoned by a third-party notice; unlike in, for instance, German law this question is not regulated by statute in Austria. In 1997 an enlarged senate of the Oberste Gerichtshof (ie the highest instance appointed to decide fundamental questions) answered this question in the affirmative with remarkable reasoning: At first glance this decision seems to come to the opposite conclusion because of its detailed discussion of domestic procedural law; however, it then makes a U-turn by

---

[15] Cf Storme 'Überall dasselbe Prozessßrecht?' in *Verfahrensgarantien im nationalen und internationalen Prozeßrecht: Festschrift für Matscher* (1993) 500 ff.

[16] *Rasu Maritima SA v Perusahaan Pertambangan Minyak Dan Gas Bumi Negara and Government of Indonesia* [1978] QB 644, [1977] 3 All ER 324, CA.

[17] SZ 70/60 = [1997] JBl 368 = [1977] ecolex 422 (Oberhammer) = [1997–8] JAP (Chiwitt–Oberhammer); cf on this Klicka 'Die Bindungswirkung bei Nebenintervention und Streitverkündung', [1997] JBl 611; Mansel 'Gerichtspflichtigkeit von Dritten. Streitverkündung und Interventionsklage' in Bajons-Mayr-Zeiler (eds) 'Die Übereinkommen von Brüssel und Lugano' (1997) 207; Rechberger 'Der österreichische OGH als (Ersatz-) Gesetzgeber' in *Wege zur Globalisierung des Rechts, Festschrift für Schütze* (1999) 711; Oberhammer 'Zur "Internationalisierung" der Rechtsfindung, dargestellt am Beispiel des Verfahrensrechts' in Bundesministerium für Justiz (ed), *Global Business und Justiz* (2000) 380 ff.

applying comparative law. Article 6(2) of the Brussels and Lugano Convention governs jurisdiction in matters relating to actions on a warranty or guarantee or third-party proceedings. Germany, Spain, Austria, and Switzerland have made a reservation in Article V of Protocol 1 to the Lugano Convention against this jurisdiction;[18] at the same time it was agreed there that any effects which judgments given in those States may have on third parties will also be recognized in the other contracting States—ie the effects of a judgment on interveners and thus precisely those effects, the existence of which was controversial under Austrian law.

In brief, the Austrian Oberste Gerichtshof drew the conclusion from this provision that judgments must also have such effects on third parties in Austria. The reasoning for this is particularly noteworthy: according to the Oberste Gerichtshof, European procedural law was to be considered 'also as a model for the interpretation of autonomous civil procedural law because its provisions ... are acceptable due to its balance'. A 'core purpose' of the Lugano Convention was 'to speed up legal unification between the contracting States'. If one were to consider matters differently in the case of third-party notices and interveners, this would lead to 'particularism which was not desired by the legislator' and to the development of 'particularistic Austrian law', which runs counter to the objective of European legal uniformity.

Three things are remarkable about this decision. First, the case had no international aspect whatsoever; secondly, the 'European-friendly interpretation' is here obviously not a means to an end to justify a result which was desired anyhow—for, apparently, originally the converse was going to be decided; and thirdly, this decision is remarkable because the Oberste Gerichtshof considers the 'Europeanization' of codified procedural law with continental European character to be one of the tasks of national court rulings. Although this decision is a particularly striking one, it is by no means an isolated example of the 'European-friendliness' of this court, especially in the field of civil procedural law.[19]

Of course, more in-depth reading of the English and Austrian decision shows the limits of such an approach: Lord Denning really only refers to the French *saisie conservatoire* and then remarks that there is something like that everywhere on the Continent; as is well known, the Mareva injunction was then understood in continental Europe to be a new 'invention' of English law. The Austrian Oberste Gerichtshof really only looks closely at German law and then cites several Swiss sources, from which it infers that

---

[18] Cf also Art 65 of Regulation (EC) 44/2001.

[19] Cf on this in general terms Oberhammer 2000 (n 17) 369 ff; id 'Internationale Rechtshängigkeit, Aufrechnung und objektive Rechtskraftgrenzen in Europa' [2002] IPRax 428 ff.

the legal situation in the procedural codes of the Swiss cantons is 'by and large' the same as in Germany; although Spain also made a reservation to Article 6(2) of the Convention, the legal situation there is not mentioned at all, and no mention is even made of the legal systems of the other Member States. This observation should not be misunderstood in any way as constituting criticism of these courts. National high courts are, after all, not research institutes for comparative law; if a judge of the Austrian Oberste Gerichtshof has to draft more than 100 decisions each year, then it is understandable if he does not also examine Spanish law. The situation here is different from the case of the European Court of Justice (ECJ)[20] or in international arbitration,[21] where the necessity to approximate the substance of diverging national concepts and the perspective of comparative law ensue from the fact alone that lawyers from various countries are brought together.[22] Here academic jurisprudence is no doubt called upon to offer appropriate 'assistance'.[23] Nowadays we still have to ask ourselves the same question as *Sacco* formulated in 1977: 'La circulation des modèles (. . .) est-elle aujourd'hui suffisamment intense pour prévaloir sur les frontières politiques et linguistiques?'[24] Although the last decades have brought a veritable boom in research in comparative law in a number of jurisdictions, nevertheless, for example, some national reforms of procedural law have nowadays been based on much less extensive preparatory comparative work than was the case in the same countries in the nineteenth century; and even at the European level there is always the risk that the legislator of regulations or directives thinks too little about the territory in which its law is supposed to flourish.

As a result of this, one cannot fail to appreciate that the comparative law approach still has to find its position in the traditional canon of methods of making legal findings. From the point of view of the German *Rechtskreis* it should be noted that, on the basis of codified law, the development of juristic methods has come a long way from the 'reception-friendly' principle of

---

[20] On the role of comparative law in civil procedural case-law of the ECJ, cf also, from a German perspective, Kropholler *Europäisches Zivilprozeßrecht* (7th edn 2002) intro, margin nos 48 ff.

[21] On the aspect of the harmonization of procedural law by the practice of international arbitration cf from a German perspective, Wagner 'Europäisches Beweisrecht— Prozessrechtsharmonisierung durch Schiedsgerichte [2001] ZEuP 455 ff.

[22] It is noteworthy here that the Liechtenstein Oberste Gerichtshof (Highest Court of Justice), as the European court of last instance which is entirely comprised of foreign—namely Austrian—judges, has already drawn conclusions in analogy to Austrian law; cf on this H Heiss 'Zur Kodifikation des liechtensteinischen internationalen Privatrechts' in Pro *iustitia et scientia: Festschrift für Kohlegger* (2000) 266 et seq.

[23] Cf this opinion of von Mehren in 'The Role of Comparative Law in the Practice of International Law' in *Festschrift für Neumayer* (1985) 485.

[24] Sacco 'Droit commun de l'Europe, et composantes du droit' in Cappelletti (ed) *New Perspectives for a Common Law in Europe* (1978) 98.

statuta stricte sunt interpretanda to the method of *Wertungsjurisprudenz*,[25] which dominates today. The comparative law approach can therefore not be an alternative to the developed understanding of methods; instead it can only exist in addition to the latter—an addition which in this context partly still has to look for, and perhaps even fight for, its place among that which has dominated up to now, by proving its argumentative authority. As *ceterum censeo* I would like to add that, particularly in the field of juridical methods, we are, after all, presently still in many aspects a long way from a European *acquis*: if legal integration brings some disorder as a transitional product, *Rechtsdogmatik* (as we call it in the German *Rechtskreis*) is, in my opinion, meant to create order to a much greater extent even than hitherto.

V

Moreover, today there already is a provision—in Article 1 of Protocol 2 to the Lugano Convention—that expressly requires national courts of the Member States to pay due account to the law of other States when interpreting the Convention. According to this provision, the courts of each contracting State shall, when applying and interpreting the provisions of the Convention, pay due account to the principles laid down by any relevant decision delivered by courts of the other contracting States concerning provisions of this Convention. Even if the ECJ's case-law on the Brussels Convention/Regulation (quite rightly) dominates the interpretation of the Lugano Convention, there are nevertheless decisions in this connection that are guided by the case-law of other national courts.

However, this is obviously done in very different ways. For instance, to define the term 'consumer' under Article 13(1) of the Lugano Convention, the Swiss Bundesgericht (Federal Court) considered and discussed not only the case-law of the ECJ but also German decisions and literature.[26] While this decision draws upon foreign case-law as a guide to help its argumentation, which should not be deviated from without good cause, the Austrian Oberste Gerichtshof took a completely different route. In a decision on the scope of application of Article 17 of the Lugano Convention[27] it agreed with a restrictive interpretation by German[28] and Italian[29] case-law and,

---

[25] Cf on this Zimmermann 'Statuta sunt stricte interpretanda? Statutes and the Common Law: A Continental Perspective' [1997] CLJ 315.

[26] BGE 121 III 336 = [1996] SZIER 84 (Volken).

[27] [1998] ecolex 694 (Oberhammer). The legal opinion expressed in this decision has, of course—like its precedents from Germany and Italy—been superseded by decisions which have since been delivered by the ECJ (cf ECJ Group Josi 412/98; Coreck 387/98); in this sense also (obiter) the Austrian Oberste Gerichtshof RdW 2002/452.

[28] Cf [1992] IPRax 377.   [29] Cf (1994) Foro italiano 2158 (Pagni).

more particularly, *only* referred to the 'harmonized application of law' required by Article 1 of Protocol 2—without any substantive reasoning! It therefore only focuses on the results of the deliberations of the German Bundesgerichtshof and the Italian Corte di Cassazione (and, what's more—because of a 'European-friendly' argument in the foreground—in so doing it came to a conclusion which severely limits the scope of application of European law). The approach by the Swiss Bundesgericht is here, in my opinion, clearly to be preferred. The point of approximating laws by observing foreign case-law cannot be to create a kind of international precedent law applying the method *prior tempore potior iure*; instead, the focus should be on the weight of the better arguments,[30] European competition between the best ideas.

VI

In a host of decisions the Austrian Oberste Gerichtshof had (additionally) applied the Lugano Convention on questions of international civil procedural law, even though it had not yet entered into force in Austria at the relevant time because it had not been ratified.[31] In one of these decisions there is a comment that summarizes the underlying understanding in order to justify this method. There the Oberste Gerichtshof remarks that the rules of foreign legal systems (and signed but not yet ratified international treaties) could also be considered to fill gaps (in codified law), to weight elements of (Austrian) rules, and to determine trends in solutions.[32]

Remarks like this of course invite legal practice to refer in their submissions in litigation to foreign precedents. It could in fact be that such cases have in recent times become more frequent. Thus, for instance, in a case before the Handelsgericht (Commercial Court) of Vienna in 2002 (which has not yet been finally concluded) the defendants referred to relevant decisions of the Italian Corte di Cassazione regarding the question whether the Austrian courts had international jurisdiction (only) because foreign courts would otherwise deliver a decision which (from an Austrian perspective) would be a breach of *ordre public* (public policy); the Handelsgericht followed their argumentation and in this connection cited the said Italian

---

[30] Cf on this Basedow 'Das BGB im künftigen europäischen Vertragsrecht. Der hybride Kodex' (2000) 200 AcP 461 ff.

[31] Cf [1995] WBl 265 = [1996] IPRax 201; SZ 65/14 = [1993] EvBl 93 = [1993] JB 666 = [1993] ZfRV 43; [1995] JBl 595 = [1995] EvBl 137 = [1995] RdW 219 = [1995] ZfRV 15.

[32] [1995] WBl 265 = [1996] IPRax 201. Cf on this decision Pfeiffer, 'Falscher vorauseilender Gehorsam in die richtige Richtung—zur "Lugano-freundlichen" Auslegung des autonomen österreichischen Zuständigkeitsrechts' [1996] IPRax 205; Oberhammer 2000 (n 17) 391 ff.

decisions in its court order.[33] This case shows firstly that the comparative law approach is already beginning to play a role in cases at first instance; I hardly think that this would have been possible twenty years ago. Secondly, this case also shows how comparative law could play a role before Austrian courts in future; not so much by the courts referring to foreign precedents *ex officio* (as in the above-mentioned cases), but rather by the parties making such submissions. The fact that more and more Austrian attorneys (but hardly any judges) have studied abroad as well as being educated in Austria might also play a role. From the perspective of legal history one thereby instinctively thinks of the history of the reception of Roman law in Germany at the threshold of the Middle Ages to early modern history. Here too the fact that attorneys who were trained in Roman law abroad cited Roman law in domestic courts (which were yet unfamiliar with Roman law) played an important role—and this was a source for two things, namely, on the one hand, chaos and, on the other hand, legal development.[34] Both options are included in the idea of national courts taking comparative law into account.

[33] Order of the Handelsgericht (Commercial Court) Vienna of 30 Dec 2002 31 Cg 26/02m (unpub).
[34] Cf on this eg Mitteis and Lieberich *Deutsches Privatrecht* (9th edn 1981), 8.

19

Comparative Law and the Courts

Geoffrey Samuel

The use of comparative law in national and international courts is a topic fraught with difficulties. These difficulties stem primarily from the notion of 'comparative law' itself—that is to say, its definition, its scope, and its context—but they also stem from the relationship between any given legal system and the various historical, geographical, and intellectual contexts of the given system itself. Thus just because the judges in, say, an English or a French court during a particular epoch, might never refer to, or seemingly interest themselves in, a foreign case, piece of legislation, or doctrinal work, it does not follow that comparative law, for the epoch in question, has no relevance or even role with regard to these courts. For comparative law is concerned with two fundamental questions. What is 'comparison'? And what is 'law'?

These questions immediately indicate that the mere citing of foreign material in a judgment, report, or argument does not amount in itself to the use of comparative law by a court. One might draw an analogy with the law school. To provide students with a definition of comparative law that is adequate to locate the precise boundaries between the subject of the definition and a range of associate subjects such as legal history, legal theory, sociology of law, Roman law, European contract law, and the like is probably impossible.[1] What can be done is to state what comparative law is not. Thus it is not, for example, an introduction to French law or to German law since such subjects do not have at their heart knowledge obtained about law through comparison. Moreover, an introduction to a foreign legal system will not necessarily enlighten the students about the epistemological issues that surround the 'law' question.[2] No doubt a study of a foreign system could broaden the student's mind about what amounts to legal knowledge. Yet there is the danger that it might also have the opposite effect inasmuch as it could consolidate a view that legal knowledge is simply a matter of rules.[3] Of course, the citing of foreign material in a national court is not exactly analogous to the introduction of courses on foreign law in a law

---

[1] See eg K Zweigert and H Kötz *An Introduction to Comparative Law* trans T Weir (3rd edn Oxford University Press 1998) 2–12.

[2] P Legrand *Le Droit comparé* (Paris PUF 1999) 32.

[3] See eg R Perrot, *Institutions judiciaires* (9th edn Paris Montchrestien 2000) para 215.

faculty, but it does go some way in stressing that great care must be taken when one talks of comparative law in the courts. Often one is not actually talking of comparative law. What is meant is that foreign material is being considered by the court, which may, or may not, draw conclusions obtained through methods that can properly be described as comparative. And even if the comparative method is adopted, this will not necessarily in itself mean that comparative law is in play. A true comparatist needs continually to be reflecting on the nature of legal knowledge itself.[4]

When one turns to this 'law' question, a whole range of issues start to emerge out of the fuzzy image that comparative law as a title seemingly creates. The first concerns the relationship in general between a specific national legal system and what Professor Legrand calls 'the other'.[5] This relationship can be of a great many kinds depending on the systems in play. However, when the national system is the English common law and the 'other' is the civil law tradition, the relationship turns out, possibly, to be rather asymmetrical. Just as equity cannot be properly defined or understood without a thorough knowledge of the common law and its history (the reverse being not quite so true, or at least different), so English law cannot today be properly comprehended without a reasonable understanding of aspects of the civil law. In other words the relationship between English law and Continental law is probably rather different from the relationship between a civil law system, as a national system, and the common law as 'other'. The reason for this is the common law's complex intellectual relationship with, above all, civilian doctrine, which has functioned, particularly during the nineteenth century, at the level both of theory—one thinks of John Austin and, later, the whole analytical tradition[6]—and of practice.

At the practical level the relationship between the common law and the civil law is, for example, of importance in understanding a number of modern categories of law. The law of contract was virtually an import,[7] citations to foreign material being particularly in evidence between 1850 and 1880, and the language of Roman law was often extended to torts.[8] In the great case of *Taylor v Caldwell*[9] much of Blackburn J's judgment is taken up with a detailed consideration of Roman and French materials. And while one cannot talk here of transplantation as such, since Blackburn J skilfully translated the civilian notions into the more home-grown idea of an implied term,[10] it would be a great mistake to think that the citation and

---

[4] Legrand (n 2) 17–23.   [5] Ibid at 10.

[6] P Stein *Legal Evolution: The Story of an Idea* (Cambridge University Press 1980) 70 ff.

[7] AB Simpson 'Innovation in Nineteenth Century Contract Law' (1975) 91 LQR 247.

[8] See G Samuel *Law of Obligations and Legal Remedies* (2nd edn London Cavendish 2001) 1057 and references therein.   [9] (1863) 122 ER 309.

[10] D Ibbetson *A Historical Introduction to the Law of Obligations* (Oxford University Press 1999) 224.

use of Continental ideas in English cases is some new phenomenon. It would be much more accurate to talk in terms of a long-term relationship between English case-law and the civil law tradition.[11]

This long-term relationship gives rise to what might be called a hidden comparative law, the expression embracing the idea of an unconscious as well as a conscious aspect. Cases such as *White v Jones*[12] and *Fairchild v Glenhaven Funeral Services Ltd*[13] are of course well known for their open and conscious references to civilian cases and both indeed may actually be cases where it would be justified to talk of comparative law (however strong or weak). Lord Goff in *Jones* certainly uses German law to construct a model of possible liability even if, in the end, he abandons everything in the pursuit of a typically English 'practical justice'. In *Fairchild* the foreign material was used, not as a source of law in any positive sense, but as a guide to where a just solution might be found.[14] It is arguable, given these attitudes to justice, that the judges were reflecting, even if only unconsciously, on the nature of law, and this in itself might raise the use of foreign material out of the category of descriptive foreign law towards some idea of comparative law as an active tool in decision-making. This reflection, it should be added, at least in the case of *Fairchild*, was not necessarily just vague philosophizing on the nature of justice. There was a real epistemological issue about how social facts were to be comprehended (methodological individualism versus holism) and this in turn can be referred back to deep-level epistemological problems in the social sciences in general.[15]

This open use of foreign material does at first sight seem to set cases like *White*, *Fairchild*, and one or two other recent decisions[16] apart from the normal run of weekly reports. Yet hidden, or at least relatively hidden, comparative law is to be found in a whole range of other cases where the foreign element might not at first sight seem evident. No doubt most restitution lawyers, even those not familiar with either Roman law or the codes, are more or less aware that the foundation and independence of their subject owes much to civilian thinking.[17] And the same could be said *mutatis mutandis* for the debate surrounding the existence of public and private law[18] or of a doctrine of abuse of rights.[19] Yet there are many less

---

[11] On this point, see T Weir 'Complex Liabilities' in *International Encyclopedia of Comparative Law* (JCB Mohr) vol 11, ch 12, para 67.

[12] [1995] 2 AC 207. [13] [2002] 3 WLR 89.

[14] See Lord Bingham, para 32.

[15] G Samuel *Epistemology and Method in Law* (Aldershot Ashgate 2003) 295–329.

[16] See eg *Greatorex v Greatorex* [2000] 1 WLR 1970.

[17] Samuel (n 8) 10–11, 387–91. Thus cases such as *Fibrosa etc v Fairbairn etc* [1943] AC 32, especially Lord Wright's judgment, could be said to have a comparative law element.

[18] See generally JWF Allison *A Continental Distinction in the Common Law: A Historical and Comparative Perspective on English Public Law* (Oxford University Press 1996).

[19] M Taggart *Private Property and Abuse of Rights in Victorian England* (Oxford University Press 2002).

dramatic areas where a relationship between common law and civil law is to be found beneath the surface of judgments. For example, Professor Beale has drawn attention in France to an English decision of the Court of Appeal that raises an issue that is of some relevance to civil lawyers, namely, the problem of *imprévision* in contract law.[20] The problem is traditionally of conceptual importance to French lawyers because of a difference of approach between the public and the private law courts.[21] Now Professor Beale makes the point that if one adopts a functional approach to comparative law an English court would appear to have arrived at the same solution as German law might have done utilizing the doctrine of *Wegfall der Geschäftsgrundlage*. Thus comparative methodology, when applied to an ordinary case of contractual interpretation (ordinary in the sense that there are no specific references to Continental cases or texts), can suddenly reveal beneath the surface of the case a hidden depth. Yet Professor Beale's example proves to be even richer when one looks at Lord Denning's judgment in the case. For the then Master of the Rolls appeared to be formulating a doctrine of change of circumstances when he indicated, at the end of his judgment, that the court could determine the agreement in such a way as to put the parties under an obligation to renegotiate the price. Of course the other two judges were not prepared to support him on this point, but the comparatist will not be slow to observe that Lord Denning's thesis has found acceptance at both a European and an international level.[22]

The idea of comparative law in the national courts is not, then, confined simply to cases where foreign materials are cited and considered. Comparative law is omnipresent in a whole range of decisions. Lord Diplock's adoption of the distinction between public and private law is one of the more famous examples;[23] but any decision that lends itself to analysis through the use of comparative methodology is, arguably, an illustration of the existence of comparative law in a national court. Perhaps this point can be developed a little further in respect of legal reasoning. In a case of 1964 the victim of a gas explosion brought an action against the public utility supplier,[24] but, because the claimant could not prove fault, the action was framed in nuisance and under the rule of *Rylands v Fletcher*.[25] The Court of Appeal rejected the claim. In justifying the refusal to recognize an absolute liability, Sellers LJ said that the supply of gas, water, and electricity 'are well-nigh a necessity of modern life' and thus it 'would seem odd

---

[20] H Beale 'La Commission Lando: Le point de vue d'un "common-law lawyer" ', in C Jamin and D Mazeaud (eds), *L'Harmonisation du droit des contrats en Europe* (Paris Economica 2001) 127, 129.   [21] See Samuel (n 8) 378–9.

[22] Principles of European Contract Law art 6.111; Unidroit Principles for International Commercial Contracts Art 6.2.3.   [23] *O'Reilly v Mackman* [1983] 2 AC 237.

[24] *Dunne v NW Gas Board* [1964] 2 QB 806.

[25] *Rylands v Fletcher* (1866) LR 1 Ex 265 (Ex); (1868) LR 3 HL 330 (HL).

that facilities so much sought after by the community and approved by their legislators should be actionable at common law because they have been brought to places where they are required and have escaped without negligence by an unforeseen sequence of mishaps'.[26] In saying this, the judge was following the comments of an earlier law lord who had observed in a case of damage resulting from escaping water that the supply of water was recognized 'as being so desirable in the interests of the community that in some form or other it is usually made obligatory in civilised countries'. However, this common lawyer had equally gone on to assert that it 'would be unreasonable for the law to regard those who install or maintain such a system of supply as doing so at their own peril, with an absolute liability for any damage resulting from its presence even when there has been no negligence'.[27] This statement is pregnant with comparative law possibilities since it not only raises the activity in issue, the supply of a public benefit, into an international realm ('civilized countries') but also frames its reasoning around the notion of the 'community interest'.

The key point here for the comparatist is the notion of an interest. This is a concept that transgresses national law to play a role in all Western legal systems and, in doing this, it has the capacity to act as a 'master-key' allowing access to legal thinking in a range of legal systems.[28] Accordingly the comparatist, furnished with this key, can compare the reasoning employed in the English gas and water cases with the kind of reasoning that might be employed in a civilian court faced with similar facts. And, with respect to France if not elsewhere, the exercise proves interesting in that the same reasoning starting point—the community interest—would result in solutions completely opposite to those arrived at in the two English decisions. In France the supply of gas or water, because it benefits the community, is, in cases where there is 'an unforeseen sequence of mishaps', subject to 'an absolute liability for any damage resulting from its presence even when there has been no negligence' (to borrow the words of the common law judges). Sellers LJ was of course of the opinion that such liability would seem odd, yet the French view is that if the community benefits from an activity then the community should equally shoulder the burdens. Why should one individual have to shoulder a risk that arises out of a community benefit? In order to achieve the equality of burdens the community, that is to say the State, will automatically pay compensation to the injured citizens.[29]

---

[26] *Dunne v NW Gas Board* [1964] 2 QB 806, 832.

[27] Lord Moulton in *Rickards v Lothian* [1913] AC 263, 281–2.

[28] F Ost *Droit et intérêt, vol 2, Entre droit et non-droit: L'intérêt* (Facultés universitaires Saint-Louis Bruxelles 1990) 10. This point is developed in Samuel ch 20 in this volume.

[29] L Neville-Brown and J Bell *French Administrative Law* (5th edn Oxford University Press 1998) 193–200.

These two English cases concerning what were then public utilities are, accordingly, just as relevant to the comparatist as *White v Jones* or the *Fairchild* decision. Moreover, this relevance can be located at several levels. At the level of concepts the comparatist can focus upon the role of an interest and thus the escaping water case becomes a decision in which comparative law is present because community interest is used as a premiss for arriving at one conclusion in one country and another conclusion in another country. This is not to suggest that 'interest' necessarily has the same cultural meaning in both systems. Yet the possibility of *mentalité* and cultural difference, or even the possibility of similarity, is exactly the kind of issue that will be of concern to comparative law. The 'comparison' and the 'law' elements of comparative law are of sufficient epistemological sophistication as to engage these kinds of practical problems in all their practical and theoretical complexity. Yet the point of entry remains the notion of an interest.

Another level of comparison is the schematic analysis of the facts. If one envisages society as nothing more than a collection of individual participants each having their own individual interests to protect and to pursue, then it is likely that collective interests might well be endowed with a certain structural weakness vis-à-vis the individual.[30] The fact that an 'individual' will include the largest and wealthiest of corporations will of course mean that in reality the community interest and the individual interest are often completely distorted.[31] Such a weakness is perhaps evident in the two public utility cases. The community interest is treated as only a very weak reasoning *unité*[32] quite incapable of effecting a transformation from fault to strict liability; the court thus 'rewards' the community of professionals and *commerçants* by treating them as if they were private individuals pursuing everyday activities.[33] In France the community interest is a much stronger *unité* partly because it is closely interwoven with the power of the State through the constitutional principle of *égalité*. Yet it is also stronger because republicanism as a political ideal means that the community has an ontological existence that is missing in England. Community interest in France is, accordingly, more than capable of effecting a transformation away from the fault principle.

This ontological (and ideological) foundation of community interest can be equally important with regard to what might be called the 'reception' of

---

[30] R Boudon and R Fillieule *Les Méthodes en sociologie* (12th edn Paris PUF 2002) 41–90.

[31] This distortion might perhaps be evident in the House of Lords' attitude towards the relationship between an individual and a bank. The individual is expected to be fully aware of the bank's financial interests: *Director General of Fair Trading v First National Bank plc* [2002] 1 AC 481.

[32] To borrow (and perhaps distort a little) Professor Atias's expression: see C Atias *Épistémologie juridique* (Paris Dalloz 2002) para 186 ff.

[33] See Samuel (n 8) 497.

certain civilian ideas. Here one is not always talking in terms of a hidden or unconscious comparative law, although some relevant cases will not necessarily openly display any European or foreign law dimension. The emphasis is on the circulation and incorporation of concepts from the 'other' and the vehicle is often European Community law. Sometimes such concepts or ideas can be assimilated without, seemingly at any rate, too many problems and perhaps one such example is proportionality. This clearly is now part of English public law.[34] Yet it may well have a role in private law because it is an idea that can function very easily at the level of the law of actions and so not only has it proved useful as a means of directly controlling the granting or withholding of certain remedies,[35] but it has the capability of acting as a new rationalizing vehicle for understanding a range of traditional cases.[36] Other concepts are more difficult. The leading example here is good faith, which, as Professor Teubner has observed, is very much context-dependent.[37] English courts may think that they can absorb this classic civilian notion,[38] but the recent case-law tells a rather different story. The rejection of a general pre-contractual duty to take into consideration the interests of the other party is of course well known.[39] But two relatively recent implied term cases are particularly revealing in that had they occurred in France the plaintiffs would probably have succeeded on the basis that the employers were under a good faith duty to provide the information that formed the focal point of the dispute.[40] The reason for this difference is again one of community interest. However, here one is not talking of the wider community, but of the contracting parties; a contract is a community enterprise between the two parties and good faith needs to be understood within this 'nouvelle philosophie'.[41] Put another way, to what *persona* does the interest notion attach? Is a court envisaging a social reality that consists simply of individuals—'there is no such thing as society'— or a social reality that is made up of cooperating subgroups themselves capable of being envisaged as a *unité*?

Good faith is valuable to the question of comparative law and the courts for another reason. It illustrates how easy it is for judges and jurists to

[34] *Gough v Chief Constable of Derbyshire Constabulary* [2002] QB 459 (DC); [2002] QB 1213 (CA).

[35] *Lock plc v Beswick* [1989] 1 WLR 1268.

[36] Thus cases such as *Hong Kong Fir Shipping Co Ltd v Kawasaki Kisen Kaisha Ltd* [1962] 2 QB 26 could be seen as proportionality decisions. But cf Beale (n 20) 131, who suggests that the case might be seen as one of abuse of rights.

[37] G Teubner 'Legal Irritants: Good Faith in British Law or How Unifying Law Ends Up in New Divergences' (1998) 61 MLR 11.

[38] See eg *Director General of Fair Trading v First National Bank plc* [2002] 1 AC 481.

[39] *Walford v Miles* [1992] 2 AC 128.

[40] *Reid v Rush & Tompkins Plc* [1990] 1 WLR 212; *University of Nottingham v Eyett* [1999] 2 All ER 437.

[41] F Gendron, *L'Interprétation des contrats* (Itée Wilson & Lafleur 2002) 148.

indulge in what might be called superficial comparative law. One has heard many times the assertion that courts in different systems, although employing quite different conceptual models or methods, usually end up arriving at the same solutions. This can sometimes be true; yet equally it can often be untrue as the gas, water, and implied term cases so clearly indicate. Moreover, merely putting the emphasis on the actual outcome of cases can be superficial in itself, even where outcomes, as between cases in two different systems, are the same. This is not to suggest that functionalism as a method is superficial; indeed this is not the case. But functionalism, despite an assertion to the contrary by one of the leading textbooks on comparative law,[42] is not the only method in comparative law. The structural scheme is of equal importance on occasions because it can reveal things that the functional scheme cannot.[43] Structuralism can reveal how a legal system operates in terms of a model of elements and relations and how these elements and relations are, in turn, embedded in the law's perception of social reality.

Take, for example, the following problem. A treasure hunter using a metal detector discovered a medieval brooch in his local park and the coroner's court adjudged it not to be treasure trove thus allowing the finder to keep possession of the article. He was sued by his local authority, who claimed that they were entitled to the brooch since it was found in a park of which they were the freeholder and in which the public were not permitted to use metal detectors. Auld LJ, delivering the main judgment in the Court of Appeal, having observed early on that 'the English law of ownership and possession, unlike that of Roman Law, is not a system of identifying absolute entitlement but of priority of entitlement',[44] went on to adjudge that the local authority had a better entitlement than the finder. Now it might well be that a civilian court could reach the same result, but for a comparatist it is unlikely that this would be why the English case is of interest. What is of interest is the structure of the model used by Auld LJ and how this structure compares with the Romanist one to be found in the civil law systems. In Roman law, as the judge pointed out, the structure is one of an absolute relation between person and thing[45] and the starting point would be a remedy *in rem* that would in turn raise a simple question. Who is the owner of the brooch? However, if one looks in more depth at the English case, not only does the whole question of ownership appear largely irrelevant—for personal property entitlement is based on a better

[42] Zweigert and Kötz (n 1) 34.

[43] Cf D Gerber 'Sculpting the Agenda of Comparative Law: Ernst Rabel and the Facade of Language' in A Riles (ed) *Rethinking the Masters of Comparative Law* (Oxford Hart 2001) 190, 205–7. For a discussion of the structural scheme in law, see Samuel (n 15) 36–308.

[44] *Waverley BC v Fletcher* [1996] QB 334, 345.

[45] Well expressed in the Code civil Art 544.

right to possession[46]—but the actual remedy in issue is the tort of conversion which, being a tort, is an action that is categorized in the law of obligations. The implications of this structural difference are quite startling for comparatists dreaming of a European Civil Code since all of the great European national codes are based on the Roman model of a rigid distinction between the law of property and the law of obligations—between, in other words, real and personal rights.

Functionalism cannot bring out this structural aspect to legal systems.[47] It cannot reveal how the finder loses the brooch to the local authority not because he lacks a direct right *in rem*, but, inter alia, because he was a trespasser in the park. Status, obligation, remedy, and property are all intermixed in the English model and in a manner that must make all thought of harmonizing personal property law a fantasy. Possession as a legal and an empirical concept is so deeply rooted in common law thinking that it transgresses the relation between *persona* and *res* (property) to exert such a major influence in the law of obligations (bailment, conversion, trespass) that, at times, *owning* and *owing* merge within the notion of entitlement. Once one functions at the level of entitlement all rights become the same; they are simply entitlements and thus a person with a mere contractual right to enter property is considered on occasions to have just as good entitlement to a proprietary (possessory) remedy as the actual possessor.[48] The point here, it must be stressed, is not to criticize English law. The point is simply to indicate how the structural models used by different legal systems can be of fundamental importance to the comparatist because it is the differences between these models that give rise to serious epistemological obstacles when it comes to harmonization of legal systems.[49] Emphasizing the functional outcomes of cases is only one aspect of comparative law.[50]

No doubt this may seem somewhat removed from comparative law in the courts. It is not. When Lord Diplock and Lord Goff talk in terms of an English law of obligations, they are not just indulging in comparative law.[51] They are, with respect, indulging in a rather superficial version of it. This is because a 'law of obligations' makes structural sense only when it is placed within the civilian institutional scheme and this scheme, which has its origins in the *Institutes of Gaius*, is nowhere reflected in the original forms of action model that acted as the foundation of the common law. Of course much has

---

[46] T Weir *Tort Law* (Oxford University Press 2002) 155.

[47] This point is developed in much more depth in G Samuel *Epistemology and Comparative Law: Contributions from the Sciences and Social Sciences* (forthcoming).

[48] *Manchester Airport Plc v Dutton* [2000] 1 QB 133.

[49] This point is discussed in a little more depth in G Samuel 'English Private Law in the Context of the Codes' in M van Hoecke and F Ost (eds), *The Harmonisation of European Private Law* (Hart Oxford 2000) 47.   [50] See generally Gerber (n 43).

[51] See *Moschi v Lep Air Services Ltd* [1973] AC 331, 346; *Henderson v Merrett Syndicates Ltd* [1995] 2 AC 145, 184.

changed since the early days, and the abolition of the forms of action during the nineteenth century certainly opened up English legal thinking to new ideas, new models, and new concepts. Yet the absence of a history of institutional learning (Blackstone excepted) means that, viewed in historical perspective, the content of English law is very much more 'open-plan' than is the case with civil law systems, where constitutional and code texts have erected solid and often impenetrable walls. Such an open-plan architecture does allow judges to erect their own walls and demolish existing ones erected by their predecessors. But when they do this, they may well be indulging in an exercise of hidden or unconscious comparative law.[52] One reason for this is that for well over a century Roman law was a requirement for the Bar and so all barristers trained before 1970 would have an outline of the Roman blueprint somewhere in their subconscious. Today it is European Union law that is compulsory, soon to be followed, perhaps, by human rights law.

This subject is—or these subjects are—no substitute, of course, for Roman law in the sense that it, or they, will not directly endow the student with a knowledge of ownership, possession, actions *in rem*, actions *in personam*, obligations, quasi-contract, and so on. Yet they may stimulate another kind of thinking. They may lead to a generation of judges for whom the law is not a matter of national systems each with their own specific concepts, relations, and symmetries (or asymmetries). Law, for them, might be a *mélange* of ideas, of schemes of intelligibility, of structures, of sub-systems, and the like.[53] Comparative law in such an intellectual environment will not necessarily be rendered irrelevant. Indeed, the opposite might be true. Comparative law will be the subconscious, if not the conscious, source of this kind of complex knowledge given its epistemological focus on comparison and on law. In addition, it will surely have its role, on the European level, of stimulating the new thinking that one comparatist has suggested is so essential to all national systems acting within European meta-legal system.[54] On further reflection, and on an historical examination of legal argumentation in the common law of the kind undertaken recently by Professor Waddams,[55] perhaps, after all, one is not talking about some possible future. Perhaps one is talking of the common law of the here and now, perhaps even of the then and now. In which case the whole question of the use of comparative law in common law courts is truly a most complex and subtle one and is an issue that stretches far beyond the citation of a few foreign cases and texts.

---

[52] One rather obvious example is Lord Atkin's use of a term such as *culpa* in *Donoghue v Stevenson* [1932] AC 562.

[53] Samuel (n 43) 295–329.

[54] C Joerges 'European Challenges to Private Law: On False Dichotomies, True Conflicts and the Need for a Constitutional Perspective' (1998) 18 Legal Studies 121.

[55] See S Waddams 'Johanna Wagner and the Rival Opera Houses' (2001) 117 LQR 431.

20

The Notion of an Interest as a Formal Concept in English and in Comparative Law

Geoffrey Samuel

The purpose of this chapter is to examine a legal concept that has not received much general attention, at least in recent years, in the United Kingdom literature: this is the notion of a legal 'interest'. It will be examined mainly in the context of English law and this examination will be extended into some specific areas of difficulty. But the chapter will also have an important comparative dimension since the concept has received some detailed attention on the Continent.[1] This comparative dimension will, to some extent, be harnessed to support the following thesis to be extracted from the analysis: that the notion of an interest is, on the one hand, *descriptively* and *explanatively* a far more important concept than the notion of a right but, on the other hand, is, institutionally and conceptually speaking, no less a formal concept than a right.

I. INTRODUCTION

There are a range of reasons why an 'interest' deserves analysis by the comparative lawyer. The notion of an interest is by its very nature one of the most central of all legal concepts since it is one that, like the legal subject (*persona*) or the legal objects (*res*), exists at one and the same time in both the legal world and the world of social reality. It is, in other words, a truly mediating concept between fact and law. Secondly, it is a notion that goes back to Roman times and thus is a legal concept that should attract the attention of the legal theorist specializing in epistemology and the comparative lawyer.[2]

---

[1] In particular from Professor François Ost: F Ost *Droit et intérêt*, vol 2, Entre le droit et non-droit: L'intérêt (Bruxelles Facultés universitaires Saint-Louis 1990). I should like to acknowledge from the outset the great debt owed to this book.
[2] R Zimmermann *The Law of Obligations: Roman Foundations of the Civilian Tradition* (Oxford University Press Oxford 1996) 35–8, 826–7.

Equally, and this is a third reason, it is a concept that connects with what must be the most famous of legal notions, that of a 'right'.[3] An interest often appears to be a kind of halfway house between a right and a remedy. The notion of an interest is, accordingly, a useful starting point for examining a range of other legal concepts. Fourthly, an interest is a notion that connects with the *persona* (legal subject) as an individual: to determine an interest is to determine a legal subject and his, her, or its expectations.[4] An interest, then, is a legal concept that can play a central role in legal thought and legal reasoning; it is a 'passport' to all areas of the law.[5] Fifthly, in having its basic roots in the world of fact rather than in the normative abstraction of law, it is a concept that would appear to lie beyond the rule. It is a concept that, itself, suggests that legal knowledge is not exclusively rule-based. Indeed, this factual dimension to the notion of an interest allows it to be used as the basis of an 'actional' scheme of intelligibility: thus in economics it represents the self-interested actor.[6] Because such an actor also has a role in the legal plan, the notion of an interest can act as a link between law and another discipline such as economics. Finally, therefore, the notion of an interest is a key means by which one can understand legal reasoning. It bridges the gap not just between legal substance and legal method, but equally between judgment and solution; it is the means by which one can have access to the thinking that lies behind the more formal elements of legal knowledge, that is to say behind rules and legal rights. It is, in brief, a key to legal knowledge.

Now the 'actional' scheme strongly suggests that interests attach to the person: that is to say, that a person acts in his or her own best interests.[7] However, from the point of view of what can be called the 'institutional system'—that is, the system of classification used first by Gaius and then by Justinian in their *Institutes* and later adopted as the structural foundation for all the modern codes[8]—the position looks different. Interest can be seen

---

[3] See eg *Chief Constable of Kent v V* [1983] 1 QB 34.

[4] JA Jolowicz 'Protection of Diffuse, Fragmented and Collective Interests in Civil Litigation: English Law' [1983] CLJ 222. Note in particular the work of Rudolf von Jhering and Rosco Pound, who both saw law as a means of serving social ends conceptualized as interests: extracts of their thinking on interests can be found in D Lloyd and M Freeman *Lloyd's Introduction to Jurisprudence* (6th edn Stevens 1994) 550–1, 570–9.

[5] Ost (n 1) 10–11.

[6] A Leroux and A Marciano *La Philosophie économique* (Paris PUF 1998) 15–18.

[7] See on this aspect R von Jhering *Law as a Means to an End*, trans I Husik (Boston 1913) where he defines interest in terms of pleasure and pain (pp. 26–7). Later he says: 'Nature herself has shown man the way he must follow in order to gain another for his purposes: it is that of *connecting one's own purpose with the other man's interest*. Upon this principle rests all our human life: the State, society, commerce and intercourse' (p. 28). Note also Rosco Pound's preference in teaching jurisprudence 'to build on Jhering's idea of interests, defining them as claims or wants or desires (or, I like to say, expectations) which men assert de facto': R Pound *Jurisprudence* (West 1959) vol 3, 15.

[8] On the institutional system and its development, see P Stein 'The Development of the Institutional System' in P Stein and A Lewis (eds) *Studies in Justinian's Institutes in Memory*

as a concept that attaches on occasions as much to 'things' (*res*) and to legal 'actions' (*actiones*) as to the *persona*. Thus one can talk of having a legal interest in land or of an interest requirement which attaches to a particular kind of legal remedy (for example, judicial review). The advantage of this institutional perspective is that it allows for an analysis of an interest from more of a 'three-dimensional' model than is the case when interest is seen uniquely from the position of the legal subject. It provides a perspective through which very different kinds of interest, or interest relationships, can emerge and as a result the institutional system is able to provide a useful conceptual starting point. However, the great strength of the 'institutional system' is that it is more than an abstract theoretical scheme; it is a *model* that, as has been argued elsewhere, seemingly has its roots as much in social fact as in a system of law.[9] Such a model functions in truth more as a halfway house between social reality and law and thus takes on the status of an object of legal science. Taken together, then, the notion of an interest and the institutional system provide a—perhaps *the*—model by which social fact, as 'constructed' by the institutional system itself, connects with law, also organized, at least on the Continent, by the institutional plan. Social 'reality', in other words, begins its connection with legal discourse through the notion of an interest; and this connection is completed through the relationship between an interest and the institutional system.

However, before turning to the notion of an interest, several points must be made not just about the limits of this present investigation but about legal concepts in general. Clearly different kinds of interests—for example, the 'best interests' of the medical patient in relation, say, to the 'sufficient interest' requirement in judicial review or to the 'property interest' in land law—will *substantively* be very different as between themselves. A full and exhaustive investigation of the notion of an interest ought, accordingly, to examine in depth these substantive differences.[10] In addition, the notion of an interest has, since Jhering, and more precisely Pound, an important role in jurisprudence (legal philosophy and theory) in that interest theory has provided the basis of what might be called a 'realist' or sociological approach to law.[11] Such an approach sees the source and definition of law

---

of *JAC Thomas* (Sweet & Maxwell 1983) 151–63; P Stein *The Character and Influence of the Roman Civil Law* (Hambledon 1988) 73–82. See also G Samuel *The Foundations of Legal Reasoning* (Maklu 1994) 171–190.

[9] G Samuel 'Classification of Obligations and the Impact of Constructivist Epistemologies' (1997) 17 LS 448.

[10] But see generally Pound (n 7).

[11] HF Jolowicz *Lectures on Jurisprudence* (Athlone 1963) 175–9. According to Pound a 'legal system attains the ends of the legal order (1) by recognising certain interests, individual, public, and social; (2) by defining the limits within which those interests shall be recognised and given effect through legal precepts developed and applied by the judicial (and today the

not in concepts and rules as such but in the mass of competing social interests, each interest being defined by Rosco Pound as 'a demand or desire or expectation which human beings, either individually or in groups or associations or relations, seek to satisfy'.[12] Pound's great contribution to the understanding of an interest is to be found in his exhaustive classification of interests together with an analysis of their substance.[13] This present investigation, perhaps surprisingly at first sight, does not intend to revisit this aspect of an interest since the aim is to approach the notion more from model coherence than from model correspondence.[14] That is to say, the purpose of this chapter is to look at an interest in terms of its role as an important element or relation in the institutional *system*; the aim is to examine an interest from the viewpoint of its relationship with other concepts and institutions. Of course serious constraints of space are one fundamental reason for this more limited analysis. Yet the point has already been made that the institutional system is a model and as such it ends up by defining social reality as much as social reality defines the model. In other words, the different kinds of interests to be investigated in this chapter gain at least part of their *substantive* quality from the institutional system itself and it is this more *formal* aspect of an interest which will form the basis of this present investigation.[15]

administrative) process according to an authoritative technique; and (3) by endeavoring to secure the interests so recognised within the defined limits' (n 7) 16.

[12] Pound (n 7) 16.

[13] Ibid 25–324. For a very brief summary or listing, see (n 11) Jolowicz 177–8. However, as this chapter will imply, Pound's classification and analysis is incomplete.

[14] A theory can be 'true' either because it corresponds with reality or because it is internally coherent and this coherence allows one to explain a phenomenon: L Solar *Introduction à l'épistémologie* (Ellipses 2000) 43–4. It may be, of course, that law is not as internally coherent as models or theories in the natural sciences, but this may be because of the difficulty in trying to reduce three-dimensional social reality to two-dimensional rules: see G Samuel *Law of Obligations and Legal Remedies* (2nd edn Cavendish 2001) 523–62.

[15] Pound's starting point is very clearly articulated: 'We begin, then, with the proposition that the law does not create these interests. It finds them pressing for recognition and security. First, a legal system classifies them and recognises a larger or smaller number. Second, it fixes the limits within which it endeavors to secure the interests so selected. . . . Third, a legal system works out means by which the interests may be secured when recognised and as delimited' (n 7) 21. This chapter does not wish to dispute as such this starting point; however, it will argue that interest is equally a formal concept as much determined by its relationship to *persona*, *res*, and *actio*. Thus it has a conceptual role that *appears* to be empirical in substance but is actually conceptual in form and this form goes far in determining the normative outcome of a case. To compare substantively, therefore, the various quite different interests is to some extent to miss the point when it comes to understanding the conceptual role of an interest. Much will depend on the relational foundation of an interest: thus an interest attaching to the *persona* or to the *actio* will by definition be very different 'substantively' from an interest which attaches to a *res*.

II. NORMATIVE AND QUASI-NORMATIVE CONCEPTS

Given this emphasis on the formal aspect of the institutional model, something must also be said about legal concepts in general. Legal concepts cannot properly be understood outside the idea of a system of reasoning and thus they attract problems not just of definition but also of how each concept relates one to another. Philosophers of science talk of 'coherence';[16] and it is worth recalling at this point the observation of one such philosopher that scientific models do not relate directly to actual facts. They function in terms of *virtual* facts, that is to say, facts schematically determined within the network of concepts that make up the model.[17] It is the model that constructs both the theory and the 'facts' and thus the model acts, to an extent at any rate, as both the science and the object of science, the external world having its relevance primarily in terms of verification. Concepts and categories are, accordingly, fundamental to scientific knowledge and the progress of each science is before anything else a genealogy of categories.[18] It has already been mentioned that the 'institutional system' acts as the basis for a similar conceptual model in legal thinking. Yet this institutional model is too abstract to give a complete account about how specific solutions are reached in judgments; other more precise concepts have a role.

However, in understanding the role of legal concepts a fundamental distinction needs to be made between 'normative' and 'quasi-normative' concepts.[19] The first group are those that are fully normative. These concepts have two basic characteristics: first they are divorced entirely from social fact and secondly they express an 'ought' (normative) situation in themselves. The two most important are 'right' and 'duty'. Thus to say that P has a right to £100 is a normative statement in itself; nothing more needs to be added to the statement in order to entitle P to a remedy for his £100. *Ubi ius ibi remedium.* The same is true, but from the other end so to speak, with respect to duty; to say that D is under a duty to pay £100 to P is a fully normative statement in itself. Rights and duties have thus become fundamental to the language of legal reasoning. In the law of tort, carelessness which causes damage to another is turned from the descriptive into the normative through the application of the concept of 'duty of care'. The defendant who negligently causes damage to the plaintiff will be liable if it can be shown that he was under a legal 'duty' to the plaintiff.[20] Similarly, a

---

[16] See generally Solar (n 14) 43–5.

[17] G-G Granger *La Science et les sciences* (2nd edn Paris PUF 1995) 49.

[18] Ibid 114.

[19] P Dubouchet *Sémiotique juridique: Introduction à une science du droit* (Paris PUF 1990) 144–5.

[20] *Donoghue v Stevenson* [1932] AC 562. Note the particularly important role of 'duty' in situations where the damage has arisen through the defendant's failure to act: *Reeves v Commissioner of Police for the Metropolis* [1999] 3 WLR 363.

bank might be unable to enforce a contract against one of its clients if it was in breach of some pre-contractual (equitable) 'duty' such as the duty to advise the client to seek independent legal advice before signing the document.[21] Occasionally a set of facts can be given their normative dimension through the use of the concept of a 'right'. In one case involving the failure of a local authority to consider a tender, for example, the plaintiff succeeded because he had more than a mere expectation: the descriptive 'expectation' had become an enforceable 'right'.[22] On other occasions, however, the court may be sceptical if the plaintiff asserts merely that he or she has a 'right' that the defendant has infringed; for rights usually have to be founded upon an existing cause of action or statutory provision.[23] Nevertheless, the position has just been modified quite drastically with the coming into force of the Human Rights Act 1998. Now that the Convention for the Protection of Human Rights and Fundamental Freedoms is part of English law, plaintiffs who feel that they have suffered harm as a result of the actions (or inactions) of a public authority, and which contravene one of the articles of the Convention, may well be able to use the notion of a 'right' as their starting point for a remedy.

A second group of concepts can be called quasi-normative. They include terms such as 'damage', 'fault', 'proximity', 'interest', and 'expectation', and are seemingly nothing but descriptive notions that express no 'ought' (normative) dimension. To say that P has suffered damage or has an interest which he wishes to protect implies in itself no entitlement to a legal remedy; it simply describes a situation.[24] In order to obtain a remedy to compensate the damage or to protect the interest something more must be shown. However, in reality such concepts can go far in themselves in suggesting that a remedy ought to be available in that the juxtaposition of several 'descriptive' elements—for example damage, fault and causation—might be enough to establish liability in damages.[25] In other words, the juxtaposition of several 'descriptive' concepts can add up to more than the sum of their parts. Indeed even a single element like 'damage' or 'interest' can be pivotal as a reasoning technique in suggesting that a remedy ought to be available. Thus in one case a Court of Appeal judge supported the granting of an interlocutory injunction partly on the basis that it would be 'ridiculous if in this present age the law is that the making of deliberately

---

[21] *Barclays Bank Plc v O'Brien* [1994] 1 AC 180.

[22] *Blackpool & Fylde Aero Club Ltd v Blackpool BC* [1990] 1 WLR 1195.

[23] *Kingdom of Spain v Christie Ltd* [1986] 1 WLR 1120, 1129. And see eg *F v Wirral MBC* [1991] 2 WLR 1132 (CA).

[24] Note, for example, the observation of Lord Oliver in *Caparo Industries plc v Dickman* [1990] 2 AC 605, 633: ' "Proximity" is, no doubt, a convenient expression so long as it is realised that it is no more than a label which embraces not a definable concept but merely a description of circumstances from which, pragmatically, the courts conclude that a duty of care exists.'   [25] See Code civil Art 1382 (herein after CC).

harassing and pestering telephone calls to a person is only actionable in the civil courts if the recipient of the calls happens to have the freehold or a leasehold proprietary interest in the premises in which he or she has received the calls'.[26] The type of 'damage' (harassment) could be said to be the motivating factor behind the intervention of the law.[27] One might note equally the irony that it was the notion of an 'interest' that was the problem facing the plaintiff in the first place: only a person with an interest in land is entitled to a remedy founded on the tort of private nuisance.[28] The daughter suffering the abusive telephone calls was living in the house of her parents and thus she had, legally speaking, no interest in the property. Accordingly, if the problem is viewed from the position of the defendant, it could be said that he was arguing that he was entitled to succeed in law because of the absence of an interest, again endowing a descriptive concept with a quasi-normative flavour.

Rights and interests are therefore closely connected when it comes to the 'provoking' of a range of 'appropriate solutions'. However, as we have equally suggested, the two notions need to be kept separate. The separation goes back to Roman law where it is recognized in the sources that an owner might have the 'right' (ius) to ill-treat his slaves, but it is not in his 'interest' (*interest*) to do so.[29] This apparent dichotomy is not just an issue of linguistic nicety: for the Romans were aware of the distinction between the rational and the empirical—law could be grasped by the mind whereas fact was chaotic[30]—and a term such as ius represented something quite different from *interest* and *utilitas*. One must not of course over-exaggerate the ability of Roman jurists when it comes to abstract theorizing; they were not systems theorists and their own structures were not without internal contradiction and methodological inconsistency. However, they had clearly reached the stage where they separated rationalized, and thus normative, legal relationships or connections from descriptive social reality and so one can find texts where the problem in issue is the marrying of some awkward example of empirical fact with an established legal institution, concept, or relationship.[31] The distinction between *ius* and *interest* is an aspect of this same intellectual process. Interest is a descriptive concept that functions within social fact, but at the same time it is a concept that connects with the normative elements in the system of legal rationality. The amount of damages payable in law was, to give another example from the Roman sources, often measured by an amount of money equivalent to the plaintiff's

[26] *Khorasandjian v Bush* [1993] QB 727, 734. However, the reasoning was subsequently criticized by the House of Lords in *Hunter v Canary Wharf Ltd* [1997] AC 655.

[27] Certainly the type of damage encouraged Parliament to intervene: see Protection from Harassment Act 1997.

[28] Confirmed in *Hunter v Canary Wharf Ltd* [1997] AC 655.

[29] D 1 6 2.   [30] D 22 6 2.   [31] See eg D 1 6 6.

(factual) interest.[32] Law and economics, to use modern thinking, meet through the mediation of an interest.

Interest was thus useful for giving expression to an individual's own economic stake, so to speak, in a society that was already both commercial and monetary in its economic foundation. One should not be surprised to find, therefore, that the notion of an interest was, at least where the assessment of damages was concerned, something that was to be defined objectively as an economic factor. Subjective feelings, for example, were things that were not easily translatable into interests.[33] However, the moment that the law did give protection to some aspect of subjective feeling, such as Roman law did with respect to dignity and dishonour,[34] these protected feelings could immediately be defined as 'interests' since private law was concerned with the protection of private interests (*utilitates*).[35] The flow between *ius* and *interest* was, accordingly, very much a two-way process in part defined by the logic of the institutional system. Interests were something that could be defined by factual, or more often economic, reality; yet they could equally be constructed by the law itself and thus projected back onto the empirical world to be given a 'reality' within social fact. This is what makes interest such a key concept in legal analysis and reasoning.

Another aspect to the notion of an interest was, and is, the way it can help give expression to institutions themselves. Thus when the Romans talked of a particular action being beneficial because it is in the 'public interest' that people should be able to use public streets without fear or danger, the concept of an interest is, in part, giving the idea of 'the public', as a group, some cohesion.[36] The notion of *utilitas publica* acted, at least in later civilian thinking, as one starting point by which the State could be conceived as an institution.[37] In turn, the expression 'in the interest of the State' was to become rather sinister in its connotation since it could so easily be used to turn the citizen into a subject. It could, in other words, be used to suppress constitutional and human rights. Modern law has also seen various subgroups within society being given cohesion through the development of notions such as the 'interests of workers' (labour law) and the 'consumer interest' (consumer law). Indeed such interests can sometimes give rise to specific bodies or officers (that is to say, institutions) whose role is to oversee and to give protection to these kinds of interests.[38] Once such official recognition is given to an interest, it then becomes easy to slip from the descriptive towards the normative and to talk in terms of rights. One can talk about workers' rights and consumer rights. There is of course an

---

[32] D 2 13 10 3. [33] D 9 2 33pr. [34] D 47 10 1 2.

[35] D 1 1 1 2. [36] D 9 3 1 1.

[37] J-L Mestre *Introduction historique au droit administratif français* (Paris PUF 1985) 98–103. [38] See eg Fair Trading Act 1973 s 2(1).

important political and philosophical edge to this movement from interest to right: for example, it is quite uncontroversial to state that the RSPCA is a body charged with looking after the interests of animals. However, to state that it is charged with a duty to protect animal rights is a different matter.

III. INTERESTS ATTACHING TO THE *PERSONA*

In truth the relationship between 'right' and 'interest' is complex because it raises questions not just of legal conceptualization but also of philosophy and theory. It is, accordingly, a relationship that in itself requires reflection.[39] However, before the theoretical issues that lie beneath the right and interest dichotomy can be properly understood, it is important that the way in which an 'interest' functions as a legal concept be equally appreciated. Only when one has an idea of the scope and flexibility, not to say utility, of the notion can one really begin to consider some of the theoretical questions. More importantly, perhaps, interest can be examined in relation to the institutional system which, as we have said, is one of the key structures by which law finds expression in social fact and social fact finds expression in law. The institutional structure and the notion of an interest, taken together, provide the model that links rules with fact; together they are the mediating notions that link the empirical and normative worlds.

The *Digest* of Roman law begins its analysis of law with the *ius personarum* on the ground that law is made for the sake of mankind.[40] Given that law is about the protection of interests (*utilitates*),[41] the *persona* equally acts as a good starting point for the examination of the notion of an interest. Indeed one might say that the law is made for the protection of personal interests with the result that if a person goes missing his or her interests remain in existence in need of protection by another *persona*.[42] These interests are of course wide-ranging and varied and if one wished to analyse all the various types and classes one would be in effect studying the whole mass of laws themselves.[43] However, the general point to be made about the notion of an interest in relation to the institution of the *persona* is that it

---

[39] See eg Pound (n 7) 338–41. Pound says that 'although it does not create the interest but recognizes and delimits it', the law 'nevertheless confers and defines these capacities, they are called legal rights in contradistinction to demands recognized in ethics or the morality of the time and place but not backed by the law which are called moral rights' (p. 338). This view of the relationship between interests and rights is, arguably, no longer epistemologically tenable since the institutional system mediates between law and fact and thus, as this present chapter seeks to establish, the law does go some way to creating interests.

[40] D 1 5 2.   [41] D 1 1 1 2.   [42] CC Art 117.

[43] Which is in effect what Pound does and this is one reason why his *Jurisprudence* covers five volumes.

can act as a vehicle for giving expression to the idea of personality itself. It can do this in two main ways. First, the notion of an interest can be used to give expression to intangible 'things' that attach intimately to the conception of a person.[44] Perhaps the two best examples to be found in French law are dignity and privacy. These are not part of a person's patrimony and so do not form part of the law of property; they are very much part of the law of persons.[45] These interests of personality do not, accordingly, attract a monetary value as such and they cannot be traded.[46] Now the fact that they are given specific protection in the Code civil obviously has the effect of endowing privacy and dignity with the status of rights rather than just interests. But as Professor Ost points out, despite this status there are still hesitations inasmuch as the Code is by no means clear as to how these rights are to be protected.[47] They are not like obligation or property rights that are given direct protection in the law of actions; instead they are more like 'interests' which can be treated as 'patrimonial' if they are invaded.[48]

This 'patrimonial interest' aspect is well brought out by an English case concerning an elderly Norwegian man who suffered a severe stroke while in England.[49] A dispute arose between the family of the man and the man's close friend: the family (defendants) wanted the man returned to Norway for care while the friend (plaintiff) wanted the man to be treated in an English private nursing home. Given the fact that the man himself was unable to communicate, the whole reasoning process had to shift from 'rights' to 'interests'. What was in the 'best interests' of the man himself? Did each of the parties have a 'legitimate interest' in the legal dispute? With respect to the second question, Millet LJ was of the view that 'unless the court is willing to entertain proceedings brought by the parties who claim the responsibility for looking after the patient it will often not be possible to bring proceedings at all'. And this would be unfortunate since 'the parties are likely to resort to self-help'.[50] This second question is essentially one where the interest attaches to the *actio* rather than the *persona*, but while

---

[44] 'Individual interests are claims or demands or desires involved in and looked at from the standpoint, of the individual life immediately as such—asserted in title of the individual life' (n 7) 23. See also R Pound *Contemporary Juristic Theory*, extracted in Lloyd and Freeman (n 4) 574: 'Individual interests are interests of personality or interests in the domestic relations or interests of substance. Interests of personality are those involved in the individual physical and spiritual existence; in one's body and life, ie security of his physical person and his bodily health, in free exertion of one's will, ie, freedom from coercion, and from deception . . . in free choice of location, in one's reputation, in freedom to contract and of entering into relations with others, in free industry . . .'. [45] CC Arts 9 (privacy), 16 (dignity).
[46] Ost (n 1) 122. Note, however, if these interests are invaded damages are awarded often via CC Art 1382 and to this extent they thus appear as patrimonial interests. Note, for example, in English law the Human Organs Transplants Act 1989 s 1.
[47] Ost (n 1) 117–24.   [48] Cf Protection of Harassment Act 1997 s 3.
[49] *In re S (Hospital Patient: Court's Jurisdiction)* [1995] 3 WLR 78.
[50] At 92.

the case is very much a law of persons problem, the inability of the rightholder himself to assert his rights in court creates structural problems. As Professor Ost recognizes with regard to the civil law tradition, the notion of a right is extremely ambiguous as a practical reasoning device when taken out of its property context.[51] It simply does not function properly when applied to 'rights' of personality since the idea of being the master of one's own body does not always find expression in legal structures. What one is really talking about, says Ost, is the protection, through a variety of means, of a 'simple interest'. This may seem a rather extraordinary conclusion given the importance, in the scale of legal values, of the human body. Human rights are fundamental[52] and one of the most fundamental of these human personality rights is the right to life. Yet even here the English case-law indicates that institutionally this can often be handled only by recourse to the notion of an interest.[53]

In the *Tony Bland* case the courts were asked to rule, in an action for a declaration, if a hospital could discontinue a life support programme for a young man who, as a result of the dreadful Hillsborough tragedy, was rendered permanently unconscious with, according to medical opinion, no chance of recovery.[54] In short, could the hospital allow the young man to die by withdrawing the feeding necessary to keep him functioning in his vegetative state? One might have thought that the starting point for this legal action would have been the *right* to life that attaches to the human *persona*, yet this was not the concept that formed the basis of the reasoning and the decision.[55] Instead the judges focused on the notion of an interest and asked what would be in the 'best interests' of Tony Bland. The reason for this shift of emphasis becomes evident when one considers the final decision reached in the case: the House of Lords came to the conclusion that it would be in the best interests of Bland if he were to be allowed to die. Had the judges approached this case in terms of *rights*, it would have been extremely difficult to conclude that Bland should be allowed to die since this would have appeared to contravene his fundamental human right to life.[56] The notion of a right would have emphasized the *persona*. However, in replacing 'right' with 'interest' the lawyers were able to effect a shift from the subjective to the objective. Tony Bland became, to use the

---

[51] Ost (n 1) 122. [52] Human Rights Act 1998.

[53] What the notion of an interest does in this situation is not so much to give effect to some pre-existing claim or demand or expectation existing empirically (although these must have some basis in fact). It gives an alternative and objective view of the conceptual (institutional) structure since the subjective view is eclipsed by the unconsciousness of the main right-holder.

[54] *Airedale NHS Trust v Bland* [1993] AC 789.

[55] See now on the relationship between the right to life and the interest of the patient: *NHS Trust A v M* [2001] 2 WLR 942.

[56] Cf Ward LJ in *In re A (Children) (Conjoined Twins: Surgical Separation)* [2001] 2 WLR 480, 537.

expression of Millet LJ in the case discussed earlier, analogous to a 'sack of potatoes' whose 'interests' were to be considered detached from the *persona* itself.

A second way in which the notion of an interest can give expression to the idea of personality is through the specific recognition of an interest, or set of interests, existing independently of the legal status of the subject him or herself. Thus in the area of family law children are deemed to have their own interests which are to be treated independently from, say, the interests of the parents.[57] And since Roman times these interests come into existence before the actual legal personality of the child itself.[58] The concept of an interest and the notion of a *persona* are therefore not interdependent in quite the same way as rights and legal personality. This *décalage* allows the notion of an interest to be extended beyond human legal subjects in a way that would be controversial if it were rights that were in issue; for example, legislation can, as we have already suggested, talk about the interests of animals without raising the kind of philosophical controversy that would inevitably result had the text talked in terms of rights.[59]

This ability to extend beyond the existence of the *persona* is particularly useful when it comes to interests that attach more to groups of human beings rather than just to the individual. These interests are often, to begin with at least, rather diffuse and may well remain legally unrecognized until given shape by attachment to some, perhaps equally diffuse, legal subject.[60] Legal 'subject' in this context must be understood in two rather different ways. The first way is simply as a category and thus the interest in issue is one that attaches to a category of persons; one talks here of 'interest groups'. Legislation is full of examples: one recent text lists various interests groups as including teachers, employers of teachers, providers of teacher training, and so on.[61] Another Act talks of the 'interests of local government, industry, agriculture and small businesses',[62] while yet another piece of legislation mentions 'persons able to represent the interests of particular kinds of litigants (for example, businesses or employees)'.[63] It would be a gross exaggeration to say that the existence of these various interests has the effect of creating new legal subjects. Accordingly the capacity of, say, a local authority to obtain an injunction in the interests of the local inhabitants does not as such turn the local community into a legal person.[64] Nevertheless, local government, agriculture, small businesses,

---

[57] Ost (n 1) 73–80; *In re L (A Child)* [2001] 2 WLR 339.
[58] D 1 5 7.
[59] Animals (Scientific Procedures) Act 1986 s 5(3)(c).
[60] See generally Jolowicz (n 4).
[61] Teaching and Higher Education Act 1998 s 1(5).
[62] Pollution Prevention and Control Act 1999 s 2(4)(c).
[63] Civil Procedure Act 1997 s 6(2)(f).
[64] Local Government Act 1972 s 222.

teachers, employers, and employees are interest groups that often find it valuable to create specific legal persons or associations to act as a focal point for the representation of their interests. Indeed, even if such groups lack any kind of legal personality, procedural rules may nevertheless give indirect recognition.[65] Sometimes these associations become so prominent that they change the symmetry of the law itself. The creation of trade unions and employers' associations had the ultimate effect of creating a new category of law: labour law is now a subject independent of the law of obligations.[66]

IV. COMMERCIAL INTERESTS

The mediation between fact, policy, and law is particularly evident in respect of two group interests that have played central roles in more recent times: the commercial and the consumer interests. The 'commercial interest' is in many respects much older than the consumer one in that a formal division has been made in civilian thinking between civil and commercial law for many centuries.[67] In English law no similar formal distinction is made and thus legal areas such as company law, contract, tort, intellectual property, and the like find themselves on the same plane. What English law does recognize is the notion of the 'commercial interest' and this notion is fundamental enough to dominate whole areas of English legal and of political thinking.

For example, the law of contract finds itself having to mediate not just between the two major interest groups of business and consumer but between different conceptions about what the interests themselves require from the law. On the one hand, the commercial interest requires 'a degree of rigidity in legal principle'[68] since businessmen 'have to look after own interests' and thus it 'is up to them to assess the probable impact of any particular clause upon their interest'.[69] On the other hand, 'commercial reality' (that is to say, interest) also requires on occasions 'a practical

---

[65] See eg W van Gerven J Lever and P Larouche *Tort Law* (Oxford Hart 2000) 248–77.

[66] In this respect the Pound thesis of pre-existing interests ultimately recognized by the law and given expression in legal rights or powers has much to commend it. There is no doubt that these interests can be said, in some form, to pre-exist empirically. All the same, the role of the institutional system must not be underestimated either; the conceptual formation of new interest groups goes far in itself in giving substantive content to the interests inasmuch as the law creates an institutional model in which these interests seemingly find expression. One is no longer focusing on the sociological facts as the foundation of the interest but the institutional model and as such the law will have as much input into the model as any social fact.

[67] See generally D Tallon 'Civil and Commercial Law' in *International Encyclopedia of Comparative Law* (JCB Mohr) vol 8, ch 2.

[68] Megaw LJ in *The Mihalis Angelos* [1971] 1 QB 164, 205.

[69] Lord Goff in *The General Capinpin* [1991] 1 Lloyd's Rep 1, 9.

approach' which, in the context of the problem in issue, means 'some flexibility in the law of contract'.[70] This apparent contradiction is perhaps more subtle than it might first appear. In the first situation the commercial interest is being viewed from the position of the individual *commerçant* who is in the business of pursuing, by negotiation, his own individual economic interest. In the second situation the law is being assessed in terms of a group interest: the 'relations of all parties to each other are commercial relations entered into for business reasons of ultimate profit'.[71] Perhaps one might distinguish these two situations by differentiating between 'business' and 'commercial' interests, the former attaching to the individual subject, the latter to a group interest. Whatever the situation, the point to stress is that 'interest', commercial or business, is the mediating element that allows the courts to adjust their reasoning in relation to the 'subject' in play.[72] Sometimes the focus will be on the individual legal subject and its particular interest;[73] at other times it will be on a more diffuse group where the court is taking notice of an interest that transcends each individual legal subject.[74] In other words the 'commercial interest' can on occasions be more of a 'general interest' that is rooted as much in the private sector as the public and thus ends up as a kind of privatized general interest set in the context of a political economy and the circulation of money.[75]

The problem for the courts, then, is to walk a delicate tightrope between the economic and political pressures[76] and it is here that the notion of an interest has its role to play in legal reasoning. Of course, not all the cases are analysed directly using the concept of an interest, but the notion is often there in the background.[77] Moreover, the notion itself can be very problematic. Those who combine in order to threaten commercial or business interests may find themselves being accused of causing harm to the public interest,[78] while the business enterprise which might appear to be

---

[70] Lord Wilberforce in *The Eurymedon* [1975] AC 154, 167.   [71] Ibid at 167.

[72] See eg *Thorne v Motor Trade Association* [1937] AC 797.

[73] As in eg *Walford v Miles* [1992] 2 AC 128.

[74] Here the question is: what is in the interests of commerce? See eg *Blackpool & Fylde Aero Club Ltd v Blackpool BC* [1990] 1 WLR 1195, 1201 ('the confident assumptions of commercial parties'). See also *Thorne v Motor Trade Association* [1937] AC 797 where the House of Lords alluded to 'business interests' (or 'trade interests') beyond the mere acquisition of money.

[75] A Jacquemin and G Schrans *Le Droit économique* (3rd edn Paris PUF 1982) 9–33.

[76] 'It is . . . apparent that whether or not a particular commercial activity is or is not in the "public interest" is very much a matter of political judgment . . . and the courts must be careful not to invade the political field and substitute their own judgment for that of the Minister': per Lord Keith in *R v Secretary of State for Trade and Industry, Ex p Lonrho Plc* [1989] 1 WLR 525, 536.

[77] This is true in *Thorne v Motor Trade Association* [1937] AC 797 where the primary issue was whether a certain threat amounted to blackmail, but the moral dimension was discussed in relation to the notion of 'business interest'.

[78] See eg *Duport Steels Ltd v Sirs* [1980] 1 WLR 142, 156–7 per Lord Diplock.

threatening the public interest may find its activity receiving support on the basis of legitimate commercial interest.[79] Indeed, a government health minister once declared (accurately), in the public interest, that most eggs produced in England were contaminated by salmonella, something that did not enhance the producers' commercial interest; the government subsequently removed the minister and paid compensation to the egg producers.[80] One association's illegitimate self-interest is another association's legitimate commercial interest. No doubt things are not quite as simple as this: the extent to which the law will recognize and protect a person's interest in earning a living, the trader's interest in trading, or the workman's interest in working is plagued by conceptual and policy difficulties.[81] Yet it is just these difficulties that invite the intervention of the court. Is the law going to endow, following the Pound analysis, an 'interest' with the status of a 'right'?[82] Some judgments raise a direct question about the nature of the business interest in play;[83] other judgments look to the interest invaded and relate this to the acts and behaviour of the defendant.[84] These latter cases raise subsidiary questions: should the pursuit of the interest be allowed on the basis that the pursuit is a 'freedom'?[85] Or should the pursuit itself of the interest be classed as 'unlawful' on the ground that it is, for example, against the 'public interest'? If the act of pursuing the interest amounts to a wrong, because it is breach of the criminal law or is a tort, the court will find little difficulty in concluding that the pursuit is unlawful. However, this does not always mean that the interest in issue is not worthy of further examination. In one case the House of Lords held that the blacking of a ship in a country where such blacking was lawful did nevertheless amount to economic duress for the purposes of the English law of unjust enrichment.[86] Yet this reasoning has the bizarre effect of saying that workers, paid slave wages in the commercial interests of their employers, will be unjustly enriching themselves at the expense of their employers if they take industrial action in pursuit of their own, surely legitimate, interests. It is cases like this that confirm that the Pound analysis of a strict dichotomy between social fact (interests) and legal conceptualization (rights) is epistemologically too simplified.

[79] See eg *Camelot Group Plc v Centaur Communications Ltd* [1999] QB 124. See also *Thorne v Motor Trade Association* [1937] AC 797.

[80] T Weir *A Casebook on Tort* (9th edn London Sweet & Maxwell 2000) 579.

[81] Ibid 567–70.   [82] (n 7) 338.

[83] See eg Lord Woolf in *Lonrho Plc v Fayed* [1990] 2 QB 479, 493.

[84] See eg *Gulf Oil (GB) Ltd v Page* [1987] Ch 327. And see *Thorne v Motor Trade Association* [1937] AC 797.

[85] *Thorne v Motor Trade Association* [1937] AC 797; *Schering Chemicals Ltd v Falkman Ltd* [1982] 1 QB 1, 22.

[86] *Dimskal Shipping Co v ITWF (The Evia Luck)* [1992] 2 AC 152.

In France it is said there has been a general 'commercialization of the law',[87] but this commercialization has, in theory at least, been defined to some extent by a much greater formalization in respect of categories. The sharp division between public and private law together with a further subdivision between civil and commercial law provides a structural pattern against which interests are measured and to some extent defined and perceived. However, given the (partially) empirical nature of an interest, it has the capacity, evidently, of transgressing these formal categories and, when it does, the threat to formalized constitutional freedoms at least becomes more evident in France, even if unstoppable.[88] In England, on the other hand, there is no formal means of separating the commercial from the public interest (as the eggs example seemingly confirms). And so there is a range of factual situations where economic and political interests become confused to the extent that the latter can get subverted by the former.[89] In fact the notion of commercial interest has found its way into the heart of English public law in as much as it has become a 'constitutional' right available to the State. Take, for example, confidential information. The lack of any formal distinction between public and private law has led to government information being protected on the ground of 'ownership' and 'privacy'[90] and private sector information being protected in the face of a strong public health interest.[91] To expose on television to the general public that a certain drug might be dangerous would, according to one appeal judge, be a 'betrayal of business confidences'.[92] Indeed restraining the press from exposing confidential information is seen by the English judiciary as 'an expression and not a negation of democracy in action'[93] in that a constitutional right to press freedom of the kind found in the United States results only in the press being 'above the law'.[94] Such an approach no doubt has the advantage of giving the judiciary much discretion in these matters.[95] However, it has to be asked if this 'interest'

---

[87] See eg C Champaud *Le Droit des affaires* (2nd edn Paris PUF 1984) 23 quoting Ripert.
[88] Jacquemin and Schrans (n 75) 35–41.
[89] See recently on this *Att-Gen v Blake* [2001] 1 AC 268.
[90] *Home Office v Harman* [1981] QB 534, 557; *Att-Gen v Guardian Newspapers* [1987] 1 WLR 1248.
[91] *Schering Chemicals Ltd v Falkman Ltd* [1982] 1 QB 1. But cf *Lion Laboratories Ltd v Evans* [1984] 2 All ER 417.
[92] Shaw LJ in *Schering Chemicals Ltd v Falkman Ltd* [1982] 1 QB 1, 27.
[93] Lord Templeman in *Att-Gen v Guardian Newspapers* [1987] 1 WLR 1248, 1299.
[94] Lord Ackner in *Att-Gen v Guardian Newspapers* [1987] 1 WLR 1248, 1306. See also *X Ltd v Morgan-Grampian (Publishers) Ltd* [1991] 1 AC 1.
[95] *Reynolds v Times Newspapers Ltd* [1999] 3 WLR 1010. One may reflect on the extent to which the Lord Archer affair will have made nonsense of the tort of defamation's role in seemingly stopping the press from being above the law. One commentator noted: 'Media lawyers know that a judge's voicing of respect for freedom of expression is usually the precursor to a judgment significantly curtailing that right': D Tench *Media Guardian* 23 July 2001, 10. See eg *Ashworth Hospital Authority v MGN Ltd* [2002] 1 WLR 2033 §38.

approach[96] will be able to withstand the shift towards 'rights' stimulated by the Human Rights Act 1998.[97] One answer is that the interest approach is very much capable of surviving if, as we shall see, the notion of a right itself can effectively be reduced, by sleight of reasoning, to an interest.

The incorporation of the European Convention for the Protection of Human Rights and Fundamental Freedoms into English law is only one aspect of the European dimension to law that will have possibly a profound influence on the traditional interrelationship of the various established interests. European Union law is another dimension having an important influence. And this influence is not just upon United Kingdom common law thinking but upon legal science more generally: the traditional Romanist dichotomy between public and private law is being rendered meaningless by an EU system of law which is, at one and the same time, a civil, a commercial, and a constitutional law.[98] Conceptually, this intermixing of legal relations and interests is less of a problem for the common lawyer in that constitutional, property, and commercial interests have, as we have already seen, long been intermingled in English legal reasoning.[99] Even local government has been judged, not by public law principles, but by rules of business ethics.[100] Such a business-like approach may, it must be said, sometimes be a good thing; but in legal reasoning it allows judges to use commercial self-interest against press freedom in a rather paradoxical way. Commercial self-interest can be seen as something to be protected against press intrusion often on the basis of preventing a betrayal of confidence.[101] Equally commercial self-interest can be used to restrain publication on the ground that the press are simply acting in their own commercial self-interest and thus are not deserving of constitutional protection.[102] Constitutional law can in consequence become subverted by the positive and negative aspects of the commercial interest. There are great dangers in this subversion. To give just one example, the British Foundry Association was reported to have said, in relation to a Freedom of Information Campaign on the environment, that they doubted whether there is a genuine public demand for environmental information. There is only a demand stimulated 'by pressure groups with little regard for the economic consequences of the fulfilment

---

[96] See eg *Lord Lowry in X Ltd v Morgan-Grampian (Publishers) Ltd* [1991] 1 AC 1, 55.

[97] *Goodwin v UK* (1996) 22 EHRR 123.

[98] C Joerges 'The Impact of European Integration on Private Law: Reductionist Perceptions, True Conflicts and a New Constitutional Perspective' [1997] ELJ 378.

[99] G Samuel 'The Impact of European Integration on Private Law: A Comment' (1998) 18 LS 167.

[100] *Roberts v Hopwood* [1925] AC 578; *Prescott v Birmingham Corporation* [1955] Ch 210; *Bromley LBC v GLC* [1983] 1 AC 768. See also D Oliver 'The Human Rights Act and Public/Private Law Divides' [2000] EHRLR 343.

[101] *Schering Chemicals Ltd v Falkman Ltd* [1982] 1 QB 1; *Camelot Group Plc v Centaur Communications Ltd* [1999] QB 124.

[102] See eg *Francome v Mirror Group Newspapers Ltd* [1984] 1 WLR 892, 898.

of their demands'.[103] The irony here is that the Association was perhaps failing to appreciate that environmental issues do not embrace only public or general interests. The environment raises the question of the possibility of an interest attaching to a group of humans—a diffuse *persona*—who do not as yet exist. In other words, how should the law accommodate the interests of future generations? And is this an issue for the civil, the constitutional, or the commercial law?

V. INTERESTS ATTACHING TO THE *ACTIO*

The 'commercial interest' might be said to have held its own, in English law, in the face of, say, the 'general interest' and indeed in the face of certain constitutional freedoms, if not rights, such as the liberty of the press. This success, needless to say, raises questions about the effectiveness and scope of interests such as the 'public interest'.[104] Is this, in the end, an interest that is to be subsumed under a more overriding notion as such the 'economic interest'? Are all interests, public and private, to be measured entirely in relation to the *homo oeconomicus*?[105] These are questions that have been examined in some detail but the effectiveness of the notion of an interest is not exhausted by reference simply to interests that attach to the *persona* and to more diffuse legal groups and classes. Interests can equally attach themselves to actions (*actiones*) and to things (*res*).

In fact these different perspectives can often be a useful approach to a comparative analysis. Take the notion of 'public interest'.[106] One way this can be given expression in its strong sense in a legal system is by attaching it to a legal subject whose primary purpose is to protect this interest and this interest alone. In French law such a subject is the Ministère public, whose role is to represent the State in criminal cases—where the Ministère public acts as the prosecutor—and the public interest in civil cases.[107] In

---

[103] *The Observer* 16 July 1989, 4.

[104] Pound talks of interests of the State as a juristic person and interests of the State as guardians of social interests: see Jolowicz (n 11) 177.

[105] For an interesting case touching on this question, see *Co-operative Insurance Society Ltd v Argyll Stores Ltd* [1998] AC 1. This case raises the issue of the relationship between the economic interests of the parties to a contract and the general public interest, and all in relation to the availability of an actio (specific performance in equity). Note, however, Pound's warning: 'We must not confuse interest as claim, as jurists use the term, with interest as advantage as economists use it' (n 7) 23.

[106] 'Public interests are the claims or demands or desires asserted by individuals involved in or looked at from the standpoint of political life—life in politically organized society. They are asserted in title of that organisation. It is convenient to treat them as the claims of a politically organized society thought of as a legal entity' Pound (n 7) 23.

[107] The Ministère public is not a person as such but a corps of *magistrats*: see generally J Volff *Le Ministère public* (Paris PUF 1998).

this latter role the Ministère public intervenes as a third party to represent the public interest alongside the private interests of the parties.[108] English law has no equivalent institution as such, although the office of the Attorney-General can be used to represent in law the public interest.[109] In addition local authorities have power to seek remedies on behalf of the interests of local inhabitants.[110] Here the notion of public interest is formally attaching to a legal subject and thus to an extent the institutional pattern is one of *persona* (legal subject) and *res* (interest). However, the procedural issue behind this pattern is more often one concerning the entitlement to bring an action in court. Who can sue to vindicate the public interest? The problem is therefore just as much one of an interest attaching to an *actio*.

The procedural point is not new and has in fact a history stretching back to the Roman *actio popularis*. These popular actions were theoretically available to any member of the public and could be brought, for example, against an owner of a building adjacent to a highway from which something had been thrown or poured causing injury to highway users.[111] Being public penal actions they were designed to protect the public interest (*utilitas publica*) in using the streets without danger,[112] but those with a particular interest (*interest*) in bringing the action would be given preference to sue.[113] This idea of restricting legal actions only to those with a legitimate interest in the proceedings has been developed into a general principle within the civil law tradition: *pas d'intérêt, pas d'action*.[114] In other words a plaintiff who wishes to bring, or defend, an action in the civil courts must either have a legitimate interest in the success or failure of the proceedings or be a person given power by statute to vindicate or defend a specified interest.[115] Thus it was once the situation in French law that an unmarried partner who had lived with a fatally injured victim of a tort could not sue the tortfeasor because the partner lacked a legitimate interest in the *actio*.[116] This interpretation has now been abandoned, but what is interesting about the legitimate interest requirement is that it can act as the basis for both a narrow and a wide view of liability. It can restrict the number of

---

[108] Nouveau code de procedure civile Art 424. For a general comparative overview see M Cappelletti *The Judicial Process in Comparative Perspective* (Oxford 1989) 268–308.

[109] See generally *Gouriet v Union of Post Office Workers* [1978] AC 435. And see also Cappelletti (108). [110] Local Government Act 1972 s 222.

[111] D 9 3 1pr. [112] D 9 3 1 1. [113] D 9 3 5 5.

[114] J-J Barbiéri *La Procédure civile* (Paris PUF 1995) 22.

[115] Nouveau code de procédure civile Art 31.

[116] One might note how, once again, this legal situation was a good example of how interest was as much dependent on the institutional system as on empirical fact. As a matter of strict social fact, the interests of a married and unmarried couple are identical; the difference is simply one of the existence and non-existence of the legal relationship of marriage. The absence of legal protection to the unmarried partner was being determined by an 'interest' whose substance was being defined entirely by reference to the law.

plaintiffs able to sue, but increase the types of damage (that is to say interests) legitimately protected.[117]

Probably a similar rule exists in English law in respect of civil proceedings,[118] although of course concepts such as 'duty of care', or the requirement of damage, often fulfil the same role and thus make superfluous any
legitimate interest provision.[119] However, statute now confers on a number
of public officers or bodies the power to seek certain remedies on behalf of
specified interests[120] and this statutory power has recently been extended to
the Consumers' Association in respect of unfair terms in consumer
contracts.[121] Yet whatever the position with regard to English private law
and legal remedies, in public law the interest rule is quite specific. A person
wishing to bring an action for judicial review must have a 'sufficient interest' in the matter.[122] In other words, in public law the law of actions is kept
separate from substantive law exclusively through the use of the notion of
an interest. An individual is entitled to commence a judicial review action
only if he has a 'sufficient interest' and this must logically be separate from
the substantial public law 'right' that will be in issue in the judicial review
claim itself.[123]

Care must thus be taken, if the distinction between right and interest is
to have any conceptual meaning, to keep 'interest' separate from 'right'. If
care is not taken here, the law of actions issue will soon become at least
partly merged with the substantive law question. And the result will be that
the question whether or not a private person can bring a legal action will
become very close to depending upon the actual substance of the claim
itself.[124] The requirement of 'sufficient interest' can, accordingly, easily
transform itself into a kind of public law preliminary question of law, or a
public law striking out action, either raising 'interest' effectively to the
status of 'right' or reducing 'right' to little more than an interest. Such a
transformation would be an error inasmuch as the purpose of the requirement is the exclusion of potential plaintiffs on the ground that there is an
insufficient connection between *persona* and *actio*. The *locus standi* question is not really something that goes to the lawfulness of an administrative
decision. Such a requirement is no doubt necessary with regard to certain
kinds of remedies where individual damage is not a precondition since it
would probably introduce into law an unacceptable insecurity if everyone

---

[117] See van Gerven et al (n 65) 125–9.
[118] *Lall v Lall* [1965] 3 All ER 330; *The Nordglimt* [1988] QB 183, 199–200.
[119] See eg Financial Services Act 1986 s 62.
[120] Ibid s 6.
[121] Unfair Terms in Consumer Contracts Regulations 1999 reg 12.
[122] Supreme Court Act 1981 s 31(3).   [123] Ibid.
[124] See eg *IRC v National Federation of Self-Employed and Small Businesses Ltd* [1982] AC
617.

had the right to challenge in court an unlawful act of another.[125] Nevertheless, the notion of sufficient interest can go well beyond the descriptive inasmuch as it can raise a question as to whether a particular interest group ought to be regarded, in effect, as a legal subject. This can become acutely conceptual in that it can raise on occasions the question of whether a group of persons can add up to more than the sum of the individuals.

Take, for example, a government minister who makes an unlawful decision that has consequences for the environment but does not actually invade the individual interest of any single individual. According to one judge the mere assertion of an interest does not give one an interest. Thus the 'fact that some thousands of people join together and assert that they have an interest does not create an interest if the individuals did not have an interest'.[126] Perhaps not, but the position is more complex than the judge seems to suggest. A wine distributor sells as litre bottles of wine bottles that in fact contain only 98 centilitres and secures for itself a huge profit. No single consumer suffers any measurable loss as far as the law is concerned, yet the buyers as a class have been deprived of a large amount of money. The same applies with respect to the environment. It may be that an unlawful decision by a minister, or an unlawful act by a commercial organization, causes no measurable invasion of any individual interest, but this does not mean that a class of persons will be unaffected. If the commercial organization profits from its unlawful act it will, without doubt, have advanced its commercial interest. Is one forced to say that this advance is cost-free since no individual interest is affected? What if a group of drugs companies launch onto the market at the same time, and at great profit to themselves, a drug that is dangerous? Does one have to wait for an individual consumer to suffer before one can say that consumers as a class has had its interest threatened?[127]

This does not of course mean that there are not difficult cases. In the *Rose Theatre* case[128] the Secretary of State for the Environment refused to class the site in the City of London where the remains of the Globe Theatre were discovered as a listed archaeological site. When the remains were first discovered, a trust company had been set up which had as its object the preservation of the remains and the making of them accessible to the public.

---

[125] *R v Secretary of State for the Environment, Ex p Rose Theatre Trust Co* [1990] 1 QB 504, 519 per Schiemann J.   [126] ibid at 520

[127] Note also there is a causal point that can arise in these kind of cases. If a consumer is injured by a drug launched onto the market by several independent drug companies but it is not possible to locate the actual company responsible for supplying the dangerous drug, does this mean that the consumer interest and the victim's private interest must suffer at no cost to the general commercial interest? See now *Fairchild v Glenhaven Funeral Services Ltd* [2002] 3 WLR 89.   [128] [1990] 1 QB 504.

The trust company sought to bring an action for judicial review in respect of the minister's refusal; however, the judge dismissed the action not just on the ground of substance, but also on the *locus standi* question. Since no individual had a sufficient interest in the matter it followed, concluded the judge, that the company created by those individuals had no standing. On closer inspection of the judgment it emerges that the judge was in fact deciding the issue not so much as one of an 'interest' but as one of 'right'. 'Where one is examining an alleged failure to perform a duty imposed by statute', said Schiemann J, 'it is useful to look at the statute and see whether it gives an applicant a *right* enabling him to have that duty performed.'[129] Now, the moment one switches from 'interest' to 'right', one is of course moving from the descriptive, or even quasi-descriptive, to the exclusively normative. However, what makes this switch dangerous in this type of case is that while judicial review might well involve a 'duty' it never involves a 'right'. The best that an individual or interest group can hope to obtain in public law is a 'legitimate expectation' and this, almost by definition, is not a right.[130] Remedies are being confused with rights.

One immediate point needs to be stressed about this case. In emphasizing this particular example it is not being suggested that the *Rose Theatre* case is a reliable authority; indeed, strictly speaking, it probably is not.[131] The point to be made is that it is an excellent example of how the substance of the interest was not actually being determined by social reality but by the conceptual model of law in play. In many situations this confusion of right and interest may not matter. The judge in the *Globe Theatre* case was not as such acting unfairly since most of his judgment is devoted to the substantive issue of whether the minister actually abused his discretion and he rejected the legal challenge on this ground. He ruled on the standing issue because that is what the parties themselves desired. However, there are other situations where the raising of an interest to the level of a right, or indeed the reduction of a right to the level of an interest, is more problematic. Freedom of speech has been described at common law as not a right but only a liberty[132] and this has given rise to a situation where even today, with the Human Rights Act 1998 on the statute book, the House of Lords is still having difficulty in asserting such a human 'right' in relation to other interests such as the public interest in receiving information or the commercial interest of the press itself.[133] In other words a fundamental human right is still seen as little more than an 'interest' to be set against other interests whose status is not actually recognized by the Convention for the

---

[129] Ibid at 520; emphasis added.
[130] *Council of Civil Service Unions v Minister for the Civil Service* [1985] AC 374.
[131] See *R v Inspectorate of Pollution, Ex p Greenpeace Ltd (No 2)* [1994] 4 All ER 329, 351.
[132] *Att-Gen v Guardian Newspapers (No 2)* [1990] AC 109, 283.
[133] See eg *Reynolds v Times Newspapers Ltd* [1999] 3 WLR 1010.

Protection of Human Rights and Fundamental Freedoms. In short some interests end up as rights, while some rights end up as interests; and this is so partly because English judicial reasoning so easily slips from one concept to the other and partly because the European Convention itself uses both notions.

VI. *ACTIO* AND ABUSE

Nothing that has been said should be taken as saying that there are never occasions when the notion of an interest, at the level of the remedy, should not be used to outflank a right. Indeed, it has already been noted that in civil law systems a rightholder is entitled to sue only if there is a legitimate interest in the proceedings. Often, by definition, if the rightholder is seeking to vindicate his right, this in itself will provide the interest. However, there are occasions when it could be said that a rightholder has no interest in enforcing his rights. The French Code civil lays down in one of its most famous articles (Article 544) that 'ownership is the right to enjoy and to dispose of things in the most absolute manner'. But the Cour de cassation has stated that this 'absolute right' is subject to the limitation that it can be exercised only in satisfaction of a 'serious and legitimate interest'.[134] Thus a landowner who grew 2-metre-high ferns on her land with the sole purpose of blocking out the light of her neighbour was held to have committed a tort and declared liable in damages to her neighbour.[135] The basis of this action for damages was not the interference with the neighbour's property or contractual right, for the neighbour did not have as such a right to light. It was the malicious behaviour of the landowner which deprived the exercise of the right to grow plants on one's land of its legitimate interest. In an earlier case the French Supreme Court had made a similar ruling with respect to a landowner who had erected 16-metre towers on his land topped with spikes with the deliberate intention of interfering with his neighbour's ballooning activities. These towers went way beyond anything needed to protect the landowner's 'legitimate interests'.[136] The importance of the two cases is that they established the doctrine of abuse of rights based on the relationship between subjective 'malice' and objective 'interest'.[137]

The theory of abuse of rights did not confine itself to the law of property but expanded into other areas of private law where, on occasions, it linked up with neighbouring concepts such as good faith.[138] Again these developments involved the notion of an interest. In the area of family law, for example,

---

[134] Cass civ 20 jan 1964; [1964] D 518.
[135] Ibid.
[136] Cass req 3 août 1915; (1917) 1 D 79.
[137] Ost (n 1) 143.
[138] J-L Bergel *Théorie générale du droit* (3rd edn Paris Dalloz 1999) 258.

abuse of family property rights by a spouse might be curtailed where the interest of the family was threatened.[139] And in contract the theory, along with good faith, helped develop the idea that each party to a contract had to consider not just their own commercial interests but the legitimate interests of the other contracting party.[140] In company law the rights and interests of shareholders might well take second place to the interests of the company as a whole.[141] What is so important about this civilian development is that while it is clearly something that focuses on the concept of a right, the actual vehicle by which the theory of abuse of right has been put into effect is the notion of an interest. As Professor Ost has stated, its positive influence is incontestable. Sometimes an interest acts as a means of curbing an excess of selfish individualism such as where the group interest takes precedence over that of the individual. Sometimes it ensures the stability of contract by stressing the common interest of the two or more parties.[142] These developments have not, it must be said, occurred without severe criticism from those who considered that the doctrine of abuse of rights amounted to the undermining of the absolute nature of a right and depriving it of its conceptual force. As Ost says, the 'consideration payable for the satisfaction of interests is the correlative weakening of subjective rights'.[143]

This ability of an interest to weaken the notion of a 'right' goes some way in explaining why the notion of a subjective right has never had the same force in English law as it has had on the Continent.[144] English law has thought more in terms of liberty rather than rights; and liberty, as Ost explains, is at the basis of the notion of an interest.[145] This lack of rights-thinking in English law has resulted equally in a lack of any formal theories of abuse of rights. Problems that would be treated as an abuse of a right in civil law tend, in England, to be solved on the basis of the law of actions (remedies) which in turn look to behaviour and reasonableness. A reasonable level of noise may become an unreasonable interference with a property interest if the noise is the result of a malicious motive.[146] In public law, equally, the emphasis is not on the rights of citizens, but on what they might reasonable expect from a public service.[147] But such a 'legitimate expectation' can nevertheless function more or less as a 'legitimate interest' with the result that a public body will not be able to enforce any of its 'private' law property or contract rights if it lacks a proper interest in its exercise.[148] These abuse cases do not in strict theory draw their normative force as such

---

[139] J-L Bergel *Théorie générale du droit* (3rd edn Paris Dalloz 1999) 258.
[140] P Malaurie and L Aynès *Les Obligations* (10th edn Paris Cujas 1999) 225–6.
[141] Ost (n 1) 86.   [142] ibid 152–3.   [143] Ibid 167.
[144] G Samuel 'Le Droit subjectif and English Law' [1987] CLJ 264.
[145] Ost (n 1) 185–6.
[146] *Christie v Davey* [1893] 1 Ch 316; *Hollywood Silver Fox Farm v Emmett* [1936] 2 KB 468.
[147] *Council of Civil Service Unions v Minister for the Civil Service* [1985] AC 374.
[148] *Wheeler v Leicester CC* [1985] AC 1054.

from the motive of the defendant since motive has been said to be irrelevant when it comes to the exercise of a property right.[149] The normative force in these cases comes from the existence of a cause of action or a remedy like judicial review. This creates a rather complex picture because motive gets relegated to a seemingly more indirect role. For example, a Court of Appeal judge was able to assert without contradiction that a 'person who has a right under a contract . . . is entitled to exercise it . . . for a good or a bad reason or no reason at all'.[150] However, it would be extremely dangerous for any lawyer to take this statement simply at face value because if malicious behaviour does lack any 'legitimate interest' or, indeed, interferes with an easily identifiable interest of another it is by no means clear that the law of remedies will be impotent.[151]

The question is whether one can go further and use the notion of an interest as a positive means of remedial intervention. A person exercises a legitimate liberty deliberately to interfere with a legitimate interest of another: will a remedy be available to the person whose legitimate interest is invaded? This question takes us to the heart of the relationship between rights, remedies, and interests, for if a court is prepared to grant a remedy it would immediately seem to flow, logically, that the interest is being transformed into a protected right.[152] It is this bootstraps circularity that gives legal reasoning its force as an informal source of law.

In particular the interest approach has been used to support the granting of injunctions. On one occasion a defendant was restrained from doing an act, not itself wrongful, simply because it interfered with the commercial interest of the plaintiff without furthering, according to the court, any interest on the part of the defendant.[153] On another occasion the Court of Appeal was prepared to restrain a defendant from exercising his liberty to use the highway on the basis that he may be tempted to invade the 'legitimate interest' of the plaintiff if he were allowed to approach the vicinity of the plaintiff's home.[154] In this latter case the starting point was the relationship between the power of the High Court to grant an injunction[155] and the 'need to protect the legitimate interests of those who have invoked its jurisdiction'.[156] Once again the defendant's 'right' to use the highway was reduced to an interest with the result that the case became one of 'two interests to be reconciled'. The reconciliation was then achieved by raising

---

[149] *Bradford Corporation v Pickles* [1895] AC 587.
[150] Pearson LJ in *Chapman v Honig* [1963] 2 QB 502, 520.
[151] See eg *Blackpool & Fylde Aero Club Ltd v Blackpool BC* [1990] 1 WLR 1195.
[152] Cf *Hubbard v Pitt* [1976] QB 142.
[153] See eg *Gulf Oil (GB) Ltd v Page* [1987] Ch 327.
[154] *Burris v Azadani* [1995] 1 WLR 1372.
[155] Supreme Court Act 1981 s 37(1).
[156] Sir Thomas Bingham MR at 1377.

the plaintiff's 'legitimate interest' to the status of a right and to reduce the defendant's to that of a 'liberty' which 'must be respected up to the point at which his conduct infringes, or threatens to infringe, the rights of the plaintiff'.[157] Finally, the liberty and right dichotomy was reduced to one of mutual legitimate interests: in restraining the defendant from temptation the court was acting not only 'in the plaintiff's interest', but also, 'indirectly, [in] the defendant's'.[158] None of this is to suggest that the Court of Appeal was wrong to grant an injunction on the facts of this case. The point is simply that the source of the law is in the circularity of the reasoning and in the manipulation of concepts like 'interest' and 'right'. There are occasions, in other words, where such bootstrap reasoning can amount to law-making in a way that has little to do with the application of rules. The source of law in this case was an 'interest', but an interest that existed as much in the reasoning process as in any social reality.

VII. DAMAGES AND INTERESTS

We have seen that interest attaches to an *actio* in two main ways. It provides a formal link between *persona* and *actio* for the purposes of actionability and the role here is essentially procedural. It can also act as a substitute 'right' where its role is to provide a substantive dimension to the availability of a remedy. Does the plaintiff have a legitimate interest in need of protection by the court? There is, however, a third, although not unrelated, way in which an interest attaches to a remedy. In damages actions the notion of an interest is used as a means of giving expression to, and categorizing, different types of harm suffered by a plaintiff. This damages role has been well described by Tony Weir:

> To cause harm means to have an adverse effect on something good. There are several good things in life, such as liberty, bodily integrity, land, possessions, reputation, wealth, privacy, dignity, perhaps even life itself. Lawyers call these goods 'interests.' These interests are all good, but they are not all equally good. This is evident when they come into conflict (one may jettison cargo to save passengers, but not vice versa, and one may detain a thing, but not a person, as security for a debt). Because these interests are not equally good, the protection afforded to them by the law is not equal; the law protects the better interests better: murder and rape are, after all, more serious crimes than theft. Accordingly, the better the interest invaded, the more readily does the law give compensation for the ensuing harm.[159]

One can see from this passage why it is tempting to reduce the whole of the law to a matter of 'interests'.[160] Law is about the protection of 'goods', or

---

[157] Sir Thomas Bingham MR at 1380.   [158] Ibid 1381.   [159] Weir (n 80) 6.
[160] See eg P Cane *Tort Law and Economic Interests* (2nd edn Oxford Clarendon Press 1996).

the avoidance of harm, and these goods or harm can be divided up, as Weir observes, into interests. Again this is an analysis that has its foundation in Roman law. In an action for the wrongful killing of a slave, the question arose as to the amount of damages that should be payable to the owner: is it just the value of the slave as a thing or is the owner entitled to a value based on the owner's 'interest' in the slave not being killed? The response was in favour of the latter: *et hoc iure utimur, ut eius quod interest fiat aestimatio.*[161]

This Roman contribution to the law of damages was of immense importance for two reasons. First, it provided a 'scientific' means of assessing compensation: damages would be payable only if an interest could be identified and valued.[162] 'Interest', in other words, was the means by which one could link descriptive categories of harm to normative principles of what a defendant ought to pay. Secondly, it provided a means of giving concrete expression to intangible 'goods', such as loss of an expected profit,[163] or intangible 'harms', such as depreciation of a collective group of objects through the destruction of a single item.[164] 'Interest' in this sense became a form of property, an intangible thing (*res incorporalis*) that in turn endowed the whole idea of an obligation with its proprietary character.[165] These ideas in turn helped transform the law of delict (tort) from a quasi-criminal law of actions, where a person who had caused harm paid a fine or penalty, to a law of actions founded on a relationship between two individuals where the idea was to re-establish harmony between two patrimonies. The development of the notion of an 'interest', in short, was virtually synonymous with the development of a sophisticated private law.

These Roman developments went far in transforming the notion of an interest from being an analytical device attached to the *actio* to a form of property seemingly capable of existing independently from the remedy. This is most evident perhaps with respect to a claim for a debt. At one level this is simply an entitlement to a remedy, but at another level it is a 'thing', that is to say an asset to be entered as a credit in the creditor's patrimony. In modern common law a debt is a form of property aptly entitled a 'thing in action' (chose in action) and this is one reason why Lord Denning MR was able to conclude that a third party was entitled to enforce her right to a debt even although she was not a party to the contract creating the debt.[166] She was, said Lord Denning, in effect enforcing an *in rem* property right that was not subject to the *in personam* privity of contract rule.[167] Of course, a

---

[161] D 9 2 21 2.   [162] See eg D 9 2 41pr.   [163] Ibid.
[164] D 92 22 1.   [165] G 2 14.
[166] *Beswick v Beswick* [1966] Ch 538 (CA); but cf [1968] AC 58.
[167] Note also how Lord Denning MR had recourse to the notion of an interest in this case: 'The general rule undoubtedly is that "no third person can sue, or be sued, on a contract to which he is not a party"; but at bottom that is only a rule of procedure. It goes to the form of

right to damages for a slave wrongfully killed or stolen by the defendant might not as such be as much of a *res* as the slave had been when alive or in the plaintiff's possession. But metaphysically speaking the right to damages comes very close to being a form of property in itself. Both are capable of being valued in monetary terms and thus both are able to be called 'interests', as we have seen from Tony Weir's observation. In fact this reduction of physical things to mere interests is post-Roman since it is clear that the Roman jurists distinguished between the thing itself (*res*) and the interest (*id quod interest*) which attached to it.[168] And one might note, also, how Weir himself advocates that tort lawyers should continue to distinguish between physical things and money. The 'deference of lawyers to economists', he laments, 'is one of the most chilling examples of *trahison des clercs* in the late twentieth century'.[169] Needless to say, the central concept used in economics is the notion of an interest.[170]

However, the sharp distinction made by the Romans between *interest* and other legal concepts such as *dominium* and *res* resulted in a remarkably creative conceptual structure. For example, where one person buys a slave that unknown to him was stolen property, both the buyer and the original owner of the slave had independent theft actions (a tort in Roman law) against the seller, despite the single *res* and unique *dominium*, since two independent interests were involved.[171] One creative possibility opened up by this separation between the concepts, together with the attachment of interest to the *actio*, is that 'interest' could be used to obtain monetary compensation for a type of loss that, of itself, would give rise to no legal claim. As Lawson points out, an 'extraordinary juristic interest attaches to the Roman slave as an entity which was at once a person and a thing'; thus 'the slave enabled the Romans to bridge the gap between damage to property and personal injuries'.[172] This may seem an odd dichotomy by today's standards, but it has to be borne in mind that the Roman law of wrongful damage (*actio legis Aquiliae*) applied only to property—things that were owned—and a person was not the owner of his own body.[173] Once the idea was established that personal injuries was an 'interest' it became possible for this interest to detach itself from the particular *actio* in which it had

---

remedy, not to the underlying right. Where a contract is made for the benefit of a third person who has a legitimate interest to enforce it, it can be enforced by the third party in the name of the contracting party or jointly with him or, if he refuses to join, by adding him as a defendant. In that sense, and it is a very real sense, the third person has a right arising by way of contract. He has an interest which will be protected by law. . . . It is different when a third person has no legitimate interest, as when . . . he is seeking to rely, not on any right given to him by the contract, but on an exemption clause': *Beswick v Beswick* [1966] Ch 538, 557; cf [1968] AC 58.

[168] D 9 2 21 2; D 47 2 27pr-2; D 47 2 50pr. And see Zimmermann (n 2) 826–7.
[169] Weir (n 80) 7.   [170] Leroux and Marciano (n 6).   [171] D 47 2 75.
[172] FH Lawson *Negligence in the Civil Law* (Oxford University Press Oxford 1955) 21.
[173] D 9 2 13pr.

been developed and to exist, if not independently, then at least as an interest that attached itself to other remedies analogous to the *actio legis Aquiliae*.[174] This is not to claim that the Romans ever protected this freeman's interest as well as they protected proprietary interests. But at least they established the idea that personal injury was a definable interest even if one was not the owner of one's own body.[175]

Another way in which the notion of an interest could stimulate a remedy in situations where there was no legal 'right' was in respect of the *persona* who might have no independent claim. One example is the unborn child, who had no legal *persona*, but who nevertheless had interests worthy of protection.[176] The more classic example is where one person is able to obtain damages for the invasion of an interest attaching to another person. This is a problem that can arise as a result of what civil lawyers call the relative effect of contract (or privity of contract in the common law). Thus in Roman law where a party promised that something would be given or done on behalf of another, no binding obligation arose since each party must promise only for himself.[177] The empirical basis for this lack of an obligation was quite clearly stated to be the absence of any interest; it is of no interest to a promisor that something be done in the interest of another.[178] However, the logic of this empirical thesis is that if there was an interest in respect both of the promisor and of the third party, then there ought to be an enforceable obligation. Now although the Romans themselves appear to have gone some way in accepting this logic,[179] the procedural technicalities of the Roman stipulation nevertheless resulted in the third party not having an *actio* and this could prima facie give rise to an unprotected interest.[180] The question arose, therefore, as to how one might indirectly give expression to such an interest. The problem was not insoluble and one way or another some third parties, both in Roman law itself and in the later civil law, were allowed to sue until, in the end, the *alteri stipulari nemo potest* concept was itself abandoned.[181] Nevertheless, what is important about this Roman law experience is the role assumed by the notion of an interest and the relationship between this concept and the availability of an *actio*.[182] Interest became the key concept not just with regard to the development of the *alteri stipulari* rule itself, but equally with respect to its exceptions and ultimate disappearance. The whole saga is perhaps a less visible, yet more subtle, example of how economics exerts its influence through a mediating common concept.

---

[174] See eg D 9 3 1pr. The amount to be claimed was fixed as a penalty, however, because no valuation could actually be made of a freeman since he was not property: D 9 3 1 5.
[175] Zimmermann (n 2) 1014–17. [176] D 1 5 7. [177] D 45 1 83pr.
[178] D 45 1 38 17. [179] D 45 1 38 20; Zimmermann (n 2) 36–7.
[180] Zimmermann (n 2) 37–9. [181] Ibid 38–45.
[182] Lord Denning MR adopted a similar form of reasoning, as has been seen: *Beswick v Beswick* [1966] Ch 538, 557.

In English law the relative independence of the law of remedies has allowed the courts to develop some indirect protection of those interests which, in themselves, have not been recognized at the level of legal rights. A leading example is *Jackson v Horizon Holidays Ltd*[183] where a father contracted with a firm of tour operators for a holiday for himself and his family. The holiday, in breach of contract, turned out to be most unsatisfactory and the father sought compensation for the mental distress suffered. The tour operator took the case to appeal, not on the basis of liability as such, but with respect to an award of damages made by the judge. This award had been quite generous even though the trial judge had stated that he could not take account of the mental distress of the family, only of the actual contractor, the father. The Court of Appeal dismissed the appeal, but Lord Denning MR considered that the amount awarded by the trial judge would have been excessive if it was meant to compensate only for the damage suffered by the father. However, when extended to include the wife and children it would not be excessive. Two interest problems were in issue here. First, there was the question of mental distress itself: was this an interest to be recognized by the law of contract? Following an earlier decision, the Court of Appeal had little difficulty in respect of this issue.[184] Secondly, there was the privity of contract problem. Lord Denning devoted much of his judgment to this question and, having examined a number of hypothetical but plausible everyday problems, concluded that the contractor ought to be able to recover damages not just for himself but for third parties whose interests were in play.

Jackson is an almost perfect example of how an interest can be protected through the law of actions.[185] The family had no substantive obligation rights under the contract, yet they received compensation thanks to the father's *actio*. One might talk, then, of an imperfect interest. This 'imperfection' was given an added dimension by the actual nature of the damage suffered. It was not a pecuniary loss as such; it was a loss of enjoyment leading to disappointment and frustration. Such an interest attaches to the *persona* rather than to any res inasmuch as it is a subjective experience that cannot easily be reduced to money. But it found expression in *Jackson* thanks only to the father's damages which were in effect increased so as to cover the family interest.[186] Another way of approaching the case, then, is to see it as a group or class interest. The imperfection arises as a result of legal technicality; the family interest could not be directly protected since the family, as a legal entity, could not sue or be sued. Only individuals, or

---

[183] [1975] 1 WLR 1468. Note now, however, the Contracts (Rights of Third Parties) Act 1999.   [184] *Jarvis v Swan's Tours* [1973] QB 233.
[185] Cf Contracts (Rights of Third Parties) Act 1999.
[186] See also *Pickett v British Rail Engineering Ltd* [1980] AC 126.

corporate groups recognized by statute, have standing vis-à-vis a legal action. Given this procedural limitation, the institutional role of the actio comes into its own inasmuch as it can indirectly recognize class or other diffuse interests that the other two institutions of person and thing cannot always acknowledge. All this, of course, can be expressed in terms of rules and principles and, as we have seen, there are some statutes that do just this in respect of certain interest groups.[187] Yet it is equally clear that the patterns in play take reasoning beyond the flat dimension of the written word. And this is equally true of the third type of interest, the interest that attaches to a *res*.

VIII. INTERESTS ATTACHING TO THE *RES*

We have seen that there are two interest aspects to *Jackson*: there is the substance of the interest itself—is mental distress an interest to be protected by the law?[188]—and there is the actionability point about whether strangers to the contract can recover. The first aspect could well be seen as something that goes beyond the mere actio (damages) and becomes a kind of 'thing'— a *res*—to be protected like an item of physical property. When viewed from this position the interest might be regarded as attaching to the *res* inasmuch as it is this 'thing' that generates the legal claim. Accordingly the whole of the law of obligations could be reconceptualized, as indeed we have seen from Tony Weir's observation, in terms of the various interests protected.[189] The law of obligations becomes, in other words, a means for translating 'interests' (the object of the law of obligations) into 'rights' (the law of obligations itself). There is, however, a more specific proprietary aspect to the notion of an 'interest'. In property law the term 'interest' is used to describe a person's specific legal relationship with an object of property; lawyers in the common law world talk of a person having a legal interest in a piece of property, a fund, or even a chattel. Here the term is being used not in its descriptive sense, but in the sense that is often much closer to that of a legal 'right' in the property.

The term 'interest' is used in its most formal property sense in land law: the 'rights' referred to in section 1(2) of the Law of Property Act 1925 are referred to not as 'estates' in land—these are dealt with by section 1(1)—but

---

[187] See eg Local Government Act 1972 s 222.

[188] One might note yet again how mental distress as an interest recognized in the law of contract is not simply a matter of the law giving expression to a pre-existing social fact. In the tort of negligence such a mental distress interest has not been recognized (*Best v Samuel Fox & Co Ltd* [1952] AC 716), again showing how the substance of the interest depends, in this situation, on the conceptual category in play.

[189] And see Cane (n 160).

as 'interests' or 'charges'.[190] These 'interests' can be analysed, as with any legal 'right', by reference to positive rules of land law and in this context they lose, if not all, certainly part of their descriptive character. In other words, the notion of an interest can in this context be defined, at the outset, as a normative concept. However, on closer examination the position turns out to be more complex since an 'interest' in another's property can include a possessory relationship and this is a relation said to have its root more in fact than in law.[191] Thus if someone finds an item of property in the street and takes it home it can be asserted that the finder has taken 'possession' of it. Moreover, the finder could even assert that he has an 'interest' in the thing to the extent that if it were to be stolen from his house he could go some way in claiming a relationship with the item were the police to recover it. Of course the legal analysis cannot, and does not, stop at this descriptive stage; it has to go on to decide whether the finder has, as a result of his former possessory relationship with the thing, an entitlement to it. Should the original owner arrive at the police station to assert his legal title, this would no doubt destroy any normative entitlement—or 'right'—that the finder might have had. But what if no owner could be traced? It may be that the finder's possessory 'interest' would entitle him to the thing over and above any other citizen (save of course the original owner).[192] In other words he would have a *right to possession* and this turns possession—and the interest that attaches to it—into a normative concept.[193]

The switch from the descriptive to the normative is usually effected through the legal *actio*—the finder will bring an action against the person in actual possession—and this will force a court into deciding who has the best *right* to possession. One might accordingly see the problem as one of an interest attaching not so much to the thing but to the remedy. This analysis is of particular importance when it comes to equitable remedies and so, for example, a person who has contracted to buy land will be able to claim specific performance of the contract should the seller refuse to perform.[194] A contract right in effect becomes a right to the thing itself and thus a kind of property right. As a leading introductory work points out, not all equitable remedies that are concerned with property actually attach to the *res* itself; some 'are personal and therefore are not equivalent to interests in property'.[195]

In the past this distinction between contractual and property interests was kept separate. For example, in the Australian case of *Cowell v Rosehill Racecourse Co Ltd*[196] the High Court of Australia distinguished between a

[190] K Gray and S Gray *Elements of Land Law* (3rd edn Butterworths 2001) 449.
[191] FH Lawson and B Rudden *The Law of Property* (2nd edn Oxford University Press 1982) 41.   [192] *Parker v British Airways Board* [1982] QB 1004.
[193] Weir (n 80) 485.   [194] Lawson and Rudden (n 191) 61–2.   [195] Ibid 63.
[196] (1937) 56 CLR 605.

contractual interest to enter the land of another and the proprietary interest of an actual owner of this land together with someone having say a leasehold or possessory right. The contractual right to enter the land of another cannot be put on the same footing as the right of someone having a proprietary interest in the land itself: for if they were put on the same footing the contractual interest would in effect become a proprietary interest; it would, to use the language of property 'rights', become a *ius in rem*. What this case is recognizing is that *in personam* and *in rem* 'interests' are quite different. However, more recently this distinction has become blurred. In *Manchester Airport Plc v Dutton*[197] an action for recovery of land was brought by a claimant whose only interest in the property was a contractual licence to occupy. The defendants argued that the action should fail because the actual plaintiff had no possessory 'right' and thus, if viewed from the traditional Romanist model, the relationship between *persona* and *res* was not strong enough to justify this particular person to the *actio*. A majority of the Court of Appeal disagreed; the relationship of a contractual right to occupy was strong enough to maintain the action. According to Laws LJ the question was one concerning the right of the plaintiff and whether this right deserved to be protected. He thus concluded:

In this whole debate, as regards the law of remedies in the end I see no significance as a matter of principle in any distinction drawn between a plaintiff whose right to occupy the land in question arises from title and one whose right arises only from contract. In every case the question must be, what is the reach of the right, and whether it is shown that the defendant's acts violate its enjoyment. If they do, and (as here) an order for possession is the only practical remedy, the remedy should be granted. Otherwise the law is powerless to correct a proved or admitted wrongdoing; and that would be unjust and disreputable. The underlying principle is in the Latin maxim (for which I make no apology), 'ubi jus, ibi sit remedium.'[198]

What is interesting about this judgment is that it illustrates very clearly how, once again in legal reasoning, legal institutions, concepts, and relationships can be recombined to produce a structure whose logic seems impeccable. The plaintiff had a 'ius' and thus should have a remedy and the fact that the actual remedy in issue was 'in rem' should not be allowed to defeat the plaintiff's remedy seeking to enforce the right. To do otherwise would be to allow oneself to be constrained by the old forms of action.[199] In a dissenting judgment Chadwick LJ was unhappy with the way a contractual relationship was being treated as sufficient to found the claim

---

[197] [2000] QB 133. [198] At 150.

[199] 'I would hold that the court today has ample power to grant a remedy to a licensee which will protect but not exceed his legal rights granted by the licence. If, as here, that requires an order for possession, the spectre of history (which, in the true tradition of the common law, ought to be a friendly ghost) does not stand in the way. The law of ejectment has no voice in the question; it cannot speak beyond its own limits': 149–50.

for possession since this relation *in personam* did not amount as such to an 'interest in land'.[200] But the trick, of course, was, in effect, to treat the notion of an 'interest' as more open-ended. By focusing upon the contractual interest bestowed upon the claimant in relation to the land and then by merging this interest with the contract itself so as to produce a 'right', the majority was able to adopt an approach that 'blurs the distinction between different types of right and different types of remedy'.[201] The result is that both 'right' and effectively 'interest' lose their meaning as formal proprietary concepts to become open-ended notions capable of hopping from the relationship between *persona* and *res* to the relationship between two personae and to the relationship between *persona* and *actio*.

It is not, however, just contractual interests that can impact upon property rights. In *Wandsworth LBC v A*[202] a local authority obtained an injunction against a parent, on the grounds of her abusive behaviour, excluding her from entering the school where her child was being educated. On appeal the Court of Appeal discharged the injunction because the local authority had not given the parent an opportunity to be heard before excluding her from the school. Buxton LJ, delivering the judgment of the Court, said that 'the local authority has an obligation in public law to educate their children' while the 'parent has a correlative interest in seeing the duties of the authority properly performed'. This does not give the parent a 'right to interfere with how the professional educators undertake their work, but it does give him an interest in being informed about their work, with the possibility of formal representations about it'. This makes the parent 'a more significant figure' than 'a mere visiting tradesman'. The Court was of the opinion that such a tradesman could be excluded from a school 'without any inhibition in public law' but a parent could not.[203]

One might note here that the key concept is the 'interest'. The parent, as the Court stressed, does not have any rights as such, but she does have an interest that puts her in a different class from other visitors. Arguably this interest is descriptive inasmuch as it arises simply out of the fact that the child is attending the school, but its quasi-normative dimension is equally relevant. This quasi-normativity does not, of course, result from any relationship with the school property and thus is a legal relationship that is completely independent from the local authority's proprietary (ownership) relationship with the land. However, it does raise an interesting question about the extent to which public law (*imperium*) can impinge upon private law *dominium*. To what extent does 'interest' act as a means of turning a central area of private law, that is to say the law of property, into a form of 'quasi-public' law? The point is an important one because 'interest' could,

---

[200] 141, 143.   [201] Kennedy LJ at 151.   [202] [2000] 1 WLR 1246.
[203] 1253.

in this situation, end up as the foundation for the only viable means of establishing a balance between the exercise of the private power of *dominium* and the constitutional and administrative control of such power. The problem has been investigated by two leading property lawyers who indicate, clearly, how, without proper consideration being given to principles of public law and their relationship with principles of private law, the exercise of *dominium* can lead to constitutional injustice.[204] The transfer of a public monopoly into the private arena, which in legal terms means a shift from *imperium* to *dominium,* has dramatic effects at the level of legal concepts since the transfer puts the corporation beyond the reach of judicial review. How are the interests of citizens to be equally translated? Kevin and Susan Gray give the example of the privatized water company able to acquire land by compulsory purchase (in the 'public interest') which in turn allows the private company to further its own commercial interest (private profit) at the expense of those individuals forced to give up their homes at below commercial value prices and at much inconvenience.[205] The so-called public and the commercial interest are advanced at the expense of the individual interest. The reverse side of this argument can be seen when private individuals, employed to run private companies operating a public service like the railway, are given huge bonuses. Here the private interest profit is justified because it will act as 'an incentive to do well' thus, presumably, enhancing the public interest.[206]

IX. MEDIATING AND COMPARATIVE DIMENSIONS OF AN INTEREST

The privatization of corporations again indicates how the notion of an interest is often as much tied up with the *persona* and the *actio* as with the *res.* Interest can, accordingly, be seen as a kind of mediating concept between the three Gaian institutions. However, when it does play such a role it can easily slip from being a descriptive concept to one that is functioning only at the level of law; it becomes an exclusionary, or negative, rather than (as with the *Wandsworth* case) a positive device.[207] A good example of this is provided by *Macaura v Northern Assurance Co.*[208] The plaintiff sold his timber assets to his 'one-man' company in return for all its shares and then, in his own name, took out fire insurance on the timber

---

[204] K Gray and S Gray 'Private Property and Public Property' in J McLean (ed) *Property and the Constitution* (Oxford Hart 1999) 11–39.   [205] Ibid 37.

[206] *The Guardian* 4 July 2001, 2.

[207] This is one important reason why an exhaustive examination of the substantive content of an interest, as important an exercise as it is (on which, see Pound (n 7)), may well fail to throw that much light on the role of an interest in legal reasoning and in the way it can provoke a particular solution in a case.   [208] [1925] AC 619.

assets. After a fire which destroyed the timber, the plaintiff tried to claim on the policy, but the insurance company successfully resisted the claim on the ground that he personally had no 'insurable interest' in the assets of the company. His only *res* were the shares. This seems a strange decision when viewed from the position of an interest as a *descriptive* concept since it is clear that the shareholder had a very real interest in the assets of the company just as a parent has an interest in the school grounds where his or her child is being educated. No doubt the decision can be justified in the narrow terms of insurance law, yet it indicates how interest can act as a negative exclusionary device even in private law. Interest is a means by which facts can be viewed holistically (commercial or consumer interests, for example) or individualistically (company and its sole shareholder) and thus is a device that helps shape the pattern of the facts themselves. 'Interest' in other words mediates not just between *persona*, *res*, and *actio* but also between each element that goes to make up the facts.

It is this ability to construct and deconstruct facts that gives the notion of an 'interest' its comparative dimension as a *formal* concept. As Professor Ost observes, the notion has the effect of undermining the traditional vision of law and fact. According to this traditional 'classical model' law is a matter of systematized and hierarchical rules waiting to be applied through the normative syllogism to sets of facts.[209] The rule is clearly distinguishable not only from the fact to which it is to be *applied*, but from the norms of other disciplines such as political, economic, and moral systems. One particular characteristic of this view of law is that there is a logic both of command and of binary articulation; in short, something is either permitted or prohibited. In addition the rules all combine so as to appear to flow from a single source, that is to say, from the legislator which represents the will of the people. The rules are characterized by their abstraction and their generality, these two characteristics in turn linking the rules to the 'universal'; a universal that is rooted in the objectivity of the social contract in which the individual is merged with the social body as a whole.[210] When law is viewed from the position of interests, however, this classical model

---

[209] This 'classical' model goes back to the Enlightenment view of legal method when law was seen as a system analogous to mathematics and thus to be applied to facts through logic (*mos geometricus*). A good description of this method is given by Professor Timsit: 'The courts are entrusted with the duty of establishing the facts from which flow the legal consequences to apply having regard to the legal system in force. Once the facts are established, a legal syllogism is enough, whereby the rule of law constitutes the major premise, the established facts as envisaged by the conditions of the rule the minor premise and the court decision the conclusion. . . . This implies that for each situation submitted to the judge there would be a legal rule applicable, that there would be only one and that this rule would be devoid of any ambiguity. . . . The legal system is, at the end of the day, assimilated to a deductive system constructed on the model of axiomatic systems existing in geometry or arithmetic': G Timsit *Thèmes et systèmes de droit* (Paris PUF 1986) 106–7. [210] Ost (n 1) 175.

soon breaks down. As a result of the 'subversive' influence of the interest, the distinction between fact and law becomes blurred and relative; facts become normative (and *formalized*) and rules become descriptive. The whole flow of the law starts to reverse and to double back on itself while, at the same time, the frontiers between law and other disciplines break down. In the world of interests things are only relative; it is always a matter of weighing one interest against another within a social context where the objectivity of the judgment no longer has much meaning since everything is a matter of negotiation. The individual is swallowed up by the various class interests of rival social groups which themselves make up the social corps.[211]

This view of law from the position of an interest is very much at odds with the official portrait of the legal rule in civil law systems, as Professor Ost indicates. Yet it is not, of course, at odds with the common law vision. The English lawyer will have no problem in envisaging law as a matter of induction rather than deduction ('from the bottom up')[212] or as a system whose frontiers are open to inputs from other disciplines.[213] There are several reasons for this difference of conceptualization. First, and foremost, the history of the civil law is largely a history of a movement towards 'axiomatized' codes of subjective rights.[214] According to this classic model the individual is the focal point of law and thus all law is to be viewed from the position of the legal subject (*persona*). No intermediate groups, as Ost points out, are allowed to perturb this vision of individual rights which exist as metaphysical conceptions relating one to another through relations of co-ordination or subordination, never through integration.[215] The common law remained untouched by the academic systematizing tendency of humanism; the absence of common law faculties, before the end of the nineteenth century, left the common law to be shaped by practice and by a legal doctrine which thought in terms of lists of actions and procedural refinements.[216] When common lawyers finally came to think in terms of rights, the most powerful theory was one that saw them as legally protected social interests.[217] Even today, the idea that rights can be 'objects' of legal claims causes difficulty[218] and the notion of a right is not something that

---

[211] Ibid 176.   [212] Ibid.

[213] One thinks in particular of the influence of economic thinking in *Co-operative Insurance Society Law v Argyll Stores Ltd* [1998] AC 1. Note also the position in family law: *In re L (A Child)* [2001] 2 WLR 339, 375.

[214] See in particular M Villey *La Formation de la pensée juridique moderne* (4th edn Montchrestien 1975).

[215] Ost (n 1) 177. One might note also how Pound's classification and analysis of interests (n 7) is rather weak on intermediate group interests.

[216] M Lobban *The Common Law and English Jurisprudence 1760–1850* (Oxford 1991) 9.

[217] O Ionescu *La Notion de droit subjectif dans le droit privé* (Bruylant 1978) 143, 148–9.

[218] See Jonathan Parker LJ in *Ashurst v Pollard* [2001] 2 WLR 722, 728.

lends itself to abstract definition.[219] Rights, even when they are recognized, tend on the whole to be only relative and contingent and this, if one follows the Ost analysis of an interest, will effectively reduce the right to an interest.[220] Rights, even with the incorporation of the European Convention on Human Rights, are things to be negotiated and traded one against another.[221] 'Rights have as their vocation to juxtapose and to arrange themselves in a hierarchical order,' observes Professor Ost; 'interests on the other hand have the tendency to merge and to dilute themselves.'[222]

One can certainly see this diluting tendency in the English case-law.[223] Take the recent *Ashworth Hospital* case[224] where the Court of Appeal (whose decision was confirmed by the House of Lords) upheld an order forcing a newspaper to disclose the name of the hospital employee who had leaked certain medical records of one of the hospital patients. There is no doubt that such a disclosure of medical records amounted to a gross breach of privacy and Lord Phillips MR (whose judgment was specifically approved by the House of Lords) was of the view that the hospital itself 'had a clear independent interest in retaining their confidentiality'. However, Article 10 of the Convention for the Protection of Human Rights and Fundamental Freedoms states that everyone has the right to freedom of expression and that this includes the right 'to receive and impart information and ideas without interference by public authority'. More specifically section 10 of the Contempt of Court Act 1981 lays down that disclosure is not to be ordered save 'in the interests of justice'. One would have thought, therefore, that this fundamental right would have protected the press from having to reveal a source. Indeed, a previous House of Lords decision ordering disclosure of sources on the basis of the interests of justice was overturned on further appeal to the European Court of Human Rights.[225] The *right* of the journalist trumped the *interest* of justice. Yet on reading Lord Phillips's judgment—in fact on reading the argument for the defence—it becomes clear that the case is not one about rights:

91. Mr Browne [counsel for the defendants] submitted that in a case such as this the English court has to follow a three-stage test. First it has to decide whether the *interests of justice* are engaged. Secondly the court has to consider as a fact whether disclosure is necessary to achieve the relevant ends of justice. Finally the court has to weigh, as a matter of discretion, the *specific interests* of the claimant against the *public interest* in the protection of journalists' confidential sources.[226]

---

[219] See eg *In re L (A Child)* [2001] 2 WLR 339.   [220] Ost (n 1) 176.
[221] See eg Lord Steyn in *Brown v Stott* [2001] 2 WLR 817, 839.
[222] Ost (n 1) 181.   [223] And note Tench's comment (n 95).
[224] *Ashworth Hospital Authority v MGN Ltd* [2001] 1 WLR 515. Confirmed [2002] 1 WLR 2033 (HL).
[225] *Goodwin v UK* (1996) 22 EHRR 123; cf *X Ltd v Morgan-Grampian (Publishers) Ltd* [1991] 1 AC 1.
[226] [2001] 1 WLR 536; emphasis added. And see Lord Woolf CJ in the House of Lords: [2001] 1 WLR 2033 §32.

The central concept here is, quite evidently, that of an interest. One should not be surprised by this since this is the language of negotiation and not vindication. Moreover, this interests approach is closely tied up with the nature of the remedy in issue: the plaintiffs were claiming disclosure through the remedy of discovery of documents and this remedy is essentially procedural. As Lord Reid has pointed out, the 'chief occasion for its being ordered was to assist a party in an existing litigation' but 'this was extended at an early date to assist a person who contemplated litigation'.[227] The result in the *Ashworth* case is that the press was not able to rely upon its right to resist the remedy of discovery. It was in effect defeated by a concept, the 'interests of justice', which, as Lord Diplock once stated, is used 'in the technical sense of the administration of justice in the course of legal proceedings in a court of law'.[228] *Ubi remedium ibi ius.* Or, to put it another way, legal rights are largely a matter of outcomes whose determination has been fought out on the terrain of remedies and procedure. On this terrain the key concept is not that of a right but of an *interest*. But, of course, this interest is as *formalized* a concept as a right, even if it does not have the same inherent normative power, and once formalized it finds itself in the same conceptual world as a right, thus able to take it on, and often defeat it.

This brings one to the second reason why the common lawyer has less difficulty than the civilian in conceptualizing law from the interest position as analysed by Professor Ost. The common lawyer simply does not reason in terms of rights. To an extent this point is evident in a number of the decisions already analysed, but it has equally been dealt with in depth elsewhere.[229] Suffice it to say, therefore, that when English judges do use the term 'right', they do so usually in a very relative way. 'The word "rights" is a highly confusing word,' said Ormrod LJ, 'which leads to a great deal of trouble if it is used loosely, particularly when it is used loosely in a court of law.'[230] One might of course say the same about an 'interest'. But two points need to be made with respect to this concept. First, an interest is much more easily identified as a source of reasoning in English law than on the Continent where the 'law' is expressed, for the most part, in codes and texts.[231] Ost, of course, identifies an interest as a viable informal source of law, but in English legal reasoning, as some of the remedy cases show, an interest is virtually a formal building block in the construction of

---

[227] *Norwich Pharmacal Co v Customs and Excise Comrs* [1974] AC 133,173.
[228] *Secretary of State for Defence v Guardian Newspapers Ltd* [1985] AC 339, 350.
[229] Samuel (n 144).
[230] *A v C* [1985] FLR 445, 455. And see also *In re L* [2001] 2 WLR 339.
[231] One could give many examples, but perhaps *Thorne v Motor Trade Association* [1937] AC 797, *Miller v Jackson* [1977] QB 966, and *Burris v Azadani* [1995] 1 WLR 1372 will suffice to support the point.

a judgment.[232] Secondly, the term 'interest', being a 'descriptive' concept, functions as much within the facts as within the law and this gives it a certain precision when compared to a right. Such precision may only be viable in the context of a particular set of facts, yet an interest remains relatively clear vis-à-vis other identified interests within any such factual situation, even if differences are as much formal, in the institutional sense, as factually substantive.[233] This endows it with its particular comparative quality inasmuch as it is capable of being *functionally* compared with interests identified in Continental analysis. Might it be possible, therefore, to relate the methods of the civilians with those of the common lawyer in abandoning any formal notion of a right and concentrating, instead, on an interest?

If the analysis pursued in this chapter is correct, it would appear that there is a common model—the institutional system—that underpins both legal traditions since the notion of an interest does appear to function in relation to *persona*, *res*, and *actio*. There are of course obvious similarities such as, for example, the 'interests of children', and such similarities have become of importance in private international law.[234] However, the point to be emphasized in the present context is not so much these more obvious similarities; the comparatist should be attempting to go beyond the linguistic term in order to see if there are cognitive structures at work which share common elements.[235] Clearly in this context the notion of an interest is promising because it suggests that the Gaian institutional elements (persons, things, and actions) are at work within the facts of both civil law and common law cases. In the civil law, as Ost illustrates, there are plenty of cases where interest has an explicit role in the reasoning and the outcome. Yet 'interest' could equally be used to illuminate those cases where the reasoning, on the surface, seems to be applying more formal normative concepts such as rights and obligations. As Ost observes, any legal system that requires a 'legitimate interest' before one can bring a legal action to vindicate a right must be a system that, in the end, is one founded on interests.[236] However, as this chapter has tried to show, the substance of these interests may not be as empirical as Roscoe Pound asserted. Or, put another way, the conceptual force of an interest is provided less by its apparent empirical substance than by its relationship with other concepts within the institutional system and it is this position in the model which goes far (as the *Rose Theatre* case and others illustrate) in actually defining the apparent empirical substance.

---

[232] See eg *Burris v Azadani* [1995] 1 WLR 1372. See also Lord Denning MR's judgment in *Miller v Jackson* [1977] QB 966. [233] See eg *Burris v Azadani* [1995] 1 WLR 1372.
[234] See eg *In re L (A Child)* [2001] 2 WLR 339.
[235] P Lagrand *Le Droit comparé* (Paris PUF 1999) 32. [236] Ost (n 1) 32.

There is, however, a more fundamental comparative and, indeed, theoretical point to be made. The notion of a 'right' in legal discourse is often inadequate as both a reasoning and an explanatory device. A right suggests an absolute normative entitlement which 'trumps' all other claims and obligations; it gives expression to the idea that an owner is entitled to his property—or to enforce a contractual 'right'—irrespective of the social and moral merits of the owner's claim. Yet in most legal disputes, or at least those beyond the law of property and debt, such an all-or-nothing approach is unrealistic. An ultra-nominalist approach whereby claims are envisaged only from the viewpoint of a vindicating individual operating in a social vacuum is not reflected in the majority of legal decisions, at least in the appeal courts.[237] What inspires a 'right', as this survey has hopefully begun to indicate, is neither a desire for description nor a need for explanation. That is to say, a right is not a concept that can be used to *describe* the methods employed by the judiciary, nor can it be used to *explain* the process of legal reasoning. Instead it is a concept inspired by ideological legitimization.[238] This is not to criticize the notion of a right, for legitimization is as valid an epistemological tool as description or explanation and, of course, a tool that is particularly useful in law because of its fundamental role in legal reasoning. The point to be made, in brief, is that social reality forces legal reasoning to slip from the metaphysical world of normative concepts towards a quasi-normative—that is to say, more descriptive—world of legal concepts which can operate within the facts themselves. What helps bind *persona* with res and with *actio* is a notion which, like them, functions at one and the same time within the world of fact and the world of norms. This is why, as this chapter has, I hope, demonstrated, the notion of an interest identifies itself both with the Gaian institutional structure and, often, with the concept of a right. Rights provide legitimization, while interests—seemingly—provide description and explanation.

CONCLUDING REMARKS

It is this descriptive and explanative ability therefore that are the keys to the central role of an interest in legal reasoning. However, this chapter has gone further than simply exposing the role of an interest behind many apparent 'rights'. It has shown that the notion of an interest is not something to be understood in terms of a list of different categories of interest defined

---

[237] And note that even in a case like *Ingram v Little* [1961] 1 QB 31 or *Moorgate Mercantile Ltd v Twitchings* [1977] AC 890 the appeal judges were split.

[238] B Valade 'De l'explication dans les sciences sociales: Holisme et individualism' in J-M Berthelot (ed) *Épistémologie de sciences sociales* (Paris PUF 2001) 368–9.

strictly in terms of their empirical content. It is not a matter of abstracting from legal analysis a public, private, commercial, state, economic, expectation, restitutionary, reliance interest (and so on), and endowing each category of interest with a linguistic definition. It is a question of modelization. That is to say, it is a matter of seeing an interest as an important *formal* relational element in the Gaian institutional system and one that helps begin to represent the complexity of social fact within the structural model of *persona*, *res*, and *actiones*. It is this model that mediates between fact, law, and reasoning, and it has been the object of this chapter to discuss case-law examples that illustrate this epistemological thesis.

Another object has been to indicate the possibilities that the notion of an interest (together with the institutional system) holds for the comparatist. However, it must be stressed by way of a final remark that any reference here to similarity between systems is not to be taken as a reference either to 'sameness' or to the possibility of harmonization. To suggest that the Gaian institutional model, together with the notion of an interest, underpin both common law and civilian analysis does not imply sameness of mentality since difference can be found in the institutional patterns adopted in different systems. This point has been illustrated in more detail elsewhere.[239] But by way of brief illustration one might refer to the different patterns in play when it comes to car accidents in France and in England. There is no doubt that there is similarity of pattern at the level of an interest attaching to the person (personal injury) or the thing (property damage). However, there is also a difference. First, in the way liability attaches in France to the relationship between *persona* and *res*— that is to say, damage done by a thing under the control of another[240]—and in England to the relationship between person and person (duty of care).[241] Thus in France the injured victim does not have the burden of proving fault. Secondly, in the way that these liability patterns are in turn to be considered within the larger context of the public or general interest vis-à-vis the individual interest. Transport is in the general interest and as a social and economic activity it carries statistically predictable risks. The *persona* upon whom this risk should finally lie is one dependent upon how interest is envisaged as a *political* fact. Should the burden rest on each individual human (individual interest) who can shift the burden only if he or she can prove individual fault? Or should the risk be on the community as an economic group (class interest) as given expression through the public law requirement of compulsory insurance? The answer may well be ideological, yet it is also epistemological.[242]

---

[239] See eg G Samuel 'Comparative Law and Jurisprudence' (1998) 47 ICLQ 817.

[240] Originally CC Art 1384 but now Loi no 85–677 du 5 juillet 1985.

[241] Reaffirmed recently: *Mansfield v Weetabix Ltd* [1998] 1 WLR 1263.

[242] That is to say, a question of legal knowledge. Legal epistemology is concerned with the question: what is it to have knowledge of law? See generally C Atias *Épistémologie juridique* (PUF Paris 1985); *Épistémologie juridique* (Paris Dalloz 2002).

Do forests exist or are there only trees? Does society exist or are there only individuals? In sociology the debate is one between methodological individualism and holism;[243] in comparative law it is between different institutional patterns.

The complexity of these patterns can be such that to see in the notion of an 'interest', and its attachment to an institutional system, similarity is dangerous. Many citizens in civil law countries found Margaret Thatcher's observation on the non-existence of society baffling.[244] Professor Legrand would say that this is due to a difference of *mentalité*.[245] However, such a difference of *mentalité* does not, as this chapter has hoped to show, imply a difference of structural elements and relations; that is to say, what might be seen as a difference of 'cognitive structures'. It implies a difference of structural patterns. Such differences, whatever the similarities at the level of the notion of an interest, should never be underestimated by the comparatist. In short, the notion of an interest is as much a concept for examining difference as it is a concept for understanding similarity. Its great value, however, is that it can act as the means of understanding difference as much at the level of social fact as at the level of abstract law. It can take comparatists (and lawyers in general) beyond the rules, and to this extent it is an undoubted 'empirical' source of law and legal reasoning.

[243] See generally Valade (n 238).
[244] Cf Lord Cooke of Thornton in McLean (ed) (n 204).
[245] P Legrand 'European Legal Systems Are Not Converging' (1996) 45 ICLQ 52.

21

Comparative Law in the German Courts

Hannes Unberath

Comparative law in the German courts is a topic that has occupied German academics with some measure of regularity.[1] The conclusions drawn are usually pessimistic in tone and, on the basis of detailed statistical evaluations, state the limited role foreign law has played so far before their courts. Yet, the significance of the topic is rapidly growing with the infiltration into German law of European law, especially in the field of private and private international law, and the increased importance of international conventions. In short: private law in Europe is in the process of reacquiring a transnational character.[2]

The purpose of this chapter is modest. Rather than giving a comprehensive overview[3] I highlight only aspects of this broad theme, hoping thus to reveal the specific problems of comparative law before national courts and offer some insights into its usefulness as a tool for the national judge. The inquiry is further limited to the areas in which comparative law has played a role in German and English private law. Comparative law may provide assistance to national courts in two quite different respects. In Section I I will discuss comparative law as a necessary tool and in Section II comparative law as a voluntary enterprise. The concluding section briefly explores the future role of comparative law.

---

[1] Eg H Kötz 'Der Bundesgerichtshof und die Rechtsvergleichung' in A Heldrich and K Hopt (eds) *50 Jahre Bundesgerichtshof* (2000) vol 2, 824; U Drobnig 'The Use of Foreign Law by German Courts' in U Drobnig and S van Erp (eds) *The Use of Comparative Law by Courts* (The Hague Kluwer Law International 1999) 127; B Grossfeld 'Vom Beitrag der Rechtsvergleichung zum deutschen Recht' (1984) 184 AcP 289; JM Mössner 'Rechtsvergleichung und Verfassungsrechtsprechung' (1974) 99 AöR 193; B Aubin 'Die rechtsvergleichende Interpretation autonom-internen Rechts in der deutschen Rechtsprechung' (1970) 34 RabelsZ 458; H Dölle 'Der Beitrag der Rechtsvergleichung zum deutschen Rechts' in *Festschrift zum 100 jährigen Bestehen des deutschen Juristentages* (1960) 19.

[2] As Professor Reinhard Zimmermann remarked in his Clarendon Lecture *Roman Law, Contemporary Law, European Law* (Oxford University Press 2001) 108. Cf Kötz (n 1) 842.

[3] See, for a recent survey in English, BS Markesinis *Comparative Law in the Courtroom and Classroom* (2003) 107.

I. COMPARATIVE LAW AS A NECESSARY TOOL

The aim of any international convention is to harmonize the law. For uniformity to be preserved it is essential to take into account its international character and the interpretation given to the convention in other Member States. A perfect illustration can be found in Article 7(1) of the Convention on Contracts for the International Sale of Goods (CISG): 'In the interpretation of this Convention, regard is to be had to its international character and to the need to promote uniformity in its application and the observance of good faith in international trade.'[4] Maritime law is an area of the law dominated by international conventions such as the Hague Rules where international practice is of paramount importance.[5] Here German courts have frequently referred to English law. This is not surprising for in this field English law has much to offer. Not only is the case-law a goldmine for any civil lawyer; often the contracts of carriage themselves incorporate English terms or concepts.[6] This area is thus a perfect example of how English law has benefited the development of international practice. Recent developments lead one to believe that this is not a one-way street. Even the more 'advanced' English system may benefit from looking at the position of German law.[7] It is interesting to note that German courts tend to cite English textbooks (eg *Scrutton on Charterparties*), the Carriage of Goods by Sea Act, or accounts of English law in German[8] rather than the case

---

[4] The degree of autonomy of the supranational source of law is increased and the importance of comparative law lessened if a supranational court is empowered with the final interpretation of the source. Such is the case with the European legislation but as Judge Lenaerts has powerfully explained, the comparative method remains essential in preparing the decisions of the European Court of Justice and the Court of First Instance (see ch 8 in this volume).

[5] BGHZ 56, 300, decision of the Bundesgerichtshof (German Supreme Court, BGH) of 28 June 1971, illustrates this point well. 'International practice' was the Court's guiding principle in deciding whether a shipper is answerable for the master of the ship in relation to the seaworthiness of the ship and in limiting the liability of a time-charterer to that of a shipowner. The latter aspect is particularly noteworthy because at the time the Brussels convention on limitation of liability of shipowners of 1957 was only about to be ratified in Germany (in England this had happened in the Merchant Shipping (Liability of Shipowners and Others) Act 1958). Thus the Court followed international practice even before the legislator had fully adapted German law (now: §486 HGB). See, for further examples, Drobnig (n 1) 135.

[6] eg BGHZ 6, 127, decision of 20 May 1952 'on deck at shipper's risk'; BGHZ 25, 250, decision of 26 Sept 1957 'Quality, contents and weight unknown'; BGHZ 29, 120, decision of 18 Dec 1958 arbitration clause; Hanseatisches Oberlandesgericht Hamburg, decision of 7 Nov 1974, MDR 1975, 406 Himalaya clause; BGH, decision of 22 Jan 1990, VersR 1990, 503 Identity of Carrier clause; BGHZ 145, 170, decision of 21 Sept 2000 carriage of goods by air). English law is also referred to when bills of ladins are to be construed; eg BGHZ 44, 303, decision of 15 Nov 1965; BGHZ 60, 102, decision of 25 Jan 1973.

[7] See *The Starsin* [2003] UKHL 12 where Lord Millett and Lord Hobhouse of Woodborough referred to German law in support of their view.

[8] The leading but now outdated commentary on maritime law by G Schaps and HJ Abraham *Seerecht* (4th edn 1978) contains detailed and elegant glosses on English case-law.

itself.[9] This hesitation to base a German decision on an English case is understandable since the German judge may not be in the best position to distinguish cases and weigh the authoritative value in the foreign system. At the same time this in itself emphasizes the need for the comparative lawyer to act as a bridge between different systems.

The second area of the law where national courts are bound to consider foreign law is international private law. Under conflict of laws rules German courts like their English counterparts may be called upon to apply foreign law. Peculiar from an English perspective may be the fact that according to the present reading given to section 293 of the Code of Civil Procedure, the court is entrusted with the task also to determine the foreign law. This explains why according to German practice the court commissions a report on the position of the foreign legal system in question.[10] However, although foreign law is here routinely applied by national courts, which in itself sometimes provides beautiful examples of cross-fertilization between the different systems,[11] the comparative method is only needed in hard cases. To give an example: according to the traditional approach of the so-called *lege fori* qualification it is necessary to compare the foreign rule with German substantive law in order to determine which specific German conflict of laws rule covers the foreign rule of substantive law.[12] Often this will not involve any difficulties. However, a more elaborate comparative approach is crucial where foreign law provides for remedies unknown to the national system. It is then essential to take into account the function of the unknown concept and compare it to the purpose of remedies in one's own system in singling out the applicable conflicts rule.[13]

---

[9] As for instance in BGHZ 60, 102.

[10] Usually from a comparative law institute such as the Max-Planck-Institut für ausländisches und internationals Privatrecht in Hamburg. Even further back goes the tradition of the Institute of Comparative Law in Munich, which under the directorship of Ernst Rabel was declared to be available for such requests as early as 1924. See 'Bekanntmachung des Bayerischen Staatsministeriums der Justiz' in *Justizministerialblatt für den Freistaat Bayern vom 21. Juli 1924* No 13326.

[11] Especially where the national judge assumes the role of his foreign counterpart in developing the law because the inquiry into foreign law does not yield an unequivocal answer. From the English jurisprudence *City of Gotha and Federal Republic of Germany v Sotheby's and Cobert Finance SA* Queen's Bench Case No 1993 C 3428 and 1997 G 185, reproduced and translated in MH Carl H Güttler and K Siehr *Kunstdiebstahl vor Gericht* (2001), offers an excellent illustration. Mr Justice Moses in deciding whether the German city of Gotha was entitled to a claim in restitution against Sotheby's in relation to a Dutch painting confiscated by Soviet authorities after the war applied German law. The elegant High Court judgment was to become the first judicial authority on the relevant provision §221 (now §198) of the German Civil Code.   [12] See Drobnig (n 1) 130.

[13] Eg the concept of *Mahr* (*Morgengabe*), existing in most Islamic systems, according to which the husband undertakes to pay the wife a certain sum upon dissolution of the marriage; cf A Heldrich 'Das juristische Kuckucksei aus dem Morgenland' [1983] IPRax 64. From the rich case-law: BGH NJW 1987, 2161, decision of 28 Jan 1987.

In the examples discussed until now comparative law is a necessary element of the judicial or legislative process. The true challenge for comparative law lies elsewhere. This is whether a comparative lawyer can succeed in persuading practitioners to consider what Lord Bingham called the wider jurisprudence[14] even in cases where national law alone is concerned. There are prominent examples in German law, where courts had recourse to comparative law either to support their view or to distance themselves from a foreign position.

One should note at the outset that German courts are less free to develop the law than their English counterparts. In civil law systems adjudication is to a great extent determined by the codal and relevant statutory regime. Law reform is a task mainly performed by the legislator.[15] On the other hand, it is a misconception to conclude that the courts are a passive part of the legal machinery, devoid of creative powers when applying the meagre dead letter of the law.[16] As the 'case-law revolution'[17] following the coming into force of the Bürgerliches Gesetzbuch (BGB) in 1900 demonstrates, there is room for creative thinking and thus also for comparative law.

An example where the courts 'corrected' the initial approach of the legislator and, interestingly for our purpose, did so under the influence of comparative material, is the development of the right to damages for privacy invasions. The fathers of the Civil Code had ruled out the possibility of damages for interference with privacy. The report of the Committee of the BGB states in uncompromising terms that it would be 'repugnant to majority opinion among the population to place non-material values on the same level as property interests and to compensate with money interference with non-material interests'.[18] By the time the (Bundesgerichtshof) German

---

[14] *Fairchild v Glenhaven Funeral Services Ltd.* [2002] UKHL 22 paras 23–32.

[15] See for a detailed analysis of the generous use of foreign material by the German legislator Markesinis (n 3) 114 ff.

[16] Rudolph von Jhering warned strongly against this type of 'positivistic' judge. See his inaugural lecture held in Vienna, 16 Oct 1868, repr in O Behrends (ed) *Ist die Jurisprudenz eine Wissenschaft?* (1998) 50.   [17] Zimmermann (n 2) 55.

[18] For details, see BS Markesinis and H Unberath *German Law of Torts* (4th edn Oxford University Press 2002) 74, 406, 472. There was some protection of privacy, though random, often incidental, and overall very limited, before the ground-breaking *Herrenreiter* case. For instance §22 *Kunsturhebergesetz* required inter alia the prior permission of the relatives of a deceased if his photograph is to be published, a provision prompted by the unsolicited publication of pictures of the body of Bismarck, see H Coing [1958] JZ 558, 559. However, the remedy was in public law. In the Bismarck case itself, RGZ 45, 170, decision of 28 Dec 1899, the Imperial Court relied on Roman law in establishing that because the photographer trespassed on the land and thus unlawfully obtained the photographs the relatives were entitled to have the photographic plates destroyed.

Federal Court reconsidered the issue in the *Herrenreiter* case in 1958,[19] the climate had dramatically changed. Two factors seem to have been decisive: the 'constitutionalization' of private law and the (comparative) academic studies available to the court. Ironically, the same two factors may initiate the introduction of a general privacy right into English law.

The Basic Law of 1949 attributed the highest value to human dignity. Only weeks before the decision in the *Herrenreiter* case the Constitutional Court had developed the theory of indirect horizontal effect of the Constitution,[20] thus bringing human dignity to the forefront in the area of private law as well. According to the *Drittwirkung* doctrine[21] the rules of private law must be interpreted in conformity with the fundamental values of the Constitution. The Bundesgerichtshof in the *Herrenreiter* case did not expressly refer to this new doctrine, but it applied its rationale when it said:

Now that the Constitution guarantees a comprehensive protection to the personality and recognizes human dignity and the right to free development of the personality as a fundamental value, it has done away with the dogma held by the original draftsmen of the BGB that there can be no civil law protection of general personality right.

The court concluded:

It would be intolerable to refuse compensation for that immaterial damage.

Foreign law was not referred to at this stage but academic writings were taken into account. There was at the time a strong current of opinion in German academic literature in favour of recognizing a general right of privacy.[22] Noteworthy in particular is the systematic treatise on the subject by Heinrich Hubmann,[23] who strongly suggested that the time was ripe for the recognition of a right of privacy and that its violation should give rise to a right to claim damages. Interestingly enough, one of his arguments was that the right of privacy was recognized in other legal systems.[24] There can

---

[19] BGHZ 26, 349, decision of 14 Feb 1958 translated in Markesinis and Unberath (n 18) 415. The plaintiff acted as a gentleman showjumper. The defendant disseminated a poster with a picture of the showjumper advertising a pharmaceutical preparation which purportedly increased sexual potency.

[20] In the famous *Lüth* case: BVerfGE 7, 198, decision of 15 Jan 1958 translated in Markesinis and Unberath (n 18) 392.

[21] See, for a comparative examination, BS Markesinis (1999) 115 LQR 47.

[22] See H Coing in *Staudinger's Kommentar zum BGB* (11th edn 1957) Vorbem §1 Rn 20 with references.

[23] *Das Persönlichkeitsrecht* (1953, 2nd edn 1967). Cited by the BGH in an earlier seminal judgment, in which the right to freely develop one's personality was recognized as one of the interests protected by the general tort provision §823 I BGB: BGHZ 24, 72, decision of 2 Apr 1957.

[24] 1st edn 38, 251; §17 of the 2nd edn gives a detailed account of the situation in Switzerland (which he regarded as a suitable model), France, Austria, and Italy. English law was also examined, though he correctly stated that English courts did not recognize a right of privacy and concluded that the situation was 'somewhat unsatisfactory'.

be no doubt that this was at the back of the mind of the judges when
Herrenreiter was decided and that the judges drew confidence from the fact
that recognizing a right of privacy had been successfully tested in other legal
systems. Thus it is not surprising that when a few years later the court was
criticized for interfering with the freedom of the press, the
Bundesgerichtshof was quick to emphasize that

in almost all legal systems in which the value of a person plays a central role
damages is recognized as an adequate remedy for invasions of privacy. Also in these
systems freedom of the press is of fundamental importance and continues to be so
despite the recoverability of damages. Therefore, the objection is unfounded that
recognizing the right to damages for violations of the right of privacy would unrea-
sonably interfere with the freedom of the press.[25]

While in these decisions the references to comparative material are fairly
general and can only be understood against the background of academic
studies available to the court, the fine-tuning of this right of privacy
prompted the German courts to examine foreign material in more detail.
Thus, following, this time expressly, the Swiss model, the court limited the
right to damages to cases in which the violation of privacy was of considerable weight.[26] In the more recent *Caroline* litigation the
Bundesgerichtshof looked once again at other jurisdictions.[27] The German
Federal Court held that the princess, even though a public figure, was entitled to privacy in places accessible to the public provided that it was obvious that the person wished to be let alone and crucially the location offered
some seclusion from the public. Thus the publication of photographs taken
in a restaurant was said to interfere with the right of privacy. The reference
here was to a decision of the Supreme Court of the United States.[28] By
contrast, photographs taken of the princess walking on the street did not
constitute an infringement of privacy. The Court explicitly rejected the
more radical French approach[29] according to which the unsolicited publication of a photograph is prohibited unless it shows the person performing
a public duty.

The privacy cases are in a number of ways a useful illustration of how
comparative law can benefit the development of the law before national
courts. First, they show how a new concept came more easily to be recognized because other legal systems had successfully incorporated it. Secondly,
the comparative method was used also on a more specific level to justify

---

[25] BGHZ 39, 124, 132, decision of 5 Mar 1963. In a similar vein the Constitutional Court
stressed that this line of cases of the BGH brought German law into line with international
developments, BVerfGE 34, 269, 291; decision of 14 Feb 1973.

[26] BGHZ 35, 363, decision of 19 Sept 1961.

[27] BGHZ 131, 332, decision of 19 Dec 1995 reproduced in Markesinis and Unberath (n 19)
444.   [28] *Katz v United States* 389 Supreme Court (1967) 347.

[29] Cour de cassation Bulletin des arrêts Chambres civiles No 98, 67.

refinements and the application to the individual case. Thirdly, the development reminds one of the present situation in English law.[30] What has taken place in Germany over many years seems—some would argue—about to begin in England. Finally, the privacy cases may be typical in so far as they suggest that the comparative method is particularly attractive when a radical departure from previous practice is at stake or a novel issue arises and the local solution is not strongly dictated by a local statute or long-established practice.

This last aspect is confirmed by two other decisions. In the first the Bundesgerichtshof rejected a wrongful life claim.[31] This time it preferred the approach adopted by the English Court of Appeal in the *McKay* case[32] to the more liberal view expressed in some American decisions. In the second the Court had to decide whether a doctor who negligently removed the only kidney of a child was liable in damages to the child's mother who donated one of her own kidneys to rescue the child.[33] However, the Bundesgerichtshof also used comparative material in other contexts in which the issues were not genuinely new but potentially controversial.[34]

Overall, however, the German record does not compare well with the recent willingness of English courts[35] to embrace foreign ideas. Professor Kötz concluded in his recent study that the number of cases where the

---

[30] See Markesinis and Unberath (n 19) 411 with references.

[31] BGHZ 35, 363, decision of 19 Sept 1961.

[32] *McKay v Essex Health Authority* [1982] 2 WLR 890.

[33] BGHZ 101, 215; decision of 30 June 1987, reproduced in Markesinis and Unberath (n 18) 660. Liability was established and the court referred to the rescue doctrine as applied in US decisions.

[34] See eg BGHZ 101, 337, decision of 16 Sept 1987 (sale of goods, reference to Swiss and US law); BGHZ 63, 140, decision of 5 Nov 1974 (liability for sport injuries, reference to French law); BGHZ 21, 112, decision of 22 June 1956, and BGHZ 24, 214, decision of 13 May 1957 (commercial agents, references to Swiss, French, Italian, and Austrian law).

[35] From the last ten years: *White v Jones* [1995] 2 AC 207 (cf W Lorenz [1995] JZ 317); *Henderson v Merrett Syndicates Ltd* [1995] 2 AC 145 (cf Markesinis and Unberath (n 18) 337); *Hunter v Canary Wharf Ltd* [1997] AC 655; *Barry v Midland Bank plc* [1998] 1 All ER 805; *Kleinwort Benson Ltd v Lincoln CC* [1999] 2 AC 349; *McFarlane v Tayside Health Board* [2000] 2 AC 59 (cf Markesinis and Unberath (n 18) 197); *Arthur JS Hall & Co v Simons* [2000] 3 WLR 543 (cf Markesinis and Unberath (n 18) 330); *Michael Douglas, Catherine Zeta-Jones, Northern and Shell plc v Hello! Ltd* [2000] EWCA Civ 353; *Alfred McAlpine Construction Ltd v Panatown Ltd* [2001] 1 AC 518 (cf H Unberath *Transferred Loss* (Hart Oxford 2003) 205); *Greatorex v Greatorex* [2000] 1 WLR 1970 (cf Markesinis (n 157); *A v National Blood Authority* [2001] EWHC QB 446; *Campbell v Mirror Group Newspapers Ltd* [2002] EWCA Civ 1373; *Fairchild v Glenhaven Funeral Services Ltd* [2002] UKHL 22; *The Starsin* [2003] UKHL 12. An overview given by K Schiemann LJ 'Aktuelle Einflüsse des deutschen Rechts auf die richterliche Fortbildung des englischen Rechts' [2003] EuR 2003, 17. This is in fact a renaissance of comparative law in England if one remembers for instance that comparative law formed part of major treatises of the 19th century, eg J Chitty *A Treatise on the Law of Contracts and Upon the Defences to Actions Thereon* (6th edn by 1857 JA Russel); C Blackburn *A Treatise on the Effect of the Contract of Sale* (1845). See, as to these developments and the reasons for the change in attitude, BS Markesinis 'Our Debt to Europe' in BS Markesinis (ed) *Clifford Chance Millennium Lectures* (2000) 37.

Bundesgerichtshof referred to foreign law without the need to do so was only around a dozen.[36] The main reason for the initial absence of wide-ranging comparative jurisprudence in Germany can be easily identified. With the emergence of the Civil Code in the year 1900, a major achievement of the Pandectist school but also comparative evaluation,[37] German scholarship and the courts focused all their energy on interpreting the Code and filling it with life. Roman law was marginalized as a study in the history of law and the comparative approach had become superfluous.[38]

Fortunately this self-imposed isolation seems to have come to end. There are hardly any major monographs nowadays that dos not include at least a comparative chapter. Practitioners' books are still a notable exception. The German legislator is increasingly anxious to bring German law into line with international practice. The recent modernization of the German law of obligations is a perfect example.[39] It is to be hoped that the courts will follow suit.

III. COMPARATIVE LAW: OUTLOOK

If a European Civil Code were ever to be adopted,[40] this would mean within the Code's scope the end of comparative law in its traditional form. However, this course of events does not seem likely. The Commission itself has abandoned the idea of a more modest Contract Code in favour of creating an optional body of EU contract law and consolidating the existing law.[41] 'Harmonization' on a large scale would not only eventually make the comparative method superfluous eventually but it would sweep away the heritage of centuries. Traditions may be worth preserving but it is equally important that legal scholarship as well as adjudication transcends the boundaries of one's own legal system. Great assistance and fresh ideas can

---

[36] Including criminal law; Kötz (n 1) 832.
[37] See Dölle (n 1) 25 ff. with references.
[38] Cf Zimmermann (n 2) 40 ff.
[39] *Gesetz zur Modernisierung des Schuldrechts vom 26.11.2001*, BGBl. I S. 3138 implementing Directive 1999/44/EC on consumer sales. The directive in turn is in part modelled after art 35 CISG. Unlike the English Sale and Supply of Goods to Consumers Regulations 2002 (cf M Bridge (2003) 119 LQR 173) the German legislator extended the approach of the directive beyond consumer sales to sale of goods generally. Moreover, the whole system of remedies for irregularities of performance was changed. See, for an account in English, R Zimmermann *Breach of Contract and Remedies Under the New German Law of Obligations*, Saggi, conferenze e seminari, vol 48 (Centro di studi e ricerche di diritto comparato e straniero 2002); for the use of comparative material for this reform: Markesinis (n 3) 114.
[40] Opinions vary from strongly in favour, O Lando 'Does the European Union Need a Civil Code?' [2003] RIW 2003, 1, to strongly against, Y Lequette 'Quelques remarques à propos du projet du code civil européen de M. von Bar' [2002] D Chron 2202.
[41] COM (2003) 68 final 12 Feb 2003.

be expected from the different study groups on European private law.[42] I would wish that the European Principles acquire the same persuasive force *in the courtroom* as the Restatements prepared by the American Law Institute, but I am sceptical whether this will be the case. The systemic differences between the European legal orders are too great to be dissolved by compromise decisions. Thus Sir Roy Goode, who was a member of the Lando Commission, has recently remarked that he accepted specific performance as a primary remedy under the Principles of European Contract Law[43] but it would be quite another thing to have this as a rule of English law.[44] In my view the most promising approach is comparative research done with the English practising lawyer in mind. Professor Basil Markesinis has called this the right packaging of foreign law.[45] If it is accompanied by making the material available in the English language,[46] this method seems most successful and worth copying in Germany.[47]

Comparative law should be presented in such a way that it appeals to a national lawyer. Its appeal will be strong if the research is directed at specific topics while at the same time the comparative lawyer undertaking the research is familiar with and ideally trained in both legal systems and understands the philosophical and historical foundations of both. This service, which comparative law can provide, should not be belittled as a minor task. Comparative law is not only a service to the national legal system. It is a cause—an end in itself. The great jurist Rudolph von Jhering remarked more than a hundred years ago in a well-known but little adhered to passage from his *Geist des römischen Rechts*:[48]

The time has gone for ever when Roman law united most of European jurisprudence. Legal scholarship is now national scholarship; the limits of legal science coincide with political borders. What a humiliating, unworthy state of affairs! Yet it is for legal scholarship to free itself from these limitations and to regain what it possessed for so long, to regain its universal character for all time to come, albeit under the different guise of comparative law. Its method will be different, its perspective wider, its judgment more mature, and thus the apparent loss will turn out to be its saviour, elevating legal science to a higher level.

---

[42] The Commission on European Private Law has recently published the third and final part of O Lando, E Clive, A Prüm and R Zimmermann (eds) *The Principles of European Contract Law*. See also the publications of the working teams of The Study Group on a European Civil Code (chairman C von Bar) and the European Group on Tort Law (Tilburg Group).

[43] Art 9: 102.

[44] In his reply to the Commission's Communication on European Contract Law, COM (2001) 398 final, available at <http://europa.eu.int/comm/consumers>.

[45] Above (n 3) 215.

[46] As done, for instance, on the web site of the Institute of Global Law, University College London <http://www.ucl.ac.uk/laws/global_law/cases/index.html>.

[47] Professor Kötz emphasizes that it is the task of the comparative lawyer to make the practitioner aware of the foreign material: above (n 1), 841.

[48] Vol 1 (5th edn 1891) 14–15.

In so far as comparative law is a service to the courts, so far as it is a means to an end the end is highly desirable. Comparative law is able to ensure that convergence between the different legal systems will emerge gradually and organically. By pursuing this path, rather than imposing extensive harmonization from above, the traditional approaches of national legal systems are preserved, and from these competing ideas the national judge will be able to choose the most compelling solution while preserving coherence within his own dear law.

Index